Classical
music
on CD

1996

Julian Haylock & Alexander Waugh

Mitchell Beazley

Classical Music on CD 1996
A Mitchell Beazley Pocket Music Guide

First published in Great Britain in 1995
by Mitchell Beazley,
an imprint of Reed Consumer Books Limited
Michelin House, 81 Fulham Road
London SW3 6RB
and Auckland, Melbourne, Singapore and Toronto

Executive Editor Sarah Polden
Coordinating Editor Anthea Snow
Data Inputting and Editor Diana Vowles
Proofreader John Bailie
Index Hilary Bird
Production Controller Juliette Butler

Jacket Photograph Reg Wilson

A CIP catalogue record for this book is available from the British
Library
ISBN 1 85732 757 8

Set in Linotype Caslon 540 and M Gill Sans
Produced by Mandarin Offset
Printed in Malaysia

Contents

Introduction

Even in these unpredictable post-recessionary times, the demand for recorded classical music shows no signs of abating. The record companies have continued to release new CDs at a rate guaranteed to confound even the most product-hungry of collectors and, as noted in last year's edition, the majors have been paying special attention to their back catalogues, ensuring that the classics of the past are steadily becoming available again at an affordable price, many of them for the very first time.

While a pronounced nostalgia for vintage recordings (along with their original covers and art work!) is a pronounced feature of the new release schedules, those collectors with more specialist tastes have also been well catered for whether it be a penchant for period instrument recordings, music of the pre-Renaissance, or the symphonic byways of the Romantic era. Most notably, there has been a resurgence of interest in contemporary music, the like of which has not been seen since the heady days of the sixties and the emergence of Boulez, Stockhausen and the Polish avant-garde.

Keeping on top of the veritable mountain of new product which is constantly emerging is very much a full-time activity, a situation which is fully reflected in the current edition which contains no fewer than 650 new entries. Countless recordings have changed catalogue number and price range, others have been reissued with different couplings, whilst a fair number have fallen by the wayside, hopefully not for long. Otherwise the general format remains unchanged from last year except for the introduction of American catalogue numbers where these differ from those normally encountered in Europe.

The compact disc was officially launched in 1983 and its success now, little more than a decade later, is so complete that most shops no longer stock black vinyl records, while the majority of recording companies have stopped making them altogether. The stylus and groove medium that dominated commercial recording since its teething days in the early part of this century has been spectacularly usurped. Cassette sales, too, have fallen during recent years with the introduction of portable CD players and in-car CD.

For those still unconverted to the compact disc medium, it might be as well to rehearse here some of its important advantages. The materials used in its manufacture and the fact that it is a non-contact medium (since the music is read by a laser beam instead of by a stylus or cassette head) make for a much more reliable and longer-lasting product than either the record or magnetic tape cassette. No more groove debris or erosion. No more crackle, hiss, wear and tear. The collector can now reap the rewards of state-of-the-art technology unspoilt by warped pressings, end-of-side distortion, misplaced central holes, mistracking and scratches.

In theory the compact disc should provide distortion-free sound enhanced by unrivalled clarity, pitch stability and wide dynamic range. In practice, unfortunately, this is not always the case. Nor is it unusual for a technically distinguished recording to be let down by disappointing musicianship. This guide is designed to point the collector towards CDs that are both technically well recorded and musically satisfying. Operas and operettas are excluded from this volume, but a companion guide, *Opera on CD*, is available for the benefit of those who want a complete classical music collection.

AW & JH

Key to Abbreviations

AAM	Academy of Ancient Music	alt	alto
ASMF	Academy of St. Martin-in-the-Fields	arr.	arranged
BPO	Berlin Philharmonic Orchestra	bar	baritone
CBSO	City of Birmingham Symphony Orchestra	bs	bass
		bsn	bassoon
COE	Chamber Orchestra of Europe	Ch	choir/chorus
CSO	Chicago Symphony Orchestra	cl	clarinet
DG	Deutsche Grammophon	cont	contralto
DHM	Deutsche Harmonia Mundi	cor ang	cor anglais
EBS	English Baroque Soloists	cvd	clavichord
ECO	English Chamber Orchestra	db	double bass
FNO	French National Orchestra	dir	director
FRNO	French Radio National Orchestra	fl	flute
HM	Harmonia Mundi	fpno	fortepiano
LAPO	Los Angeles Philharmonic Orchestra	gmba	viola da gamba
LCP	London Classical Players	gtr	guitar
LGO	Leipzig Gewandhaus Orchestra	hn	horn
LPO	London Philharmonic Orchestra	hp	harp
LSO	London Symphony Orchestra	hpd	harpsichord
NPO	New Philharmonia Orchestra	kbd	keyboard
NRO	National Radio Orchestra	lte	lute
NYPO	New York Philharmonic Orchestra	mez	mezzo-soprano
ORTF	Orchestre Radiodiffusion et Télévision Française	min.	minor
		narr	narrator
OSR	Orchestre de la Suisse Romande	ob	oboe
PJWE	Philip Jones Wind Ensemble	orch.	orchestrated
RLPO	Royal Liverpool Philharmonic Orchestra	org	organ
		perc	percussion
ROHO	Royal Opera House Orchestra (Covent Garden)	pno	piano
		rec	recorder
RPO	Royal Philharmonic Orchestra	sax	saxophone
SFSO	San Francisco Symphony Orchestra	sop	soprano
SNO	Scottish National Orchestra	synth	synthesizer
VCM	Vienna Concentus Musicus	tbn	trombone
VPO	Vienna Philharmonic Orchestra	ten	tenor
		tpt	trumpet
CO	chamber orchestra	trb	treble
O	orchestra	vcl	cello
PO	philharmonic orchestra	vib	vibraphone
RSO	radio symphony orchestra	vla	viola
SO	symphony orchestra	vln	violin
YO	youth orchestra		

Key to Symbols

O	Orchestral (including concertos)
C	Chamber
S	Solo instrument
V	Vocal (including choral/orchestral works)
◇	Authentic (recording made on original instruments)
*	Links corresponding pieces with performers
[A]	Analogue
[D]	Digital
F	Full price (over £10)
M	Mid-price (£6–£10)
B	Budget price (under £6)

How to use this book

This guide is not a catalogue: every CD listed is a recommendation. In order to find out which is the best recording of any given piece of classical music, simply look up the work under its composer, and the CD listed will be the one to buy. Occasionally, more than one outstanding recommendation is given, leaving the collector free to choose according to the suitability of the couplings. If the works/couplings are identical, then the first version listed should be considered the guide's first choice. Look out for the ✧ (authentic) sign: sometimes two recommendations have been given so as to offer a choice to those who prefer authentic performances on period instruments to modern instruments in certain repertoire (see below).

Composers are listed in alphabetical order. On the same line as the composer's name are the composer's dates and country of birth followed (in rare cases) by the composer's adopted country: eg HANDEL, George Frideric (1685–1759) Germany/England.

Under each composer the CDs are divided and listed according to the following categories in the following order: Orchestral (including concertos), Chamber, Solo instrumental and Vocal (including choral/orchestral works). (See Key to Symbols on page 5.) Where there is more than one type of music on a disc, the disc will be listed under the category that includes the first-named work. Where a particular performer appears on only one particular work on a disc, asterisks (*) have been used to link the performer with the corresponding piece.

Each CD entry is listed as follows:

1. the name of the piece(s) with, where helpful, the type of piece in brackets: eg (tone poem), (cantata), etc;

2. the names of soloists, chorus, orchestra/conductor. After the soloists' or singers' names their instrument or vocal range is given in brackets;

3. where there are also pieces on the CD by one or more additional composer(s) these are listed in brackets: eg (+ Reich: *Variations for Wind*);

4. the record company, the CD reference number (see below), the number of CDs (if more than one), whether the recording was originally digital or analogue (see below), and the price range.

Period instrument recordings As music written before c.1600 (Medieval and Renaissance) is nowadays almost inevitably recorded using period instruments (certainly the bulk of the recommendations in this guide), we have limited the authentic sign (✧) to music of the Baroque, Classical and mainstream Romantic periods (c.1600–1760, c.1760–1830 and c.1830–1915 respectively). However, with keyboard instruments the whole question of authenticity is so complex and hotly debated that in the case of solo instrumental music the authentic sign has been used only with regard to the Classical and early Romantic fortepiano.

If a required piece cannot be found It should be noted that the contents of each CD are listed with its most prominent, important or popular piece first. Other works thereafter are listed alphabetically. Certain works may be found tucked away under one of the composer's more famous or important compositions. Malcolm Arnold's *Tam O'Shanter* overture, for instance, can be found under his Symphony No. 1. With more than 10,000 pieces recommended in this guide it is worth browsing as the required work is sure to be listed somewhere! If you are unsure as to the composer try the Index of Selected Works on pages 252–56.

[A] & [D] analogue and digital recordings Analogue [A] means that the recording was made on magnetic tape. Digital [D] means that the music was recorded onto some form of computer tape, usually Digital Audio Tape (DAT) or video tape. The advantage of a digital recording is that, in theory, there should be no deterioration in sound quality between the music when it is recorded in the studio and when it is played on a CD at home, whereas analogue recordings are prone to tape noise, pre- and post-echo known as 'print through', harmonic distortion and tape wear.

All CDs have a three-letter digital/analogue symbol on them which is usually found on the back cover. These symbols have led to a great deal of misunderstanding, which is why this guide employs the simple one-letter symbols [A] and [D]. The standard explanation for the three-letter coding is as follows:

DDD: digital tape recorder used during session recording, mixing and/or editing, and mastering (transcription);

ADD: analogue tape recorder used during session recording, digital tape recorder used during subsequent mixing and/or editing and during mastering (transcription);

AAD: Analogue tape recorder used during session recording and subsequent mixing and/or editing; digital tape recorder used during mastering (transcription).

Since the CD is itself a digital format, the final letter must always be a D and can therefore be ignored. Similarly, the second letter (the editing) is not necessary since, if the original recording was analogue, a digital edit does not improve its analogue shortcomings any more than the final digital transfer onto CD. The only letter of interest is therefore the first one, which denotes whether the original studio recording was made onto digital or analogue tape.

CD reference numbers These are invaluable when buying or ordering a CD. Many shops order and replace their stock using computerized systems which are entirely reliant on the numbers supplied by the record companies and can find a disc more quickly and easily using a number than a disc title. During the age of the LP, disc numbers could vary markedly from one country to another, but the arrival of the CD has led to greater standardization. However, US numbers occasionally differ from those commonly encountered in Europe and elsewhere. These are indicated in the text for the first time in this latest 1996 edition.

About the recommendations The recommendations in this guide have been chosen for technical and artistic merit, for faithfulness to the composer's score and, of course, for truth and clarity in sound engineering. Because the CD is a state-of-the-art digital sound medium, this guide recommends, where possible, only recordings that have used stereo recording technology. For this reason, mono recordings (despite often spellbinding artistic interpretations) have been largely excluded except where an excellent stereo alternative could not be found. (For a selective list of outstanding mono recordings, see pages 248–51) By buying only those CDs recommended in this guide, the classical music enthusiast will be able to build a collection which not only avoids any unnecessary and expensive duplication of works, but will provide a lifetime's listening pleasure.

100 Essential Works

With such a bewildering variety of classical music to choose from, it is difficult for the beginner to know quite where to begin; it is hoped that the following highly selective list will help get things off to a flying start. Whilst the works listed below are by no means all amongst the greatest of their kind ever composed, they are certainly amongst the most popular, and once sampled it is hoped they will encourage further listening, leading to a lifetime of rewarding investigation and revelation.

ALBINONI
Adagio in G minor

ALLEGRI
Miserere mei

J.S. BACH
Brandenburg Concerto No. 2
Orchestral Suite No. 3
Toccata and Fugue in D minor, BWV565
Mass in B minor

BARBER
Adagio for Strings

BARTÓK
Concerto for Orchestra

BEETHOVEN
Piano Concerto No. 5 (Emperor)
Violin Concerto
Symphony No. 5
Piano Sonata No. 14 (Moonlight)

BERLIOZ
Symphonie fantastique

BIZET
Carmen: Suites

BORODIN
Prince Igor: Polovtsian Dances

BRAHMS
Piano Concerto No. 1
Violin Concerto
Symphony No. 2

BRITTEN
Young Person's Guide to the Orchestra

BRUCH
Violin Concerto No. 1

BRUCKNER
Symphony No. 4 (Romantic)

JANÁČEK
Sinfonietta

LISZT
Piano Concerto No. 1
Piano Sonata in B minor

MAHLER
Symphony No. 4

MENDELSSOHN
Violin Concerto in E minor
Symphony No. 4 (Italian)

MOZART
Horn Concerto No. 4
Piano Concerto No. 23
Serenade No. 13 (Eine kleine Nachtmusik)
Symphony No. 40
Mass No. 19 (Requiem)

MUSSORGSKY
Night on a Bare Mountain
Pictures at an Exhibition

ORFF
Carmina Burana

PACHELBEL
Canon and Gigue

PROKOFIEV
Classical Symphony (No. 1)
Peter and the Wolf

RACHMANINOV
Piano Concerto No. 2
Symphony No. 2

RAVEL
Boléro
Pavane pour une infante défunte

RESPIGHI
Pines of Rome

RIMSKY-KORSAKOV
Scheherazade

RODRIGO
Concierto de Aranjuez

ROSSINI
Overtures

SAINT-SAËNS
Carnival of the Animals
Symphony No. 3 (Organ)

SATIE
Gymnopédie No. 1

SCHUBERT
Symphony No. 5
Piano Quintet (Trout)
Die schöne Müllerin

SCHUMANN
Piano Concerto
Kinderszenen

SHOSTAKOVICH
Symphony No. 5

SIBELIUS
Violin Concerto
Finlandia

JOHANN STRAUSS II
Blue Danube

RICHARD STRAUSS
Also sprach Zarathustra
Don Juan

STRAVINSKY
Firebird
Petrushka
Rite of Spring

TCHAIKOVSKY
Piano Concerto No. 1
Violin Concerto
Nutcracker
Romeo and Juliet Overture
Sleeping Beauty
Swan Lake
Symphony No. 5

VAUGHAN WILLIAMS
Fantasia on Greensleeves
Fantasia on a Theme of Thomas Tallis

VERDI
Overtures

VIVALDI
The Four Seasons, Op. 8/1-4

WAGNER
Operatic excerpts

WEBER
Overtures

Editors' Choice

THE BEST OF RECENT CLASSICAL MUSIC RELEASES ON CD

BEST OVERALL RECORDING

Barber: *Violin Concerto, Op. 14*; Korngold: *Violin Concerto*; *Much Ado about Nothing: Suite*
Shaham (vln), LSO, Previn
DG 429 886-2 [D] F

It was an inspired idea to couple together two of the most indelibly tuneful concertos composed this century. Gill Shaham pulls out all the stops, tossing off even the most demanding pyrotechnics with effortless grace and security, whilst handling the many skin-tingling moments with rapturous intensity. Swashbuckling support from a clearly inspired LSO/Previn partnership, captured in superbly detailed and impactful sound.

BEST MEDIEVAL RECORDING

The Spirits of England and France, Vol. 1: Pykini, Machaut, Pérotin, etc.
Gothic Voices, Page
Hyperion CDA 66739 [D] F

A stunning collection of sacred and secular music composed during the later Middle Ages. Christopher Page's Gothic Voices wear their scholarship lightly, bringing a frisson and electric communication to these pieces unrivalled by any other group currently working in this sphere. Here the music of Machaut and his contemporaries emerges not as a series of historical curiosities but as part of a vital and highly articulate musical tradition.

BEST RENAISSANCE RECORDING

Gesualdo: *17 Madrigals*
Arts Florissants Vocal & Instrumental Ensembles, Christie
HM HMC90 1268 [D] F

Although strictly speaking a reissue at full price, this disc's very special qualities mark it out as an essential purchase. Don Carlo Gesualdo, Prince of Venosa, led a life that was as colourful as his music, at one point successfully arranging for the murder of his wife and her lover. These madrigals represent the apex of 16th-century modernity, using harmonic idioms so advanced for their time that Stravinsky claimed to have learnt much from them. Exemplary performances and recording.

BEST BAROQUE RECORDING

Bach: *Violin Concertos: in A min, BWV1052*; *in F min., BWV1056*; *Violin and Oboe Concerto in C min., BWV1060*; *Oboe d'amore Concerto in A, BWV1055*
Wallfisch (vln/dir), Robson (ob/dir), Age of Enlightenment O
Virgin VC5 45095-2 (US: 45095) [D] F

With the exception of the Violin and Oboe Concerto, these are all reconstructions of original concertos, now lost, on which Bach is known to have based his solo harpsichord concertos. They could hardly wish for more persuasive advocacy than they receive here from Elizabeth Wallfisch and her gifted period instrument colleagues, whose devotion to these matchless scores shines through every bar.

BEST CLASSICAL RECORDING

Haydn: *Symphonies Nos. 82-87 (Paris)*
Tafelmusik, Weil
Sony CD66295; CD662966, 2 separately available CDs [D] **F**

Ideas as to how this music may have sounded in Haydn's day have altered radically even during the last decade, with the established ongoing cycles from Hogwood and Goodman differing in many important respects. Now Bruno Weil joins the fold with a pair of discs which elicit the sheer joy and humanity of Haydn's inspiration like no other. This is gloves-off authenticism at its most spectacular and a glittering triumph for all concerned.

BEST ROMANTIC RECORDING

Liszt: *A Faust Symphony*
Seiffert (ten), Prague Philharmonic Male Ch., BPO, Rattle
EMI CDC5 55220-2 (US: CDC 55220) [D] **F**

If this scorching new recording of Liszt's wayward master-piece is anything to go by, the combination of Britain's finest conductor and arguably the world's finest orchestra has exceptional potential. The BPO respond to Rattle's direction with an uninhibited vitality and exuberance not normally associated with this orchestra, while eliciting a tonal resource and corporate virtuosity to silence criticism. A major achievement.

BEST 20TH-CENTURY RECORDING

Debussy: *La Mer; Nocturnes; Jeux, *Première Rhapsodie*
*Cohen (cl), Cleveland O, Boulez
DG 439 896-2 [D] **F**

Boulez's ongoing series of recordings for DG look set to become one of the recorded milestones of the digital age. Here the Cleveland Orchestra play with a refinement typical of this most meticulous of conductors. Every phrase, every texture is balanced within an inch of its life, and yet a strong sense of personal identification with the music in hand is unerringly conveyed throughout. This superb recording represents the art of interpretation at its most exquisite.

BEST CONTEMPORARY RECORDING

MacMillan: *Busqueda; Visitatio sepulchri*
Scottish CO, Bolton, *MacMillan
RCA Catalyst 09026 62669-2 [D] **F**

James MacMillan is now firmly established as one of British contemporary music's leading lights, as is triumphantly confirmed by this second disc of his music in RCA's enterprising new Catalyst series. Don't be put off by the pop-style image cultivation; his is a serious and instantly recognizable compositional voice, one which successfully combines thoroughly up-to-date aesthetics with an ear-grabbing communicability.

BEST CONCERTO RECORDING

Prokoviev: *Violin Concerto No. 1 in D, Op. 19*; Shostakovich: *Violin Concerto No. 1 in A min., Op. 77*
Vengarov (vln), LSO, Rostropovich
Teldec 4509 98143-2 [D] **F**

While no one would deny that the Prokoviev concerto features anything but the work of a master violinist, the star attraction here is a performance of Shostakovich's bleak and rather forbidding First Violin Concerto which leaves no stone unturned. Even the classic Oistrakh/Mitropoulos recording cannot compete with the appalling desolation and searing emotional hammer blows dealt by this unforgettable account.

BEST SYMPHONY RECORDING

Vaughan Williams: *Symphonies Nos. 1-9*; *Flos campi*; *Serenade to Music*
Various soloists, RLPO, Handley
EMI Eminence CD-BOX VW1 (US: Classics for Pleasure CDBOX VW1), 6 CDs [D] M

Although strictly speaking it is only the coupling of the 6th and 9th symphonies which is new to the catalogue this year (CD-EMX2230; US: CDM 65455), this retrospective boxed set of Vernon Handley's complete VW cycle is a most distinguished achievement. Handley directs this repertoire with a skill and understanding unmatched anywhere in the world today, and these inspirational RLPO readings have been captured in superbly atmospheric sound. A treasurable bargain.

BEST ORCHESTRAL RECORDING

Martin: *Symphonie*; *Symphonie Concertante*; *Passacaglia*
LPO, Bamert
Chandos CHAN 9312 [D] F

Chandos are once again to be applauded for their enterprising endeavours on behalf of unjustifiably neglected figures, in this case the great Swiss composer Frank Martin. Unquestionably a creative artist of the utmost distinction, Martin has long had to contend with dedicated if not particularly sophisticated recorded advocacy. Bamert and the LPO at last do these masterpieces of the orchestral repertoire real justice, and have been accorded resplendent sound quality to match.

BEST CHAMBER RECORDING

Fauré: *Violin Sonatas: No. 1 in A, Op. 13*; *No. 2 in E min., Op. 108*; *Morceau de concours*; *Andante, Op. 75*; *Romance, Op. 28*; *Berceuse, Op. 16*
Amoyal (vln), Rogé (pno)
Decca 436 866-2 (US: London 436 866-2) [D] F

Fauré's music is amongst the most elusive of all the great composers. Legion are the artists who have had little success in the recording studio when entering into his artistic domain. It was therefore a particularly happy idea to combine two of the most sensitive and highly attuned of all Fauré interpreters in a programme devoted entirely to the works for violin and piano. The results are nothing short of ravishing. Unimpeachable sound.

BEST PIANO RECORDING

Scriabin: *Preludes: Op. 2/2*; *Op. 9/1*; *Opp. 11, 13, 15, 16 & 17*
Fergus-Thompson (pno)
ASV CDDCA 919 [D] F

A dream of a record which captures artistry of an altogether exceptional order in alluring sound. Pieces which in many hands sound obtuse, even abrupt, are handled with a sensitivity and inimitable sense of timing to make the listener draw breath. Throughout, Fergus-Thompson handles colour and texture like a master painter, ravishing the ear with a tantalising exhibition of highly sensual musicscapes. Unmissable.

BEST ORGAN RECORDING

Messiaen: *Complete Organ Works*
Weir (org)
Collins 70312, 7 CDs [D] **M**

Once upon a time, the hugely simplistic and distinctly unfashionable image of Messiaen pottering about in the countryside notating birdsong was met by a certain degree of critical awkwardness. Those years are now thankfully well behind us, and Gillian Weir's achievement in collecting together all Messiaen's extant organ works is a truly virtuoso tour-deforce. There is no finer introduction to Messiaens's unique soundworld in the present catalogue.

BEST VOCAL RECORDING

Tchaikovsky: *19 Songs*
Borodina (mez), Gergieva (pno)
Philips 442 013-2 [D] **F**

Tchaikovsky's songs are at last coming into their own, with a significant number of recitals having appeared over the last couple of years. None of them, however, quite match this superb collection from the gifted young mezzo-soprano Olga Borodina. She brings all the richness and tonal resource one would expect from a master Russian singer, coupled with a sensitivity to mood which is altogether rarer.

BEST STEREO REISSUE

Shostakovich: *String Quartets Nos. 1–15*
Shostakovich Quartet
Olympia OCD 5009, 5 CDs [A] **M**

A revelatory set which constantly reveals fresh insights into even the most familiar of these fifteen masterworks. By adopting a relatively straightforward approach, entirely free of interpretative mannerisms, with a tendency towards fastish tempi, the Shostakovich Quartet succeed more than any other ensemble in underlining the cycle's purely Classical virtues. Superlative playing, unique interpretations, fine recording quality.

BEST MONO REISSUE

Rachmaninov: *Piano Concerto No. 2; *Rhapsody on a theme of Paganini; Scherzo from Mendelssohn's 'A Midsummer Night's Dream' (trans. Rachmaninov); Preludes Nos. 1, 6, 16, 21 & 23; Moment Musical No. 4*
Moiseiwitsch (pno), LPO, Goehr, *Cameron
APR 5505 [A] **F**

A legendary set of performances from one of the greatest Rachmaninov exponents of all time. Rachmaninov himself was so in awe of this recording of the Second Concerto that he considered it superior even to his own. The Paganini Rhapsody also remains for many the version which still finds all comers wanting. As if further evidence was needed, the Mendelssohn Scherzo transcription and Preludes feature pianism at an altogether exalted level.

Stop Press

The following CDs were issued too late for inclusion in the main text.

BARTOK

Divertimento; Dance Suite; Hungarian Sketches; 2 Pictures
CSO, Boulez
DG 445 825-2 [D] **F**

BEETHOVEN

Piano Sonatas Nos. 8–11
Brendel (pno)
Philips 442 774-2 [D] **F**

GLASS

String Quartets Nos. 2–5
Kronos Quartet
Nonesuch 7559 79356-2 [D] **F**

HAYDN

String Quartets, Op. 77; Berio: *Notturno (Quartetto III)*
Alban Berg Quartet
EMI CDC5 55191-2 (US: CDC 55191) [D] **F**

MARTINŮ

Piano Concertos Nos. 2–4
Firkusny (pno), Czech PO, Pešek
RCA 09026 61934-2 [D] **F**

MAXWELL DAVIES

*Symphony No. 5; *Five Klee Pictures; Chat Moss; Cross Lane Fair
*Philharmonia O, BBC PO, Maxwell Davies
Collins 14602 [D] **F**

MOZART

String Quartet in G, K387; *String Quintet in G minor, K516
Lindsay Quartet, *P. Ireland (vla)
ASV CDDCA 923 [D] **F**

SCHUMANN

Kinderszenen, Op. 15; Kreisleriana, Op. 16; Humoresque, Op. 20
Lupu (pno)
Decca 440 496-2 [D] **F**

TCHEREPNIN

Piano Concertos Nos. 1, 4 & 5
McLachlan (pno), Chethams SO, Clayton
Olympia OCD 440 [D] **F**

WEBER

Piano Concertos: No. 1 in C; No. 2 in Eb; Konzertstück in F min.
Demidenko (pno), Scottish CO, Mackerras
Hyperion CDA 66729 [D] **F**

WEILL

Violin Concerto; Hindemith: *Septet for wind;* Toch: *Five Pieces for wind and percussion, Op. 83*
Tetzlaff (vln/dir), Deutsche Kammerphilharmonie Soloists
Virgin VC5 45056-2 [D] **F**

Recommended Recordings

ADAM, Adolphe (1803–1856) FRANCE

O *Le Corsaire* (ballet) ECO, Bonynge
Decca 430 286-2 (US: London 430 286-2), 2 CDs [D] **F**

Giselle (ballet) ROHO, Bonynge
Decca 433 007-2 (US: London 433 007-2), 2 CDs [D] **M**

ADAMS, John (born 1947) USA

O *Chamber Symphony; Grand Pianola Music* Alley, Sutherland
(pnos), London Sinfonietta, Adams
Elektra-Nonesuch 7559 79219-2 (US: 79219-2) [D] **F**

*Fearful Symmetries; *The Wound-dresser* *Sylvan (bar), St.
Luke's O, Adams
Elektra-Nonesuch 7559 79218-2 (US: 79218-2) [D] **F**

*Harmonielehre; The Chairman Dances; Tromba Lontana; Short
Ride in a Fast Machine* CBSO, Rattle
EMI CDC5 55051-2 (US: CDC 55051) [D] **F**

Shaker Loops SFSO, de Waart
(+ Reich: *Variations*)
Philips 412 214-2 [A] **F**

S *Bump; Cerulean; Coast; Disappointment Lake; Hoodoo Zephyr;
Tourist Song; Tundra* Adams (synth)
Elektra-Nonesuch 7559 79311-2 (US: 79311-2) [D] **F**

V *Harmonium* SFSO & Ch, de Waart
ECM 821 465-2 [A] **F**

ADDINSELL, Richard (1904–1977) ENGLAND

O *Warsaw Concerto* Ortiz (pno), RPO, Atzmon
(+ Gershwin: *Rhapsody in Blue*; Gottschalk: *Grande fantaisie*;
Liszt: *Fantasia on Hungarian Themes*; Litolff: *Concerto
symphonique No. 4*)
Decca 430 726-2 (US: London 430 726-2) [D] **M**

ALAIN, Jehan (1911–1940) FRANCE

S *Complete Organ works* M-C Alain (org)
Volume 1
Erato 2292 45402-2 [D] **F**
Volume 2
Erato 2292 45508-2 [D] **F**

ALBÉNIZ, Isaac (1860–1909) SPAIN

S *Cantos de España, Op. 232: Córdoba; Mallorca, Op. 202; Suite
española, Op. 47: Cádiz; Cataluña; Granada; Sevilla* Bream (gtr)
(+ Granados: *Guitar works*)
RCA 09026 61608–2 [D] **F**

Iberia (complete); *Navarra; Suite española, Op. 47*
de Larrocha (pno)
Decca 417 887-2 (US: London 417 887-2), 2 CDs [D] **F**

D'ALBERT, Eugen (1864–1932) GERMANY

O *Piano Concertos: No. 1 in B min., Op. 2; No. 2 in E, Op. 12* Lane
(pno), BBC Scottish SO, Francis
Hyperion CDA 66747 [D] **F**

ALBINONI, Tomaso (1671–1751) ITALY

O   *Adagio in G min.* (arr. Giazotto) Orpheus CO
DG 429 390-2 [D] **F** (see collections – *Popular Baroque*)

12 Concerti a cinque, Op. 5 Carmirelli (vln), I Musici
Philips 442 658-2 [D] **M**

*12 Concerti a cinque, Op. 7; Sinfonie e concerti a cinque, Op. 2: Nos.
5 & 6* Holliger (ob), Bourgue (ob), I Musici
Philips 432 115-2, 2 CDs [D] **F**

12 Concerti a cinque, Op. 7: Nos. 2, 3, 5, 6, 8, 9, 11 & 12 Holliger
(ob/dir), Elhorst (ob), Berne Camerata
DG Archiv 427 111-2 [A] **M**

12 Concerti a cinque, Op. 9: Nos. 1, 4, 6, 7, 10 & 12 Ayo (vln),
Holliger (ob), Bourgue (ob), Garatti (hpd), I Musici
Philips 426 080-2 [A] **M**

12 Concerti a cinque, Op. 9: Nos. 2, 3, 5, 8, 9 & 11 Holliger (ob),
Bourgue (ob), Garatti (hpd), I Musici
Philips 434 157-2 [A] **M**

Trumpet Concerto in C Wilbraham (tpt), ASMF, Marriner
(+ Haydn: *Trumpet Concerto;* Hummel: *Trumpet Concerto;* L.
Mozart: *Trumpet Concerto;* Telemann: *2 Oboe and Trumpet
Concerto No. 1*)
Decca 417 761-2 (US: London 417 761-2) [A] **M**

C   *Sonate da camera, Op. 4; Trattenimenti Armonici per camera, Op. 6*
Wallfisch (vln), Locatelli Trio
♦ Hyperion CDA 66831/2, 2 CDs [D] **F**

ALFVÉN, Hugo (1872–1960) SWEDEN

O   *Swedish Rhapsodies Nos. 1-3; A Legend of the Skerries, Op. 20; King
Gustav Adolf II (Suite), Op. 49: Elegy* Iceland SO, Sakari
Chandos CHAN 9313 [D] **F**

*Symphony No. 1 in F min., Op. 7; Drapa, Op. 27; Revelation
Cantata, Op. 31: Andante Religioso; Swedish Rhapsody No. 2
(Uppsala-rapsodi), Op. 24* Stockholm PO, Järvi
BIS BIS-CD 395 [D] **F**

*Symphony No. 2 in D, Op. 11; Swedish Rhapsody No. 1
(Midsummer Vigil), Op. 19* Stockholm PO, Järvi
BIS BIS-CD 385 [D] **F**

*Symphony No. 3 in E, Op. 23; Swedish Rhapsody No. 3
(Dalarapsodi), Op. 47; The Prodigal Son* (ballet): *Suite*
Stockholm PO, Järvi
BIS BIS-CD 455 [D] **F**

*Symphony No. 4 in C min., Op. 39; En Skärgådssägen, Op. 20
*Högman (sop), *Ahnsjö (ten), Stockholm PO, Järvi
BIS BIS-CD 505 [D] **F**

Symphony No. 5; Bergakungen: Suite; Gustav II Adolf: Elegy
Royal Stockholm PO, Järvi
BIS BIS-CD 585 [D] **F**

ALKAN, Valentin (1813–1888) FRANCE

O   *Concerti da camera Nos. 1 & 2, Op.10/1 & 2* Hamelin (pno),
BBC Scottish SO, Brabbins
(+Henselt: *Piano Concerto in F min.*, etc.)
Hyperion CDA 66717 [D] **F**

S *12 Études, Op. 35: Allegro barbaro; 12 Études dans les tons mineurs, Op. 39: Comme le vent; En rhythme molossique; Scherzo diabolico; Le festin d'Ésope; Grande sonate: Les quatre âges, Op. 33; 25 Preludes, Op. 31: La chanson de la folle au bord de la mer* Smith (pno)
EMI CDM7 64280-2 (US: Angel CDM 64280) [A] **M**

12 Études dans les tons mineurs, Op. 39: Scherzo diabolico; Gigue et air de ballet dans le style ancien, Op. 24; 3 Marches, Op. 37/1; 2 Nocturnes, Op. 57/1; Quatrième recueil de chants, Op. 67: Barcarolle; Saltarelle, Op. 23; Sonatine, Op. 61; Zorcico (danse ibérienne) Ringeissen (pno)
HM HMA 190 927 [A] **M**

25 Préludes dans les tons majeurs et mineurs, Op. 31 Mustonen (pno)
(+ Shostakovich: *24 Preludes*)
Decca 433 055-2 (US: London 433 055-2) [D] **F**

13 Prières, Op. 64; Petits préludes; Impromptu, Op. 69 Bowyer (org)
Nimbus NI 5089 [D] **F**

ALLEGRI, Gregorio (1582–1652) ITALY

V *Miserere mei* Stamp (sop), Tallis Scholars, Phillips
(+ Mundy: *Vox patris caelestis*; Palestrina: *Missa Papae Marcelli*)
Gimell CDGIM 339 [A] **F**

ALWYN, William (1905–1985) ENGLAND

O *Autumn Legend; Lyra Angelica; Pastoral Fantasia; Tragic Interlude* Masters (hp), Daniel (cor ang), Tees (vla), City of London Sinfonia, Hickox
Chandos CHAN 9065 [D] **F**

Concerti Grossi Nos. 1–3; Oboe & Harp Concerto Daniel (ob), City of London Sinfonia, Hickox
Chandos CHAN 8866 [D] **F**

Film Music: The Fallen Idol: Suite; The History of Mr. Polly; Odd Man Out: Suite; The Rake's Progress: Calypso LSO, Hickox
Chandos CHAN 9243 [D] **F**

*Symphony No. 1; *Piano Concerto No. 1* *Shelley (pno), LSO, Hickox
Chandos CHAN 9155 [D] **F**

Symphony No. 2; Derby Day; Fanfare for a Joyful Occasion; The Magic Island; Overture to a Masque LSO, Hickox
Chandos CHAN 9093 [D] **F**

*Symphony No. 3; *Violin Concerto* *Mordkovitch (vln), LSO, Hickox
Chandos CHAN 9187 [D] **F**

Symphony No. 4; Elizabethan Dances; Festival March LSO, Hickox
Chandos CHAN 8902 [D] **F**

*Symphony No. 5; *Piano Concerto No. 2; Sinfonietta* *Shelley (pno), LSO, Hickox
Chandos CHAN 9196 [D] **F**

C *Clarinet Sonata; Oboe Sonata; Flute Sonata; Sonata Impromptu for violin and viola; Divertimento for solo flute; 'Crepuscule' for solo harp* Farrall (cl), Daniel (ob), Hill (fl), Chen (vln), McFarlane

(vla), Jones (hp), Drake (pno)
Chandos CHAN 9197 [D] **F**

C   *String Quartets Nos. 1 & 2* Quartet of London
Chandos CHAN 9219 [D] **F**

*String Quartet No. 3; String Trio; *Rhapsody for Piano Quartet*
*Willison (pno), Quartet of London
Chandos CHAN 8440 [D] **F**

S   *12 Preludes; Fantasy-Waltzes* Ogdon (pno)
Chandos CHAN 8399 [D] **F**

V   *Song Cycles: Invocations; *A Leave-Taking* Gomez (sop),
Constable (pno); *Rolfe Johnson (ten), Johnson (pno)
Chandos CHAN 9220 [D] **F**

ANDERSON, Leroy (1908–1975) USA

O   *23 Orchestral Miniatures* Eastman-Rochester Pops O, Fennell
Philips Mercury 432 013-2 [A] **M**

ARENSKY, Anton (1861–1906) RUSSIA

O   *Piano Concerto in F min., Op. 2; Fantasia on Russian Folksongs,
Op. 48* Coombs (pno), BBC Scottish SO, Maksymiuk
(+ Bortkiewicz: *Piano Concerto No. 1*)
Hyperion CDA 66624 [D] **F**

Variations on a Theme of Tchaikovsky, Op. 35a English String O,
Boughton
Nimbus NI 5347 [D] **F** (see collections – *String Favourites*)

C   *String Quartet in A min. for violin, viola & 2 cellos, Op. 35*
Raphael Ensemble
(+ Tchaikovsky: *Souvenir de Florence*)
Hyperion CDA 66648 [D] **F**

Piano Trios: No. 1 in D min., Op. 32; No. 2 in F min., Op. 73
Beaux Arts Trio
Philips 442 127-2 [D] **F**

Suites for 2 pianos Nos. 1-4 Coombs (pno), Munro (pno)
Hyperion CDA 66755 [D] **F**

ARNE, Thomas (1710–1778) ENGLAND

O   *6 Favourite Concertos* Nicholson (kbds), Parley of Instruments,
Holman
✧ Hyperion CDA 66509 [D] **F**

8 Overtures AAM, Hogwood
✧ L'Oiseau-Lyre 436 859-2 [A] **F**

V   *Cymon and Iphegenia* (cantata); *The Desert Island* (stage play):
What tho' his guilt; Frolick and free (cantata); *The Morning*
(cantata); *Jenny; Much Ado about Nothing* (stage play): *Sigh no
more, ladies; Thou soft flowing Avon* (ode); *The winter's amusement:
The lover's recantation* Kirkby (sop), Morton (ten), Parley of
Instruments, Goodman
✧ Hyperion CDA 66237 [D] **F**

ARNOLD, Malcolm (born 1921) ENGLAND

O   *Clarinet Concerto No. 1, Op. 20; Flute Concerto No. 1, Op. 45;
Horn Concerto No. 2, Op. 58; Double Violin Concerto, Op. 77*
Collins (cl), Jones (fl), Watkins (hn), Sillito (vln), Fletcher
(vln), London Musici, Stephenson
Conifer CDCF 172 [D] **F**

○ *Clarinet Concerto No. 2; Flute Concerto No. 2; Horn Concerto No. 1; Piano Duo Concerto* Collins (cl), Jones (fl), Watkins (hn), Nettle & Markham (pno duo), London Musici, Stephenson
Conifer CDCF 228 [D] **F**

Guitar Concerto Bream (gtr), Melos Ensemble, Arnold (+Bennett: *Guitar Concerto*; Rodrigo: *Concierto de Aranjuez*)
RCA 09026 61598-2 [A] **M**

*Concerto for 2 Pianos (3 hands), Op. 104; Carnival of Animals, Op. 72; A Grand, Grand Overture, Op. 57; Symphony No. 2, Op. 40 *Nettle & Markham (pnos), RPO, Handley
Conifer CDCF 240 [D] **F**

Viola Concerto, Op. 108; Concerto for 28 Players; Larch Trees; Serenade for Small Orchestra, Op. 26 Golani (vla), London Musici, Stephenson
Conifer CDCF 211 [D] **F**

4 Cornish Dances, Op. 91; 8 English Dances Opp. 27 & 33; 4 Irish Dances, Op. 126; 4 Scottish Dances, Op. 59; Solitaire (ballet): *Sarabande and Polka* LPO, Arnold
Lyrita SRCD 201 [A] **F**

Overtures: *Beckus the Dandipratt, Op. 5; Commonwealth Christmas, Op. 64; The Fair Field, Op. 110; The Smoke, Op. 21; A Sussex Overture, Op. 31* LPO, Arnold
Reference RRCD-48 [D] **F**

Sinfoniettas Nos. 1–3; Flute Concerto No. 1; Oboe Concerto Beckett (fl), Messiter (ob), London Festival O, Pople
Hyperion CDA 66332 [D] **F**

Symphonies: Nos. 1, Op. 22; No.2, Op. 40 LSO, Hickox
Chandos CHAN 9335 [D] **F**

Symphonies: No. *2, Op. 40; No. 5, Op. 74; Peterloo Overture, Op. 97 CBSO, Arnold; *Bournemouth SO, Groves
EMI CDM7 63368-2 (US: Angel CDM 63368) [A] **M**

Symphonies: No. 3, Op. 63; No. 4, Op. 71 LSO, Hickox
Chandos CHAN 9290 [D] **F**

Symphony No. 6; *Fantasy on a Theme of John Field; Sweeney Todd Suite; Tam O'Shanter Overture *Lill (pno), RPO, Handley
Conifer CDCF 224 [D] **F**

Symphonies: Nos. 7, Op. 113; No. 8, Op. 124 RPO, Handley
Conifer CDCF 177 [D] **F**

C *Divertimento, Op. 37; Duo, Op. 10; Flute Sonata, Op. 121; Oboe Quartet, Op. 61; Quintet, Op. 7; 3 Shanties, Op. 4* Nash Ensemble
Hyperion CDA 66173 [D] **F**

Duo for 2 Cellos, Op. 85; Piano Trio, Op. 54; Viola Sonata No. 1, Op. 17; 5 Violin Pieces, Op. 84; Violin Sonatas: No. 1, Op. 15; No. 2, Op. 43 Nash Ensemble
Hyperion CDA 66171 [D] **F**

Clarinet Sonatina; Bassoon Fantasia, Op. 86; Clarinet Fantasia, Op. 87; Flute Fantasia, Op. 89; Horn Fantasia, Op. 88; Oboe Fantasia, Op. 90; Flute Sonatina, Op. 19; Oboe Sonatina, Op. 28; Recorder Sonatina, Op. 41; Trio, Op. 6 Nash Ensemble
Hyperion CDA 66172 [D] **F**

String Quartets: No. 1, Op. 23; No. 2, Op. 118 McCapra Quartet
Chandos CHAN 9112 [D] **F**

ARRIAGA, Juan (1806–1826) SPAIN

C *String Quartets: No. 1 in D min.; No. 2 in A; No. 3 in E♭*
Chilingirian Quartet
(+ Wikmanson: *Quartet No. 2*)
CRD 3312/3, 2 CDs [A] **F**

AUBER, Daniel (1782–1871) FRANCE

O Opera Overtures: *The Bronze Horse; Fra Diavolo; La Muette de
Portici* Detroit SO, Paray
(+ Suppé: *Overtures*)
Philips Mercury 434 309-2 [A] **M**

AVISON, Charles (1709–1770) ENGLAND

O *12 Concerti after Domenico Scarlatti* ASMF, Marriner
Philips 438 806-2, 2 CDs [A] **B**
Brandenburg Consort, Goodman
◇ Hyperion CDA 66891/2, 2 CDs [D] **F**

BACH, Carl Philipp Emanuel (1714–1788) GERMANY

O *Cello Concertos: in A min., H432; in B♭, H436; in A, H439*
Bylsma (vcl), Age of Enlightenment O, Leonhardt
◇ Virgin VC7 59541-2 (US: CDC 59541) [D] **F**

Flute Concertos: in D min., H426; in G, H445; in A, H438
Stinton (fl), St. John's O, Lubbock
Collins 13732 [D] **F**

6 Sinfonias, H657–62: in G; in B♭; in C; in A; in B min.; in E
English Concert, Pinnock
◇ DG Archiv 415 300-2 [D] **F**

C *3 Flute Quartets (Trio Sonatas), H537–9: in A min.; in D; in G;
Flute Sonata in G, H564* Les Adieux
◇ DHM GD 77052 (US: Editio Classica 77052-2) [A] **M**

The Complete Flute Sonatas B. Kuijken (fl), van Asperen (hpd)
◇ Sony CD 53964, 2 CDs [D] **F**

*Sinfonia a tre voci in D, H585; Trio Sonatas: in B♭, H584; in C
min., H579; Viola da Gamba Sonata in D, H559; 12 Variations in
D min. on La Folia, H263* Purcell Quartet
◇ Hyperion CDA 66239 [D] **F**

S *Fantasias: in C, H291; in F♯ min. (Freye Fantasie), H300; Rondo
in C min., H283; Keyboard Sonatas: in A min., H30; in E min.,
H281; in C, H47; 12 Variations in D min. on La Folia, H263*
Staier (hpd)
DHM RD 77025 (US: 77025-2) [A] **F**

*6 Keyboard Sonatas (Prussian), H24–2 ; 6 Keyboard Sonatas
(Wurttemberg), H30–34 & 36* van Asperen (hpd)
Teldec 9031 77623-2, 2 CDs [D] **F**

V *Die letzten Leiden des Erlösers (The Last Sufferings of the Saviour)*
(Passion cantata), *H776* Schlick (sop), de Reyghere (sop),
Patriasz (cont), Prégardien (ten), van Egmond (bass), Ghent
Collegium Vocale, La Petite Bande, Kuijken
◇ DHM GD 77042 (US: Editio Classica 77042-2), 2 CDs [A] **M**

Magnificat in D, H772 Palmer (sop), Watts (cont), Tear (ten),
Roberts (bs), King's College Ch, ASMF, Ledger
(+ J.S. Bach: *Magnificat*)
Decca 421 148-2 (US: London 421 148-2) [A] **M**

BACH, Johann Christian (1735–1782) GERMANY

O *6 Keyboard Concertos, Op. 1; 6 Keyboard Concertos, Op. 7* Haebler
(fpno), Vienna Capella Academica, Melkus
Philips 438 712-2, 2 CDs [A] **B**

*Symphonies: Op. 6/1-6; Op. 18/1-6; Op. 9/1-3; Overture: La
calamità* Netherlands CO
Philips 442 275-2, 2 CDs [A] **F**

*Symphonies: in E♭, Op. 18/1, in D, Op. 18/4; in G min., Op. 6/6;
Sinfonia Concertante in C, T289/4; Adriano in Siria (opera):
Overture, Standage* AAM, Standage
◇ Chandos CHAN 0540 [D] **F**

C *Quintets, T301/1: No. 1 in C; No. 6 in D; T304/6: No. 1 in D;
Sextet in C, T302/1* English Concert
◇ DG Archiv 423 385-2 [D] **F**

S *6 Sonatas, T341/1* Wooley (fpno)
◇ Chandos CHAN 0543 [D] **F**

BACH, Johann Christoph Friedrich (1732–1795) GERMANY

C *Cello Sonata in A* Bylsma (vcl), van Asperen (hpd)
(+ J.S. Bach: *Viola da Gamba Sonatas Nos. 1–3*)
◇ Sony CD 45945 [D] **F**

BACH, Johann Sebastian (1685–1750) GERMANY

O *Brandenburg Concertos Nos. 1–6, BWV1046–51* Tafelmusik,
Lamon
◇ Sony CD 66289, 2 CDs [D] **F**
COE
DG 431 660-2 2 CDs [D] **F**

Harpsichord Concerti Nos. 1–8 Koopman (hpd/dir), Amsterdam
Baroque O
◇ Erato 4509 91930-2, 2 CDs [D] **B**

Harpsichord Concerto No. 3 in D, BWV1054 Mustonen
(pno/dir), Deutsche Kammerphilharmonie
(+Beethoven: *Piano Concerto in D*)
Decca 443 118-2 (US: London 443 118-2) [D] F

*Double Harpsichord Concerti Nos. 1–3; Triple Harpsichord
Concerti Nos. 1 & 2; Triple Concerto for Flute, Violin &
Harpsichord in A min., BWV1044; Quadruple Harpsichord
Concerto in A min., BWV1065* Koopman (hpd/dir), Mathot,
Marisaldi, Mustonen (hpds), Manze (vln), Hazelzet (fl),
Amsterdam Baroque O
◇ Erato 4509 91929-2, 2 CDs [D] **B**

*Violin Concertos Nos. 1 in A min., BWV1041, & 2 in E, BWV1042;
*Double Violin Concerto in D min., BWV1043; **Violin and Oboe
Concerto in D min., BWV1060* Grumiaux (vln), *Krebbers (vln),
**Holliger (ob), Solistes Romands, Gerecz; **NPO, De Waart
Philips 420 700-2 [A] **M**

*Violin Concertos: No. 1 in A min., BWV1041, & 2 in E, BWV1042;
*Double Violin Concerto in D min., BWV1043; **Triple Violin
Concerto in D, BWV1064* Wallfisch (vln), *Bury (vln),
**Beznosiuk (vln), **Mackintosh (vln), Age of
Enlightenment O
◇ Virgin VC7 59319-2 (US: CDC 59319) [D] **F**

*Violin Concertos: in A min, BWV1052; in F min., BWV1056; Violin
and Oboe Concerto in C min., BWV1060; Oboe d'amore Concerto in*

A, BWV1055
EDITORS' CHOICE: Wallfisch (vln/dir), Robson (ob/dir), Age of
Enlightenment O
◇ Virgin VC5 45095-2 (US: 45095) [D] **F**

O *Orchestral Suites Nos. 1–4, BWV1066–9* Amsterdam Baroque O,
Koopman
◇ DHM RD 77864 (US: 77864-2), 2 CDs [D] **F**
Bennett (fl), ASMF, Marriner
Decca 430 378-2 (US: London 430 378-2) [A] **M**

C *The Art of Fugue, BWV1080* Koopman, Mathot (hpds)
Erato 4509 96387-2 [D] **F**

Flute Sonatas Nos. 1–6, BWV 1030–5 Galway (fl), Moll (hpd),
Cunningham (vla da gmb)
RCA 09026 62555-2 [D] **F**

A Musical Offering, BWV 1079 Moroney (hpd), Cook (hpd), See
(fl), Holloway (vln), Linden (vcl)
◇ HM HMC90 1260 [D] **F**

Trio Sonatas Nos. 1–4, BWV1036–9 London Baroque
◇ HM HMC 90 1173 [D] **F**

Viola da Gamba Sonatas Nos. 1–3, BWV1027–9 Bylsma (vcl),
van Asperen (hpd)
(+ J.C.F. Bach: *Cello Sonata in A*)
◇ Sony CD 45945 [D] **F**
Maisky (vcl), Argerich (pno)
DG 415 471-2 [D] **F**

10 Violin Sonatas, BWV1014–1023 Grumiaux (vln), Jaccotet
(hpd)
Philips 426 452-2, 2 CDs [A] **M**

S *Cello Suites Nos. 1–6, BWV1007–12*
Schiff (vcl)
EMI CDS7 47471-8 (US: Angel CDCC 47471), 2 CDs [D] **F**
Bylsma (vcl)
◇ Sony CD 48047, 2 CDs [D] **F**

*Lute Suites Nos. 1–4, BWV995–7; 1006a; Fugue, BWV1000;
Prelude, Fugue and Allegro, BWV998; Prelude, BWV999*
Kirchhof (lte)
◇ Sony CD 45858, 2 CDs [D] **F**

Solo Violin Sonatas and Partitas Nos. 1–6, BWV1001–6
Grumiaux (vln)
Philips 438 736-2, 2 CDs [A] **B**
Kuijken (baroque vln)
◇ RCA GD 77043 (US: Editio Classica 77043-2), 2 CDs [A] **M**

The Art of Fugue, BWV1080 Moroney (hpd)
◇ HM HMC90 1169/70, 2 CDs [D] **F**

*Chromatic Fantasia and Fugue in D min., BWV903; Fantasias: in
C min., BWV906; in G min., BWV917; in C min., BWV919;
Fantasia and Fugue in A min., BWV904; Preludes: in A min.,
BWV922; in C min., BWV921; Preludes and Fugues: in A min.,
BWV894; in F, BWV901; in G, BWV902a* Staier (hpd)
DHM RD 77039 (US: 77039-2) [A] **F**

*Chromatic Fantasia and Fugue in D min., BWV903; 4 Duets,
BWV802–5; Italian Concerto in F, BWV971; Partita in B min.,
BWV831* Rousset (hpd)
L'Oiseau-Lyre 433 054-2 [D] **F**

S *English Suites Nos. 1–6, BWV806–11* Gilbert (hpd)
HM HMC90 1074/5, 2 CDs [D] **F**

*French Suites Nos. 1–6, BWV812–7; Suite in A min., BWV818a;
Suite in E♭, BWV819* Moroney (hpd)
Virgin VCD7 59011-2 (US: CDCC 59011), 2 CDs [D] **F**

Goldberg Variations, BWV988 Cole (hpd)
Virgin VER5 61153-2 (US: 61153) [D] **M**
Gavrilov (pno)
DG 435 436-2 [D] **F**

*15 Inventions in 2 Parts, BWV772–86; 15 Inventions in 3 Parts,
BWV787–801; 6 Little Preludes, BWV933–8* Koopman (hpd)
Capriccio 10210 [D] **F**

*15 Two-part Inventions, BWV772-786; 15 Three-part Sinfonias,
BWV787-801; Fantasia in C min., BWV906; Fantasia and Fugue
in D min., BWV903* Hewitt (pno)
Hyperion CDA 66746 [D] **F**

*Partitas Nos. 1–6, BWV825–830; Italian Concerto, BWV971;
Overture in the French Style in B min., BWV831* Staier (hpd)
DHM 05472 77306-2 [D] **F**

Partitas Nos. 1–6, BWV825–30; 10 Preludes & Fugues
Gould (pno)
Sony CD 52597, 2 CDs [A] **M**

7 Toccatas, BWV910–916 Gould (pno)
Sony CD 52612, 2 CDs [A] **M**

The Well-tempered Clavier: Books Nos. 1 & 2, BWV846–893
Tilney (cvd)
Hyperion CDA 66351/4, 4 CDs [D] **F**
Gould (pno)
Book 1:
Sony CD 52600, 2 CDs [A] **M**
Book 2:
Sony CD 52603, 2 CDs [A] **M**

*Keyboard transcriptions by Busoni, Le Fleming, Hess, Kempff, Liszt,
Lord Berners and Rachmaninov* Fergus-Thompson (pno)
ASV CDDCA 759 [D] **F**

*Complete Organ Works Vol. 1: 3 Fantasias, BWV562, 570, 572; 3
Fantasias and Fugues, BWV537, 542, 561; 6 Fugues, BWV575–7,
579 (On a Theme of Corelli), 581, 946; Kleines harmonisches
Labyrinth; Passacaglia and Fugue in C min.; Pedal-Exercitium; 8
Preludes and Fugues, BWV531–3, 535, 548–551; Toccata, Adagio
and Fugue in C; 3 Toccatas and Fugues, BWV538 (Dorian), 540,
565 (in D min.); 2 Trios, BWV583, 585* Hurford (org)
Decca 421 337-2 (US: London 421 337-2), 3 CDs [A] **M**

*Complete Organ Works Vol. 2: 20 Chorale Preludes, BWV669–678,
680–689; 24 Kirnberger Chorale Preludes, BWV690–713; Prelude
and Fugue in E♭ (St. Anne), BWV552; 6 Trio Sonatas,
BWV525–530* Hurford (org)
Decca 421 341-2 (US: London 421 341-2), 3 CDs [A] **M**

*Complete Organ Works Vol. 3: Canonic Variations on 'Von Himmel
Hoch'; 3 Chorale Partitas, BWV766–8; 21 Chorale Preludes,
BWV645-650 (Schubler), 726–740; 2 Chorale Variations,
BWV770–1; Organ Concertos Nos. 1–6, BWV592–597*
Hurford (org)
Decca 421 617-2 (US: London 421 617-2), 3 CDs [A] **M**

S *Complete Organ Works Vol. 4: 35 Chorale Preludes, BWV714, 719, 742, 957, 1090–1120 (Arnstadt/Yale Manuscript); 18 Chorale Preludes, BWV651–658 (Leipzig), 663–668, 714–725* Hurford (org)
Decca 421 621-2 (US: London 421 621-2), 3 CDs [D/A] **M**

Complete Organ Works Vol. 5: Allabreve in D, BWV589; Aria in F, BWV587; Canzona in D min., BWV588; 2 Fantasias, BWV563, 571; 3 Fugues, BWV574, 578, 580; Pastorale in F, BWV590; 3 Preludes, BWV567–9; 10 Preludes and Fugues, BWV534, 535a (unfinished), 536, 539, 541, 543–7; 8 Short Preludes and Fugues, BWV553–60; Prelude, Trio and Fugue in Bb; Toccata and Fugue in E; 3 Trios, BWV584, 586, 1027a; Ricercare (Musical Offering) Hurford (org)
Decca 425 631-2 (US: London 425 631-2), 3 CDs [A] **M**

Complete Organ Works Vol. 6: Orgelbüchlein (46 Chorale Preludes) BWV599–644; 22 Chorale Preludes, BWV620a, 741–8, 751–2, 757–763, 765, Anh. 55; Fugue in G min. Hurford (org)
Decca 425 635-2 (US: London 425 635-2), 2 CDs [A] **M**

Aus tiefer Not, BWV1099; Organ Concerto No. 1 in G, BWV592; Erbarme dich, BWV721; Fantasia and Fugue in G min., BWV542; Pastorale in F, BWV590; Trio Sonata in Eb, BWV525; Toccata and Fugue in B min., BWV565 Bowyer (org)
Nimbus NI 5280 [D] **F**

Organ Concertos Nos. 1–5, BWV592–6 Preston (org)
DG 423 087-2 [D] **F**

Organ Concerto No. 2 in A min., BWV593; Prelude and Fugue in D min., BWV539; Fugue in G, BWV576; Aria in F, BWV587; Christ lag in Todesbanden, BWV718; Jesus, meine Zuversicht, BWV728; Christ ist erstanden, BWV746; Toccata and Fugue in F, BWV540 Bowyer (org)
Nimbus NI 5400 [D] **F**

Organ Concerto No. 5 in D min., BWV596; Partita on 'Sei gegrüsset', BWV768; Preludes and Fugues: in F min., BWV534; in A min., BWV543; Trio Sonata No. 2 in C min., BWV526 Bowyer (org)
Nimbus NI 5290 [D] **F**

Organ Concerto No. 5 in D min, BWV596; Aria in F, BWV587; Trio Sonata No. 5, BWV 529; Toccata, Adagio and Fugue in C, BWV564; Vater unser im Himmelreich, BWV737; Der Tag, ist so freundenreich, BWV 719; Nun danket alle Gott, BWV657; Fantasia super Valet will ich der geben, BWV735; Nun freut euch, lieben Christen gmein, BWV734 Hurford (org)
EMI Eminence CD-EMX 2226 (US: Classics for Pleasure CDEMX 2226) [D] **M**

Fantasia in G, BWV572; Fantasia and Fugues in C min., BWV537; in G min., BWV542; in C min., BWV562; Preludes and Fugues in D, BWV 532; in F min., BWV534; in A, BWV536; in G, BWV541; in A min., BWV543; in B min., BWV544; in C, BWV545; in C min., BWV546; in C, BWV547; in E min. (Wedge), BWV548; in Eb (St. Anne), BWV552 Herrick (org)
Hyperion CDA 66791/2, 2 CDs [D] **F**

Fantasia and Fugue in G min., BWV542; Passacaglia & Fugue in C min., BWV582; 6 Schubler Chorales, BWV645–50; Toccata, Adagio & Fugue in C, BWV564; Toccata & Fugue in F, BWV540 Preston (org)
DG 435 381-2 [D] **F**

S *Fantasia con imitatione in B min., BWV563; Fugue in A, BWV950;*
Fugue in B min., BWV951; Fugue in C min., BWV575; 8 'Short'
Preludes and Fugues, BWV553–560; Toccata in G min., BWV915;
Toccata in G, BWV916 Bowyer (org)
Nimbus NI 5377 [D] **F**

Orgelbüchlein, BWV599–644 Herrick (org)
Hyperion CDA 66756 [D] **F**

Passacaglia and Fugue in C min., BWV582; Toccata, Adagio and
Fugue in C, BWV564; Toccatas and Fugues: in D min., BWV565;
in F, BWV540; in D min. (Dorian), BWV538 Herrick (org)
Hyperion CDA 66434 [D] **F**

Prelude and Fugue in E min., BWV548; Passacaglia in C min.,
BWV582; Pastorella, BWV590; Piece d'orgue, BWV572; 3 Choral
Preludes, BWV691, 727 & 734 Kee (org)
Chandos CHAN 0510 [D] **F**

Prelude and Fugues: in D, BWV532; in A, BWV536; in G,
BWV541; Fugue in G, BWV577; Trio Sonata No. 5 in C, BWV529;
Chorale Preludes: Ein feste Burg, BWV720; Gelobet seist du,
BWV697 & 722; In dulci jubilo, BWV751 & 729; Von Himmel
hoch, BWV738 Bowyer (org)
Nimbus NI 5289 [D] **F**

6 Trio Sonatas, BWV525–530 Preston (org)
DG 437 835-2 [D] **F**

Toccata and Fugue in D min., BWV565; Passacaglia and Fugue in
C min., BWV582; Prelude and Fugue in G, BWV541; Fugues: in G
(Gigue), BWV577; in B min., BWV579; Pastorale in F, BWV590; 4
Chorale Preludes Hurford (org)
EMI Eminence CD-EMX 2218 (US: Classics for Pleasure CDEMX
2218) [D] **F**

Trio Sonata No. 6 in G, BWV560; Toccata, Adagio & Fugue in C,
BWV564; Prelude & Fugue in E min, BWV533; Prelude & Fugue
in G min., BWV535; Toccata in E, BWV566; Trio in G min., BWV
584; Fantasia super Valet will ich der geben, BWV735; Valet will
ich der geben, BWV736; Partita Wenn wir in hochsytein Noten sen, BWV
Anh.78 Bowyer (org)
Nimbus NI 5423 [D] **F**

V *Ascension Oratorio; Cantatas BWV43 & 44* Schlick (sop),
Patriasz (mez), Prégardien (ten), Kooy (bs), Collegium Vocale,
Herreweghe
◇ HM HMC90 1479 [D] **F**

Complete Sacred Cantatas, BWV 1–199 Various artists, VCM,
Harnoncourt; Leonhardt Consort, Leonhardt
◇ Teldec 4509 91765-2, 60 CDs [A/D] **B**

Volume 1, BWV1–19
◇ Teldec 4509 91755-2, 6 CDs [A] **M**

Volume 2, BWV20–36
◇ Teldec 4509 91756-2, 6 CDs [A] **M**

Volume 3, BWV37–60
◇ Teldec 4509 91757-2, 6 CDs [A] **M**

Volume 4, BWV61–78
◇ Teldec 4509 91758-2, 6 CDs [A] **M**

Volume 5, BWV79–99
◇ Teldec 4509 91759-2, 6 CDs [A] **M**

V   *Volume 6, BWV100–117*
    ◇ Teldec 4509 91760-2, 6 CDs [A] **M**

    Volume 7, BWV119–137
    ◇ Teldec 4509 91761-2, 6 CDs [A] **M**

    Volume 8, BWV138–162
    ◇ Teldec 4509 91762-2, 6 CDs [A/D] **M**

    Volume 9, BWV163–182
    ◇ Teldec 4509 91763-2, 6 CDs [A] **M**

    Volume 10, BWV183–199
    ◇ Teldec 4509 91764-2, 6 CDs [A] **M**

Cantatas: The Complete Archiv Series Various Artists, Munich Bach O & Ch, Richter
DG Archiv 439 368-2, 26 CDs [A] M

Cantatas: BWV4, 56 & 82 Fischer-Dieskau (bar), Munich Bach O & Ch, Richter
DG Archiv 427 128-2 [A] M

Cantatas: BWV8, 78 & 99 Bach Ensemble, Rifkin
◇ L'Oiseau-Lyre 421 728-2 [D] **F**

Cantatas: BWV26, 80 & 116 Mathis (sop), Schmidt (sop), Schreier (ten), Fischer-Dieskau (bar), Munich Bach O & Ch, Richter
DG Archiv 427 130-2 [A] M

Cantatas: BWV36, 61 & 62 Argenta (sop), Lang (mez), Rolfe Johnson (ten), Bär (bar), Monteverdi Ch, EBS, Gardiner
◇ DG Archiv 437 327-2 [D] **F**

Cantatas: BWV39, 93 & 107 Mellon (sop), Brett (alto), Crook (ten), Kooy (bs), Collegium Vocale, Herreweghe
◇ Virgin VC7 59320-2 (US: CDC 59320) [D] **F**

Cantatas, BWV51, 82a & 199 Argenta (sop), Ensemble Sonnerie, Huggett
◇ Virgin VC5 45038-2 (US: 45038) [D] **F**

Cantatas: BWV51, 78 & 140 Bach Ensemble, Rifkin
◇ L'Oiseau-Lyre 443 188-2 [D] **M**

Cantatas: BWV54, 169 & 170 Bowman (alt), King's Consort, King
◇ Hyperion CDA 66326 [D] **F**

Cantatas: BWV73, 105 & 131 Mellon (sop), Lesne (alt), Crook (ten), Kooy (bs), Collegium Vocale, Herreweghe
◇ Virgin VC7 59237-2 (US: CDC 59237) [D] **F**

Cantatas: BWV82, 159 & 170 Baker (mez), Tear (ten), Shirley-Quirk (bar), ASMF, Marriner
Decca 430 260-2 (US: London 430 260-2) [A] M

Cantatas, BWV 84, 202 & 209 Argenta (sop), Ensemble Sonnerie, Huggett
◇ Virgin VC5 45059-2 (US: 45059) [D] **F**

Cantatas: BWV106, 118 & 198 Argenta (sop), Chance (alt), Rolfe Johnson (ten), Varcoe (bar), Monteverdi Ch, EBS, Gardiner
◇ DG Archiv 429 782-2 [D] **F**

V *Cantatas: BWV140 & 147* Holton (sop), Chance (alt), Rolfe
Johnson (ten), Varcoe (bar), Monteverdi Ch, EBS, Gardiner
✧ DG Archiv 431 809-2 [D] **F**

Cantatas: BWV202 (Wedding), 209, 211 (Coffee) & 212 (Peasant)
Ameling (sop), English (ten), Nimsgern (bs), Collegium
Aureum
✧ DHM GD 77151 (US: Editio Classica 77151-2), 2 CDs [A] **M**

Cantatas: BWV206 & 207a Ziesak (sop), Chance (alt),
Prégardien (ten), Kooy (bs), Stuttgart Chamber Ch, Concerto
Cologne, Bernius
✧ Sony CD 46492 [D] **F**

Cantata: BWV208: Was mir behagt (Hunt) Smith (sop), Kirkby
(sop), Davies (ten), George (bs), Parley of Instruments,
Goodman
✧ Hyperion CDA 66169 [D] **F**

Christmas Oratorio, BWV248 Rolfe Johnson (ten), Argenta
(sop), von Otter (mez), Blochwitz (ten), Bär (bar), Monteverdi
Ch, EBS, Gardiner
✧ DG Archiv 423 232-2, 2 CDs [D] **F**

Easter Oratorio, BWV249; Cantata, BWV11 Frimmer (sop),
Popken (alt), Prégardien (ten), Wilson Johnson (bs), Age of
Enlightenment O & Ch., Leonhardt
✧ Philips 442 119-2 [D] **F**

20 Lieder from Schmelli's Song-book Schreier (ten), Richter (org)
DG 427 131-2 [A] **M**

Magnificat in D, BWV243
Kirkby (sop), Bonner (sop), Chance (alt), Ainsley (ten), Varcoe
(bar), Collegium Musicum 90 O & Ch, Hickox
(+ Vivaldi: *Gloria in D, RV589; Ostro picta*)
✧ Chandos CHAN 0518 [D] **F**
Palmer (sop), Watts (cont), Tear (ten), Roberts (bs), King's
College Ch, ASMF, Ledger
(+ C.P.E. Bach: *Magnificat*)
Decca 421 148-2 (US: London 421 148-2) [A] **M**

Mass in A, BWV234; Mass in G min., BWV235; Sanctus, BWV238
Mellon (sop), Lesne (alt), Prégardien (ten), Kooy (bs),
Collegium Vocale, Herreweghe
✧ Virgin VC7 59587-2 (US: CDC 59587) [D] **F**

Mass in B min., BWV232 Argenta (sop), Dawson (sop), Hall
(sop), Kwella (sop), Morgan (mez), Chance (alt), Stafford (alt),
Milner (ten), Evans (ten), Varcoe (bar), Monteverdi Ch, EBS,
Gardiner
✧ DG Archiv 415 514-2, 2 CDs [D] **F**
Ameling (sop), Minton (mez), Watts (cont), Krenn (ten),
Krause (bs), Stuttgart CO, Munchinger
Decca 440 609-2 (US: London 440 609-2), 2 CDs [A] **B**

Mass in F, BWV233; Mass in G, BWV236 Mellon (sop), Lesne
(alt), Prégardien (ten), Kooy (bs), Collegium Vocale,
Herreweghe
✧ Virgin VC7 59634-2 (US: CDC 59634) [D] **F**

Motets, BWV225–230 Stuttgart Chamber Ch, Stuttgart
Baroque O, Bernius
✧ Sony CD 45859 [D] **F**

St. John Passion, BWV245 Schlick (sop), Wessel (cont), de
Mey (ten), Kooy (bs), Netherlands Bach Ch, Amsterdam

Baroque O, Koopman
◇ Erato 4509 94675-2, 2 CDs [D] **F**

V *St. Matthew Passion, BWV244* Rolfe Johnson (ten), Schmidt
(bar), Bonney (sop), Monoyios (sop), von Otter (mez), Chance
(alt), Crook (ten), Bär (bar), Hauptmann (bs), Monteverdi Ch,
EBS, Gardiner
◇ DG Archiv 427 648-2, 3 CDs [D] **F**
Pears (ten), Fischer-Dieskau (bar), Schwarzkopf (sop),
Ludwig (mez), Gedda (ten), Berry (bs), Philharmonia Ch & O,
Klemperer
EMI CMS7 63058-2 (US: CDMC 63058), 3 CDs [A] **M**

BALAKIREV, Mily (1837–1910) RUSSIA

O *Piano Concertos: No. 1 in F# min., No. 2 in E♭* Binns (pno),
English Northern PO, Lloyd-Jones
(+ *Rimsky-Korsakov: Piano Concerto*)
Hyperion CDA 66640 [D] **F**

Symphony No. 1 in C; Second Overture on Russian Themes
Philharmonia O, Svetlanov
Hyperion CDA 66493 [D] **F**

*Symphony No. 2 in D min.; Tamara (symphonic poem); Overture
on 3 Russian Themes* Philharmonia O, Svetlanov
Hyperion CDA 66586 [D] **F**

S *Islamey* Gavrilov (pno)
(+ *Prokofiev: Piano Concerto No. 1, etc.; Tchaikovsky: Piano
Concerto No. 1, etc.*)
EMI CDM7 64329-2 (US: CDM 64329) [A] **M**

Piano Sonata in B♭ min.; The Lark Fergus-Thompson (pno)
(+ *Scriabin: 2 Poems; Piano Sonata No. 3; Vers la flamme*)
Kingdom KCLCD 2001 [D] **F**

BANTOCK, Granville (1868–1946) ENGLAND

O *Celtic Symphony; Hebridean Symphony; The Sea Reivers; The Witch
of Atlas* RPO, Handley
Hyperion CDA 66450 [D] **F**

Pagan Symphony; Fifne at the Fair; 2 Heroic Ballads RPO,
Handley
Hyperion CDA 66630 [D] **F**

BARBER, Samuel (1910–1981) USA

O *Cello Concerto, Op. 22; *Cello Sonata, Op. 6; Adagio for Strings,
Op. 11* Kirshbaum (vcl), Scottish CO, Saraste
Virgin VC5 59565-2 (US: 59565) [D] **F**

**Piano Concerto, Op. 38; Symphony No. 1, Op. 9; Souvenirs
(ballet), Op. 28: Suite* *Browning (pno), St Louis SO, Slatkin
RCA RD 60732 (US: 60732-2) [D] **F**

Violin Concerto, Op. 14
EDITORS' CHOICE: Shaham (vln), LSO, Previn
(+*Korngold: Violin Concerto, etc.*)
DG 429 886-2 [D] **F**

Essays for Orchestra Nos. 1–3 Detroit SO, Järvi
(+ *Ives: Symphony No. 1*)
Chandos CHAN 9053 [D] **F**

Medea (ballet), Op. 23: Suite Eastman-Rochester O, Hanson
(+ *Gould: Fall River Legend: Suite; Spirituals*)
Philips Mercury 432 016-2 [A] **M**

O *Medea's Meditation & Dance of Vengeance, Op. 23a; Music for a Scene from Shelley, Op.7; Under the Willow Tree* Detroit SO, Järvi (+Chadwick: *Symphony No. 3*)
Chandos CHAN 9253 [D] **F**

Symphony No. 1, Op. 9; Adagio for Strings, Op. 11; Essays Nos. 1 & 2; Music for a Scene from Shelley, Op. 7; School for Scandal Overture Baltimore SO, Zinman
Argo 436 288-2 [D] **F**

Symphony No. 2, Op. 19; Adagio for Strings, Op. 11 Detroit SO, Järvi
(+ Bristow: *Symphony in F# min.*)
Chandos CHAN 9169 [D] **F**

C *String Quartet, Op. 11* Emerson Quartet
(+ Ives: *String Quartets Nos. 1 & 2*)
DG 435 864-2 [D] **F**

S *The Complete Piano Music* Parkin (pno)
Chandos CHAN 9177 [D] **F**

Piano Sonata in Eb, Op. 26 Lawson (pno)
(+ Carter: *Piano Sonata;* Copland: *Piano Sonata;* Ives: *Three-page Sonata*)
Virgin VC7 59008-2 (US: 59008) [D] **F**

V *Agnus Dei* Corydon Singers, Best
(+ Bernstein: *Chichester Psalms;* Copland: *In the Beginning*, etc.)
Hyperion CDA 66219 [D] **F**

The Complete Songs Studer (sop), Hampson (bar), Browning (pno), Emerson Quartet
DG 435 867-2, 2 CDs [D] **F**

BARTÓK, Béla (1881–1945) HUNGARY/USA

O *Concerto for Orchestra; *Dance Suite; *2 Portraits; *Mikrokosmos* (arr.): *Bourée; From the Diary of a Fly* LSO, *Philharmonia Hungarica, Dorati
Philips Mercury 432 017-2 [A] **M**

Concerto for Orchestra; 4 Pieces, Op. 12 CSO, Boulez
DG 437 826-2 [D] **F**

Piano Concertos Nos. 1–3 Anda (pno), Berlin RSO, Fricsay
DG 447 398-2 [A] **M**

Viola Concerto; Music for Strings, Percussion and Celeste Christ (vla), BPO, Ozawa
DG 437 993-2 [D] **F**

Violin Concertos Nos. 1 & 2 Midori (vln), BPO, Mehta
Sony CD 45941 [D] **F**

Violin Concerto No. 2; Rhapsodies Nos. 1 & 2 Takezawa (vln), LSO, Tilson Thomas
RCA 09026 61675-2 [D] **F**

Dance Suite; *Music for Strings, Percussion and Celeste; The Wooden Prince NYPO, *BBC SO, Boulez
(+Scriabin: *Poem of Ecstasy*)
Sony CD 64100, 2 CDs [A] **M**

Divertimento for Strings; Music for Strings, Percussion and Celeste; Miraculous Mandarin (ballet): *Suite* CSO, Solti
Decca 430 352-2 (US: London 430 352-2) [D] **F**

O   *Hungarian Sketches; Romanian Folkdances* Minneapolis SO, Dorati
(+ Kodály: *Dances from Galanta*, etc.)
Philips Mercury 432 005-2 [A] **M**

  The Wooden Prince (ballet); *Cantata profana* Aler (ten), Tomlinson (bar), CSO & Ch, Boulez
DG 435 863-2 [D] **F**

C   *Contrasts; Rhapsodies Nos. 1 & 2; Romanian Folkdances; Solo Violin Sonata* Collins (cl), Osostowicz (vln), Tomes (pno)
Hyperion CDA 66415 [D] **F**

  44 Duos Kiss (vln), Balogh (vln)
Hyperion CDA 66453 [D] **F**

  String Quartets Nos. 1–6 Emerson Quartet
DG 423 657-2, 2 CDs [D] **F**

  Violin Sonata No. 1 Kremer (vln), Argerich (pno)
(+ Janáček: *Sonata;* Messiaen: *Theme & Variations*)
DG 427 351-2 [D] **F**

  Sonata for 2 Pianos and Percussion Argerich, Freire (pnos), Sadlo, Guggeis (perc)
(+Ravel: *Rapsodie espagnole; Ma mère l'oye*)
DG 439 867-2 [D] **F**

S   *Allegro barbaro; 2 Romanian Dances; 3 Hungarian Folksongs from Csik; 4 Dirges; Suite; Romanian Christmas Carols; 3 Studies; 3 Rondos on Folktunes; First Term at the Piano* Kocsis (pno)
Philips 442 016-2 [D] **F**

  14 Bagatelles; 2 Elegies; 3 Hungarian Folk Tunes; 6 Romanian Folk Dances; Sonatina Kocsis (pno)
Philips 434 104-2 [D] **F**

  10 Easy Pieces; For Children (1945 revised version); *15 Hungarian Peasant Songs; Romanian Folkdances; Piano Sonata; Sonatine; Out of Doors* Béroff (pno)
EMI CZS5 68101-2 (US: CDMB 68101), 2 CDs [A] **B**

  Mikrokosmos (complete); *For Children* (original version) Ranki (pno)
Teldec 9031 76139-2, 3 CDs [D] **F**

BAX, Arnold (1883–1953) ENGLAND

O   **Cello Concerto; Cortège; Mediterranean; Overture to a Picaresque Comedy; Prelude for a Solemn Occasion* *R. Wallfisch (vcl), LPO, Thomson
Chandos CHAN 8494 [D] **F**

  *Violin Concerto; A Legend; Romantic Overture; Golden Eagle (incidental music) *Mordkovitch (vln), LPO, Thomson
Chandos CHAN 9003 [D] **F**

  The Garden of Fand; The Happy Forest; November Woods; Summer Music Ulster O, Thomson
Chandos CHAN 8307 [D] **F**

  Tone poems: *In the Faery Hills; Into the Twilight; Roscatha; The Tale the Pine-trees knew* Ulster O, Thomson
Chandos CHAN 8367 [D] **F**

  Northern Ballad No. 2; Spring Fire; Symphonic Scherzo RPO, Handley
Chandos CHAN 8464 [D] **F**

O *Saga Fragment; Winter Legends* Fingerhut (pno), LPO, Thomson
Chandos CHAN 8484 [D] **F**

Symphonies Nos. 1–7 LPO, Ulster O, Thomson
Chandos CHAN 8906/10 [D] **M**

Symphony No. 1 in E♭; Christmas Eve on the Mountains (tone poem) LPO, Thomson
Chandos CHAN 8480 [D] **F**

Symphony No. 2 in E min./C; Nympholept (tone poem) LPO, Thomson
Chandos CHAN 8493 [D] **F**

Symphony No. 3; 4 Orchestral Sketches: Dance of the Wild Irravel; Paean LPO, Thomson
Chandos CHAN 8454 [D] **F**

Symphony No. 4; Tintagel (tone poem) Ulster O, Thomson
Chandos CHAN 8312 [D] **F**

Symphony No. 5 in C♯ min.; Russian Suite LPO, Thomson
Chandos CHAN 8669 [D] **F**

Symphony No. 6; Festival Overture LPO, Thomson
Chandos CHAN 8586 [D] **F**

Symphony No. 7; Songs: Eternity; Glamour; A Lyke-Wake; Slumber Song Hill (ten), LPO, Thomson
Chandos CHAN 8628 [D] **F**

*Tintagel; Christmas Eve; Festival Overture; Nympholept; 4 Orchestral Sketches: Dance of the Wild Irravel; Paean LPO,*Ulster O, Thompson
Chandos CHAN 9168 [D] **F**

C *Cello Sonata in E♭; Sonatina in D; Legend-Sonata in F♯ min.; Folk-Tale* Gregor-Smith (vcl), Wrigley (pno)
ASV CDDCAA 896 [D] **F**

Piano Trio in B♭ Borodin Trio
(+ Bridge: *Piano Trio No. 2*)
Chandos CHAN 8495 [D] **F**

Oboe Quintet Francis (ob), English Quartet
(+ Holst: *Air and Variations; 3 Pieces;* Jacob: *Oboe Quartet;* Moeran: *Fantasy Quartet*)
Chandos CHAN 8392 [D] **F**

Clarinet Sonata Hilton (cl), Swallow (pno)
(+ Bliss: *Clarinet Quintet;* Vaughan Williams: *6 Studies*)
Chandos CHAN 8683 [D] **F**

Violin Sonatas: No. 1 in E; No. 2 in D Gruenberg (vn), McCabe (pno)
Chandos CHAN 8845 [D] **F**

String Quartet No. 2; *Piano Quintet Norris (pno), Mistry Quartet
Chandos CHAN 8795 [D] **F**

S *Apple Blossom Time; Burlesque; The Maiden with the Daffodil; Nereid; O Dame Get Up and Bake Your Pies; On a May Evening; The Princess's Rose Garden; Romance; 2 Russian Tone Pictures; Sleepy Head* Parkin (pno)
Chandos CHAN 8732 [D] **F**

S *Country Tune; Lullaby; Piano Sonatas Nos. 1 & 2; Winter Waters*
Parkin (pno)
Chandos CHAN 8496 [D] **F**

*A Hill Tune; In a Vodka Shop; Piano Sonatas Nos. 3 & 4; Water
Music* Parkin (pno)
Chandos CHAN 8497 [D] **F**

Rhapsodic Ballad R. Wallfisch (vcl)
(+ Bridge: *Cello Sonata;* Delius: *Cello Sonata;* Walton:
Passacaglia)
Chandos CHAN 8499 [D] **F**

BEASER, Robert (born 1954) USA

O *Chorale Variations; *The Seven Deadly Sins; **Piano Concerto*
*Opalach (bs), **Paul (pno), American Composers O, Davies
Argo 440 337-2 [D] **F**

BEETHOVEN, Ludwig van (1770–1827) GERMANY

O *Piano Concertos Nos. 1–5; *Triple Concerto in C, Op. 56* Fleisher
(pno), Cleveland O, Szell; *Stern (vln), Rose (vcl), Istomin
(pno), Philadelphia O, Ormandy
Sony CD 48397, 3 CDs [A] **F**

Piano Concertos Nos. 1–5 Pollini (pno), BPO, Abbado
DG 439 770-2, 3 CDs [D] **F**

*Piano Concertos Nos. 1–4; *Violin Romances Nos. 1 & 2*
Kovacevich, BBC SO, C. Davis; *Grumiaux (vln),
Concertgebouw O, Haitink
Philips 442 577-2, 2 CDs [A] **B**

Piano Concertos: No. 1 in C, Op. 15; No. 2 in Bb, Op. 19
Kovacevich (pno), BBC SO, C. Davis
Philips 422 968-2 [A] **B**

Piano Concertos: No. 2 in Bb, Op. 19; No. 4 in G, Op. 58 Fleisher
(pno), Cleveland O, Szell
Sony CD 48165 [A] **B**

Piano Concertos: No. 3 in C min., Op. 37; No. 4 in G, Op. 58
Kempff (pno), BPO, Leitner
DG 419 467-2 [A] **M**

*Piano Concerto No. 5 in Eb (Emperor), Op. 73; *Triple Concerto in
C, Op. 56* Fleisher (piano), Cleveland O, Szell; *Stern (vln),
Rose (vcl), Istomin (pno), Philadelphia O, Ormandy
Sony CD 46549 [A] **B**

*Piano Concerto No. 5 in Eb, Op.73 (Emperor); Piano Concerto in
D, Op. 61a (arr. of Violin Concerto); Violin Concerto: Triple
Concerto* Kovacevich (pno), Grumiaux (vln), Szeryng (vln),
Krebbers (vln), Arrau (pno), C. Davis, Haitink, Inbal
Philips 442 580-2, 2 CDs [A] **B**

*Piano Concerto No. 5 in Eb (Emperor), Op. 73; *Fantasia in C
min., Op. 80* Tan (fpno), *Schütz Ch, LCP, Norrington
◇ EMI CDC7 49965-2 (US: Angel CDC 49965) [D] **F**

Piano Concerto in D , Op. 61a (arr. of Violin Concerto) Mustonen
(pno), Deutsche Kammerphilharmonie, Saraste
(+Bach: *Harpsichord Concerto No. 3*)
Decca 443 118-2 (US: London 443 118-2) [D] **F**

Violin Concerto in D, Op. 61 Schneiderhan (vln), BPO, Jochum
(+Mozart: *Violin Concerto No. 5*)
DG 447 403-2 [A] **M**

○ *Triple Concerto in C, Op. 56* Oistrakh (vln), Rostropovich (vcl),
Richter (pno), BPO, Karajan
(+Brahms: *Double Concerto*)
EMI CDM7 64744-2 (US: Angel CDM 64744) [A] **M**

*Concerto Movement for Violin and Orchestra in C, Wo05; Romance
No. 1 in G, Op. 40* Kremer (vln), LSO, Tchakarov
(+ Schubert: *Konzertstück*, etc.)
DG 431 168-2 [A] **M**

The Creatures of Prometheus (ballet) Orpheus CO
DG 419 608-2 [D] **F**

Complete Overtures: *Consecration of the House, Op. 124;
Coriolan, Op. 62; The Creatures of Prometheus, Op. 43; Egmont,
Op. 84; Fidelio; King Stephen, Op. 117; Leonoras Nos. 1–3; Name
Day, Op. 115; The Ruins of Athens, Op. 113* BPO, Karajan
DG 427 256-2, 2CDs [A] **M**

Symphonies Nos. 1–9
Margiono (sop), Remmert (cont), Schasching (ten), Holl (bs),
A. Schoenberg Ch, COE, Harnoncourt
Teldec 2292 46452-2, 5 CDs [D] **F**
NDR SO, Wand
RCA 74321 20277-2, 5 CDs [D] **M**

Symphonies Nos. 1–9 (includes interview with Gardiner)
Monteverdi Ch., Orchestre Révolutionnaire et Romantique,
Gardiner
❖ **DG Archiv 439 900-2, 5 CDs** [D] **F**

Symphonies: No. 1 in C, Op. 21; No. 2 in D, Op. 36 18th Century
O, Bruggen
❖ **Philips 434 029-2** [D] **F**

*Symphonies: No. 1 in C, Op. 21; No. 6 in F (Pastoral), Op. 68;
Egmont: Overture, Op. 84a* Cleveland O, Szell
Sony CD 46532 [A] **B**

Symphonies: No. 2 in D, Op. 36; No. 4 in B♭, Op. 60
Philharmonia O, Klemperer
EMI CDM7 63355-2 (US: Angel CDM 63355) [A] **M**

Symphonies: No. 2 in D, Op. 36; No. 8 in F, Op. 93 LCP,
Norrington
❖ **EMI CDC7 47698-2 (US: Angel CDC 47698)** [D] **F**

Symphony No. 3 in E♭ (Eroica), Op. 55; Grosse Fuge in B♭, Op. 133
Philharmonia O, Klemperer
EMI CDM7 63356-2 (US: Angel CDM 63356) [A] **M**

Symphony No. 3 in E♭ (Eroica), Op. 55; Overtures: *Fidelio,
Op. 72b; Coriolan, Op. 62* Chicago SO, Reiner
RCA 09026 60962-2 [A] **M**

*Symphony No. 4 in B♭, Op. 60; Symphony No. 7 in A, Op. 92; King
Stephen, Op. 117: Overture* Cleveland O, Szell
Sony CD 48158 [A] **B**

Symphonies: No. 5 in C min., Op. 67; No. 7 in A, Op. 92 VPO,
Kleiber
DG 447 400-2 [A] **M**

*Symphonies: No. 5 in C min., Op. 67; No. 8 in F, Op. 93; Fidelio:
Overture, Op. 72a* BPO, Karajan
DG 419 051-2 [A] **M**

O *Symphonies: No. 6 in F (Pastoral), Op. 68; No. 8 in F, Op. 93*
COE, Harnoncourt
Teldec 9031 75709-2 [D] F

Symphony No. 9 in D min. (Choral), Op. 125
Tomowa-Sintow (sop), Baltsa (mez), Schreier (ten), van Dam
(bs-bar), Vienna Singverein, BPO, Karajan
DG 415 832-2 [A] M
Dawson (sop), Van Nes (cont), Rolfe Johnson (ten), Schulte
(bs), Lisbon Gulbenkian Ch., 18th Century O, Bruggen
✧ **Philips 438 158-2 [D] F**

Wellingtons Sieg, Op. 91; *Egmont: Incidental Music; **Marches:
WoO29 in Bb; WoO24 in D; WoO18 in F; WoO19 in F; WoO20 in
C; Ecossaise in D; WoO22 *Janowitz (sop), BPO, Karajan;
**BPO Wind Ensemble, Priem-Bergrath
DG 419 624-2 [A] F

C *Cello Sonatas Nos. 1-5; *Complete Variations* Rostropovich (vcl),
Richter (pno); *Gendron (vcl), Françaix (pno)
Philips 442 565-2, 2 CDs [A] M

Cello Sonatas: No. 1 in F, Op. 5/1; No. 2 in G min., Op. 5/2
Bylsma (vcl), Bilson (fpno)
✧ **Elektra Nonesuch 7559 79152-2 (US: 79152-2) [D] F**

Cello Sonatas Nos. 3–5 Bylsma (vcl), Bilson (fpno)
✧ **Elektra-Nonesuch 7559 79236-2 (US: 79236-2) [D] F**

Cello Sonatas: No. 3 in A, Op. 69; No. 5 in D, Op. 105/2 Du Pré
(vcl), Bishop (pno)
EMI CDM7 69179-2 (US: Angel CDM 69179) [A] M

Grosse Fuge, Op. 133 Hagen Quartet
(+Schubert: *String Quintet*)
DG 439 774-2 [D] F

Piano Quartet in Eb, Op. 16 Ax (pno), Stern (vln), Laredo (vla),
Ma (vcl),
(+ Schumann: *Piano Quartet*)
Sony CD 53339 [D] F

Piano and Wind Quintet, Op. 16 Perahia (pno), Black (ob), King
(cl), Halstead (hn), Sheen (bsn)
(+ Mozart: *Piano and Wind Quintet*)
Sony CD 42099 [D] F

Piano Trios Nos. 1–11 Istomin (pno), Stern (vln), Rose
(vcl)
Sony CD 46738, 4 CDs [A] M

Piano Trios: No. 1 in Eb, Op. 1/1; No. 3 in C min., Op. 1/3;
Variations, Op. 44 Castle Trio
✧ **Virgin VC7 59590-2 (US: CDC 59590) [D] F**

Piano Trios: No. 1 in C min. Op. 1/1; No. 5 in D (Ghost), Op. 70/1
Chung Trio
EMI CDC7 54579-2 (US: CDC 54579) [D] F

Piano Trios: No. 2 in G, Op. 1/2; No. 4 in Bb, Op. 11; in Eb
WoO38 Castle Trio
✧ **Virgin VC7 59220-2 (US: CDC 59220) [D] F**

Piano Trios: No. 4 in Bb, Op. 11; No. 7 in Bb (Archduke), Op. 97
Chung Trio
EMI CDC5 55187-2 (US: CDC 55187) [D] F

C *Piano Trios: No. 7 in Bb (Archduke), Op. 97 ; No. 9 in Bb, WoO39;*
No. 11 in G, Op. 121a (Kakadu Variations) Castle Trio
◇ Virgin VC7 59044-2 (US: 59044) [D] **F**

*Septet in Eb, Op. 20; *Wind Sextet in Eb, Op. 71* Vienna Octet;
*Vienna Wind Soloists
Decca 436 653-2 (US: London 436 653-2) [D] **F**

Serenade in D, Op. 8; String Trio in Eb, Op. 3 L'Archibudelli
◇ Sony CD 53961 [D] **F**

*String Quartets: Nos. 1–6, Op. 18; *String Quintet in C Op. 29*
Tokyo String Quartet; *Zukerman (vla)
RCA 09026 61286-2, 3 CDs [D] **F**

String Quartets: No. 1 in F, Op. 18/1; No. 12 in Eb, Op. 127
Orford Quartet
Delos DE 3031 [D] **F**

String Quartets: Nos. 2-4, Op. 18/2-4 Végh Quartet
Auvidis Valois V4402 [A] **M**

String Quartets: No. 5 in A, Op. 18/5; No. 7 in F (Rasumovsky),
Op. 59/1 Orford Quartet
Delos DE 3033 [D] **F**

String Quartets: No. 6 in Bb, Op. 18/6; No. 16 in F, Op. 135;
Grosse Fuge, Op. 133 Orford Quartet
Delos DE 3038 [D] **F**

String Quartets: Nos. 7–11, Opp. 59/1–3 (Rasumovsky); 74; 95
Italian Quartet
Philips 420 797-2, 3CDs [A] **M**

String Quartets (Razumovsky): Nos. 7-9, Op. 59/1-3 Lindsay
Quartet
ASV CDDCS 207, 2 CDs [D] **M**

String Quartets: No. 10 in Eb (harp), Op. 74; No. 11 in F min.
(Serioso), Op. 95 Cleveland Quartet
Telarc CD 80351 [D] **F**

String Quartets: No. 11 in F min. (Serioso), Op. 95 & 15 in A min.,
Op. 132 Végh Quartet
Auvidis Valois V4406 [A] **M**

String Quartets: Nos. 12–16, Opp. 127, 130–132, 135; Grosse Fuge
in Bb, Op. 133
Lindsay Quartet
ASV CDDCS 403, 4 CDs [D] **F**

String Quartet No. 13 in Bb, Op. 130; Grosse Fuge in Bb, Op. 133
Végh Quartet
Auvidis V4407 [A] **F**
Lindsay Quartet
ASV CDDCA 602 [D] **F**

String Quartets: No. 14 in C# min., Op. 131; No. 16 in F, Op. 135
Végh Quartet
Auvidis V4408 [A] **F**
(arr.) VPO, Bernstein
DG 435 779-2 [A/D] **F**

String Quartets: No. 15 in A min., Op. 132; No. 16 in F, Op. 135
Talich Quartet
Calliope CAL 9639 [A] **F**

String Quintet in C, Op. 29; Septet in Eb, Op. 20 Hausmusik
◇ EMI CDC7 54656-2 (US: CDC 54656) [D] **F**

C *3 String Trios, Op. 9: No. 1 in G; No. 2 in D; No. 3 in C min.*
L'Archibudelli
◇ Sony CD 48190 [D] **F**

Violin Sonatas Nos. 1–10 Perlman (vln), Ashkenazy (pno)
Decca 421 453-2 (US: London 421 453-2), 4 CDs [A] **M**

Violin Sonatas Nos. 1–3 Kremer (vln), Argerich (pno)
DG 415 138-2 [D] **F**

Violin Sonatas: No. 4 in A min., Op. 23; No. 5 in F (Spring),
Op. 24 Kremer (vln), Argerich (pno)
DG 419 787-2 [D] **F**

Violin Sonatas: No. 5 in F (Spring), Op. 24; No. 8 in G, Op. 30/3;
No. 9 in A (Kreutzer), Op. 47 Zukerman (vln), Barenboim
(pno)
EMI CDM7 64631-2 (US: CDM 64631) [A] **M**

Violin Sonatas Nos. 6–8, Op. 30/1–3 Kremer (vln), Argerich
(pno)
DG 445 652-2 [D] **F**

Wind Octet in E♭, Op. 103; Wind Quintet in E♭ H19; Rondino in E♭,
WoO25; Wind Sextet in E♭, Op. 71 COE Wind Soloists
ASV CDCOE 807 [D] **F**

Wind Octet in E♭, Op.103; Rondino in E♭, WoO25; March in B♭,
WoO29; Duo in C, WoO27/1; Sextet in E♭, Op.71 Mozzafiato,
Neidich
◇ Sony CD 53367 [D] **F**

S *Bagatelles Nos. 1–24* Kovacevich (pno)
Philips 426 976-2 [A] **B**

Bagatelles Nos. 1–24; Fantasia in G min., Op. 77; 7 Variations on
'God Save the King', WoO78; 5 Variations on 'Rule Britannia',
WoO79 Tan (fpno)
◇ EMI CDC7 54526-2 (US: Angel CDC 54526) [D] **F**

Piano Sonatas Nos. 1–32 (complete)
Barenboim (pno)
EMI CZS7 62863-2 (US: CDMB 62863), 10 CDs [A] **M**

Piano Sonatas Nos.1–3, Op.2/1–3 Brendel (pno)
Philips 442 124-2 [D] **F**

Piano Sonatas: No. 3 in C, Op. 2/3; No. 4 in E♭, Op. 7; No. 27
in E min., Op. 90 Richter (pno)
Olympia OCD 336 [D] **F**

Piano Sonatas: No. 5 in C min., Op. 10/1; No. 10 in G, Op. 14/2;
No. 19 in G min., Op. 49/1; No. 20 in G, Op. 49/2 Gilels
(pno)
DG 419 172-2 [D] **F**

Piano Sonatas: Nos. 5–7, Op. 10 Lortie (pno)
Chandos CHAN 9101 [D] **F**

Piano Sonatas: No. 7 in D, Op. 10/3; No. 18 in E♭, Op. 31/3; 15
Variations and Fugue on an Original Theme in E♭ (Eroica), Op. 35
Gilels (pno)
DG 423 136-2 [D] **F**

Piano Sonatas: No. 8 in C min. (Pathétique), Op. 13; No. 13 in E♭,
Op. 27/1; No. 14 in C♯ min. (Moonlight), Op. 27/2; No.15 in D
(Pastoral), Op. 28; No. 24 in F♯, Op. 78 Kempff (pno)
DG 415 834-2 [A] **M**

S *Piano Sonatas: No. 8 in C min., Op.13 (Pathétique); No. 23 in F min., Op.57 (Appassionata); No. 31 in Ab, Op. 110* Gilels (pno)
DG 439 426-2 [A/D] **B**

Piano Sonatas: Nos. 9 & 10, Op. 14/1 & 2; No. 24 in F#, Op. 78; No. 27 in E min., Op. 90; No. 28 in A, Op. 101 Jando (pno)
Naxos 8.550162 [D] **B**

Piano Sonatas: No. 12 in Ab, Op. 26; No. 13 in Eb, Op. 27/1; No. 14 in C# min. (Moonlight), Op. 27/2; No. 19 in G min., Op. 49/1 Brendel (pno)
Philips 438 863-2 [D] **F**

Piano Sonatas: No. 14 in C# min. (Moonlight), Op. 27/2; No. 21 in C (Waldstein), Op. 53; No. 23 in F min. (Appassionata), Op. 57 Pletnev (pno)
Virgin VC7 59247-2 (US: CDC 59247) [D] **F**

Piano Sonatas: No. 15 in D (Pastoral), Op. 28; No. 17 in D min. (Tempest), Op. 31/2 Gilels (pno)
DG 419 161-2 [A] **F**

Piano Sonatas: Nos. 17 in D min. (Tempest), & 18 in Eb, Op. 31/2 & 3; No. 26 in Eb (Les adieux), Op. 81a Perahia (pno)
Sony/CBS CD 42319 [D] **F**

Piano Sonatas: No. 17 in D min. (Tempest), Op. 31/2; No. 25 in G, Op. 79; No. 28 in A, Op. 101 Gelber (pno)
Denon CO-75245 [D] **F**

Piano Sonatas: No. 21 in C (Waldstein), Op. 53; No. 23 in F min. (Appassionata), Op. 57; No. 26 in Eb (Les adieux), Op. 81a Gilels (pno)
DG 419 162-2 [A] **F**

Piano Sonatas No. 21 in C (Waldstein), Op. 53; No. 23 in F min. (Appassionata), Op. 57; No. 26 in Eb (Les adieux), Op. 81a Tan (fpno)
◇ Virgin VER5 61160-2 (US: 61160) [D] **M**

Piano Sonatas: No. 21 in C (Waldstein), Op. 53; No. 22 in F, Op. 54; No. 28 in A, Op. 101; Andante in F, WoO57 Brendel (pno)
Philips 438 472-2 [D] **F**

Piano Sonata No. 23 in F minor, Op. 57 (Appassionata) Richter (pno)
(+ Brahms: *Piano Concerto No. 2*)
RCA 07863 56519-2 [A] **M**

Piano Sonatas: No. 27 in E min., Op. 90; No. 28 in A, Op. 101; No. 32 in C min., Op. 111 Kovacevich (pno)
EMI CDC7 54599-2 (US: CDC 54599) [D] **F**

Piano Sonatas Nos. 27–32 Rosen (pno)
Sony CD 53531, 2 CDs [A] **B**

Piano Sonatas: Nos. 28–32 Pollini (pno)
DG 419 199-2, 2 CDs [A] **F**

Piano Sonata No. 29 in Bb (Hammerklavier), Op. 106 Gilels (pno)
DG 410 527-2 [A] **F**

Piano Sonatas: No. 30 in E, Op. 109; No. 31 in Ab, Op. 110 Gilels (pno)
DG 419 174-2 [A] **F**

33 Variations on a Waltz by Diabelli, Op. 120 Kovacevich (pno)
Philips 422 969-2 [A] **B**

S   *33 Variations on a Waltz by Diabelli, Op. 120; Piano Sonata No.
    28 in A, Op. 101* Donohoe (pno)
    EMI CDC7 54792-2 (US: CDC 54792) [D] **F**

    *6 Variations on an Original Theme in F, Op. 34; 15 Variations and
    a Fugue on an Original Theme in Eb (Eroica), Op. 35; 2 Rondos,
    Op. 51; Bagatelle No. 25 in A min., Für Elise, WoO59* Lortie
    (pno)
    Chandos CHAN 8616 [D] **F**

V   *An die ferne Geliebte* (song cycle), *Op. 98; 8 Lieder* Fischer-
    Dieskau (bar), Demus (pno)
    (+ Brahms: *Lieder*)
    DG 415 189-2 [A] **F**

    *Bundeslied, Op. 122; Elegischer Gesang, Op. 118; King Stephen, Op.
    117; Meeresstille und glückliche Fahrt, Op. 112; Opferlied, Op. 121b*
    Ambrosian Singers, LSO, Tilson Thomas
    Sony/CBS CD 76404 [D] **F**

    Mass in C, Op. 86; Meeresstille und glückliche Fahrt, Op. 112
    Dunn (sop), Zimmermann (mez), Beccaria (ten), Krause (bar),
    Ernst-Senff Chamber Ch, Berlin RSO & Ch, Chailly
    Decca 417 563-2 (US: London 417 563-2) [D] **F**

    Missa Solemnis in D, Op. 123
    Janowitz (sop), Ludwig (mez), Wunderlich (ten), Berry (bs),
    Vienna Singverein, BPO, Karajan
    (+ Mozart: *Mass No. 16*)
    DG 423 913-2, 2 CDs [A] **M**
    Margiano (sop), Robbin (mez), Kendall (ten), Miles (bs),
    Monteverdi Ch, Orchestre Révolutionnaire et Romantique,
    Gardiner
    ◇ DG Archiv 429 779-2 [D] **F**

BELLINI, Vincenzo (1801–1835) ITALY

O   *Oboe Concerto in Eb* Lord (ob) ASMF, Marriner
    (+ Cherubini: *Horn Sonata;* Donizetti: *String Quartet;* Rossini:
    String Sonatas)
    Decca 443 838-2 (US: London 443 838-2), 2 CDs [A] **B**

BEN-HAIM, Paul (1897–1974) GERMANY/ISRAEL

O   *Violin Concerto* Perlman (vln), Israel PO, Mehta
    (+ Castelnuovo-Tedesco: *Violin Concerto No. 2*)
    EMI CDC7 54296-2 (US: CDC 54296) [D] **F**

    Sweet Psalmist of Israel Marlowe (hpd), Stavrache (hp), NYPO,
    Bernstein
    (+ Bloch: *Sacred Service;* Foss: *Song of Songs*)
    Sony CD 47533, 2 CDs [A] **M**

BENJAMIN, George (born 1960) ENGLAND

O   *Antara* London Sinfonietta, Benjamin
    (+ Boulez: *Dérive; Mémoriale;* Harvey: *Song Offerings*)
    Nimbus NI 5167 [D] **F**

    *At First Light; **A Mind of Winter; ***Ringed by the flat Horizon
    *Hulse (ob), **Walmsley-Clark (sop), ***Archibald (cl),
    London Sinfonietta, Benjamin; ***Pople (vcl), BBC SO,
    Elder
    Nimbus NI 5075 [D] **F**

S   *Piano Sonata* Benjamin (pno)
    Nimbus NI 1415 [D] **M**

BENNETT, Richard Rodney (born 1936) ENGLAND

O *Guitar Concerto* Bream (gtr), Melos Ensemble, Atherton
(+ Arnold: *Guitar Concerto*; Rodrigo: *Concierto de Aranjuez*)
RCA 09026 61598-2 [A] **M**

BERG, Alban (1885–1935) AUSTRIA

O *Chamber Concerto; *4 Clarinet Pieces; Piano Sonata* Barenboim
(pno), Zukerman (vln), *Pay (cl), Ensemble
InterContemporain, Boulez
DG 423 237-2 [A] **M**

Violin Concerto Szeryng (vln), Bavarian RSO, Kubelik
(+ Schoenberg: *Piano and Violin Concertos*)
DG 431 740-2 [A] **M**
Zehetmair (vln), Philharmonia O, Holliger
(+Hartmann: *Concerto funèbre;* Janáček: *Violin Concerto*)
Teldec 2292 46449-2 [D] **F**

Lyric Suite; 3 Orchestral Pieces, Op. 6 BPO, Karajan
(+ Schoenberg: *Pelleas und Melisande* etc.; Webern:
5 Movements, etc.)
DG 427 424-2, 3 CDs [A] **M**

*3 Orchestral Pieces, Op. 6; *Lulu: Symphonic Suite* *Pilarczyk
(sop), LSO, Dorati
(+ Schoenberg: *5 Pieces;* Webern: *5 Pieces*)
Philips Mercury 432 006-2 [A] **M**

*3 Orchestral Pieces Op. 6; *Lulu: Symphonic Suite; *5 Orchestral
Songs Op. 4* *Price (sop), LSO, Abbado
DG 423 238-2 [A] **M**

C *Lyric Suite; String Quartet, Op. 3* LaSalle Quartet
(+ Schoenberg: *String Quartets Nos. 1–4*, etc.; Webern:
6 Bagatelles, etc.)
DG 419 994-2, 4 CDs [A] **M**

Lyric Suite; String Quartet, Op. 3 Alban Berg Quartet
EMI CDC5 55190-2 (US: Angel CDC 55190) [D] **F**

V *4 Lieder, Op. 2* Fischer-Dieskau (bar), Reimann (pno)
(+ Schoenberg: *Gurrelieder* etc.; Webern: *Lieder*)
DG 431 744-2, 2 CDs [A] **M**

BERIO, Luciano (born 1925) ITALY

O *Chemins Nos. II & IV; Corale; Points on the Curve to Find;
Ritorno degli snovidenia* Ensemble InterContemporain,
Boulez
Sony CD 45862 [D] **F**

Corale; Requies; Voci Chiarappa (vln), London Sinfonietta,
Berio
RCA RD 87898 (US: 7898-2) [D] **F**

*Eindrücke; *Sinfonia* Pasquier (vln), *New Swingle Singers,
FNO, Boulez
Erato 2292 45228-2 [D] **F**

V *Formazione; *Folk Songs; **Sinfonia* *van Nes (mez),
**Electric Phoenix, Royal Concertgebouw O, Chailly
Decca 425 832-2 (US: London 425 832-2) [D] **F**

Coro Cologne Radio Ch & SO, Berio
DG 423 902-2 [A] **F**

BERKELEY, Lennox (1903–1989) ENGLAND

O *Guitar Concerto* Bream (gtr), Monteverdi O, Gardiner
(+ Brouwer: *Concerto elegiaco;* Rodrigo: *Concierto de Aranjuez)*
RCA 09026 61605-2 [A] **M**

*Symphony No. 3; Canzonetta; Divertimento; Mont Juic; Partita;
Serenade* LPO, Berkeley
Lyrita SRCD 226 [A] **F**

BERKELEY, Michael (born 1948) ENGLAND

O *Clarinet Concerto; Flighting;* *'*Père du doux repos . . .*' Johnson
(cl), *Herford (bar), Northern Sinfonia, Edwards
ASV CDDCB 1101 [D] **M**

BERLIOZ (1803–1869) FRANCE

O *Harold in Italy, Op. 16;* **Rêverie et caprice, Op. 8* Menuhin
(vla/*vln), Philharmonia O, C. Davis, *Pritchard
EMI CDM7 63530-2 (US: Angel CDM 63530) [A] **M**

Overtures: *Béatrice et Bénédict; Benvenuto Cellini; Le Carnaval
romain; Le Corsaire; Les Troyens* (excerpts)*; Roméo et Juliette:
Queen Mab Scherzo* Boston SO, Munch
(+ Saint-Saëns: *Le rouet d'Omphale)*
RCA 09026 61400-2 [A] **M**

Overture: *Béatrice et Bénédict* Boston SO, Munch
(+ d'Indy: *Symphonie sur un chant;* Franck: *Symphony in D min.)*
RCA GD 86805 (US: 6805-2) [A] **M**

**Roméo et Juliette* (dramatic symphony), *Op. 17; Symphonie
funèbre et triomphale, Op. 15* *Quivar (sop), *Cupido (ten),
*Krause (bar), Tudor Singers, Montreal SO & Ch, Dutoit
Decca 417 302-2 (US: London 417 302-2), 2 CDs [D] **F**

Symphonie fantastique; Overtures: *Le Corsaire; Le Carnaval
romain; Hungarian March; Trojan March* Detroit SO, Paray
Philips Mercury 434 328-2 [A] **M**

Symphonie fantastique, Op. 14; **Lélio, Op. 14b* *Topart (narr),
*Burles (ten), *Gedda (ten), ORTF, Martinon
EMI CZS7 62739-2 (US: CDMB 62739), 2 CDs [A] **M**

Symphonie fantastique, Op. 14
LCP, Norrington
◇ EMI CDC7 49541-2 (US: Angel CDC 49541) [D] **F**
BPO, Karajan
DG 415 325-2 [A] **F**

V *39 Melodies* von Otter (mez), Pollet (sop), Aler (ten), Allen
(bar), Garben (pno), Muhlbach (hp), Sollscher (gtr), Thedeen
(vcl), Schenk (hn), Gast (hn), Stockholm Royal Opera Ch.
DG 435 860-2, 3 CDs [D] **F**

La Damnation de Faust (dramatic legend), *Op. 24* Veasey
(mez), Gedda (ten), Bastin (bs), Ambrosian Singers,
Wandsworth School Boys' Ch, LSO & Ch, C. Davis
Philips 416 395-2, 2 CDs [A] **F**

L'Enfance du Christ (sacred trilogy), *Op. 25* Murray (mez),
Tear (ten), Wilson-Johnson (bar), Best (bs), King's College
Ch, RPO, Cleobury
EMI CDS7 49935-2 (US: Angel CDCC 49935), 2 CDC [D] **F**

Messe solenelle Brown (sop), Viala (ten), Cachemaille (bar),
Monteverdi Ch, Orchestre Révolutionnaire et Romantique,

Gardiner
◇ Philips 442 137-2 [D] **F**

*La Mort de Cléopâtre; *Hermine; Overtures: Béatrice et Bénédict;
Le Roi Lear* *Plowright (sop), Philharmonia O, Rouchon
ASV CDDCA 895 [D] **F**

Requiem (Grande messe des morts), Op. 5; Overtures: *Benvenuto
Cellini; Le Carnaval romain, Op. 9; Le Corsaire, Op. 21* Pavarotti
(ten), Ernst-Senff Ch, BPO, Levine
DG 429 724-2, 2 CDs [D] **F**

*Les Nuits d'été, Op. 7; La belle voyageuse, Op. 2/4; La captive,
Op. 12; Le chasseur danois, Op. 19/6; Le jeune pâtre breton,
Op. 13/4; Tristia, Op. 18: La mort d'Ophélie; Zaïde, Op. 19/1*
Fournier (sop), Montague (mez), Robbin (mez), Crook (ten),
Cachemaille (bar), Lyon Opera O, Gardiner
Erato 2292 45517-2 [D] **F**

Te deum, Op. 22 Araiza (ten), LSO Ch, LPO Ch, European
Community YO, Abbado
DG 410 696-2 [D] **F**

BERNSTEIN, Leonard (1918–1990) USA

*Candide Overture; Facsimile; Fancy Free; On the Town: 3 Dance
Episodes & Complete; On the Waterfront; *Trouble in Tahiti; West
Side Story: Symphonic Dances* Various artists, NYPO,
*Columbia Wind Ensemble, Bernstein
Sony CD 47154, 3 CDs [A] **M**

Prelude, Fugue and Riffs Stolzman (cl), LSO, Leighton-Smith
(+ Copland: *Clarinet Concerto;* Corigliano: *Clarinet Concerto;*
Stravinsky: *Ebony Concerto*)
RCA 09026 61360-2 [D] **F**

*Symphonies Nos. 1–3; Prelude, Fugue and Riffs; Serenade (after
Plato's Symposium); Chichester Psalms* Various artists, NYPO,
Bernstein
Sony CD 47162, 3 CDs [A] **M**

West Side Story: Symphonic Dances: Candide Overture NYPO,
Bernstein
(+Gershwin: *Rhapsody in Blue*, etc.)
Sony CD 47529 [A] **M**

Chichester Psalms Corydon Singers, Best
(+ Barber: *Agnus Dei;* Copland: *In the Beginning*, etc.)
Hyperion CDA 66219 [D] **F**

*Dybbuk; *Mass (for the death of President Kennedy)* Johnson (bar),
Ostendorf (bs), NY City Ballet O; *Titus (bar), Scribner Ch,
Berkshire Boys' Ch, Studio Orchestra, Bernstein
Sony CD 47158, 3 CDs [A] **M**

17 Songs Alexander (sop), Crone (pno)
Etcetera KTC 1037 [D] **F**

BERWALD, Franz (1796–1868) SWEDEN

*Piano Concerto in D; Violin Concerto, Op. 2; Festival of the
Bayaderes; Serious & Joyful Fancies; The Queen of Golconda:
Overture* Migdal (pno), Tellefson (vln), RPO, Björling
EMI CDM5 65073-2 (US: Angel CDM 65073) [A] **M**

Symphonies Nos. 1–4 Gothenburg SO, Järvi
DG 415 502-2, 2 CDs [D] **F**

C   *Grand Septet in B♭* Nash Ensemble
(+ Hummel: *Septet in D min.*)
CRD 3344 [A] **F**

BIBER, Heinrich (1644–1704) BOHEMIA

C   *Harmonia artificiosa-ariosa (7 partitas)* Purcell Quartet
 ◇ Chandos CHAN 0575/6, 2 CDs [D] **F**

  Mensa sonara; Sonata violino representativa in A Goebel
(vln/dir), Cologne Musica Antiqua
 ◇ DG Archiv 423 701-2 [D] **F**

  Mystery Sonatas Holloway (vln), Moroney (hpd),
Tragicomedia
 ◇ Virgin VCD7 59551-2 (US: CDCC 59551), 2 CDs [D] **F**

  *Violin Sonatas Nos. 1–8; Sonata Representativa; Sonata 'La
Pastorella'; Passacaglia for solo violin; Passacaglia for solo lute*
Romanesca
 ◇ Harmonia Mundi HMU90 7134-5, 2 CDs [D] **F**

BIRTWISTLE, Harrison (born 1934) ENGLAND

O   **Antiphonies; Nomos; An Imaginary Landscape* *MacGregor
(pno), Radio PO, Gielen; BBC SO, Daniel
Collins 14142 [D] **F**

  *Carmen Arcadiae Mechanicae Perpetuum; Secret Theatre; Silbury
Air* London Sinfonietta, Howarth
Etcetera KTC 1052 [D] **F**

  The Triumph of Time; Gawain's Journey Philharmonia O,
Howarth
Collins 13872 [D] **F**

  Earth Dances BBC SO, Eötvös
Collins 20012 [D] **M**

BIZET, Georges (1838–1875) FRANCE

O   *L'Arlésienne (complete incidental music); Jeux d'enfants*
Consort of London, Haydon Clark
Collins 11412 [D] **F**

  L'Arlésienne: Suites Nos. 1 & 2; Carmen: Suites Nos. 1 & 2
Montreal SO, Dutoit
Decca 417 839-2 (US: London 417 839-2) [D] **F**

  La Jolie fille de Perth: Suite; Jeux d'enfants; Patrie (overture),
Op. 9; L'Arlésienne: Suite No. 1; Carmen: Suite No. 1 Paris O,
Barenboim
EMI CDM7 64869-2 (US: Angel CDM 64869) [A] **M**

  Patrie (overture), *Op. 19; Roma* (symphony) Toulouse
Capitole O, Plasson
EMI CDC5 55057-2 (US: CDC 55057) [D] **F**

  Symphony in C ASMF, Marriner
(+ Prokofiev: *Symphony No. 1*; Stravinsky: *Pulcinella Suite*)
Decca 417 734-2 (US: London 417 734-2) [A] **M**

S   *Nocturne No. 1 in D; Variations chromatiques, Op. 3* Gould (pno)
(+ Grieg: *Piano Sonata;* Sibelius: *3 Lyric Pieces, Op. 41; Sonatines
Nos. 1–3, Op. 67*)
Sony CD 52654, 2 CDs [A] **M**

BLAKE, Howard (born 1938) ENGLAND

O *Clarinet Concerto* King (cl), ECO, Blake
(+ Lutoslawski: *Dance Preludes;* Seiber: *Clarinet Concertino*)
Hyperion CDA 66215 [D] **F**

*Piano Concerto; **Diversions; Toccata *Blake (pno),
Philharmonia O, Willcocks; **Cohen, Philharmonia O, Blake
Sony CDHB3 [D] **F**

*Violin Concerto (The Leeds); A Month in the Country; Sinfonietta
*Edinger (vln), English Northern Philharmonia, Daniel
ASV CDDCA 905 [D] **F**

BLISS, Arthur (1891–1975) ENGLAND

O *Adam Zero* (ballet): *excerpts; Hymn to Apollo; Mêlée Fantasque;
Rout; *Serenade; **The World is Charged with the Grandeur of God*
LSO, Bliss, *Priestman; **Woodland (sop), Shirley-Quirk
(bar), LSO Wind & Brass Ensemble, Ambrosian Singers,
Ledger
Lyrita SRCD 225 [A] **F**

Checkmate (ballet): *Suite* English Northern PO, Lloyd-Jones
(+ Lambert: *Horoscope;* Walton: *Façade*)
Hyperion CDA 66436 [D] **F**

A Colour Symphony; Metamorphic Variations BBC Welsh SO,
Wordsworth
Nimbus NI 5294 [D] **F**

**Cello Concerto; Introduction & Allegro; Meditations on a Theme of
John Blow* *Cohen (vcl), RPO, Wordsworth
Argo 443 170-2 [D] **F**

*Piano Concerto; March (Homage to a Great Man) *Fowke (pno),
RLPO, Atherton
Unicorn-Kanchana UKCD 2029 [D] **M**

Music for Strings; *Pastorale (Lie strewn the white flocks) *Jones
(sop), Haslam (fl), Sinfonia Ch, Northern Sinfonia, Hickox
Chandos CHAN 8886 [D] **F**

C *Clarinet Quintet* Hilton (cl), Lindsay Quartet
(+ Bax: *Clarinet Sonata;* Vaughan Williams: *6 Studies*)
Chandos CHAN 8683 [D] **F**

String Quartets: No. 1 in Bb; No. 2 Delmé Quartet
Hyperion CDA 66178 [D] **F**

**Viola Sonata; Piano works: 2 Interludes; 4 Masks; Toccata;
Triptych* Vardi (vla), Sturrock (pno)
Chandos CHAN 8770 [D] **F**

S *Bliss (a one-step); Miniature Scherzo; The Rout Trot; Piano Sonata;
Study; Suite; Triptych* Fowke (pno)
Chandos CHAN 8979 [D] **F**

V *A Birthday Song for a Royal Child; *Mar Portugues; River Music;
**The Shield of Faith; ***The World is Charged with the Grandeur
of God* *Hay (sop), *Carter (alt), **Bowen (ten), ***Finzi
Wind Ensemble, Finzi Singers, Spicer
Chandos CHAN 8980 [D] **F**

Morning Heroes Westbrook (narr), RLPO & Ch, Groves
EMI CDM7 63906-2 (US: Angel CDM 63906) [A] **M**

BLOCH, Ernest (1880–1959) SWITZERLAND/USA

O *America* (epic rhapsody); *Concerto Grosso No.1* Seattle
Symphony & Chorale, Schwarz
Delos DE 3135 [D] **F**

*Concerti grossi Nos. 1 & 2; *Schelomo* *Miquelle (vcl), Eastman-
Rochester O, Hanson
Philips Mercury 432 718-2 [A] **M**

Violin Concerto; Baal Shem Guttman (vln), RPO, Serebrier
(+ Serebrier: *Momento psicologico; Poema elegiaca*)
ASV CDDCA 785 [D] **F**

*Three Jewish Poems; *Two Last Poems. . . (Maybe . . .); Evocations*
*Still (fl), New Zealand SO, Sedares
Koch 3-7232-2 [D] **F**

From Jewish Life Isserlis (vcl), Moscow Virtuosi, Spivakov
(+Tavener: *Eternal Memory*)
RCA 09026 61966-2 [D] **F**

Schelomo Harnoy (vcl), LPO, Mackerras
(+ Bruch: *Adagio on Celtic Themes*, etc.)
RCA RD 60757 (US: 60757-2) [D] **F**

Symphony in C# minor; Schelomo Thedeen (vcl), Malmö SO,
Markiz
BIS BIS-CD 576 [D] **F**

C *Violin Sonatas Nos. 1 & 2; Baal Shem* Friedman (vln), Schiller (pno)
ASV CDDCA 714 [D] **F**

V *Sacred Service* Merrill (bar), Metropolitan Synagogue & New
York Community Church Chs, NYPO, Bernstein
(+ Ben-Haim: *Sweet Psalmist of Israel*; Foss: *Song of Songs*)
Sony CD 47533, 2 CDs [A] **M**

BLOMDAHL, Karl-Birger (1916–1968) SWEDEN

O *Symphonies Nos. 1–3* Swedish RSO, Segerstam
BIS BIS-CD 611 [D] **F**

BOCCHERINI, Luigi (1743–1805) ITALY

O *Cello Concertos Nos. 1–12* Geringas (vcl), Padua CO, Giuranna
Claves CD50-8814/6, 4 CDs [D] **F**

*Cello Concertos: No. 3 in D, G476; No. 11 in C, G573; Symphony in
C min., G519; Symphony in D, G521; Notturno (Octet) No. 4 in G*
Bylsma (vcl), Tafelmusik, Lamon
◇ Sony CD 53121 [D] **F**

6 Symphonies, G503–8 NPO, Leppard
Philips 438 314-2, 2 CDs [A] **M**

Symphonies: in D min., G506; in F, G512; in C min., G519 AAM,
Hogwood
◇ L'Oiseau-Lyre 436 993-2 [D] **F**

C *Guitar Quintets Nos. 1–9* P. Romero (gtr), ASMF Chamber
Ensemble
Philips 438 769-2, 2 CDs [A] **M**

6 Oboe Quintets, G431–6 Francis (ob), Allegri Quartet
Decca 433 173-2 (US: London 433 173-2) [A] **M**

C *String Quintets: in F min., G274; in E, G275; in D, G276*
Smithsonian Chamber Players
✧ DHM RD 77159 (US: 77159-2) [D] **F**

String Sextets, G454, 455 & 459 Ensemble 415
✧ Harmonia Mundi HMC90 1478 [D] **F**

Cello Sonatas: Nos. 2 & 8–11; *6 Fugues for 2 Cellos, G73 Bylsma
(vcl), *Slowik (vcl), van Asperen (hpd)
✧ Sony CD 53362 [D] **F**

*Cello Sonatas: in C, G17; in E♭, G10; in C min., G2; in A, G4; in
B♭, G565* Lester (vcl), Watkin (vcl), Nwanoku (db)
✧ Hyperion CDA 66719 [D] **F**

BORODIN, Alexander (1833–1887) RUSSIA

O *Prince Igor* (opera): *Polovtsian Dances* LSO, Dorati
(+ Rimsky-Korsakov: *Capriccio espagnol*, etc.)
Philips Mercury 434 308-2 [A] **M**

*Symphonies Nos. 1–3; In the Steppes of Central Asia; Nocturne for
Strings* (arr.); *Prince Igor: Overture & Polovtsian Dances*
Gothenburg SO, Järvi
DG 435 757-2, 2 CDs [D] **F**

*Symphonies: No. 1 in E♭; No. 2 in B min.; In the Steppes of Central
Asia* RPO, Ashkenazy
Decca 436 651-2 (US: London 436 651-2) [D] **F**

C *String Quartets Nos. 1 & 2* Borodin Quartet
EMI CDC7 47795-2 (US: Angel CDC 47795) [A] **F**

S *Petite Suite* Edlina (pno)
(+Tchaikovsky: *The Seasons*)
Chandos CHAN 9309 [D] **F**

V *Complete Songs; Prince Igor* (without Act 3) Christoff (bs),
Tcherepnin (pno), Lamoureux O, Tzipine
EMI CMS7 63386-2 (US: CDMB 63386), 3 CDs [A] **M**

BORTKIEWICZ, Sergei (1877–1952) RUSSIA/AUSTRIA

O *Piano Concerto No. 1 in B♭, Op. 16* Coombs (pno), BBC Scottish
SO, Maksymiuk
(+ Arensky: *Piano Concerto; Fantasia on Russian Folksongs*)
Hyperion CDA 66624 [D] **F**

BOUGHTON, Rutland (1878–1960) ENGLAND

O **Oboe Concerto; Symphony No. 3 in B min.* *Francis (ob), RPO,
Handley
Hyperion CDA 66343 [D] **F**

V *Bethlehem* (choral drama) Holst Singers, New London
Children's Ch., Melville
Hyperion CDA 66690 [D] **F**

BOULEZ, Pierre (born 1925) FRANCE

O *Dérive; *Mémoriale* *Bell (fl), London Sinfonietta, Benjamin
(+ Benjamin: *Antara;* Harvey: *Song Offerings*)
Nimbus NI 5167 [D] **F**

Éclat-Multiples; *Rituel: In memoriam Bruno Maderna
Ensemble InterContemporain, *BBC SO, Boulez
Sony CD 45839 [A] **M**

O *Figures, Doubles, Prismes; *Le Soleil des eaux; **Le Visage nuptial*
*/**Bryn-Julson (sop), **Laurence (mez), */**BBC Singers,
BBC SO, Boulez
Erato 2292 45494-2 [D] **F**

   Messagesquisse; Notations Nos. 1–4; Rituel Paris O, Barenboim
   Erato 2292 45493-2 [D] **F**

S *Piano Sonatas Nos. 1–3* Helffer (pno)
   Astrée Auvidis E7716 [A] **F**

   Piano Sonata No. 2 Pollini (pno)
   (+ Prokofiev: *Piano Sonata No. 7;* Stravinsky: *3 Movements from
   Petrushka;* Webern: *Variations*)
   DG 447 431-2 [A] **M**

V *Le Marteau sans maître; Notations pour piano; Structures pour
   deux pianos; Livre II* Ensemble InterContemporain, Boulez
   Sony/CBS CD 42619 [D] **F**

   Pli selon pli Bryn-Julson (sop), BBC SO, Boulez
   Erato 2292 45376-2 [D] **F**

BOYCE, William (1711–1779) ENGLAND

O *12 Overtures: Nos. 1–9* Cantilena, Shepherd
   Chandos CHAN 6531 [A] **M**

   12 Overtures: Nos. 10–12; Concerti grossi: in B♭; in B min.; in E♭
   Cantilena, Shepherd
   Chandos CHAN 6541 [A] **M**

   8 Symphonies, Op. 2 English Concert, Pinnock
   ✧ DG Archiv 419 631-2 [D] **F**

V *Solomon (serenata)* Mills (sop), Crook (ten), Parley of
   Instruments & Ch, Goodman
   ✧ Hyperion CDA 66378 [D] **F**

BRAHMS, Johannes (1833–1897) GERMANY

O *Piano Concertos Nos. 1 & 2; 7 Fantasias Op. 116* Gilels (pno),
   BPO, Jochum
   DG 419 158-2, 2 CDs [A] **F**

   *Piano Concertos Nos. 1 & 2; Ballades, Op. 10; Piano Pieces,
   Op. 76; Scherzo, Op. 4* Kovacevich (pno), LSO, C. Davis
   Philips 442 109-2, 2 CDs [A] **M**

   Piano Concerto No. 1 in D min., Op. 15; *2 Lieder, Op. 91
   Kovacevich (pno), LPO, Sawallisch; *Murray (mez), Imai
   (vla), Kovacevich (pno)
   EMI CDC7 54578-2 (US: CDC 54578) [D] **F**

   *Piano Concerto No. 1 in D min., Op. 15; 4 Ballades, Op. 10
   Gilels (pno), *BPO, Jochum
   DG 439 979-2 [A] **M**

   *Piano Concerto No. 2 in B♭, Op. 83; 7 Piano Pieces, Op. 116
   Gilels (pno), *BPO, Jochum
   DG 435 588-2 [A] **M**

   Piano Concerto No. 2 in B♭, Op. 83 Richter (pno), CSO,
   Leinsdorf
   (+ Beethoven: *Piano Sonata No. 23*)
   RCA 07863 56519-2 [A] **M**

   Violin Concerto in D, Op. 77; *Double Concerto in A min., Op. 102
   Stern (vln), *Rose (vcl), Philadelphia O, Ormandy
   Sony CD 46335 [A] **B**

O *Violin Concerto in D, Op. 77*
Szeryng (vln), LSO, Dorati
(+ Khachaturian: *Violin Concerto*)
Philips Mercury 434 318-2 [A] **M**
Little (vln), RLPO, Handley
(+ Sibelius: *Violin Concerto*)
EMI Eminence CD-EMX 2203 (US: Classics for Pleasure CDEMX 2203) [D] **M**

Double Concerto in A min., Op. 102 Oistrakh (vln), Rostropovich (vcl), Cleveland O, Szell
(+Beethoven: *Triple Concerto*)
EMI CDM7 64744-2 (US: Angel CDM 64744) [A] **M**

21 Hungarian Dances VPO, Abbado
DG 410 615-2 [D] **F**

10 Hungarian Dances; Variations on a Theme by Haydn, Op. 56a
LSO, Dorati
(+ Enescu: *Romanian Rhapsody No. 2*)
Philips Mercury 434 326-2 [A] **M**

Serenades: No. 1 in D, Op. 11; No. 2 in A, Op. 16
Concertgebouw O, Haitink
Philips 432 510-2 [A] **M**

Symphonies Nos. 1–4 NDR SO, Wand
RCA 74321 20283-2, 2 CDs [D] **M**

Symphony No. 1 in C min., Op. 61; Academic Festival Overture, Op. 80; Tragic Overture, Op. 81;
Philharmonia O, Klemperer
EMI CDM7 69651-2 (US: Angel CDM 69651) [A] **M**

*Symphony No. 1 in C min., Op. 68; *Gesang der Parzen* Berlin Radio Ch., BPO, Abbado
DG 431 790-2 [D] **F**

*Symphony No. 2 in D, Op. 73; *Alto Rhapsody, Op. 53*
*Lipovsek (cont), *Ernst-Senff Ch, BPO, Abbado
DG 427 643-2 [D] **F**
*Ludwig (mez), Philharmonia O & *Ch, Klemperer
EMI CDM7 69650-2 (US: Angel CDM 69650) [A] **M**

Symphonies: No. 3 in F, Op. 90; No. 4 in E min., Op. 98
BPO, Karajan
DG 437 645-2 [A] **M**

*Symphony No. 3 in F, Op. 90; Tragic Overture, Op. 81; *Schicksalslied, Op. 54* Ernst-Senff Ch, BPO, Abbado
DG 429 765-2 [D] **F**

Symphony No. 4 in E min., Op. 98 VPO, C. Kleiber
DG 400 037-2 [A] **F**

C *Cello Sonatas: No. 1 in E min., Op. 38; No. 2 in F, Op. 99; 7 Songs* (arr. Mork) Mork (vcl), Lagerspetz (pno)
Virgin VC5 45052-2 (US: 45052) [D] **F**

Clarinet Quintet in B min., Op. 115 de Peyer (cl), Melos Ensemble
(+ Mozart: *Clarinet Quintet*)
EMI CDM7 63116-2 (US: Angel CDM 63116) [A] **M**

*Clarinet Quintet in B min., Op. 115; *Clarinet Trio in A min., Op. 114* King (cl), Gabrieli Quartet; *Georgian (vcl), *Benson (pno)
Hyperion CDA 66107 [D] **F**

C   *Clarinet Sonatas: No. 1 in F min., Op. 120/1; No. 2 in E♭,
    Op. 120/2* de Peyer (cl), Pryor (pno)
    Chandos CHAN 8563 [D] **F**

    *Clarinet Trio, Op. 114; Horn Trio, Op. 40; *Piano Trios Nos.
    1–3 Opp. 8, 87 & 101* Leister (cl), Donderer (vcl), Seifert (hn),
    Eschenbach (pno), Drolc (vln), *Trio di Trieste
    DG 437 131-2, 2 CDs [A] **M**

    Horn Trio in E♭, Op. 40 Tuckwell (hn), Perlman (vln),
    Ashkenazy (pno)
    (+ Franck: *Violin Sonata;* Saint-Saëns: *Romance;* Schumann:
    Adagio and Allegro)
    Decca 433 695-2 (US: London 433 695-2) [A] **M**

    Hungarian Dances Nos. 1–21; 16 Waltzes, Op. 39 Tal,
    Groethuysen (pno duo)
    Sony CD 53285 [D] **M**

    Piano Quartets Nos. 1–3 Ax (pno), Stern (vln), Laredo (vla),
    Ma (vcl)
    Sony CD 45846, 2 CDs [D] **F**

    Piano Quartets Nos. 1 & 3 Rubinstein (pno), Guaneri Quartet
    RCA GD 85677 (US: 5677-2) [A] **M**

    Piano Quintet in F min., Op. 34 Vladar (pno), Artis Quartet
    (+Schumann: *Piano Quintet*)
    Sony CD 58954 [D] **F**

    Piano Trios Nos. 1–3; Piano Trio in A, Op. posth. Trio Fontenay
    Teldec 9031 76036-2, 2 CDs [D] **F**

    Piano Trios Nos. 1 & 2 Suk (vln), Starker (vcl), Katchen (pno)
    Decca 421 152-2 (US: London 421 152-2) [A] **M**

    *Piano Trio No. 2; *Cello Sonata No.2; **Scherzo in C min., Op. 5*
    **Suk (vln), *Starker (vcl), Katchen (pno)
    Decca 425 423-2 (US: London 425 423-2) [A] **M**

    String Quartets Nos. 1–3 Melos Quartet
    (+ Schumann: *String Quartets Nos. 1–3*)
    DG 423 670-2, 3 CDs [D] **F**

    String Quartets: No. 1 in C min., Op. 51/1; No. 3 in B♭, Op. 67
    Borodin Quartet
    Teldec 4509 90889-2 [D] **F**

    *String Quartet No. 2 in A min., Op. 51/2; *Piano Quintet in F min.,
    Op. 34* *Virzaladze (pno), Borodin Quartet
    Teldec 4509 97461-2 [D] **F**

    String Quintets: No. 1 in F, Op. 88; No. 2 in G, Op. 111 BPO
    Octet
    Philips 426 094-2 [A] **M**

    String Sextets: No. 1 in B♭, Op. 18; No. 2 in G, Op. 36
    Raphael Ensemble
    Hyperion CDA 66276 [D] **F**

    *Variations on a Theme of Haydn, Op. 56b; Sonata for 2 Pianos in F
    min., Op. 34b; Waltzes, Op. 39/1-5* Argerich, Rabininovitch
    (pnos)
    Teldec 4509 92257-2 [D] **F**

    *Viola Sonatas: No. 1 in F min., Op. 120/1; No. 2 in E♭, Op. 120/2;
    Scherzo (from the FAE Sonata) Zukerman (vla/*vln),
    Barenboim (pno)
    DG 437 248-2 [A] **M**

C *Violin Sonatas Nos. 1–3* Suk (vln), Katchen (pno)
Decca 421 092-2 (US: London 421 092-2) [A] **M**

S *Complete Piano Music*
Katchen (pno)
Decca 430 053-2 (US: London 430 053-2), 6 CDs [A] **M**

Piano Pieces, Opp. 116–119 Kempff (pno)
DG 437 249-2 [A] **M**

*Piano Pieces, Opp. 116-119; Variations on a Theme of Handel;
Variations on a Theme of Paganini* Kovacevich (pno), Varsi
(pno), Harasiewicz (pno)
Philips 442 589-2, 2 CDs [A] **B**

*3 Piano Pieces, Op. 117; 6 Piano Pieces, Op. 118; 4 Piano Pieces,
Op. 119; 2 Rhapsodies, Op. 79* Lupu (pno)
Decca 417 599-2 (US: London 417 599-2) [A] **F**

6 Piano Pieces, Op. 118; 2 Rhapsodies, Op. 79; 16 Waltzes, Op. 39
Kovacevich (pno)
Philips 420 750-2 [D] **F**

Piano Sonatas: No. 1 in C, Op. 1; No. 2 in F# min., Op. 2
Richter (pno)
Decca 436 457-2 (US: London 436 457-2) [A] **F**

*Piano Sonata No. 3 in F min., Op. 5; Theme and Variations in
D min.* Lupu (pno)
Decca 417 122-2 (US: London 417 122-2) [A] **F**

Piano Sonata No. 3 in F min., Op. 5; 3 Intermezzi, Op. 117
Ax (pno)
Sony CD 45933 [D] **F**

*25 Variations and Fugue on a Theme by G.F. Handel, Op. 24;
6 Piano Pieces, Op. 118; 2 Rhapsodies, Op. 79* Ax (pno)
Sony CD 48046 [D] **F**

*11 Chorale Preludes, Op. 122; O Traurigkeit (chorale prelude
and fugue in A min., with original version); Fugue in Ab min.
(with original version); Preludes and Fugues in A min. & G min.*
Bowyer (org)
Nimbus NI 5262 [D] **F**

V *Begräbnisgesang, Op. 13; Gesang der Parzen, Op. 89; Nänie,
Op. 82; Alto Rhapsody, Op. 53; Schicksalslied, Op. 54* van Nes
(cont), SFSO & Ch, Blomstedt
Decca 430 281-2 (US: London 430 281-2) [D] **F**

Deutsche Volkslieder Schwarzkopf (sop), Fischer-Dieskau (bar),
Moore (pno)
EMI CDS7 49525-2 (US: CDCC 49525), 2 CDs [A] **F**

*4 Ernste Gesänge; Alte liebe; Auf dem Kirchofe; Feldeinsamkeit;
Heimweh II; Nachklang; Verzagen* Fischer-Dieskau (bar),
Demus (pno)
(+ Beethoven: *Lieder*)
DG 415 189-2 [A] **F**

4 Ernste Gesänge, Op. 121; 10 Lieder Fassbaender (mez),
Leonskaya (pno)
(+Schumann: *Liederkreis, Op. 39*)
Teldec 9031 74872-2 [D] **F**

German Requiem, Op. 45
Margiono (sop), Gilfry (bar), Monteverdi Ch, Orchestre
Révolutionnaire et Romantique, Gardiner

✧ Philips 432 140-2 [D] **F**
Schwarzkopf (sop), Fischer-Dieskau (bar), Philharmonia O
& Ch, Klemperer
EMI CDC7 47238-2 (US: Angel CDC 47238) [A] **F**

V *18 Liebeslieder Wältzer, Op. 52; 15 Neue Liebeslieder Wältzer,*
Op. 56; 3 Quartets, Op. 64 Mathis (sop), Fassbaender (mez),
Schreier (ten), Fischer-Dieskau (bar), Engel (pno),
Sawallisch (pno)
DG 423 133-2 [D] **F**

25 Lieder Ameling (sop), Jansen (pno)
Hyperion CDA 66444

23 Lieder Norman (sop), *Christ (vla), Barenboim (pno)
DG 413 311-2 [D] **F**

25 Lieder von Otter (mez), Forsberg (pno)
DG 429 727-2 [D] **F**

Motets: *Opp. 10, 12, 27, 30, 37, 74, 109–110* (complete)
Corydon Singers, Best
Hyperion CDA 66389 [D] **F**

Die schöne Magelone, Op. 33 Fassbaender (mez/narr),
Leonskaya (pno)
Teldec 4509 890854-2 [D] **F**

BRIAN, Havergal (1876–1972) ENGLAND

O *Symphony No. 1 (Gothic)* Jenisová (sop), Pecková (cont),
Dolezal (ten), Mikuláš (bs), various choirs, Czech RSO
(Bratislava), Slovak PO, Lenárd
Marco Polo 8.2323280/1, 2CDs [D] **F**

Symphony No. 3 BBC SO, Friend
Hyperion CDA 66334 [D] **F**

Symphonies Nos. 4 (Siegeslied) & 12 Jenisova, Various Chs.,
Bratislava RSO, Leaper
Marco Polo 8.223447 [D] **F**

Symphonies Nos. 17 & 32; In Memoriam; Festal Dance Irish
National SO, Leaper
Marco Polo 8.223481 [D] **F**

*Symphony No. 18; *Violin Concerto; Jolly Miller Overture*
*Bisengaliev (vln), BBC Scottish SO, Friend
Marco Polo 8.223479 [D] **F**

Symphonies Nos. 7 & 31; The Tinker's Wedding RLPO,
Mackerras
EMI CDM7 64717-2 (US: CDM 64717) [A] **M**

BRIDGE, Frank (1879–1941) ENGLAND

O *Cherry Ripe; 2 Entr'actes; An Irish Melody (Londonderry Air);*
Lament; Sally in our Alley; Sir Roger de Coverley; There is a Willow
grows aslant a Brook English String O, Boughton
(+Finzi: *Eclogue;* Parry: *English Suite*)
Nimbus NI 5366 [D] **F**

Suite for Strings
ECO, Garforth
(+ Ireland: *Downland Suite*, etc.)
Chandos CHAN 8390 [D] **F**
English String O, Boughton
(+ Butterworth: *The Banks of Green Willow*, etc.; Parry:

Lady Radnor's Suite)
Nimbus NI 5068 [D] **F**

O *Phantasm* Stott (pno), RPO, Handley
(+ Ireland: *Piano Concerto;* Walton: *Sinfonia Concertante*)
Conifer CDCF 175 [D] **F**

C *Cello Sonata in D min.* R. Wallfisch (vcl), P. Wallfisch (pno)
(+ Bax: *Rhapsodic Ballad;* Delius: *Cello Sonata;* Walton:
Passacaglia)
Chandos CHAN 8499 [D] **F**

Elegy; Scherzetto Lloyd Webber (vcl), McCabe (pno)
(+ Ireland: *Cello Sonata;* Stanford: *Cello Sonata No. 2*)
ASV CDDCA 807 [D] **F**

Phantasie Trio in C min. Hartley Piano Trio
(+ Clarke: *Piano Trio;* Ireland: *Phantasie Trio*)
Gamut GAMCD 518 [D] **F**

Piano Trio No. 2 Borodin Trio
(+ Bax: *Piano Trio in Bb*)
Chandos CHAN 8495 [D] **F**

String Quartets: No. 1 in E min.; No. 3 Brindisi Quartet
Continuum CCD 1035 [D] **F**

String Quartets: No. 2 in G min.; No. 4 Brindisi Quartet
Continuum CCD 1036 [D] **F**

S *Arabesque; Capriccios Nos. 1 & 2; A Dedication; A Fairy Tale
(Suite); Gargoyle; Hidden Fires; 3 Improvisations; In Autumn;
3 Miniature Pastorals Sets Nos. 1 & 2; A Sea Idyll; Winter Pastoral*
Jacobs (pno)
Continuum CCD 1016 [D] **F**

*Berceuse; Canzonetta (Happy South); 4 Characteristic Pieces;
Dramatic Fantasia; Étude rhapsodique; Lament; Pensées fugitives 1;
3 Pieces; 3 Poems; Scherzettino; Vignettes de Marseille (Suite)*
Jacobs (pno)
Continuum CCD 1018 [D] **F**

*Graziella; The Hour-glass (Suite); 3 Lyrics; 3 Miniature Pastorals
Set 3; Miniature Suite; 3 Sketches; Piano Sonata* Jacobs (pno)
Continuum CCD 1019 [D] **F**

BRITTEN, Benjamin (1913–1976) ENGLAND

O *An American Overture, Op. 27;* **Ballad of Heroes; The Building of
the House* (overture), *Op.97; Canadian Carnival* (overture),
Op. 19; ***4 Chansons françaises;* ****Diversions;* ***Occasional
Overture, Op. 38; Praise we great men;* ***/*****Scottish Ballad,
Op. 26; Sinfonia da Requiem, Op. 20; Suite on English Folktunes,
Op. 90;* ****Young Apollo, Op. 16* *Tear (ten), **Gomez (sop),
***Donohoe (pno), Hargan (sop), King (mez), White (bs),
****Fowke (pno), CBSO & Ch, Rattle
EMI CDS7 54270-2 (US: CDCB 54270), 2 CDs [D] **F**

**Cello Symphony, Op. 68; Sinfonia da Requiem, Op. 20;* ***Cantata
Misericordium, Op. 69* NPO, Britten; *Rostropovich (vcl),
ECO, Britten; **Pears (ten), Fischer-Dieskau (bar), LSO &
Ch, Britten
Decca 425 100-2 (US: London 425 100-2) [A] **M**

Cello Symphony, Op. 68 Ma (vcl), Baltimore SO, Zinman
(+Maxwell Davies: *Violin Concerto*)
Sony CD 58928 [D] **M**

O *Piano Concerto in D, Op. 13; Violin Concerto in D min., Op. 15*
Richter (pno), Lubotsky (vln), ECO, Britten
Decca 417 308-2 (US: London 417 308-2) [A] **M**

Diversions (for the Piano Left Hand) Fleisher (pno), Boston SO,
Ozawa
(+ Prokofiev: *Piano Concerto No. 4*; Ravel: *Piano Concerto for the
Left Hand*)
Sony CD 47188 [D] **F**

*Gloriana: Symphonic Suite; Peter Grimes: 4 Sea Interludes; The
Prince of the Pagodas: Pas de six* RLPO, Yuasa
EMI Eminence CD-EMX 2231 (US: Classics for Pleasure CDEMX
2231) [D] **M**

*Matinées musicales; Soirées musicales; *Peter Grimes: Four Sea
Interludes; *Young Person's Guide to the Orchestra* National PO,
Bonynge; *LSO, Britten
Decca 425 659-2 (US: London 425 659-2) [D/A] **M**

Peter Grimes (opera): *4 Sea Interludes and Passacaglia; Variations
on a Theme of Frank Bridge; Young Person's Guide to the Orchestra*
BBC SO, A. Davis
Teldec 9031 73126-2 [D] **F**

Prince of the Pagodas, Op. 57 (ballet in 3 acts) London
Sinfonietta, Knussen
Virgin VCD7 59578-2 (US: CDCB 59578), 2 CDs [D] **F**

*Simple Symphony, Op. 4; Variations on a Theme of Frank Bridge,
Op. 10; *Young Person's Guide to the Orchestra, Op. 34* ECO,
*LSO, Britten
Decca 417 509-2 (US: London 417 509-2) [A] **F**

C *2 Insect Pieces for Oboe and Piano; 6 Metamorphoses after Ovid for
Solo Oboe; Suite for Harp; Tit for Tat; Folksong arrangements:
Bird Scarer's Song; Bonny at Morn; David of the White Rock;
Lemady; Lord! I married me a wife; She's like a Swallow* Watkins
(ob), Ledger (pno), Ellis (hp), Shirley-Quirk (bar)
Meridian CDE 84119 [D] **F**

*String Quartets Nos. 1–3; String Quartet in D; Rhapsody; Phantasy
for String Quartet; Phantasy for Oboe and String Trio; Quartettino;
Elegy for Solo Viola; 3 Divertimenti; Alla marcia* Endellion
Quartet
EMI CMS5 65115-2 (US: CDMC 65115), 3 CDs [D] **M**

String Quartet No. 3, Op. 94 Lindsay Quartet
(+ Tippett: *String Quartet No. 4*)
ASV CDDCA 608 [D] **F**

**Cello Sonata, Op. 65; Cello Suites Nos. 1, Op. 72, & 2, Op. 80*
Rostropovich (vcl), *Britten (pno)
Decca 421 859-2 (US: London 421 859-2) [A] **M**

S *Cello Suite No. 3* Isserlis (vcl)
(+ Tavener: *The Protecting Veil; Thrinos*)
Virgin VC7 59052-2 (US: 59052) [D] **F**

V *The Complete Choral Works* Various artists, The Sixteen,
Christophers
Volume 1: *A Boy was Born; Gloriana: Choral Dances; 5 Flower
Songs; Hymn to St Cecilia*
Collins 12862 [D] **F**
Volume 2: *Antiphon; Te Deum in C; Wedding Anthem; Rejoice in
the Lamb; Sycamore Tree; Ballad of Little Musgrave; Advance*

Democracy; Sacred and Profane
Collins 13432 [D] **F**

V Volume 3: *Missa Brevis; Festival Te Deum; Jubilate Deo in C;
Hymn to St Peter; Hymn to the Virgin; Hymn of St Columba; Sweet
was the Song; New Year Carol; Shepherd's Carol; Ceremony of
Carols*
Collins 13702 [D] **F**

Complete Orchestral Song Cycles Lott (sop), Bryn-Julson (sop),
Langridge (ten), Lloyd (hn), Murray (mez), ECO, Northern
Sinfonia, Bedford
Collins 70372, 2 CDs [D] **F**

Complete Folksong Arrangements Anderson (pno), Nathan
(sop), MacDougall (ten), Martineau (pno), Lewis (hp), Ogden
(gtr)
Hyperion CDA 66941/2, 2 CDs [D] **F**

21 Folksong Arrangements Pears (ten), Britten (pno)
Decca 430 063-2 (US: London 430 063-2) [A] **M**

A Birthday Hansel, Op. 92; Canticles Nos. 1–5; Sweeter than Roses
(Purcell arr. Britten) Pears (ten), Hahessy (alt), Bowman (alt),
Shirley-Quirk (bar), Tuckwell (hn), Ellis (hp), Britten (pno)
Decca 425 716-2 (US: London 425 716-2) [A] **M**

*A Boy was Born, Op. 3; Festival Te Deum, Op. 32; Rejoice in the
Lamb, Op. 30; A Wedding Anthem, Op. 46* Unwin (trb), Seers
(sop), Chance (alt), Coxwell (sop), Salmon (ten), Hayes (bs),
Trotter (org), Corydon Singers, Westminster Cathedral Ch,
Best
Hyperion CDA 66126 [A] **F**

**Cantata Academica, Op. 62; **Hymn to St. Cecilia, Op. 27;
***Spring Symphony, Op. 44* *Vyvyan (sop), Watts (cont),
Pears (ten), Brannigan (bs), LSO & Ch, Britten; **London
Symphony Ch, Malcolm; ***Vyvyan (sop), Proctor (cont),
Pears (ten), Emanuel School Boys' Ch, ROHO & Ch, Britten
Decca 436 396-2 (US: London 436 396-2) [A] **M**

*Canticles Nos. 1–5; (Purcell arr. Britten) An Evening Hymn; In the
Deep, Dismal Dungeon of Despair; Let the Dreadful Engines*
Chance (alt), Rolfe Johnson (ten), Opie (bar), Williams (hp),
Thompson (hn), Vignoles (pno)
Hyperion CDA 66498 [D] **F**

*A Ceremony of Carols, Op. 28; Deus in adjutorium; Hymn of St.
Columba; Hymn to the Virgin; Jubilate Deo in Eb; Missa Brevis
in D* Williams (hp), O'Donnel (org), Westminster Cathedral
Ch, Hill
Hyperion CDA 66220 [D] **F**

**A Ceremony of Carols; *Hymn to St. Cecilia; Jubilate Deo in C;
Missa brevis in D; Rejoice in the Lamb; Te Deum in C King's
College Ch, Cambridge, Ledger, *Willcocks
EMI CDM7 64653-2 (US: Angel CDC 47709) [A] **M**

*Les Illuminations, Op. 18; *Nocturne, Op. 60; **Serenade for
Tenor, Horn and Strings, Op. 31* Pears (ten), ECO; *Wind
soloists, LSO strings; **Tuckwell (hn), Britten
Decca 436 395-2 (US: London 436 395-2) [A] **F**

Saint Nicholas, Op. 42; Hymn to St. Cecilia, Op. 27 Rolfe
Johnson (ten), Corydon Singers, Warwick University Ch,
ECO, Best
Hyperion CDA 66333 [D] **F**

V   *Spring Symphony; Peter Grimes* (opera): *Four Sea Interludes*
Armstrong (sop), Baker (mez), Tear (ten), LSO & Ch, Previn
EMI CDM7 64736-2 (US: CDM 64736) [A] **M**
War Requiem, Op. 66 Vishnevskaya (sop), Pears (ten), Fischer-
Dieskau (bar), Bach Ch, Highgate School Ch, Melos
Ensemble, LSO & Ch, Britten
Decca 414 383-2 (US: London 414 383-2), 2 CDs [A] **F**

*War Requiem, Op. 66; Sinfonia da Requiem; *Ballad of Heroes*
Harper (sop), Langridge (ten), Shirley-Quirk (bar), *Hill (ten),
St. Paul's Cathedral Choristers, LSO & Ch, Hickox
Chandos CHAN 8983/4, 2 CDs [D] **F**

BROUWER, LEO (born 1939) CUBA

O   *Guitar Concerto No. 3 (Concerto elegiaco)* Bream (gtr), RCA
Victor CO, Brouwer
(+L. Berkeley: *Guitar Concerto;* Rodrigo: *Concierto de Aranjuez*)
RCA 09026 61605-2 [A] **M**

BRUCH, Max (1838–1920) GERMANY

O   *Adagio on Celtic Themes, Op. 56; Ave Maria, Op. 61; Canzone.
Op. 55; Kol Nidrei, Op. 47* Harnoy (vcl), LPO, Mackerras
(+ Bloch: *Schelomo; Hebrew Rhapsody*)
RCA RD 60757 (US: 60757-2) [D] **F**

*Violin Concertos Nos. 1–3; Adagio appassionato, Op. 57; In
Memoriam, Op. 65; Konzertstücke, Op. 84; Romanze, Op. 41;
Scottish Fantasy, Op. 46; Serenade, Op. 75* Accardo (vln), LGO,
Masur
Philips 432 282-2, 3 CDs [A] **M**

Violin Concerto No.1 in G min., Op. 26 Lin (vln), Chicago SO,
Tilson Thomas
(+Mendelssohn: *Violin Concerto in E min.;* Vieuxtemps: *Violin
Concerto No. 5*)
Sony CD 64250 [D] **M**

Violin Concerto No. 2 in D min., Op. 44; Scottish Fantasy, Op. 46
Perlman (vln), Israel PO, Mehta
EMI CDC7 49071-2 (US: Angel CDC 49071) [D] **F**

Kol Nidrei, Op. 47 Haimowitz (vcl), CSO, Levine
(+ Lalo: *Cello Concerto;* Saint-Saëns: *Cello Concerto No. 1*)
DG 427 323-2 [D] **F**

Symphonies Nos. 1–3; Swedish Dances, Op. 63 LGO, Masur
Philips 420 932-2, 2 CDs [D] **F**

BRUCKNER, Anton (1824–1896) AUSTRIA

O   *Symphonies Nos. 1–9*
BPO, Karajan
DG 429 648-2, 9 CDs [A] **M**
BPO, Bavarian RSO, Jochum
DG 429 079-2, 9 CDs [A] **M**

Symphony in F min. Frankfurt RSO, Inbal
Teldec 2292 72300-2 [D] **F**

Symphony No. 0 in D min.; Overture in G min. Berlin RSO, Chailly
Decca 421 593-2 (US: London 421 593-2) [D] **F**

*Symphonies: No. 1 in C min.; *No. 5 in B♭* BPO, Karajan
DG 415 985-2, 2 CDs [D/*A] **F**

O *Symphony No. 1 in C min.; *Te Deum* *Norman (sop), *Minton (mez), *Rendall (ten), *Ramey (bs), CSO & Ch., Barenboim
DG 435 068-2 [A] **M**

Symphony No. 2 in C min. BPO, Karajan
DG 415 988-2 [D] **F**

Symphony No. 3 in D min. VPO, Böhm
Decca 425 032-2 (US: London 425 032-2) [A] **M**

Symphony No. 4 in E♭ (Romantic)
BPO, Barenboim
Teldec 9031 73272-2 [D] **F**
VPO, Böhm
Decca 425 036-2 (US: London 425 036-2) [A] **M**

Symphony No. 5 in B♭; *Te Deum *Mattila (sop), *Mentzer (mez), *Cole (ten), *Holl (bs), *Bavarian Radio Ch, VPO, Haitink
Philips 422 342-2, 2 CDs [D] **F**

Symphony No. 6 in A NPO, Klemperer
EMI CDM7 63351-2 (US: Angel CDM 63351) [A] **M**

Symphony No. 7 in E
BPO, Barenboim
Teldec 9031 77118-2 [D] **F**
VPO, Karajan
DG 429 226-2 [D] **F**

Symphony No. 8 in C min.
VPO, Karajan
DG 427 611-2, 2 CDs [D] **F**

Symphony No. 9 in D min.
BPO, Barenboim
Teldec 9031 72140-2 [D] **F**
BPO, Karajan
DG 429 904-2 [A] **M**

C *String Quartet; String Quintet; Intermezzo in D min.; Rondo in C min.* L'Archibudelli
Sony CD 66251 [D] **F**

V *Masses Nos. 1–3; Afferentur regi; Ave Maria; Christus factus est; Ecce sacerdos magnus; Locus iste; Os justi; Pange lingua; Psalm 150; Te deum; Tota pulchra es; Vexilla regis; Virga Jesse* Various artists, Berlin Deutsche Opera Ch, Bavarian RSO & Ch, BPO, Jochum
DG 423 127-2, 4 CDs [A] **M**

Mass No. 1 in D min.; Te Deum Rodgers (sop), Wyn-Rogers (cont), Lewis (ten), Miles (bs), O'Donnell (org), Corydon Singers & O, Best
Hyperion CDA 66650 [D] **F**

Mass No. 2 in E min.; Libera me; *2 Aequali *Sheen (tbn), *Brenner (tbn), *Brown (tbn), ECO Wind Ensemble, Corydon Singers, Best
Hyperion CDA 66177 [D] **F**

Mass No. 3 in F min.; Psalm 150 Booth (sop), Rigby (mez), Ainsley (ten), Howell (bs), Corydon Singers & O, Best
Hyperion CDA 66599 [D] **F**

Motets: Afferentur regi; Ave Maria (1861); Christus factus est; Ecce sacerdos magnus; Inveni David; Locus iste; Os justi; Pange lingua; Tota pulchra es; Vexilla regis; Virga Jesse Corydon

Singers, Best
Hyperion CDA 66062 [D] **F**

V *Requiem in D min.; Psalms 112 & 114* Rodgers (sop), Denley
(mez), Davies (ten), George (bs), Trotter (org), Corydon
Singers, ECO, Best
Hyperion CDA 66245 [A] **F**

BURGON, Geoffrey (born 1941) ENGLAND

V *At the round Earth's imagined corners; But have been found again;
Laudate Dominum; Magnificat; Nunc dimittis; A Prayer to the
Trinity; Short Mass; This World; Two Hymns to Mary* Chichester
Cathedral Ch, Thurlow
Hyperion CDA 66123 [D] **F**

BUSH, Geoffrey (born 1920) ENGLAND

C *Air and Round-O; Dialogue; Trio; Wind Quintet* Bennett (fl),
Black (ob), King (cl), Sheen (bsn), O'Neill (bsn), Lloyd (hn),
Bush (pno)
Chandos CHAN 8819 [D] **F**

V *The End of Love* (song cycle); *Greek Love Songs; A Little Love
Music; 3 Songs of Ben Jonson; Songs of Wonder* Luxon (bar),
Cahill (mez), Partridge (ten), Bush (pno)
Chandos CHAN 8830 [D] **F**

*Farewell, Earth's Bliss; A Menagerie; 4 Songs from 'The
Hesperides'; A Summer Serenade* Varcoe (bar), Thomson (ten),
Parkin (pno), Westminster Singers, City of London Sinfonia,
Hickox
Chandos CHAN 8864 [D] **F**

BUSONI, Ferruccio (1866–1924) ITALY/GERMANY

O *Piano Concerto, Op. 39* Donohoe (pno), BBC Singers, BBC SO,
Elder
EMI CDC7 49996-2 (US: Angel CDC 49996) [D] **F**

Turandot Suite, Op. 41 La Scala PO, Muti
(+ Casella: *Paganiniana;* Martucci: *Giga, Notturno; Novelette*)
Sony CD 53280 [D] **F**

C *Violin Sonatas: No. 1 in E min., Op. 29; No. 2 in E min. Op. 36a*
Mordkovitch (vln), Postnikova (pno)
Chandos CHAN 8868 [D] **F**

S *Fantasia contrappuntistica; Fantasia after J.S. Bach; Toccata,
Fantasia, Ciacona* Ogdon (pno)
Altarus CCD 1006 [A] **F**

*Suite Campestre; Berceuse; Elegy No. 1; Klavierstuck, Op. 33b/4;
Nach der Wendung; Machiotte Medioevali; Sonatinas Nos. 4 & 6;
2 Bach Chorale Transcriptions* Stephenson (pno)
Olympia OCD 461 [D] **F**

BUTTERWORTH, George (1885–1916) ENGLAND

O *The Banks of Green Willow; 2 English Idylls; A Shropshire Lad*
(rhapsody) English String O, Boughton
(+ Bridge: *Suite for Strings;* Parry: *Lady Radnor's Suite*)
Nimbus NI 5068 [D] **F**

V *A Shropshire Lad* (song cycle) Luxon (bar), Willison (pno)
(+ Vaughan Williams: *10 Blake Songs,* etc.)
Decca 430 368-2 (US: London 430 368-2) [A] **M**

BUXTEHUDE, Dietrich (c.1637–1707) GERMANY/DENMARK

C *Trio Sonatas, Op. 1 Nos. 2, 4 & 6; Op. 2 Nos. 2 & 3* Trio Sonnerie
⬦ ASV CDGAU 110 [D] **F**

The Complete Organ Works Saorgin (org)
HM HMX 2901484/8, 5 CDs [A] **B**

BYRD, William (1543–1623) ENGLAND

Galliards: BK 34, 53 & 55; Pavans: BK 17, 54 & 74; Pavans and Galliards: BK 2–3, 14, 29–32, 60, 70–71 & 114; Preludes: BK 1 & 115 Moroney (hpd)
HM HMC90 1241-2, 2 CDs [A] **F**

My Lady Nevells Booke (complete) Hogwood (hpd)
L'Oiseau-Lyre 430 484-2, 3 CDs [A] **F**

✓ 3 Anthems: *Praise our Lord; Sing joyfully; Turn our Capacity;* 15 Motets: *Attolite portas; Ave verum corpus; Beata virgo; Christus resurgens; Emendemus in melius; Laudibus in sanctis; Mass Propers Nos. 1 (Gaudeamus omnes) & 3 (Justorum animae); Non vos relinquam; O magnum misterium; O quam suavis; Plorans plorabit; Siderum rector; Solve iubente Deo; Veni sancte spiritus; Visita quaesumus* Cambridge Singers, Rutter
Collegium COLCD 110 [D] **F**

Cantiones sacrae: Book 1 New College Ch, Higginbottom
CRD 3420 [D] **F**

Cantiones sacrae: Book 2 New College Ch, Higginbottom
CRD 3439 [D] **F**

Complete Consort Music Wilson (lte) Fretwork
Virgin VC5 45031-2 (US: 45031) [D] **F**

Great Service in F; Lift up your heads; O clap your hands; O Lord, make thy servant; Sing joyfully unto God King's College Ch, Farnes (org), Cleobury
EMI CDC7 47771-2 (US: Angel CDC 47771) [D] **F**

Masses for 3, 4 and 5 Voices Westminster Cathedral Ch, Hill
Argo 430 164-2 [D] **F**

CAGE, John (1912–1992) USA

C *Sixteen Dances for Soloist and Company of 3* Ensemble Modern, Metzmacher
RCA 09026 61574-2 [D] **F**

In a Landscape; Music for Marcel Duchamp; Souvenir; A Valentine Out of Season; Suite for Toy Piano; Bacchanale; Prelude for Meditation; Dream Drury (kbds)
RCA 09026 61980-2 [D] **F**

String Quartet LaSalle Quartet
(+ Lutoslawski: *String Quartet;* Mayuzami: *Prelude;* Penderecki: *String Quartet*)
DG 423 245-2 [A] **M**

CANTELOUBE, Joseph (1879–1957) FRANCE

✓ *Chants d'Auvergne: Series 1–5; *Chants des Pays basques; *Chants du Languedoc; *Chants paysans* Davrath (sop), Studio O, de la Roche, *Kinsley
Vanguard 08.8002.72 (US: OVC 8001/02), 2 CDs [A] **M**

V   *Songs of the Auvergne* (selection) Upshaw (sop), Lyons Opera
     O, Nagano
     Erato 4509 96559-2 [D] **F**

CARPENTER, John Alden (1876–1951) USA

S   *Danza; 5 Diversions; Impromptu; Little Dancer; Little Indian;
     Minuet; Nocturne; Piano Sonata; Polonaise américaine; Tango
     américaine; Twilight Reverie* Oldham (pno)
     New World NWCD 328/9-2, 2 CDs [D] **F**

CARTER, Elliot (born 1908) USA

O   **Piano Concerto; Variations for Orchestra* *Oppens (pno),
     Cincinnati SO, Gielen
     New World NWCD 347-2 [A] **F**

     Concerto for Orchestra; *Violin Concerto; Three Occasions *Bohn
     (vln), London Sinfonietta, Knussen
     Virgin VC7 59271-2 (US: CDC 59271) [D] **F**

C   *String Quartets Nos. 1–4; *Duo for Violin and Piano* Juilliard
     Quartet; *Mann (vln), Oldfather (pno)
     Sony CD 47229, 2 CDs [D] **F**

     *Cello Sonata; Gra; Enchanted Preludes; Duo; Scrivo in Vento;
     Changes; Con Leggerezza; Pensosa; Riconoscenza per Goffredo
     Petrassi* Group for Contemporary Music
     Bridge BCD 9044 [D] **F**

S   *Piano Sonata* Lawson (pno)
     (+ Barber: *Piano Sonata;* Copland: *Piano Sonata;* Ives: *Three-
     page Sonata*)
     Virgin VC7 59008-2 (US: 59008) [D] **F**

CARVER, Robert (c.1490–1550) SCOTLAND

V   *Complete Sacred Choral Music* Capella Nova, Tavener
     ASV CDGAX 319, 3 CDs [D] **F**

CASELLA, Alfredo (1883–1947) ITALY

O   *Paganiniana, Op. 65* La Scala PO, Muti
     (+ Busoni: *Turandot Suite;* Martucci: *Giga, Notturno; Novelette*)
     Sony CD 53280 [D] **F**

CASKEN, John (born 1949) ENGLAND

O   *Darting the Skiff; Maharal Dreaming; Vaganza* Northern
     Sinfonia, Casken
     Collins 14242 [D] **F**

CASTELNUOVO-TEDESCO, Mario (1895–1968) ITALY/USA

O   *Guitar Concerto No. 1, Op. 99* Hall (gtr), LMP, Litton
     (+ Paganini: *Violin Concerto No. 2;* Sarasate: *Zigeunerweisen*)
     Decca 440 293-2 (US: London 440 293-2) [D] **F**

     Violin Concerto No. 2 (I Profeti) Perlman (vln), Israel PO,
     Mehta
     (+ Ben-Haim: *Violin Concerto*)
     EMI CDC7 54296-2 (US: CDC 54296) [D] **F**

CATALANI, Alfredo (1854-1893) ITALY

S   *10 Impressioni; 9 Piano Pieces* Spada (pno)
     ASV CDDCA 921 [D] **F**

CENTER, Ronald (1913–1973) SCOTLAND

S *6 Bagatelles; Piano Sonata; Suite: Children at Play* McLachlan
(pno)
(+ piano works by Scott and Stevenson)
Olympia OCD 264 [D] **F**

CHABRIER, Emmanuel (1841–1894) FRANCE

O *España; Bourrée fantasque; Gwendoline: Overture; Marche joyeuse;
Le Roi malgré lui; Danse slave; Fête polonaise; Suite pastorale*
Detroit SO, Paray
(+ Roussel: *Suite in F*)
Philips Mercury 434 303-2 [A] **M**

S *Complete Works for Solo Piano, Piano Duet and Two Pianos*
Barbizet (pno), Hubeau (pno)
Erato 4509 95309-2, 2 CDs [A] **M**

CHADWICK, George (1854–1931) USA

O *Symphony No. 2 in B♭, Op. 21; Symphonic Sketches* Detroit SO,
Järvi
Chandos CHAN 9334 [D] **F**

Symphony No. 3 in F Detroit SO, Järvi
(+Barber: *Vanessa*, etc.)
Chandos CHAN 9253 [D] **F**

CHAMINADE, Cécile (1857–1944) FRANCE

S *Air à danser; Air de ballet; Contes bleues No. 2; Danse créole; 6
Études de concert: Autumne; Feuillets d'album: Valse arabesque;
Guitare; Lisonjera; Lolita; Minuetto; Pas d'écharpes; Pas des
sylphes; 6 Pièces humoristiques: Autrefois; Pierrette; 6 Romances sans
paroles: Souvenance, Idylle, & Méditation; Sérénade; Sous le
masque; Toccata* Parkin (pno)
Chandos CHAN 8888 [D] **F**

CHARPENTIER, Marc-Antoine (1643–1704) FRANCE

C *Andromède; Sonate à 8; Suite à 4* London Baroque, Medlam
◇ HM HMC 901244 [D] **F**

V Motets: *Alma Redemptoris; Amicus meus; Ave regina; Ecce panis
angelorum; Hei mihi infelix; O crux ave spes unica; O vere, o bone; O
vos omnes; Popule meus; Salve regina; Solva vivebat I and II*
Concerto vocale
◇ HM HMA90 1149 [A] **F**

Caecilia, virgo et martyr; Filius prodigus; Magnificat Benet (sop),
Laplénie (ten), Reinhard (bs), Les Arts Florissants, Christie
◇ HM HMC90 066 [D] **F**

*In navitatem Domini nostri Jesus Christi, H414; Pastorale sur la
naissance de notre Seigneur Jésus Christ, H483* Les Arts
Florissants Vocal & Instrumental Ensembles, Christie
◇ HM HMC90 1082 [A] **F**

*In navitatem Domini nostri Jesus Christi, H416; Pastorale sur la
naissance de notre Seigneur Jésus Christ, H482* Les Arts
Florissants Vocal & Instrumental Ensembles, Christie
◇ HM HMC90 5130 [A] **F**

*3 Leçons de Ténèbres, H96–98: 9 Tenebrae Responsaries Nos. 1–3,
H111–113* Concerto Vocale
◇ HM HMC90 1005 [A] **F**

Leçons de Ténèbres: Office di Jeudi Saint Il Seminario Musicale
◇ Virgin VC5 45075-2 (US: 45075) [D] **F**

V *3 Leçons de Ténèbres du Vendredy Sainct, H105–6 & 110*
Concerto Vocale
◇ HM HMC90 1007 [A] **F**

Litanies de la Vierge, H83; Missa Assumpta est Maria, H11; Te Deum, H146 Les Arts Florissants Vocal & Instrumental Ensembles, Christie
◇ HM HMC90 1298 [D] **F**

Miserere; O Deus, O salvator noster; Oculi omnium; Paravit Dominus in judico Mellon (sop), Poulenard (sop), Ledroit (sop), Kendall (ten), Kooy (bs), Chapelle Royale O & Ch, Herreweghe
◇ HM HMC90 1185 [D] **F**

CHAUSSON, Ernest (1855–1899) FRANCE

O *Poème, Op. 25*
Perlman (vln), Paris O, Martinon
(+ Ravel:*Tzigane;* Saint-Saëns: *Havanaise; Introduction and Rondo capriccioso*)
EMI CDC7 47725-2 (US: Angel CDC 47725) [A] **F**
Kremer (vln), LSO, Chailly
(+ Milhaud: *Le Boeuf sur le toit: Le Printemps;* Satie: *Choses vues à droite et à gauche;* Vieuxtemps: *Fantasia appassionata*)
Philips 432 513-2 [A] **M**

*Symphony in Bb, Op. 20; *Poème, Op. 25* *Oistrakh (vln), Boston SO, Munch
(+ Saint-Saëns: *Introduction and Rondo capriccioso*)
RCA GD 60683 (US: 09026 60683-2) [A] **M**

C *Concerto for Piano, Violin and String Quartet, Op. 21* Maazel (vln), Margalit (pno), Cleveland O Quartet
Telarc CD 80046 [D] **F**

Piano Quartet in A, Op. 30; Piano Trio in G min., Op. 3 Les Musiciens
HM HMA90 1115 [A] **M**

S *Quelques Danses, Op. 26; Paysage, Op. 38* Hubeau (pno)
(+ Franck: *Prelude, Aria et Finale*, etc.)
Erato 4509 92402-2 [D] **F**

V *Chanson perpétuelle; **Poème de l'amour et de la mer; ***5 Mélodies, Op. 2: Le charme, Le colibri, La dernière feuille, Sérénade italienne, Les papillons* Norman (sop), *Monte Carlo Quartet, Dalberto (pno); **Monte Carlo PO, Jordan; ***Dalberto (pno)
Erato 2292 45368-2 [D] **F**

CHÁVEZ, Carlos (1899–1978) MEXICO

O *Symphonies Nos. 1 (Sinfonía de Antígona) & 4 (Romantic)* RPO, Bátiz
(+ Revueltas: *Caminos; Música para charlar; Ventanas*)
ASV CDDCA 653 [D] **F**

CHERUBINI, Luigi (1760–1842) ITALY

O Overtures: *Les Abencérages; Elisa; Les deux journées; Medée; Overture in G* ASMF, Marriner
EMI CDC7 54438-2 (US: CDC 54438) [D] **F**

C *Horn Sonata No. 2 in F* Tuckwell (hn), ASMF, Marriner
(+ Bellini: *Oboe Concerto;* Donizetti: *String Quartet;* Rossini: *String Sonatas*)
Decca 443 838-2 (US: London 443 838-2), 2 CDs [A] **B**

String Quartets Nos. 1–6 Melos Quartet
DG 429 185-2, 3 CDs [A] **M**

V *Coronation Mass in A; *Coronation Mass in G; Marche religieuse;
Requiem in C min.; **Requiem in D min.* Ambrosian Singers,
Philharmonia Ch, Philharmonia O, *LPO & Ch, **NPO, Muti
EMI CMS7 63161-2 (US: CDMB 63161), 4 CDs [D/A] **M**

CHOPIN, Frédéric (1810–1849) POLAND

O *Piano Concertos Nos. *1 & **2; Andante Spianato et Grande
Polonaise* (solo version); *4 Ballades; Barcarolle* (mono and stereo
versions); *Berceuse* (mono and stereo versions); *Boléro;
Fantaisie; Fantaisie-impromptu; 3 Impromptus; 51 Mazurkas; 21
Nocturnes; 3 Nouvelles études; 6 Polonaises; Polonaise-fantaisie; 24
Préludes; 4 Scherzi; Piano Sonatas Nos. 2* (mono and stereo
versions) *& 3; Tarantelle; 19 Waltzes* Rubinstein (pno), *New
SO of London, Skrowaczewski; **Symphony of the Air,
Wallenstein
RCA GD 60822 (US: 60822-2), 11 CDs [A] **M**

*Piano Concertos: No. 1 in E min., Op. 11; Piano Concerto No. 2 in
F min., Op. 21* Zimerman (pno), LAPO, Giulini
DG 415 970-2 [A] **F**

**Piano Concerto No. 1 in E min., Op. 11; Ballade No. 1 in G min.,
Op. 23; Nocturnes Nos. 4, 5, 7 & 8; Polonaise No. 6 in Ab, Op. 53*
Pollini (pno), *Philharmonia O, Kletzki
EMI CDM7 64354-2 (US: CDM 64354) [A] **M**

*Piano Concerto No. 2 in F min., Op. 21; Andante spianato and
Grande Polonaise, Op. 22; *Fantasia on Polish Airs, Op. 13*
Rubinstein (pno), Symphony of the Air, Wallenstein;
*Philadelphia O, Ormandy
RCA GD 60404 (US: 60404-2) [A] **M**

Les Sylphides (ballet arr.) National PO, Bonynge
(+ Respighi: *Boutique fantasque*)
Decca 430 723-2 (US: London 430 723-2) [D] **M**

C *Piano Trio in G min., Op. 8; Cello Sonata in G minor, Op. 65;
Polonaise brillante in C, Op. 3; **Polonaise brillante in C, Op. 3*
(solo piano version) *Frank (vln), Ma (vcl), Ax (pno),
**Osinska (pno)
Sony CD 53112 [D] **F**

S *Albumleaf; Allégro de concert; Andantino; Barcarolle; Berceuse;
Boléro; 2 Bourrées; Cantabile; Contredanse; 3 Écossaises; Fugue in
A min.; *Funeral March; Galop maquis; Hexameron Variations;
Introduction and Allegro in E; Introduction and Rondo;
*Introduction and Variations (1826) for 2 pianos; Introduction and
Variations, Op. 12; Largo; 3 Nouvelles études; Rondos, Opp. 1 & 5;
Rondo in C; Piano Sonata No. 1; Souvenir de Paganini; Tarantelle*
Vladimir Ashkenazy (pno), *Vovka Ashkenazy (pno)
Decca 421 035-2 (US: London 421 035-2), 2 CDs [A/D] **F**

*Ballades Nos. 1–4; Barcarolle; 27 Etudes; 10 Mazurkas; 12
Nocturnes; 2 Polonaises; 25 Preludes; Scherzo No. 3; Piano Sonatas
Nos. 2 & 3; Tarantelle* Perlemuter (pno)
Nimbus NI 1787, 6 CDs [A/D] **F**

*Ballades Nos. 1-4; Waltzes, Opp. 18 & 42; Nocturne in F, Op.
15/1; Mazurkas, Opp. 7/3, 17/4 & 33/2; Études, Opp. 10/3 & 4*
Perahia (pno)
Sony CD 64339 [D] **F**

S *Ballades Nos. 1–4; Piano Sonata No. 3 in B min., Op. 58*
Demidenko (pno)
Hyperion CDA 66577 [D] F

Études, Opp. 10 & 25 Pollini (pno)
DG 413 794-2 [A] F

*12 Études, Op. 10; Ballades Nos. 1 & 4; Berceuse; Scherzo No. 4;
3 Waltzes Op. 64* Donohoe (pno)
EMI CDC7 54416-2 (US: CDC 54416) [D] F

*Impromptus Nos. 1–3; Fantaisie-impromptu, Op. 66; Andante
Spianato et Grande Polonaise, Op. 22; Barcarolle, Op. 60; Berceuse,
Op. 57; Boléro, Op. 19; 3 Nouvelles études; Tarantelle, Op. 43*
Rubinstein (pno)
RCA RD 89911 (US: 5617-2) [A] F

Mazurkas Nos. 1–51 Rubinstein (pno)
RCA RD 85171 (US: 5614-2), 2 CDs [A] F

Nocturnes Nos. 1–21 Barenboim (pno)
DG 437 464-2, 2 CDs [A] B
Nos. 1–19 Rubinstein (pno)
RCA RD 89563 (US: 5613-2), 2 CDs [A] F

Polonaises Nos. 1–16 Ashkenazy (pno)
Decca 421 032-2 (US: London 421 032-2), 2 CDs [D] M

Polonaises Nos. 1–7 Rubinstein (pno)
RCA RD 89814 (US: 5615-2) [A] F

Preludes Nos. 1–26; Barcarolle; Polonaise No. 6 Argerich (pno)
DG 415 836-2 [A] M

*Scherzi Nos. 1–4; Introduction and Variations on a German air
(Der Schweizerbub); Variations on 'Là ci darem la mano', Op. 2*
Demidenko (pno)
Hyperion CDA 66514 [D] F

Piano Sonatas: Nos. 1–3; 4 Mazurkas, Op. 17; 5 Études
Andsnes (pno)
Virgin VCK7 59072-2 (US: 59072), 2 CDs [D] B

Piano Sonatas: No. 2 in B♭ min., Op. 35; No. 3 in B min., Op. 58
Pollini (pno)
DG 415 346-2 [D] F

Piano Sonata No. 3 in B min., Op. 58; 12 Mazurkas Kissin (pno)
RCA 09026 62542-2 [D] F

Waltzes Nos. 1–18 Pommier (pno)
Erato 4509 92887-2 [D] F

CLARKE, Rebecca (1886–1979) ENGLAND

C *Piano Trio* Hartley Piano Trio
(+ Bridge: *Phantasie Trio in C min.*; Ireland: *Phantasie Trio*)
Gamut GAMCD 518 [D] F

*Chinese Puzzle; Lullaby; Midsummer Moon; *18 Songs* *Wright
(sop), Rees (vln/vla), Sturrock (pno)
Gamut GAMCD 534 [D] F

CLEMENTI, Muzio (1752–1832) ITALY/ENGLAND

O **Piano Concerto in C; 2 Symphonies, Op. 18; Menuetto pastorale*
*Spada (pno), Philharmonia O, D'Avalos
ASV CDDCA 802 [D] F

○   *Symphonies: No. 1 in C; No. 3 (Great National); Overture in C* Philharmonia O, D'Avalos
ASV CDDCA 803 [D] **F**

  Symphonies: No. 2 in D; No. 4 in D; Overture in D Philharmonia O, D'Avalos
ASV CDDCA 804 [D] **F**

S   *Keyboard Sonatas: in F min., Op. 13/6; in B♭, Op. 24/2 (Rondo); in F♯ min., Op. 25/5; in A, Op. 33/3; in G min., Op. 34/2; Sonatina in C, Op. 36/3* Horowitz (pno)
RCA GD 87753 (US: 7753-2) [A] **M**

CLÉRAMBAULT, Louis-Nicolas (1676–1749) FRANCE

V   *Cantatas: La Mort d'Hercule; La Muse de l'Opéra; Orphée; Pirame et Tisbé* Rime (sop), Rivenq (bar), Fouchécourt (bs), Les Arts Florissants O, Christie
✧ HM HMA190 1329 [D] **F**

COATES, Eric (1886–1957) ENGLAND

○   *Ballad; By the Sleepy Lagoon; London Suite; Three Bears Phantasy; Three Elizabeths Suite* East of England O, Nabarro
ASV CDWHL 2053 [D] **M**

  By the Sleepy Lagoon; Calling all Workers; Cinderella; Dambusters March; From Meadow to Mayfair Suite; London Again; London Suite; The Merrymakers; Music Everywhere; *Saxo-Rhapsody; Summer Days Suite: At the Dance; Three Bears Phantasy; Three Elizabeths Suite; The Three Men: Man From the Sea; Wood Nymphs *Brymer (sax), RLPO, Groves; CBSO, Kilbey; LSO, Mackerras
Classics for Pleasure CD-CFPD 4456, 2 CDs [A] **B**

✓   *20 Songs* Rayner Cook (bar), Terroni (pno)
ASV CDWHL 2081 [D] **M**

COLERIDGE-TAYLOR, Samuel (1875–1912) ENGLAND

✓   *Scenes from 'The Song of Hiawatha' (cantata), Op. 30* Field (sop), Davies (ten), Terfel (bs-bar), Welsh National Opera O & Ch, Alwyn
Argo 430 356-2, 2 CDs [D] **F**

COOKE, Arnold (born 1906) ENGLAND

≡   *Clarinet Quintet* King (cl), Britten Quartet
(+ Frankel: *Clarinet Quintet;* Maconchy: *Clarinet Quintet;* Holbrooke: *Eilen Shona*)
Hyperion CDA 66428 [D] **F**

CONSTANTINESCU, Paul (1909–1963) ROMANIA

○   **Piano Concerto; Symphony* Lasi Moldova PO, Baciu; *Gheorghiu (pno), Cluj-Napoca PO, Simon
Olympia OCD 411 [D] **F**

COPLAND, Aaron (1900–1990) USA

○   *Las Agachadas; Appalachian Spring; Billy the Kid (Suite); *Clarinet Concerto; Danzón Cubano; El Salón México; Fanfare for the Common Man; John Henry; Letter from Home; **Lincoln Portrait; Music for Movies; Our Town; Outdoor Overture; Quiet City; Rodeo: 4 Dance Episodes; Symphony No. 3* *Goodman (cl), **Fonda (narr), New England Conservatory Ch, LSO, NPO, Columbia SO, Copland
Sony CD 46559, 3 CDs [A] **M**

O *Appalachian Spring; Billy the Kid* (complete); **Danzón Cubano;*
*El Salón México LSO, *Minneapolis SO, Dorati
Philips Mercury 434 301-2 [A] **M**

*Appalachian Spring; 3 Latin-American Sketches; Music for the
Theatre; Quiet City* St. Paul CO, Wolff
Teldec 229246314-2 [D] **F**

Clarinet Concerto Stolzman (cl), LSO, Leighton-Smith
(+Bernstein: *Prelude, Fugue & Riffs;* Corigliano: *Clarinet
Concerto;* Stravinsky: *Ebony Concerto*)
RCA 09026 61360-2 [D] **F**

**Piano Concerto; Dance Symphony; Music for the Theatre;*
***Organ Symphony; 2 Pieces for Strings; Short Symphony;
Statements; Symphonic Ode* *Bernstein (pno),
**Power Biggs (org), NYPO, LSO, Copland,
Bernstein
Sony CD 47232, 2 CDs [A] **M**

*Connotations; Dance Panels; Down a Country Lane; Inscape; Latin-
American Sketches; Music for a Great City; Orchestral Variations;
Preamble for a Solemn Occasion; *Red Pony Suite* NPO, LSO,
Copland; *NYPO, Bernstein
Sony CD47236, 2 CDs [A/D] **M**

*Fanfare for the Common Man; Billy the Kid: Suite; Rodeo: 4 Dance
Episodes; Appalachian Spring* NYPO, Bernstein
Sony CD 47543 [A] **M**

*Film Music from: The Red Pony; The City; Of Mice and Men; Our
Town; North Star; The Heiress; Prairie Journal* (Music for Radio)
St. Louis SO, Slatkin
RCA 09026 61699-2 [D] **F**

*Grogh (ballet); *Hear Ye! Hear Ye!* (ballet); *Prelude for Chamber
Orchestra* *Cleveland O, London Sinfonietta, Knussen
Argo 443 203-2 [D] **F**

**Lincoln Portrait; Fanfare for the Common Man;* ***Canticle of
Freedom; Outdoor Overture* *Jones, Seattle SO & **Chorale,
Schwarz
(+Harris: *American Creed*, etc.)
Delos DE 3140 [D] **F**

Rodeo (complete); *El Salón México; Danzón Cubano; Billy the Kid*
(complete) Baltimore SO, Zinman
Argo 440 639-2 [D] **F**

Symphony No. 3; Music for a Great City St. Louis SO, Slatkin
RCA RD 60149 (US: 60149-2) [D] **F**

S *The Complete Solo Piano Music* Smit (pno)
Sony CD 66345, 2 CDs [D/A] **F**

4 Piano Blues; Rodeo; Old American Songs (transcribed Marks);
Variations Marks (pno)
Nimbus NI 5267 [D] **F**

Piano Sonata Lawson (pno)
(+ Barber: *Piano Sonata;* Carter: *Piano Sonata;* Ives: *Three-page
Sonata*)
Virgin VC7 59008-2 (US: 59008) [D] **F**

V *Alone; My Heart is in the East; Night; Old American Songs: Sets 1 &
2; Old Poem; Pastorale; 12 Poems of Emily Dickinson; Poet's Song;
A Summer Vacation* Alexander (sop), Vignoles (pno)
Etcetera KTC 1100 [D] **F**

V *In the Beginning;* Motets: *Help us, O Lord; Have Mercy on us, O my Lord; Sing ye praises to our King* Corydon Singers, Best
(+ Barber: *Agnus Dei;* Bernstein: *Chichester Psalms*)
Hyperion CDA 66219 [D] **F**

*Old American Songs (orchestral version), *Sets 1 & 2;* ***8 Poems of Emily Dickinson; Billy the Kid* *Hampson (bar), **Upshaw (sop), St Paul CO, Wolff
Teldec 9031 77310-2 [D] **F**

CORELLI, Arcangelo (1653–1713) ITALY

O *12 Concerti grossi, Op. 6*
English Concert, Pinnock
◇ DG Archiv 423 626-2, 2 CDs [D] **F**
ASMF, Marriner
Decca 443 862-2 (US: London 443 862-2), 2 CDs [A] **B**

C *12 Trio Sonatas, Op. 1; 12 Trio Sonatas, Op. 2* Purcell Quartet, Lindberg Trio
◇ Chandos CHAN 0515/ CHAN 0516, 2 separate CDs [D] **F**

12 Trio Sonatas from Opp. 3 & 4 Purcell Quartet
◇ Chandos CHAN 0526 [D] **F**

12 Violin Sonatas, Op. 5 Locatelli Trio
◇ Hyperion CDA 66381/2, 2 CDs [D] **F**

CORIGLIANO, John (born 1938) USA

O *Clarinet Concerto* Stolzman (cl), LSO, Leighton-Smith
(+ Bernstein: *Prelude, Fugue & Riffs;* Copland: *Clarinet Concerto;* Stravinsky: *Ebony Concerto)*
RCA 09026 61360-2 [D] **F**

Flute Concerto; Voyage Galway (fl), Eastman PO, Effron
RCA 07863 56602-2 [D] **F**

Piano Concerto Lefevre (pno), Pacific SO, St. Clair
(+Ticheli: *Radiant Voices; Postcard)*
Koch 3-7250-2 [D] **F**

Symphony No. 1 CSO, Barenboim
Erato 2292 45601-2 [D] **F**

COUPERIN, François (1668–1733) FRANCE

C *Concerts Royaux Nos. 1-4; 9th Ordre: Allemande; 15th Ordre: Musete de choisi, Musete de Taverni* Sithsonian Chamber Players, Slowik
◇ DHM 05472 77327-2 [D] **F**

Les Nations Cologne Musica Antiqua
◇ DG Archiv 427 164-2, 2 CDs [D] **M**

S *L'Art de toucher le clavecin; Livre de clavecin – Book 1 (Ordres 1–5)*
Gilbert (hpd)
HM HMA 190 351/3, 3 CDs [A] **M**

Livres de clavecin Book 2 (Ordres 6–12); L'Art de toucher de clavecin
Baumont (hpd)
Erato 4509 96364-2, 3 CDs [D] **F**
Rousset (hpd)
Harmonia Mundi HMC90 1447-49, 3 CDs [D] **F**

Livre de clavecin – Book 3 (Ordres 13–19)
Gilbert (hpd)
HM HMA 190 357/8, 2 CDs [A] **M**

Baumont (hpd)
Erato 4509 92859-2, 2 CDs [D] **F**

S *Livres de clavecin – Book 4 (Ordres 20–27)* Rousset (hpd)
HM HMC90 1445/6, 2 CDs [D] **F**

Messe à l'usage ordinaire des paroisses; Messe pour les couvents de
réligieux et réligieuses (with plainchant) Saorgin (org)
REM Editions REM 311104, 2 CDs [D] **F**

V *Domine salvum; Doux liens de mon coeur; Jacunda vox Ecclesiae;*
Laetentur coeli et exultet; Lauda Sion; Magnificat; O misterium
ineffabile; Regina coeli laetare; Tantum ergo; Venite exultemus;
Victoria! Christo resurgenti Feldman (sop), Poulenard (sop),
Reinhart (bs), Linden (gmba), Moroney (hpd)
✧ HM HMA190 1150 [A] **F**

3 Leçons de ténèbres; Magnificat; Victoria! Christo resurgenti
van der Sluis (sop), Laurens (mez), Monteilhet (lte), Muller
(gmba), Boulay (hpd)
✧ Erato 2292 45012-2 [D] **F**

COUPERIN, Louis (c.1626–1661) FRANCE

S *Complete Harpsichord Works (Volumes 1–5)* Maroney (hpd)
HM HMA 190 1124/7, 4 CDs [D] **M**

Harpsichord Suites: in A min.; C; F; Pavane in F♯
Leonhardt (hpd)
DHM GD 77058 (US: Editio Classica 77058-2) [A] **M**

COWELL, Henry (1897–1965) USA

O *Persian Set; Hymn and Fuguing Tune No. 2; American Melting Pot;*
Air; Old American Country Set; Adagio Manhattan CO, Clark
Koch 3-7220-2 [D] **F**

CRESTON, Paul (1906–1985) USA

O *Symphony No. 3 (Three Mysteries), Op. 48; *Partita, Op. 12; Out of*
the Cradle; Invocation and Dance, Op. 58 *Goff (fl), *Talvi (vln),
Seattle SO, NY Ch S, Schwarz
Delos DE 3114 [D] **F**

Symphony No. 5, Op. 64; Toccata, Op. 68; Choreographic Suite,
Op. 86a Seattle SO, NY Ch S, Schwarz
Delos DE 3127 [D] **F**

CRUMB, George (born 1929) USA

C *Madrigals – 4 Books; Music for a Summer Evening (Makrokosmos*
III) Musica Varia, Dahlman (pno), Lindgren (pno), Asikainen
(perc), Kuisma (perc)
BIS BIS-CD 261 [D] **F**

CRUSELL, Bernhard (1775–1838) FINLAND/SWEDEN

O *Bassoon Concertino in B♭; *Introduction, Theme and Variations on*
a Swedish Air, Op. 12; Sinfonia Concertante for Bassoon, Clarinet
and Horn in B♭, Op. 3 Hara (bsn), *Korsimaa-Hursti (cl),
Lanzky-Otto (hn), Tapiola Sinfonietta, Vänskä
BIS BIS-CD 495 [D] **F**

*Clarinet Concertos: No. 1 in E♭, Op. 1; *No. 2 in F min., Op. 5;*
***No. 3 in B♭, Op. 11*
Johnson (cl), RPO, Herbig; *ECO, Groves; **ECO, Schwarz
ASV CDDCA 784 [D] **F**
Pay (cl), Age of Enlightenment O
✧ Virgin VC7 59287-2 (US: 59287) [D] **F**

C *Clarinet Quartets Nos. 1–3* King (cl), Members of the Allegri Quartet
Hyperion CDA 66077 **[A] F**

CZERNY, Carl (1791–1857) AUSTRIA

C *Fantaisie in F min., Op. 226; Grande sonate brillante in C, Op. 10; Grande sonate in F min., Op. 178; Ouverture caractéristique et brillante in B min., Op. 54* Tal, Groethuysen (pno duo)
Sony CD 45936 **[D] F**

DANIEL-LESUR, (Jean Yves) (born 1908) FRANCE

O *Le cantique des cantiques; *In paradisum; La vie intérieure; Messe du jubile* *Filsell (org), BBC Symphony Ch., Jackson
(+ Messiaen: *O sacrum convivium*)
ASV CDDCA 900 **[D] F**

DAWSON, William Levi (born 1899) USA

O *Negro Folk Symphony* Detroit SO, Jarvi
(+ Ellington: *Harlem;* Still: *Symphony No. 2*)
Chandos CHAN 9226 **[D] F**

DEBUSSY, Claude (1862–1918) FRANCE

O *La Boîte à joujoux* (ballet) Ulster O, Tortelier
(+ Ravel: *Ma Mère l'Oye*)
Chandos CHAN 8711 **[D] F**

Images Boston SO, Munch
(+Ravel: *Boléro*, etc.)
RCA 09026 61956 2 **[A] M**

Images; Prélude à l'après-midi d'un faune; Printemps Cleveland O, Boulez
DG 435 766-2 **[D] F**

Images: Iberia (only) CSO, Reiner
(+ Ravel: *Alborada*, etc.)
RCA GD 60179 (US: 60179-2) **[A] M**

La Mer; *Berceuse héroïque; Danse sacrée et danse profane; Jeux; Images; Marche écossaise; Nocturnes; Prélude à l'après-midi d'un faune; Première rhapsodie Concertgebouw O, Haitink, *van Beinum
Philips 438 742-2, 2 CDs **[A] B**

La Mer; Prélude à l'après-midi d'un faune BPO, Karajan
(+ Ravel: *Boléro; Daphnis et Chloë Suite No. 2*)
DG 427 250-2 **[A] M**

La Mer CSO/Reiner
(+ Rimsky-Korsakov: *Scheherazade*)
RCA GD 60875 (US: 09026 60875-2) **[A] M**

La Mer; Nocturnes; Jeux, *Première Rhapsodie
EDITORS' CHOICE: *Cohen (cl), Cleveland O, Boulez
DG 439 896-2 **[D] F**

Nocturnes; Le Martyre de Saint Sébastien: 2 Fanfares and Symphonic Fragments; Printemps Orchestre & Ch de Paris, Barenboim
DG 435 069-2 **[A] M**

Petite Suite; Children's Corner Suite (orch. Caplet) Ulster O, Tortelier
(+ Ravel: *Le Tombeau de Couperin; Valses nobles et sentimentales*)
Chandos CHAN 8756 **[D] F**

C *Arrangements for two pianos of music by Debussy, Schumann, Saint-Saëns, Tchaikovsky & Wagner* Heisser (pno), Pludermacher (pno)
Erato 4509 93209-2 [D] **F**

Danse sacrée et danse profane; En blanc et noir; Linderaja; Nocturnes (arr. Ravel); *Prélude à l'après-midi d'un faune* Coombs (pno), Scott (pno)
Hyperion CDA 66468 [D] **F**

Ballade; En blanc et noir; Cortège et air de danse; 6 Épigraphes antiques; Linderaja; Marche écossaise; Petite suite; Prélude à l'après-midi d'un faune; Symphony in B min. Alfons & Aloys Kontarsky (pno)
(+ Ravel: *Piano duet works*)
DG 427 259-2, 2 CDs [A] **M**

Cello Sonata; Flute, Viola and Harp Sonata; Violin Sonata; Syrinx; Chansons de Bilitis Nash Ensemble
Virgin VC7 59604-2 (US: 59604) [D] **F**

Cello Sonata Rostropovich (vcl), Britten (pno)
(+ Schubert: *Arpeggione Sonata;* Schumann: *5 Stücke in Volkston*)
Decca 417 833-2 (US: London 417 833-2) [A] **M**

Piano Trio in G Borodin Trio
(+ Martin: *Piano Trio;* Turina: *Piano Trio No. 1*)
Chandos CHAN 9016 [D] **F**

String Quartet in G min. Carmina Quartet
(+ Ravel: *String Quartet*)
Denon CO-75164 [D] **F**

Violin Sonata Takezawa (vln), de Silva (pno)
(+ Ravel: *Violin Sonata [1827];* Saint-Saëns: *Violin Sonata No. 1*)
RCA 09026 61386-2 [D] **F**

S *Ballade; Berceuse héroïque; Danse (Tarantelle styrienne); Danse bohémienne; D'un cahier d'esquisses; Élégie; Hommage à Haydn; L'isle joyeuse; Masques; Mazurka; Morceau de concours; Nocturne; Page d'album; Le petit nègre; La plus que lente; Rêverie; Valse romantique* Fergus-Thompson (pno)
ASV CDDCA 711 [D] **F**

Children's Corner Suite; Estampes; Images: Books I & II; Pour le piano Fergus-Thompson (pno)
ASV CDDCA 695 [D] **F**

Children's Corner Suite; Images: Books I & II Michelangeli (pno)
DG 415 372-2 [A] **F**

Études: Books I & II Uchida (pno)
Philips 422 412-2 [D] **F**

Images: Books I & II; 2 Arabesques; Berceuse héroïque; D'un cahier d'esquisses; Hommage à Haydn; L'isle joyeuse; Page d'album; Rêverie Kocsis (pno)
Philips 422 404-2 [D] **F**

24 Preludes (Books 1 & 2) Zimerman (pno)
DG 435 773-2, 2 CDs [D] **F**

Préludes: Book 1; 2 Arabesques; Images oubliées Fergus-Thompson (pno)
ASV CDDCA 720 [D] **F**

Préludes: Book 2; Suite bergamasque Fergus-Thompson (pno)
ASV CDDCA 723 [D] **F**

S *Suite bergamasque; Estampes; Images oubliées; Pour le piano*
Kocsis (pno)
Philips 412 118-2 [D] **F**

*Suite bergamasque; Children's Corner, Images; Arabesques; Preludes:
Bk. 1; Pour le piano; Estampes; L'Isle joyeuse; Rêverie* Roge (pno)
Decca 443 021-2 (US: London 443 021-2), 2 CDs [A] **B**

V *Ariettes oubliées; 5 poèmes de Charles Baudelaire; Chansons de
Bilitis* Stutzmann (cont), C. Collard (pno)
(+ Ravel: *Histoires naturelles*)
RCA RD 60899 (US: 09026 60899-2) [D] **F**

*La Damoiselle élue; *L'Enfant prodigue* Cotrubas (sop), Maurice
(mez), *Norman (sop), *Carreras (ten), South German Radio
Women's Ch, Stuttgart RSO, Bertini
Orfeo C012 821A [D] **F**

Le Martyre de Saint Sébastien McNair (sop), Murray (mez),
Stutzmann (cont), LSO & Ch, Tilson Thomas
Sony CD 48240 [D] **F**

DELALANDE, Michel-Richard (1657–1726) FRANCE

O *13 Sinfonies pour les soupers du Roi* Simphonie du Marais, Reyne
◇ HM HMC90 1337/40, 4 CDs [D] **F**

V Motets: *Confitebimur tibi, Deus, S59; Jubilate Deo, S9; Te Deum,
S32* van der Sluis (sop), Brunner (sop), Ragon (ten),
Honeyman (ten), Delétré (bs), Nantes Vocal Ensemble,
Grande Écurie, Colleaux
◇ Erato 2292 45608-2 [D] **F**

Motets: *Confitebor tibi Domine, S56; De Profundis, S23; Miserere,
S120* Fisher (sop), Johnston (trb), Daniels (alt), Smith (ten),
Varcoe (bar), New College Ch, King's Consort, Higginbottom
◇ Erato 2292 45014-2 [D] **F**

Motets: *Dies irae, S31; Misere
re mei Deus secundum, S27* Perillo (sop), Kwella (sop), Crook
(ten), Lamy (ten), Harvey (bs), Chapelle Royale O & Ch,
Herreweghe
◇ HM HMC90 1352 [D] **F**

Regina coeli, S53; De Profundis, S23; Cantate domino, S72 Ex
Cathedra Chamber Ch. & Baroque O, Skidmore
◇ ASV CDGAU 141 [D] **F**

DELIBES, Léo (1836–1891) FRANCE

O *Coppélia* (complete) Lyon Opera Orchestra, Nagano
Erato 4509 91730-2, 2 CDs [D] **F**

Sylvia (ballet) NPO, Bonynge
(+ Massenet: *Le Cid*)
Decca 425 475-2 (US: London 425 475-2), 2 CDs [A] **M**

DELIUS, Frederick (1862–1934) ENGLAND

O *Appalachia* (incl. rehearsal); *Brigg Fair; In a Summer Garden; On
Hearing the First Cuckoo in Spring; Hassan: La Calinda; Song
Before Sunrise; Late Swallow; Walk to the Paradise Garden;
Irmelin: Prelude; A Song of Summer; Fennimore and Gerda:
Intermezzo* Tear (ten), Jenkins (ten), Ambrosian Singers, Halle
O, LSO, Barbirolli
EMI CMS5 65119-2 (US: CDMB 65119), 2 CDs [A] **M**

*Brigg Fair; Dance Rhapsody No. 2; Florida (suite); Fennimore and
Gerda: Intermezzo; Irmelin: Prelude; Marche caprice; On Hearing*

the First Cuckoo in Spring; Over the hills and far away; Sleigh ride;
A song before sunrise; *Songs of Sunset; Summer evening; Summer
night on the river *Forrester (cont), *Cameron (bar),
*Beecham Choral Society, RPO, Beecham
EMI CDS7 47509-8 (US: CDCB 47509), 2 CDs [A] **F**

○ Brigg Fair; Eventyr; In a Summer Garden; A Song of Summer
Hallé O, Handley
Classics for Pleasure CD-CFP4568 [A] **B**

Brigg Fair; In a Summer Garden; On Hearing the First Cuckoo in
Spring; Summer Night on the river; A Village Romeo and Juliet:
Walk to the Paradise Garden BBCSO, A. Davis
Teldec 4509 90845-2 [D] **F**

Cello Concerto; *Double Concerto; Paris (The song of a great city)
R. Wallfisch (vcl), *Little (vln), RLPO, Mackerras
EMI Eminence CD-EMX 2185 (US: Classics for Pleasure CDEMX
2185) [D] **F**

Violin Concerto; Légende; Suite Holmes (vln), RPO, Handley
Unicorn-Kanchana DKPCD 9040 [D] **F**

*Violin Concerto; 2 Aquarelles; Dance Rhapsodies Nos. 1 & 2;
Fennimore and Gerda: Intermezzo; Irmelin: Prelude; On Hearing
the First Cuckoo in Spring; Summer night on the river *Little
(vln), Welsh National Opera O, Mackerras
Argo 433 704-2 [D] **F**

Fennimore and Gerda: Intermezzo; Irmelin: Prelude; Koanga: La
Calinda; On hearing the first cuckoo in spring; Sleigh ride; A Song
before sunrise; Summer Night on the River; A Village Romeo and
Juliet: The Walk to the Paradise Garden LPO, Handley
Classics for Pleasure CD-CFP 4304 [A] **B**

*Piano Concerto; Dance Rhapsody No. 1; Lebentanz; Paris (The
song of a great city) *Fowke (pno), RPO, Del Mar
Unicorn-Kanchana DKPCD 9108 [D] **F**

Dance Rhapsody No. 2; *An Arabesque; **Songs of Sunset
Walker, */Allen, **Ambrosian Singers, RPO, Fenby
Unicorn-Kanchana DKPCD 9063 [D] **F**

Florida (suite); North Country Sketches Ulster O, Handley
Chandos CHAN 8413 [D] **F**

C Cello Sonata R. Wallfisch (vcl), P. Wallfisch (pno)
(+ Bax: Rhapsodic Ballad; Bridge: Cello Sonata; Walton:
Passacaglia)
Chandos CHAN 8499 [D] **F**

String Quartet Brodsky Quartet
(+ Elgar: String Quartet)
ASV CDDCA 526 [D] **F**

V Songs: Autumn; Avant que tu ne t'en ailles; Chanson d'automne; Le
ciel est par-dessus le toit; I-Brasil; Il pleure dans mon coeur; In the
garden of the Seraglio; Irmelin Roise; Let springtime come; La lune
blanche; Silken shoes; So white, so soft; To daffodils; Twilight fancies;
The Violet; Young Venevil; Piano works: *3 Preludes; *Zum
Carnival (polka) *Parkin (pno), Lott (sop), Walker (mez),
Rolfe Johnson (ten), Fenby (pno)
Unicorn-Kanchana DKPCD 2041 [D] **F**

Hassan (incidental music) Hill (ten), Rayner-Cook (bar),
Bournemouth Sinfonietta & Ch, Handley

EMI Eminence CD-EMX 2207 (US: Classics for Pleasure CDEMX 2207) [D] **M**

v *A Mass of Life; Songs of Sunset; An Arabesque* Harper (sop), Watts (cont), Tear (ten), Luxon (bar), LPO & Ch, RLPO & Ch, Groves
EMI CMS7 64218-2 (US: ZDMB-64218), 2 CDs [A] **M**

Sea Drift; Songs of Farewell; Songs of Sunset Burgess (mez), Terfel (bar), Waynflete Singers, Southern Voices, Bournemouth SO & Ch., Hickox
Chandos CHAN 9214 [D] **F**

Song of the High Hills; Songs: The Bird's Story; Le ciel est par-dessus le toit; I-Brasil; Il pleure dans mon coeur; Let springtime come; La lune blanche; To Daffodils; Twilight fancies; Wine roses Lott (sop), Walker (mez), Rolfe Johnson (ten), Ambrosian Singers, RPO, Fenby
Unicorn-Kanchana DKPCD 9029 [D] **F**

DIAMOND, David (born 1915) USA

o *Symphony No. 1; *Violin Concerto; The Enormous Room* *Talvi (vln), Seattle SO, Schwarz
Delos DE 3119 [D] **F**

Symphonies Nos. 2 & 4; Concerto for Small Orchestra Seattle SO, Schwarz
Delos DE 3093 [D] **F**

Symphony No. 3; *Kaddish; Psalm; Romeo and Juliet (incidental music) *Starker (vcl), Seattle SO, Schwarz
Delos DE 3103 [D] **F**

Symphony No. 8; TOM (ballet); *This Sacred Ground* *Parce (bar), *Seattle Girls' Ch., *Northwest Boychoir, Seattle Symphony & *Chorale, Schwarz
Delos DE 3141 [D] **F**

DOHNÁNYI, Ernö (1877–1960) HUNGARY

o *Piano Concertos: No. 1 in E min., Op. 5; No. 2 in B min., Op. 42* Roscoe (pno), BBC Scottish SO, Glushchenko
Hyperion CDA 66684 [D] **F**

Variations on a Nursery Theme, Op. 25; 6 Concert Studies, Op. 28: No. 6 (Capriccio) in F min. Wild (pno), NPO, von Dohnányi (+ Tchaikovsky: *Piano Concerto No. 1*)
Chesky CD 13 [A] **F**

c *Piano Quintets: No. 1 in C min., Op. 1; No. 2 in Eb min., Op. 26; Suite in the Old Style, Op. 24* Roscoe (pno), Vanbrugh Quartet
ASV CDDCA 915 [D] **F**

s *Pastorale; 4 Pieces, Op. 2; 3 Pieces, Op. 23; 4 Rhapsodies, Op. 11* Roscoe (pno)
ASV CDDCA 863 [D] **F**

DONIZETTI, Gaetano (1797–1848) ITALY

c *String Quartet in D* (arr. Marriner) ASMF, Marriner (+ Bellini: *Oboe Concerto;* Cherubini: *Horn Sonata;* Rossini: *String Sonatas*)
Decca 443 838-2 (US: London 443 838-2), 2 CDs [A] **B**

v *Requiem* Cortez (mez), Pavarotti (ten), Bruson (bar), Washington (bs), Verona Areana O & Ch., Fackler
Decca 425 043-2 (US: London 425 043-2) [A] **M**

DOWLAND, John (c.1563–1626) ENGLAND

C *Lachrimae (1604)* Fretwork
Virgin VC5 45005-2 (US: 45005) [D] **F**

12 Pieces of Consort Music Extempore String Ensemble, Weigand
Hyperion CDA 66010 [D] **F**

V *First Booke of Songes* Consort of Musicke, Rooley
L'Oiseau-Lyre 421 653-2 [A] **F**

Second Booke of Songes Consort of Musicke, Rooley
L'Oiseau-Lyre 425 889-2 [A] **F**

Third Booke of Songes Consort of Musicke, Rooley
L'Oiseau-Lyre 430 284-2 [A] **F**

DUKAS, Paul (1865–1935) FRANCE

O *L'apprenti sorcier* BPO, Levine
(+ Saint-Saëns: *Symphony No. 3*)
DG 419 617-2 [D] **F**

Symphony in C; Polyeucte Overture BBC PO, Tortelier
Chandos CHAN 9225 [D] **F**

S *Piano Sonata in E♭ min.; La Plainte, au loin, du faune; Prélude élégiaque; Variations, interlude et finale sur un thème de Rameau* Fingerhut (pno)
Chandos CHAN 8765 [D] **F**

DUPARC, Henri (1848–1933) FRANCE

V *17 Mélodies* Walker (mez), Allen (bar), Vignoles (pno)
Hyperion CDA 66323 [D] **F**

DUPRÉ, Marcel (1886–1971) FRANCE

O *Organ Symphony in G min., Op. 25* Murray (org), RPO, Ling
(+ Rheinberger: *Organ Concerto No. 1*)
Telarc CD 80136 [D] **F**

S *Symphonie-Passion, Op. 23; Évocation, Op. 37* Castagnet (org)
Sony CD 57485 [D] **F**

Chorale and Fugue, Op. 57; 2 Ésquisses, Op. 41; 3 Preludes and Fugues, Op. 7; Le Tombeau de Titelouze, Op. 38: Te lucis ante terminum; Placare Christe servulis; Variations sur un vieux Noël, Op. 20 Scott (org)
Hyperion CDA 66205 [D] **F**

DURUFLÉ, Maurice (1902–1986) FRANCE

S *Fugue sur le Carillon des heures de la Cathédrale de Soissons; *Prélude, Adagio et Chorale varié sur le Veni Creator, Op. 4; Prélude et Fugue sur le nom d'Alain; Prélude sur l'introït de l'Épiphanie; Scherzo, Op. 2; Suite, Op. 5* *St. Paul's Men's Ch, Scott (org)
Hyperion CDA 66368 [D] **F**

V *Requiem, Op. 9; 4 Motets sur des thèmes grégoriens, Op. 10* Murray (mez), Allen (bar), Trotter (org), Corydon Singers, ECO, Best
Hyperion CDA 66191 [D] **F**

DUSSEK, Johann (1760–1812) BOHEMIA

S *Piano Sonatas, Op. 35/1–3; Op. 31/2 in D* Staier (fpno)
◇ DHM 05472 77286-2 (US: 77286-2) [D] **F**

DUTILLEUX, Henri (born 1916) FRANCE

O *Cello Concerto* Rostropovich (vcl), Paris O, Baudo
(+ Lutoslawski: *Cello Concerto*)
EMI CDC7 49304-2 (US: Angel CDC 49304) [A] **F**

*Violin Concerto (L'arbre des songes); **Cello Concerto (Tout un monde lointain) *Amoyal (vln), **Harrell (vcl), FNO, Dutoit
Decca 444 398-2 (US: London 444 398-2) [D] **F**

Symphonies Nos. 1 & 2 BBC PO, Tortelier
Chandos CHAN 9194 [D] **F**

C *Sonate pour Piano; Figures de resonances; 3 Préludes; Strophes sur le nom de SACHER; 'Ainsi la nuit'; Sonnets de Jean Cassou; Les Citations* Joy (pno), Dutilleux (pno), Geringas (vcl), Quatuor Sine Nomine, Cachemaille (bar), Bourgue (ob), Dreyfuss (hpd), Cazuran (db), Balet (perc)
Erato 4509 91721-2, 2 CDs [D] **F**

DVOŘÁK, Antonin (1841–1904) BOHEMIA

O Overtures: *Carnaval; Hussite; In Nature's Realm; My Home; Othello;* Symphonic poems: *The Golden Spinning-wheel; The Noon Witch; Symphonic Variations; The Water Goblin; The Wild Dove*
Bavarian RSO, Kubelik
DG 435 074-2, 2 CDs [A] **M**

Cello Concerto in B min. Rostropovich (vcl), BPO, Karajan
(+ Tchaikovsky: *Variations on a Rococo Theme*)
DG 447 413-2 [A] **M**

Cello Concerto in B min.; Rondo in G min.; Silent Woods Ma (vcl), BPO, Maazel
Sony CD 42206 [D] **F**

Piano Concerto in G min. Firkušný (pno), Czech PO, Neumann
(+ Janáček: *Capriccio; Concertino*)
RCA RD 60781 (US: 09026 60781-2) [D] **F**

Violin Concerto in A min.; Romance in F min.; Carnaval Overture
Midori (vln), NYPO, Mehta
Sony CD 44923 [D] **F**

10 Legends, Op. 59; Nocturne in B, Op. 40; *Romance in F min., Op. 11 *Gonley (vln), ECO, Mackerras
EMI Eminence CD-EMX 2232 (US: Classics for Pleasure CDEMX 2232) [D] **M**

Serenade for Strings in E; Serenade for Wind in D min. COE, Schneider
ASV CDCOE 801 [D] **F**

Serenade for Strings in E BPO, Karajan
(+ Tchaikovsky: *Serenade for Strings*)
DG 400 038-2 [D] **F**

Serenade for Wind in D min. Nash Ensemble
(+ Kramář: *Octet-Partitas in B♭ and E♭*)
CRD 3410 [A] **F**

16 Slavonic Dances Bavarian RSO, Kubelik
DG 419 056-2 [A] **M**

Symphonies Nos. 1–9; *Carnival Overture; *Scherzo capriccioso; *The Wild Dove BPO, *Bavarian RSO, Kubelik
DG 423 120-2, 6 CDs [A] **M**

O *Symphony No. 1 in C min. (The Bells of Zlonice); *Legends Nos. 1–5*
Slovak PO, *Slovak RSO, Gunzenhauser
Naxos 8.550266 [D] **B**

Symphony No. 2 in B♭; *Legends Nos. 6–10 Slovak PO, *Slovak RSO, Gunzenhauser
Naxos 8.550267 [D] **B**

Symphony No. 3 in E♭; Carnival Overture; Scherzo capriccioso
RLPO, Pesek
Virgin VC7 59257-2 (US: 59257) [D] **F**

Symphony No. 4; *10 Biblical Songs *Rayner-Cook (bar), SNO, Järvi
Chandos CHAN 8608 [D] **F**

Symphony No. 5; Othello; Symphonic Variations Oslo PO, Jansons
EMI CDC7 49995-2 (US: Angel CDC 49995) [D] **F**

Symphony No. 6; The Noon Witch SNO, Järvi
Chandos CHAN 8350 [D] **F**

Symphonies: No. 7 in D min.; No. 8 in G; & No. 9 in E min. (New World); *The Wild Dove BPO, *Bavarian RSO, Kubelik
(+Smetana: *Vltava*)
DG 439 663-2, 2 CDs [A] **B**

Symphonies: No. 7 in D min.; No. 8 in G LSO, Dorati
Philips Mercury 434 312-2 [A] **M**

Symphony No. 8 in G; Symphonic Variations LPO, Mackerras
EMI Eminence CD-EMX 2216 (US: Classics for Pleasure CDEMX 2216) [D] **M**

Symphony No. 9 in E min., (New World); *Slavonic Dances: Op. 46/1, 2, 7 & 8; Op. 72/8 BPO, *Bavarian RSO, Kubelik
DG 439 436-2 [A] **B**

C *5 Bagatelles* Domus
(+ Martinů: *Piano Quartet;* Suk: *Piano Quartet*)
Virgin VC7 59245-2 (US: CDC 59245) [D] **F**

From the Bohemian Forest; 10 Legends Thorson, Thurber
(pno duo)
Olympia OCD 363 [A] **F**

Piano Quartets: No. 1 in D; No. 2 in E♭ Domus
Hyperion CDA 66287 [A] **F**

Piano Quintet in A, Op. 81 Curzon (pno), VPO Quartet
(+ Franck: *Piano Quintet*)
Decca 421 153-2 (US: London 421 153-2) [A] **M**
Frankl (pno), Lindsay Quartet
(+Martinů: *Piano Quintet*)
ASV CDDCA 889 [D] **F**

Piano Trios: Nos. 1–4 Trio Fonterey
Teldec 9031 76458-2, 2 CDs [D] **F**

Romance in F min.; 2 Waltzes Lindsay Quartet
(+ Smetana: *String Quartets Nos. 1 & 2*)
ASV CDDCA 777 [D] **F**

4 Romantic Pieces; Violin Sonata in F; Violin Sonatina in G Suk
(vln), Holaček (pno)
Supraphon 11 0703-2 [A] **M**

16 Slavonic Dances Thorson, Thurber (pno duo)
Olympia OCD 362 [A] **F**

C *String Quartets Nos. 1–14; Andante appassionato in F; Cypresses; Quartet Movement in F; 2 Waltzes* Prague Quartet
DG 429 193-2, 9 CDs [A] **M**

String Quartets: No. 9 in D min.; No. 12 in F (American) Britten Quartet
EMI CDC7 54413-2 (US: CDC 54413) [D] **F**

String Quartets: No. 10 in Eb; No. 14 in Ab Lindsay Quartet
ASV CDDCA 788 [D] **F**

String Quartet No. 10 in Eb Vanburgh Quartet
(+ Janáček: *String Quartets Nos. 1 & 2*)
Collins 13812 [D] **F**

String Quartets: No. 12 in F (American); No. 13 in G Lindsay Quartet
ASV CDDCA 797 [D] **F**

*String Quartet No. 12 in F (American); *String Quintet in Eb* Janáček Quartet, *Vienna Octet members
Decca 425 537-2 (US: London 425 537-2) [A] **M**

String Quintet in Eb; String Sextet in A Raphael Ensemble
Hyperion CDA 66308 [D] **F**

S *Dumka in C min.; Furiant in G min.; 13 Poetic Tone Pictures; Theme with Variations; 8 Waltzes* Howard (pno)
Chandos CHAN 9044 [D] **F**

Theme with Variations; Poetic Tone Pictures Kvapil (pno)
Unicorn Kanchana DKCPD 9137 [D] **F**

V *10 Biblical Songs; Cypresses* (song collection) Langridge (ten), Kvapil (pno)
Unicorn-Kanchana DKPCD 9115 [D] **F**

Mass in D Ritchie (sop), Giles (alt), Byers (ten), Morton (ten), Christ Church Cathedral Ch, Cleobury (org), Preston
(+ Liszt: *Missa Choralis*)
Decca 430 364-2 (US: London 430 364-2) [A] **M**

Requiem; 10 Biblical Songs Fischer-Dieskau (bar), Demus (pno), Soloists, Czech PO, Ancerl
DG 437 377-2, 2 CDs [A] **B**

*Stabat Mater; *10 Legends* Mathis (sop), Reynolds (mez), Ochman (ten), Shirley-Quirk (bar), Bavarian RSO & Ch, Kubelik; *ECO, Kubelik
DG 423 919-2 [A] **M**

DYSON, George (1883–1964) ENGLAND

O *At the Tabard Inn Overture; *In Honour of the City; **Sweet Thames, run softly* *Roberts (bar), **RCM Chamber Ch, RPO, Willcocks
Unicorn-Kanchana UKCD 2013 [D] **M**

*Concerto da Camera; Concerto da Chiesa; *Concerto Leggiero* *Parkin (pno), City of London Sinfonia, Hickox
Chandos CHAN 9076 [D] **F**

Symphony in G City of London Sinfonia, Hickox
Chandos CHAN 9200 [D] **F**

C *3 Rhapsodies (for string quartet)* Divertimenti
(+ Howells: *String Quartet*)
Hyperion CDA 66139 [D] **F**

V *Prelude and Postlude; *Psalm-tune Variations on I Was Glad;
*Voluntary of Praise; Benedicte; Evening Service in D; Hail,
Universal Lord; Live forever, glorious Lord; Morning Service in F;
Valour; Vespers St. Catherine's College Ch, Rees (dir/*org)
Unicorn-Kanchana UKPCD 9065 [D] **F**

The Blacksmiths; The Canterbury Pilgrims: Suite; Quo Vadis:
Nocturne; 3 Rustic Songs; Song on May Morning; A Spring
Garland; A Summer Day: Suite; To Music Mackie (ten), RCM
Chamber Ch, RPO, Willcocks
Unicorn-Kanchana DKPCD 9061 [D] **F**

ELGAR, Edward (1857–1934) ENGLAND

O *3 Bavarian Dances, Op. 27; Chanson de matin, Op. 15 No. 2;
Chanson de nuit, Op. 15 No. 1; Dream Children, Op. 43; Salut
d'amour, Op. 12; Sérénade lyrique; Soliloquy; Sospiri, Op. 70;
Sursum Corda, Op. 11 Bournemouth Sinfonietta, Del Mar,
Hurst
Chandos CHAN 6544 [A] **M**

Cockaigne Overture, Op. 40; Introduction and Allegro, Op. 47;
Serenade in E min., Op. 20; Variations on an Original Theme
(Enigma), Op. 36 BBC SO, A. Davis
Teldec 9031 73279-2 [D] **F**

*Cello Concerto in E min.; Froissart, Op. 19; In the South (Alassio),
Op. 50; Introduction and Allegro, Op. 47 *Tortelier (vcl), LPO,
Boult
EMI CDM7 69200-2 (US: CDM 69200) [A] **M**

Cello Concerto in E min., Op. 85; *Sea Pictures Du Pré (vcl),
*Baker (mez), LSO, Barbirolli
EMI CDC7 47329-2 (US: Angel CDC 47329) [A] **F**

Violin Concerto in B min., Op. 61; Introduction and Allegro, Op. 47
Takezawa (vln), Bavarian RSO, C. Davis
RCA 09026 61612-2 [D] **F**

Violin Concerto in B min., Op. 61 Kennedy (vln), LPO, Handley
EMI Eminence CD-EMX 2058 (US: Classics for Pleasure CDEMX
2058) [D] **M**

Dream Children; Wand of Youth, Suites Nos. 1 & 2; Starlight
Express Hagley (sop), Terfel (bs-bar), Welsh National Opera
O, Mackerras
Argo 433 214-2 [D] **F**

Falstaff (symphonic study), Op. 68; *Variations on an Original
Theme (Enigma), Op. 36 Halle, *Philharmonia O, Barbirolli
EMI CDM7 69185-2 (US: Angel CDM 69185) [A] **F**

*Introduction and Allegro, Op. 47; Serenade in E min., Op. 20
*Allegri Quartet, Sinfonia of London, Barbirolli
(+ Vaughan Williams: Fantasia on Thomas Tallis; Fantasia on
Greensleeves)
EMI CDC7 47537-2 (US: Angel CDC 47537) [A] **F**

Symphonies: No. 1 in Ab, Op. 55; No. 2 in Eb, Op. 63; Cockaigne
Overture, Op. 40; In the South, Op. 50 LPO, Solti
Decca 443 856-2 (US: London 443 856-2), 2 CDs [A] **B**

Symphony No. 1 in Ab, Op. 55; Cockaigne Overture, Op. 40
Philharmonia O, Barbirolli
EMI CDM7 64511-2 (US: CDM 64511) [A] **M**

O *Symphony No.2 in E♭, Op. 63; *Sea Pictures* *Jones (mezzo), RPO, Mackerras
Argo 443 321-2 [D] **F**

Variations on an Original Theme (Enigma), Op. 36; Pomp and Circumstance Marches Nos. 1–5, Op. 39 RPO, Del Mar
DG 429 713-2 [A] **M**

C *Piano Quintet in A min., Op. 84; String Quartet in E min., Op. 83; In Moonlight for viola and piano* Lane (pno), Boyd (vla), Vellinger String Quartet
EMI Eminence CD-EMX 2229 (US: Classics for Pleasure CDEMX 2229) [D] **M**

String Quartet in E min., Op. 83 Brodsky Quartet
(+ Delius: *String Quartet*)
ASV CDDCA 526 [D] **F**

Violin Sonata in E min., Op. 82; Canto populare; Chanson de matin, Op. 15/2; Chanson de nuit, Op. 15/1; Mot d'amour; Salut d'amour, Op. 12; Sospiri, Op. 70; (6) Very easy melodious exercises in the First Position, Op. 22 Kennedy (vln), Pettinger (pno)
Chandos CHAN 8380 [A] **M**

Complete Music for Wind Quintet Athena Ensemble
Volume 1: Harmony Music Nos. 1 & 5; Intermezzo; Adagio cantabile; Andante con variazione
Chandos CHAN 6553 [A] **M**
Volume 2: Harmony Music Nos. 2–4; 6 Promenades; 4 Dances
Chandos CHAN 6554 [A] **M**

S *Adieu; Carissima; Chantant; Concert Allegro; Danse pensée; Dream Children; Griffinesque; In Smyrna; May Song; Minuet; Pastourelle; Presto; Serenade; Skizze; Sonatina (1889 and 1931 versions)* Pettinger (pno)
Chandos CHAN 8438 [D] **F**

V *Angelus, Op. 56; Ave Maria, Op. 2/2; Ave maris stella ,Op. 2/3; Ave verum corpus, Op. 2 No. 1; Ecce sacerdos magnus; Fear not, O Land; Give unto the Lord, Op. 74; Great is the Lord, Op. 67; I sing the birth; Lo! Christ the Lord is born; O hearken thou, Op. 64; O salutaris hostia I, II & III* Worcester Cathedral Ch, Partington (org), Hunt
Hyperion CDA 66313 [D] **F**

The Apostles (oratorio), Op. 49 Hargan (sop), Hodgson (cont), Rendall (ten), Roberts (bar), Terfel (bs-bar), Lloyd (bs), LSO & Ch, Hickox
Chandos CHAN 8875/6, 2 CDs [D] **F**

Caractacus, Op. 35; Severn Suite, Op. 87 Howarth (sop), Davies (ten), Roberts (bar), Wilson-Johnson (bar), Roberts (bs), Miles (bs) LSO & Ch, Hickox
Chandos CHAN 9156/7, 2 CDs [D] **F**

Coronation Ode, Op. 44; The Spirit of England, Op. 80 Cahill (sop), *Collins (cont), *Rolfe Johnson (ten), *Howell (bs), SNO & Ch, Gibson
Chandos CHAN 6574 [A] **M**

The Dream of Gerontius; Sea Pictures Baker (mez), Lewis (ten), Borg (bs), Hallé & Sheffield Philharmonic Chs, Ambrosian Singers, Hallé O, Barbirolli
EMI CMS7 63185-2 (US: CDMB 63185), 2 CDs [A] **M**

V *The Kingdom, Op. 51; Sospiri, Op. 70; Sursum corda, Op. 11*
Marshall (sop), Palmer (mez), Davies (ten), Wilson-Johnson
(bar), LSO & Ch, Hickox
Chandos CHAN 8788/9, 2 CDs [D] **F**

The Light of Life, Op. 29 Howarth (sop), Finnie (cont), Davies
(ten), Shirley-Quirk (bs), LSO & Ch, Hickox
Chandos CHAN 9208 [D] **F**

*The Music Makers, Op. 69; Dream Children, Op. 43; Elegy for
Strings, Op. 58; Sursum corda, Op. 11; Sospiri, Op. 70; Chanson de
matin, Op. 15/2; Chanson de nuit, Op. 15/1; Salut d'amour, Op. 12*
Ribby (sop), BBC SO & Ch., A Davis
Teldec 4509 92374-2 [D] **F**

26 Partsongs Swallow (pno), Ballard (vln), Thurlby (vln),
Worcester Cathedral Ch, Donald Hunt Singers, Hunt
Hyperion CDA 66271/2, 2 CDs [D] **F**

22 Partsongs Finzi Singers, Spicer
Chandos CHAN 9269 [D] **F**

ELLINGTON, Duke (1899–1974) USA

O *Harlem* Detroit SO, Järvi
(+ Dawson: *Negro Folk Symphony;* Still: *Symphony No. 2*)
Chandos CHAN 9226 [D] **F**

The River: Suite (Orch. Collier) Detroit SO, Järvi
(+ Still: *Symphony No. 1*)
Chandos CHAN 9154 [D] **F**

ENESCU, George (1881–1955) ROMANIA

O *2 Romanian Rhapsodies, Op. 11: No. 1* LSO, Dorati
(+ Liszt: *Hungarian Rhapsodies Nos. 1–6*)
Philips Mercury 432 015-2 [A] **M**

Romanian Rhapsody No. 2 LSO, Dorati
(+ Brahms: *16 Hungarian Dances; Haydn Variations*)
Philips Mercury 434 326-2 [A] **M**

*Symphony No. 3 in C; *Poème roumain, Op. 1* Romanian
National Radio O & *Ch., Andreescu
Olympia OCD 443 [D] **F**

C *Piano Quartets: No. 1 in D, Op. 16; No. 2 in D min., Op. 30*
Piedemonte (pno), Voces Quartet
Olympia OCD 412 [A] **F**

String Quartets: No. 1 in E♭, Op. 22/1; No. 2 in G, Op. 22/2 Voces
Quartet
Olympia OCD 413 [D] **F**

*Violin Sonatas: No. 2 in F min., Op. 6; No. 3 in A min., Op. 25;
Sonata Movement* A. Oprean (vln), J. Oprean (pno)
Hyperion CDA 66484 [D] **F**

FALLA, Manuel de (1876–1946) SPAIN

O *El amor brujo* (ballet); *The Three-Cornered Hat* (ballet) Boky
(sop), Tourangeau (mez), Montreal SO, Dutoit
Decca 410 008-2 (US: London 410 008-2) [D] **F**

*Nights in the Gardens of Spain; *El amor brujo* (ballet); The Three-
Cornered Hat* (ballet): *Suite* Soriano (pno), Paris Conservatoire
O, de Burgos; *de los Angeles (mez), Philharmonia O, Giulini
EMI CDM7 64746-2 (US: Angel CDM 69037) [A] **M**

Complete Solo Piano Works Heisser (pno)
Erato 2292 45481-2 [D] **F**

AURÉ, Gabriel (1845–1924) FRANCE

*Ballade, Op. 19; **Caligula, Op. 52; ***Élégie, Op. 24; **Les Djinns, Op. 12; *Fantasie, Op. 111 *Collard (pno), **Alex Bourbon Vocal Ensemble, ***Tortelier (vcl), Toulouse Capitole O, Plasson
EMI CDC7 47939-2 (US: CDC 47939) [D] **F**

*Fantaisie, Op. 79; Masques et bergamasques suite, Op. 112; Pavane, Op. 50; Pelléas et Mélisande suite (incidental music), *Op. 80* *Bennett (fl), ASMF, Marriner
Decca 410 552-2 (US: London 410 552-2) [D] **F**

Piano Quartets: No. 1 in C min., Op. 15; No. 2 in G min., Op. 45
Ax (pno), Stern (vln), Laredo (vla), Ma (vcl)
Sony CD 48066 [D] **F**

Piano Quintets: No. 1 in D min., Op. 89; No. 2 in C min., Op. 115
Domus
Hyperion CDA 66766 [D] **F**

Piano Trio in D min., Op. 120; *La Bonne Chanson, Op. 61
*Walker (mez), Nash Ensemble
CRD 3389 [A] **F**

Cello Sonata No. 2 in G min., Op. 117; Après un rêve; Berceuse, Op. 16; Élégie, Op. 24; Papillon, Op. 77; Romance, Op. 69; Sicilienne, Op. 78 Isserlis (vcl), Devoyon (pno)
Hyperion CDA 66235 [D] **F**

Violin Sonatas: No. 1 in A, Op. 13; No. 2 in E min., Op. 108; Morceau de concours; Andante, Op. 75; Romance, Op. 28; Berceuse, Op. 16
EDITORS' CHOICE: Amoyal (vln), Roge (pno)
Decca 436 866-2 (US: London 436 866-2) [D] **F**

Ballade in F♯, Op. 49; Mazurka in B♭, Op. 32; 3 Songs without Words, Op. 17; 4 Valses caprices Crossley (pno)
CRD 3426 [D] **F**

Barcarolles Nos. 1–13; *Dolly Suite, Op. 56; Impromptus Nos. 1–5; Mazurka in B♭, Op. 32; 8 Pièces brèves, Op. 84; 3 Songs without Words, Op. 17; *Souvenir de Bayreuth; 4 Valses caprices Collard (pno), *Rigutto (pno)
EMI CZS7 62687-2 (US: CDMB 62687), 2 CDs [A] **B**

Barcarolles Nos. 1–13 Crossley (pno)
CRD 3422 [A] **F**

Impromptus Nos. 1–5; 9 Preludes, Op. 103; Theme and Variations in C♯ min., Op. 73 Crossley (pno)
CRD 3423 [D] **F**

Nocturnes Nos. 1–13; 8 Pièces brèves, Op. 84 Crossley (pno)
CRD 1106/7, 2 CDs [A] **F**

16 Mélodies Baker (mez), Parsons (pno)
Hyperion CDA 66320 [D] **F**

Requiem; Ave verum corpus, Op. 65/1; Cantique de Jean Racine, Op. 11; Messe basse; Tantum ergo, Op. 65/2 Seers (sop), Poulenard (sop), George (bs), Corydon Singers, Best
Hyperion CDA 66292 [D] **F**

FELDMAN, Morton (1926–1987) USA

C *Piano and String Quartet (1985)* Takahashi (pno), Kronos Quartet
Elektra-Nonesuch 7559 79320-2 (US: 79320-2) [D] **F**

String Quartet Contemporary Music Group
Koch 37251-2 [D] **F**

FERGUSON, Howard (born 1908) NORTHERN IRELAND

C *Octet, Op. 4; Violin Sonata No. 2, Op. 10; 5 Bagatelles, Op. 9*
Chilingirian (vln), Benson (pno), Nash Ensemble
(+ Finzi: *Elegy*)
Hyperion CDA 66192 [D] **F**

4 Short Pieces, Op. 6 King (cl), Benson (pno)
(+ Finzi: *5 Bagatelles;* Hurlstone: *4 Characteristic Pieces;*
Stanford: *Clarinet Sonata, Op. 129*)
Hyperion CDA 66014 [D] **F**

V *The Dream of the Rood, Op. 19; Overture for an Occasion, Op. 16;*
2 Ballads, Op. 1; Partita, Op. 5a Dawson (sop), Rayner Cook
(bar), LSO & Ch, Hickox
Chandos CHAN 9082 [D] **F**

FIBICH, Zdenek (1850–1900) BOHEMIA

O *Symphonies: No. 2 in Eb, Op. 38; No. 3 in E min., Op. 53* Detroit
SO, Järvi
Chandos CHAN 9328 [D] **F**

FIELD, John (1782–1837) IRELAND

O *Piano Concertos: No. 2 in Ab; No. 3 in Eb* O'Conor (pno),
Scottish CO, Mackerras
Teldec CD-80370 [D] **F**

S *Nocturnes Nos. 1–18* O'Rourke (pno)
Chandos CHAN 8719/20, 2 CDs [D] **F**

16 Piano Pieces O'Rourke (pno)
Chandos CHAN 9315 [D] **F**

FINZI, Gerald (1901–1956) ENGLAND

O *Cello Concerto in A min., Op. 40* R. Wallfisch (vcl), RLPO,
Handley
(+ Leighton: *Veris gratia*)
Chandos CHAN 8471 [D] **F**

*Clarinet Concerto in C min., Op. 31; Love's Labours Lost
(incidental music), *Op. 21: Suite; Prelude in F min., Op. 25;*
Romance in Eb, Op. 11 *Hacker (cl), English String O,
Boughton
Nimbus NI 5101 [D] **F**

Eclogue Jones (pno), English String O, Boughton
(+Bridge: *Cherry Ripe*, etc.; Parry: *English Suite*)
Nimbus NI 5366 [D] **F**

C *5 Bagatelles, Op. 23* King (cl), Benson (pno)
(+ Ferguson: *4 Short Pieces, Op. 6;* Hurlstone: *4 Characteristic*
Pieces; Stanford: *Clarinet Sonata, Op. 129*)
Hyperion CDA 66014 [D] **F**

Elegy in F, Op. 22 Chilingirian (vln), Benson (pno)
(+ Ferguson: *Octet, Op. 4; Violin Sonata No. 2; 5 Bagatelles*)
Hyperion CDA 66192 [D] **F**

All this night, Op. 33; 3 Anthems: God is gone up, Op. 27/2; Lo, the full, final sacrifice, Op. 26; Magnificat, Op. 36; 7 Partsongs, Op. 17; 3 Short elegies, Op. 5; Though did'st delight mine eyes, Op. 32; White-flowering days, Op. 37 Bickett (org), Finzi Singers, Spicer
Chandos CHAN 8936 [D] **F**

Song cycles: *Before and After Summer, Op. 16; Earth and Air and Rain, Op. 15; Till Earth Outwears, Op. 19a; I Said to Love, Op. 19b; A Young Man's Exhortation, Op. 14* Hill (ten), Varcoe (bar), Benson (pno)
Hyperion CDA 66161/2, 2 CDs [D] **F**

*Intimations of Immortality Op. 29; *Grand Fantasia & Toccata, Op. 38* Langridge (ten), *Shelley (pno), RLPO & Ch, Hickox
EMI CDM7 64720-2 (US: CDM 64720) [D] **M**

FITKIN, Graham (born 1963) ENGLAND

Hook; Mesh; Stub; Cud Ensemble Bash; Icebreaker; Delata Saxophone Quartet; John Harle Band
Argo 440 216-2 [D] **F**

Log; Line; Loud Piano Circus
Argo 436 100-2 [D] **F**

Slow; Huoah; Frame Fitkin & Sutherland (kbds), Smith Quartet
Argo 433 690-2 [D] **F**

Aract; Fervent; Piano Pieces: 91; very early 92; early 92; mid 92; late 92; very late 92; 93; Hard Fairy; Blue; Fract Fitkin, Alberga, Lenehan (pnos), Harle (sop sax)
Argo 444 112-2 [D] **F**

FOSS, Lucas (born 1922) USA

Song of Songs Tourel (sop), NYPO, Bernstein
(+ Ben-Haim: *Sweet Psalmist of Israel;* Bloch: *Sacred Service*)
Sony CD 47533, 2 CDs [A] **M**

FOULDS, John (1880–1939) ENGLAND

April–England; Le Cabaret (overture); Hellas, a Suite of Ancient Greece; 3 Mantras; Pasquinade Symphonique No. 2 LPO, Wordsworth
Lyrita SRCD 212 [D] **F**

Dynamic Triptych, Op. 88 Shelley (pno), RPO, Handley
(+ Vaughan Williams: *Piano Concerto*)
Lyrita SRCD 211 [A] **F**

FRANÇAIX, Jean (born 1912) FRANCE

L'Horloge de flore (suite) de Lancie (ob), LSO, Previn
(+ Ibert: *Symphonie Concertante;* Satie: *Gymnopédies Nos. 1 & 3;* R. Strauss: *Oboe Concerto*)
RCA GD 87989 (US: 7989-2) [A] **M**

*String Trio; Wind Quintets Nos. 1 & 2; *Cor Anglais Quartet* *Marwood Ensemble, Haffner Wind Ensemble of London
Collins 14382 [D] **F**

FRANCK, César (1822–1890) BELGIUM/FRANCE

Le chasseur maudit (symphonic poem); Les Éolides (symphonic poem); Psyché (orchestral sections) Basle PO, Jordan
Erato 2292 45552-2 [D] **F**

Psyché (symphonic poem) RTB-BRT Ch., Liège O, P. Strauss
EMI CDM5 65162-2 (CDM 65162) [A] **M**

O *Symphonic Variations; Symphony in D min.* *Firkusny (pno),
   RPO, Flor
   RCA RD 60146 (US: 60146-2) [D] **F**

   Symphony in D min. CSO, Monteux
   (+ Berlioz: *Béatrice et Bénédict Overture;* d'Indy: *Symphonie sur u.
   chant*)
   RCA GD 86805 (US: 6805-2) [A] **M**

C *Piano Quintet in F min.* Curzon (pno), VPO Quartet
   (+ Dvořák: *Piano Quintet in A, Op. 81*)
   Decca 421 153-2 (US: London 421 153-2) [A] **M**

   String Quartet in D Ensemble César Franck
   Koch Schwann 3-1053-2 [D] **F**

   Violin Sonata in A Perlman (vln), Ashkenazy (pno)
   (+ Brahms: *Horn Trio;* Saint-Saëns: *Romance Op. 67;*
   Schumann: *Adagio and Allegro*)
   Decca 433 695-2 (US: London 433 695-2) [A] **F**

S *Prélude, aria et finale; Prélude, choral et fugue; Danse lente; Les
   Plaintes d'une poupée* Hubeau (pno)
   (+ Chausson: *Quelques danses,* etc.)
   Erato 4509 92402-2 [D] **F**

   *Prélude, aria et finale; Prélude, choral et fugue; Prelude, fugue et
   variation, Op. 18; Danse lente; Choral No. 3* Crossley (pno)
   Sony CD 58914 [D] **F**

   *3 Chorales; Fantaisie in A; Fantaisie in C, Op. 16; Final in B♭,
   Op. 21; Grande pièce symphonique in F♯ min., Op. 17; Pastorale in
   E, Op. 19; Pièce héroïque in B min.; Prélude, fugue and variation in
   B min., Op. 18; Prière in C♯ min., Op. 20* Murray (org)
   Telarc CD 80234, 2CDs [D] **F**

V *Rédemption* Uria-Monzon (mez), Wilson (spkr), Orfeon
   Donostiarra, Toulouse Capitole O, Plasson
   EMI CDC5 55056-2 (US: CDC 55056) [D] **F**

FRANKEL, Benjamin (1906–1973) ENGLAND

C *Clarinet Quintet, Op. 28* King (cl), Britten Quartet
   (+ Cooke: *Clarinet Quintet;* Maconchy: *Clarinet Quintet;*
   Holbrooke: *Eilen Shona*)
   Hyperion CDA 66428 [D] **F**

FRESCOBALDI, Girolamo (1583–1643) ITALY

S *The Complete Toccatas* Hogwood (hpd)
   L'Oiseau-Lyre 436 197-2, 2 CDs [D] **F**

GABRIELI, Andrea (c1510–1586) ITALY

V *Intonationi: del primo tono; del settimo tono; *Benedictus Dominus
   Deus; Missa a 12; O sacrum convivium* *O'Donnell, Roberts
   (orgs), Gabrieli Consort, Gabrieli Players, McCreesh
   (+G. Gabrieli: *Sacrae symphoniae,* etc.; Works by Benedetti &
   Thomsen)
   ◇ Virgin VC7 59006-2 (US: 59006) [D] **F**

GABRIELI, Giovanni (1557–1612) ITALY

V *Canzoni Nos. I, IV, VII & VIII; Sacrae symphoniae: 3 Canzoni a
   septimi toni; *Intonationi: del quinto tono; del ottavo tono; Sonatas
   Nos. XVIII & XIX; Sonata per tre violini; Deus qui beatum
   Dominum; Omnes gentes plaudite manibus* *O'Donnell, Roberts
   (orgs), Gabrieli Consort, Gabrieli Players, McCreesh

(+A. Gabrieli: *Intonationi*, etc.; Works by Benedetti &
Thomsen)
✧ Virgin VC7 59006-2 (US: 59006) [D] **F**

GADE, Niels (1817–1890) DENMARK

o *Symphonies: No. 1 in C min., Op. 5; No. 8 in B min., Op. 47*
Stockholm Sinfonietta, Järvi
BIS BIS-CD 339 [D] **F**

   Symphonies: No. 2 in E, Op. 10; No. 7 in F, Op. 45 Stockholm
Sinfonietta, Järvi
BIS BIS-CD 355 [D] **F**

   Symphonies: No. 3 in A min., Op. 15; No. 4 in B♭, Op. 20
Stockholm Sinfonietta, Järvi
BIS BIS-CD 338 [D] **F**

   *Symphonies: *No. 5 in D min., Op. 25; No. 6 in G min., Op. 32*
*Pöntinen (pno), Stockholm Sinfonietta, Järvi
BIS BIS-CD 356 [D] **F**

GAUBERT, Philippe (1879–1941) FRANCE

C *Ballade; Berceuse; 2 Esquisses; Fantaisie; Madrigal; Morceau
symphonique; Nocturne et allegro scherzando; Romance; Sicilienne;
Sonatas Nos. 1–3; Sonatine; Suite; Sur l'eau* Milan (fl), Brown (pno)
Chandos CHAN 8981/2, 2 CDs [D] **F**

GEMINIANI, Francesco (1687–1762) ITALY

o *6 Concerti grossi, Op. 2; 12 Concerti grossi* (based on Corelli's Op.
5): *Nos. 3 & 5* Tafelmusik, Lamon
✧ Sony CD 48043 [D] **F**

   6 Concerti grossi, Op. 3 I Musici
Philips 438 145-2 [D] **F**

   6 Concerti grossi, Op. 7 ASMF, Brown
ASV CDDCA 724 [D] **F**

C *12 Concerti grossi* (based on Corelli's Op. 5): *No. 12 in D min.
(La Folia); 6 Trio Sonatas* (arr. from *Violin Sonatas, Op. 1 Nos.
7–12): No. 3 in F; No. 5 in A min.; No. 6 in D min.; 12 Violin
Sonatas, Op. 1: No. 3 in E min.; 12 Violin Sonatas, Op. 4: No. 12
in A* Purcell Quartet
✧ Hyperion CDA 66264 [D] **F**

   6 Cello Sonatas, Op. 5 Pleeth (vcl), Webb (vcl), Hogwood (hpd)
✧ L'Oiseau-Lyre 433 192-2 [A] **F**

GERMAN, Edward (1862–1936) ENGLAND

o *Welsh Rhapsody* SNO, Gibson
(+ Harty: *With the Wild Geese;* MacCunn: *Land of Mountain and
Flood;* Smyth: *The Wreckers Overture*)
Classics for Pleasure CDCFP 4635 [A] **B**

GERSHWIN, George (1898–1937) USA

o *An American in Paris; *Piano Concerto in F; *Rhapsody in Blue;
Variations on 'I Got Rhythm' *Wild (pno), Boston Pops O,
Fiedler
RCA 74321 17906-2 [A] **B**

   *Rhapsody in Blue; Second Rhapsody; 3 Preludes; For Lily Pons;
Short Story; Sleepless Night; Violin Pieces* Tilson Thomas
(pno/dir), LAPO
Sony/CBS CD 39699 [D] **F**

O *Rhapsody in Blue; An American in Paris* Bernstein (pno/dir), NYPO
(+Bernstein: *West Side Story; Symphonic Dances; Candide Overture*)
Sony CD 47529 [A] **M**

Rhapsody in Blue K. & M. Labèque (pnos), Cleveland O, Chailly
(+ Addinsell: *Warsaw Concerto;* Gottschalk: *Grande fantaisie;* Liszt: *Fantasia on Hungarian Themes;* Litolff: *Concerto symphonique No. 4*)
Decca 430 726-2 (US: London 430 726-2) [D] **M**

S *Gershwin Songbook; Impromptu in 2 Keys; Merry Andrew; 3 Preludes; Rialto Ripples; Three-Quarter Blues* Achatz (pno)
BIS BIS-CD 404 [D] **F**

Piano transcriptions (arr. Wild): Fantasy on 'Porgy and Bess'; Improvisation in the form of a Theme and 3 Variations on 'Someone to watch over me'; 7 Virtuoso Études: I Got Rhythm; Lady be Good; Liza; Embraceable You; Somebody Loves Me; Fascinatin' Rhythm; The Man I Love Wild (pno)
Chesky CD 32 [D] **F**

V *Song Collection* Hendricks (sop), K. & M. Labèque (pnos)
Philips 416 460-2 [D] **F**

GESUALDO, Carlo (c.1561–1613) ITALY

V *Aestimatus sum; Astiterunt reges terrae; Ave, dulcissima Maria; Ave, regina coelorum; Ecce quomodo moritur; Jerusalem, surge; Maria, mater gratiae; O vos omnes; Plange quasi virgo; Precibus et meritis beatae Maria; Recessit pastor noster; Sicut ovis; Sepulto domino* Tallis Scholars, Phillips
Gimmell CDGIM 015 [D] **F**

17 Madrigals
EDITORS' CHOICE: Arts Florissants Vocal & Instrumental Ensembles, Christie
HM HMC90 1268 [D] **F**

GIBBONS, Orlando (1583–1625) ENGLAND

V *Complete Organ Music; Anthems: If ye be risen again with Christ; O Lord, in Thy wrath rebuke me not; Almighty God, who by Thy Son; We praise Thee, O Father; God so loved the world; O God the King of glory* Wooley (org), St John's College Ch., Robinson
Chandos CHAN 0559 [D] **F**

Almighty and everlasting God; Come, kiss me; First Service: Magnificat; Nunc dimittis; Hosanna to the Son of David; Lift up your heads; Now shall the praises of the Lord; O Lord of Hosts; O thou the central orb; Second Service: Magnificat; Nunc dimittis; See, see the word is incarnate; Sing of joy unto the Lord; This is the record of John; Organ works: Fantasia; Fantasia in D min.; Voluntary Butt (org), King's College Ch, London Early Music Group, Ledger
ASV CDGAU 123 [D] **F**

GINASTERA, Alberto (1916–1983) ARGENTINA

O *Harp Concerto, Op. 25* Masters (hp), City of London Sinfonia, Hickox
(+ Glière: *Harp Concerto; Coloratura Soprano Concerto*)
Chandos CHAN 9094 [D] **F**

S *The Complete Solo Piano Music & Chamber Music with Piano*
Lupu (vln), Natola-Ginastera (vcl), Portugheis (pno), Bingham
Quartet
Volume 1
ASV CDDCA 865 [D] **F**
Volume 2
ASV CDDCA 880 [D] **F**
Volume 3
ASV CDDCA 902 [D] **F**

GIULIANI, Mauro (1781–1829) ITALY

O *Guitar Concerto in A, Op. 30* Fernández (gtr), ECO, Malcolm
(+ Vivaldi: *Concerto, RV93*, etc.)
Decca 417 617-2 (US: London 417 617-2) [D] **F**

C *Duo concertante, Op. 25; Gran duetto concertante, Op. 52; Serenade,
Op. 19* Yamashita (gtr), Galway (fl), Swenson (vln)
RCA 09026 60237-2 [D] **F**

GLASS, Philip (born 1937) USA

O *Anima Mundi* (film score) Various artists, Riesman
Elektra-Nonesuch 7559 79329-2 (US: 79329-2) [D] **F**

Violin Concerto Kremer (vln), VPO, von Dohnányi
(+ Schnittke: *Concerto grosso No. 5*)
DG 437 091-2 [D] **F**

Low Symphony (with Bowie & Eno) Brooklyn PO, Davies
Philips 438 150-2 [D] **F**

C *Dances 1–5* Philip Glass Ensemble, Riesman
Sony CD 44765, 2 CDs [A] **F**

S *Mad Rush; Metamorphosis 1–5; Wichita Vortex Sutra* Glass (pno)
Sony CD 45576 [D] **F**

V *Itaipu; The Canyon* Atlanta SO & Ch, Shaw
Sony CD 46352 [D] **F**

GLAZUNOV, Alexander (1865–1936) RUSSIA

O **Violin Concerto in A min., Op. 82* Heifetz (vln), RCA Victor
SO, Hendl
(+ Prokofiev: *Violin Concerto No. 2;* Sibelius: *Violin Concerto*)
RCA RD 87019 (US: RCD1 7019) [A] **F**

Raymonda (ballet – highlights) SNO, Järvi
Chandos CHAN 8447 [D] **F**

The Sea (fantasy), *Op. 28; Spring, Op. 34* SNO, Järvi
(+ Kalinnikov: *Symphony No. 1*)
Chandos CHAN 8611 [D] **F**

The Seasons (ballet); **Violin Concerto* *Shumsky (vln), SNO,
Järvi
Chandos CHAN 8596 [D] **F**

Symphonies: No. 1 in E (Slavyanskaya), Op. 5; No. 5 in B♭, Op. 55
Bamberg SO, Järvi
Orfeo C093101A [D] **F**

*Symphony No. 2 in F♯ min., Op. 16; Concert Waltz No. 1 in D,
Op. 47* Bamberg SO, Järvi
Orfeo C148101A [D] **F**

Symphony No. 3 in D, Op. 33; Concert Waltz No. 2 in F, Op. 51
Bamberg SO, Järvi
Orfeo C157101A [D] **F**

o *Symphonies: No. 4 in Eb, Op. 48; No. 7 in F (Pastoral'naya), Op. 77* Bamberg SO, Järvi
Orfeo C148201A [D] **F**

Symphony No. 6 in C min., Op. 58; Lyric Poem, Op. 12 Bamberg SO, Järvi
Orfeo C157201A [D] **F**

Symphony No. 8 in Eb, Op. 83; Overture Solennelle, Op. 73; Wedding Procession in Eb Bamberg SO, Järvi
Orfeo C093201A [D] **F**

c *Novelettes Nos. 1–4* Shostakovich Quartet
(+ Glinka: *String Quartets*)
Olympia OCD 524 [D] **F**

String Quartets Nos. 3 & 5; Kuranta Shostakovich Quartet
Olympia OCD 525 [D] **F**

String Quartets Nos. 6 & 7 Shostakovich Quartet
Olympia OCD 526 [D] **F**

s *Grand Concert Waltz in Eb, Op. 41; Piano Sonatas: No. 1 in Bb min., Op. 74; No. 2 in Eb, Op. 75* Howard (pno)
Pearl SHECD 9538 [A] **F**

GLIÈRE, Reyngo'ld (1875–1956) RUSSIA

o *Harp Concerto; Coloratura Soprano Concerto* Masters (hp), Hulse (sop), City of London Sinfonia, Hickox
(+ Ginastera: *Harp Concerto*)
Chandos CHAN 9094 [D] **F**

Symphony No. 1 in Eb, Op. 8; The Red Poppy (ballet): Suite BBC PO, Downes
Chandos CHAN 9160 [D] **F**

Symphony No. 2 in C min., Op. 25; The Zaporozhy Cossacks, Op. 64 BBC PO, Downes
Chandos CHAN 9071 [D] **F**

Symphony No. 3 (Il'ya Mouromets), Op. 42 BBC PO, Downes
Chandos CHAN 9041 [D] **F**

GLINKA, Mikhail (1804–1857) RUSSIA

o *Ruslan and Lyudmila (opera): Overture* CSO, Reiner
(+ Prokofiev: *Lieutenant Kijé; Alexander Nevsky*)
RCA GD 60176 (US: 60176-2) [A] **M**

c *Grand Sextet in Eb* Capricorn
(+ Rimsky-Korsakov: *Piano and Wind Quintet*)
Hyperion CDA 66163 [A] **F**

String Quartets: in F; in D Shostakovich Quartet
(+ Glazunov: *Novelettes*)
Olympia OCD 524 [D] **F**

Viola Sonata Bashmet (vla), Muntian (pno)
(+ Roslavets: *Viola Sonata No.1*; Shostakovich: *Viola Sonata*)
RCA 09026 61273-2 [D] **F**

GODOWSKY, Leopold (1870–1938) POLAND/USA

s Piano transcriptions: Godowsky: *Passacaglia; Alt Wien;* Schubert: *Das Wandern; Ungeduld; Gute Nacht; Rosamunde: Ballet Music; Moments musicaux No. 3 in F min.;* Weber: *Invitation to the Dance, J260;* J. Strauss II: *Artist's Life, Op. 316* De Waal (pno)
Hyperion CDA 66496 [D] **F**

GOEHR, Alexander (born 1932) ENGLAND

O *. . . a musical offering (J.S.B. 1985), Op. 46; Lyric Pieces, Op. 35; Sinfonia, Op. 42; *Behold the Sun* (concert aria) *Thames (sop), *Holland (vib), London Sinfonietta, Knussen
Unicorn-Kanchana DKPCD 9102 [D] **F**

Metamorphosis Dance, Op. 36; Romanza, Op. 24 Welsh (vcl), RLPO, Atherton
Unicorn-Kanchana UKCD 2039 [D] **M**

V *The Death of Moses* Chance (alt), Richardson (bar), Leonard (sop), Rangarajan (ten), Robinson (bs), Cambridge University Ch, Instrumental Ensemble, S. Cleobury
Unicorn-Kanchana DKPCD 9146 [D]

GOLDMARK, Karoly (1830–1915) AUSTRO-HUNGARY

O *'Rustic Wedding' Symphony, Op. 26; Sakuntala Overture, Op. 13* RPO, Butt
ASV CDDCA 791 [D] **F**

GORECKI, Henryk (born 1933) POLAND

O *Symphony No. 1 (1959), Op. 14; Choros I, Op. 20; 3 Pieces in Olden Style* Krakow PO, Bader
Koch Schwann 3-1041-2 [D] **F**

Symphony No. 3, Op. 36 Upshaw (sop), London Sinfonietta, Zinman
Elektra-Nonesuch 7559 79282-2 (US: 79282-2) [D] **F**

C *String Quartets: No. 1 (Already it is Dusk); No. 2 (Quasi una fantasia)* Kronos Quartet
Elektra Nonesuch 7559 79319-2 (US: 79319-2) [D] **F**

V *Beatus Vir; Old Polish Music; Totus Tuus* Sotrojev (bs), Prague Philharmonic Ch, Czech PO, Nelson
Argo 436 835-2 [D] **F**

*Miserere, Op. 44; Amen, Op. 35; Euntes ibant et flebant, Op. 32; *Wislo Moja, Wislo Szara, Op. 46; *Szeroka Woda, Op. 39* *Lira Chamber Ch., Chicago Symphony Chorus, Chicago Lyric Opera Chorus, Nelson
Elektra-Nonesuch 7559 79348-2 (US: 79348-2) [D] **F**

GOTTSCHALK, Louis (1829–1869) USA

O *Grande fantaisie triomphale sur l'hymne national brésilien* Ortiz (pno), RPO, Atzmon
(+ Addinsell: *Warsaw Concerto;* Gershwin: *Rhapsody in Blue;* Liszt: *Fantasia on Hungarian Themes;* Litolff: *Concerto symphonique No. 4*)
Decca 430 726-2 (US: London 430 726-2) [D] **M**

S *Ballade; Berceuse; Caprice-Polka; Grand Scherzo; La Jota aragonèse; Manchega; Marche de nuit; Misère du trovatore; Pasquinade; Polka in A♭; Polka in B♭; La Savane; Scherzo romantique; Souvenir d'Andalousie; Souvenir de Lima; Suis-moi! Ynes* Martin (pno)
Hyperion CDA 66697 [D] **F**

Ballade No. 6; Le Bananier; Le Banjo; Canto del Gitano; Columbia: caprice américain; Danza; La Mancenillier; Mazurka; Minuit à Seville; Ojos Criollos; Romance; Souvenir de la Havane; Souvenir de Puerto Rico; Union Martin (pno)
Hyperion CDA 66459 [D] **F**

S *Bamboula; Le Bananier; Le Banjo; The Dying Poet; The Last Hope; The Maiden's Blush; Ojos Criollos; Pasquinade; Le Savane; Souvenir d'Andalousie; Souvenir de Porto Rico; Suis-moi!; Tournament Galop; Union* List (pno)
Vanguard 08.4051.71 (US: OVC 4051) [A] **M**

GOULD, Morton (born 1913) USA

O *American Symphonette No. 2; Columbia – Broadsides for Orchestra on Columbian Themes; Viola Concerto; Flourishes and Galop; Housewarming; Soundings; Symphony of Spirituals* Glazer (vla), Louisville O, Mester
Albany TROY 013/4, 2 CDs [D] **F**

Fall River Legend (ballet): *Suite; Spirituals* Eastman-Rochester O, Hanson
(+ Barber: *Medea: Suite*)
Philips Mercury 432 016-2 [A] **M**

V *A capella; Of Time and the River; *Quotations* Gregg Smith Singers, Smith; *NY Society O & Ch, Goodwin
Koch 3-7026-2 [D] **F**

GOUNOD, Charles (1818–1893) FRANCE

O *Symphonies: No. 1 in D; No. 2 in E♭* Toulouse Capitole O, Plasson
EMI CDM7 63949-2 (US: CDM 63949) [A] **M**

V *Biondina* (song cycle); *29 Songs* Lott (sop), Murray (mez), Rolfe Johnson (ten), Johnson (pno)
Hyperion CDA 66801/2, 2 CDs [D] **F**

Messe solennelle de Sainte Cécile
Seefried (sop), Stolze (ten), Uhde (bar), Czech PO & Ch, Markevitch
DG 427 409-2 [A] **M**

Mors et vita Hendricks (sop), van Dam (bs), Denize (cont), Aler (ten), Orféon Donostiarra, Toulouse Capitale O, Plasson
EMI CDS7 54459-2 (US: Angel CDCC 54459), 2 CDs [D] **F**

GRAINGER, Percy (1882–1961) AUSTRALIA/USA

O *Blithe Bells; Country Gardens' Green Bushes; Handel in the Strand; Mock Morris; Molly on the Shore; My Robin is to the Greenwood Gone; Shepherd's Hey; Spoon River; Sussex Mummers' Christmas Carol; Youthful Rapture; Youthful Suite: Rustic Dance; Eastern Intermezzo* Bournemouth Sinfonietta, Montgomery
Chandos CHAN 6542 [A] **M**

S Arrangements of: Bach: *Blithe bells;* Brahms: *Cradle Song;* Dowland: *Now, O now, I needs must part;* Elgar: *Nimrod;* Foster: *Lullaby; The rag-time girl;* Gershwin: *Love walked in; The man I love;* Rachmaninov: *Finale of the Second Piano Concerto [abridged];* R. Strauss: *Ramble on the last love-duet from 'Der Rosenkavalier';* Tchaikovsky: *Opening of the First Piano Concerto Paraphrase on the Waltz of the Flowers;* Traditional (Chinese): *Beautiful fresh flower* Jones (pno)
Nimbus NI 5232 [D] **F**

29 Folksong Arrangements Jones (pno)
Nimbus NI 5244 [D] **F**

GRANADOS, Enrique (1867–1916) SPAIN

Cuentos de la juventud, Op. 1: Dedicatoria; 12 Danzas españolas Nos. 4 & 5; 15 Tonadillas al estilo antiguo: La maja de Goya; 7 Valses poéticos Bream (gtr)
(+ Albéniz: *Guitar works*)
RCA 09026 61608-2 [D] **M**

Danza lenta; 6 Escenas románticas; 6 Piezas sobre cantos populares españoles Rajna (pno)
CRD 3322 [A] **F**

12 Danzas españolas, Op. 37 de Larrocha (pno)
Decca 414 557-2 (US: London 414 557-2) [D] **F**

Goyescas (suite) de Larrocha (pno)
Decca 411 958-2 (US: London 411 958-2) [A] **F**

GRECHANINOV, Alexander (1864–1956) RUSSIA

String Quartet No. 1 in G, Op. 2 Shostakovich Quartet
(+ Tchaikovsky: *String Quartet No. 3*, etc.)
Olympia OCD 522 [A] **F**

Liturgy of St. John Chrysostom, Op. 13/1 Cantus Sacred Music Ensemble, Arshavskaya
Olympia OCD 447 [D] **F**

The Seven Days of Passion Russian State Symphonic Capella, Polyansky
Chandos CHAN 9303 [D] **F**

GRIEG, Edvard (1843–1907) NORWAY

Complete Orchestral Works Various artists, Gothenburg SO & Ch., Järvi
DG 437 842-2, 6 CDs [D] **F**

Piano Concerto in A min., Op. 16 Kovacevich (pno), BBC SO, C. Davis
(+ Schumann: *Piano Concerto*)
Philips 412 923-2 [A] **F**

Piano Concerto in A min., Op. 16 (original version); *Larviks-Polka; 23 Short Piano Pieces* Derwinger (pno), Norrköping SO, Hirokami
BID BIS-CD 619 [D] **F**

Cradle Song, Op. 68/5; 2 Elegiac Melodies, Op. 34; Holberg Suite, Op. 40; 2 Melodies, Op. 53; 2 Norwegian Melodies, Op. 63 Norwegian CO, Tønnesen
BIS BIS-CD 147 [D] **F**

Holberg Suite, Op. 40; 2 Norwegian Melodies, Op. 63 Moscow Soloists, Bashmet
(+ Tchaikovsky: *Serenade for Strings*)
RCA RD 60368 (US: 60368-2) [D] **F**

Lyric Suite, Op. 54; Norwegian Dances, Op. 35; Symphonic Dances, Op. 64 Gothenburg SO, Järvi
DG 419 431-2 [D] **F**

Peer Gynt (incidental music); *Sigurd Jorsalfar* (incidental music), *Op. 56* Bonney (sop), Eklof (mez), Sandve (ten), Malmberg (bar), Holmgren (bar), Gosta Ohlin's Vocal Ensemble, Pro Musica Chamber Ch, Gothenburg SO, Järvi
DG 423 079-2, 2 CDs [D] **F**

O *Peer Gynt: Suites Nos. 1 & 2; Holberg Suite, Op. 40; Sigurd Jorsalfar; Suite, Op. 56* BPO, Karajan
DG 419 474-2 [A/D] **M**

Symphony in C min.; Funeral March; In Autumn (concert overture), *Op. 11; Old Norwegian Melody with Variations, Op. 51* Gothenburg SO, Järvi
DG 427 321-2 [D] **F**

C *String Quartet No. 1 in G min., Op. 27; String Quartet No. 2 in F,* **Andante con moto in C min. for piano trio; Fugue in F min.* **Roling (pno), Raphael Quartet
Olympia OCD 432 [D] **F**

Cello Sonata in A min., Op. 36; Intermezzo Mork (vcl), Thibaudet (pno)
(+Sibelius: *2 Pieces, Op. 77; 4 Pieces, Op. 78; Malinconia, Op. 20*)
Virgin VC5 45034-2 (US: 45034) [D] **F**

Violin Sonatas Nos. 1–3 Kang (vln), Pontinen (pno)
BIS BIS-CD 647 [D] **F**

S *Complete Piano Music* Oppitz (pno)
Volume 1
RCA 09026 61568-2, 3 CDs [D] **F**
Volume 2
RCA 09026 61569-2, 4 CDs [D] **F**

4 Album Leaves, Op. 28; 2 Improvisations on Norwegian Folksongs, Op. 29; 25 Norwegian Folksongs and Dances, Op. 17; 3 Pictures, Op. 19 Knardahl (pno)
BIS BIS-CD 108 [D] **F**

Ballade, Op. 24; Peer Gynt Suites Nos. 1 & 2; Sigurd Jorsalfar: Suite Knardahl (pno)
BIS BIS-CD 109 [D] **F**

Elegiac Melodies; Holberg Suite; 2 Nordic Melodies, Op. 63; Olav Trygvason; Valses Caprices, Op. 37 Knardahl (pno)
BIS BIS-CD 110 [D] **F**

6 Lyric Pieces, Op. 65; 19 Norwegian Folksongs, Op. 66 Braaten (pno)
Victoria VCD 19032 [D] **F**

10 Norwegian Melodies; 42 Norwegian Folk Songs & Dances; Halvorsen: 'Entry of the Boyars' (arr. Grieg) Braaten (pno)
Victoria VCD 19035 [D] **F**

Lyric Pieces Books 1–4 Katin (pno)
Unicorn-Kanchana UKCD 2033 [D] **M**

Lyric Pieces Books 5–7 Katin (pno)
Unicorn-Kanchana UKCD 2034 [D] **M**

Lyric Pieces Books 8–10 Katin (pno)
Unicorn-Kanchana UKCD 2035 [D] **M**

Lyric Pieces (selection) Gilels (pno)
DG 419 749-2 [A] **F**

Piano Sonata, Op. 7 Gould (pno)
(+ Bizet: *Nocturne No. 1; Variations chromatiques, Op. 3; Sibelius: 3 Lyric Pieces, Op. 41; Sonatines Nos. 1–3, Op. 67*)
Sony CD 52654, 2 CDs [A] **M**

V *Bergliot, Op. 42; The Mountain Thrall, Op. 32; Before a Southern Convent, Op. 20; 7 Songs* Bonney (sop), Stene (cont), Hagegard

(bar), Tellefsen (narr), Gothenburg SO & Ch, Järvi
DG 437 519-2 [D] **F**

V   *Olav Trygvason, Op. 50; Bergliot, Op. 42; Funeral March in Memory of Rikard Nordraak, CW 117* Fjelstad (narr), Kringleborn (a Woman), Stene (The Sibyl), Vollestad (A High Priest), Trondheim SO & Ch., Ruud
Virgin VC5 45051-2 (US: 45051) [D] **F**

Song Recitals
Von Otter (mez), Forsberg (pno)
DG 437 521-2 [D] **F**
Hagegård (bar), Jones (pno)
RCA 09026 61630-2, 2 CDs [D] **F**
Hirsti (sop), Sandve (ten), Skram (bar), Jansen (pno)
Victoria VCD 19044 [D] **F**

7 Children's Songs, Op. 61; 19 Songs from Garborg's 'Haugtussa'
Hirsti (sop), Skram (bar), Jansen (pno)
Victoria VCD 19040 [D] **F**

GRIFFES, Charles (1884–1920) USA

O   *Pleasure-Dome of Kubla Khan, Op. 8; The White Peacock; *Poem; 3 Tone Pictures, Op. 5; Bacchanale* *Goff (fl), Seattle SO, Schwarz
(+Taylor: *Through the Looking Glass*)
Delos DE 3099 [D] **F**

S   *3 Fantasy Pieces, Op. 6; Piano Sonata in F♯ min.; 3 Tone Pictures, Op. 5* Landes (pno)
(+ Macdowell: *Piano Sonata No. 4*)
Koch 37045-2 [D] **F**

Piano Sonata in F♯ min. Lawson (pno)
(+ Ives: *Piano Sonata No. 1*; Sessions: *Piano Sonata No. 2*)
Virgin VC7 59316-2 (US: 59316) [D] **F**

V   *17 Songs* Hampson (bar), Guzelimian (pno)
(+Songs by Ives & MacDowell)
Teldec 9031 72168-2 [D] **F**

GROFÉ, Ferdinand (1892–1972) USA

O   *Grand Canyon Suite* Pittsburgh SO, Maazel
(+Herbert: *Hero and Leander*, etc.)
Sony CD 52491 [D] **F**

GUBAIDULINA, Sofia (born 1931) RUSSIA

O   **Introitus: Concerto for Piano & Orchestra; Sonata; Chaconne; Musical Toys* Haefliger (pno), *NDR Radio PO, Klee
Sony CD 53960 [D] **F**

*Offertorium (Violin Concerto); *Hommage à T.S. Eliot* Kremer (vln), Boston SO, Dutoit; *Various artists
DG 427 336-2 [D] **F**

C   *Garden of Joy and Sadness; String Trio; The Seven Last Words*
Various artists
Philips 434 041-2 [D] **F**

V   *Jetzt immer Schnee; Perception* Kleindienst (sop), Lorenz (bar), Stasov (spkr), Netherlands Chamber Ch., Schönberg Ensemble, de Leeuw
Philips 442 531-2 [D] **F**

GURNEY, Ivor (1890–1937) ENGLAND

S *Nocturne in A♭; Nocturne in B; A Picture; Prelude in C; Prelude in C min.; Prelude in D♭; Prelude in F♯; 5 Preludes; Revery; To E.H.M.* Gravill (pno)
Gamut GAMCD 516 [D] **F**

V Song cycles: *Ludlow and Teme; The Western Playland* Thompson (ten), Varcoe (bar), Delmé Quartet, Burnside (sop) (+ Vaughan Williams: *On Wenlock Edge*)
Hyperion CDA 66385 [D] **F**

HAAS, Pavel (1899–1944) CZECHOSLOVAKIA

C *String Quartets: No. 2 (From the Monkey Mountains), Op. 7; No. 3, Op. 15* Hawthorne Quartet (+ Krasa: *String Quartet*)
Decca 440 853-2 (US: London 440 853-2) [D] **F**

HADLEY, Patrick (1899–1973) ENGLAND

V *Lenten Cantata; The Cup of Blessing; I Sing of a Maiden; My Beloved Spake; A Song for Easter* Ainsley (ten), Sweeney (bs), Gonville & Caius College Ch, Webber (+ Rubbra: *Choral works*)
ASV CDDCA 881 [D] **F**

HAHN, Reynaldo (1875–1947) VENEZUELA/FRANCE

O *Le bal de Béatrice d'Este: Suite* New London O, Corp (+ Poulenc: *Aubade; Sinfonietta*)
Hyperion CDA 66347 [D] **F**

V *17 Melodies* Hill (ten), Johnson (pno)
Hyperion CDA 66045 [D] **F**

HANDEL, George Frideric (1685–1759) GERMANY/ENGLAND

O *Alcina: Overture; Acts I & II: Suites; Il pastor fido: Suite; Terpsichore: Suite* EBS, Gardiner
◇ Erato 2292 45378-2 [A] **M**

  Oboe Concertos Nos. 1–3; Concerto Grosso in C (Alexander's Feast), HWV318; Sonata à cinque in B♭, HWV288 Reichenberg (ob), English Concert, Pinnock
◇ DG Archiv 415 291-2 [A] **F**

  6 Organ Concerti, Op. 4; Organ Concerti: in F (Cuckoo and the Nightingale), HWV295; in A, HWV296; Triumph of Time and Truth; Sinfonia Hurford (org), Concertgebouw CO, Rifkin
Decca 430 569-2 (US: London 430 569-2), 2 CDs [A] **M**

  6 Organ Concerti, Op. 7; Organ Concerti: in D min., HWV304; in F, HWV305a Hurford (org), Concertgebouw CO, Rifkin
Decca 433 176-2 (US: London 433 176-2), 2 CDs [A] **M**

  6 Organ Concerti, Op. 4; 6 Organ Concerti, Op. 7; Organ Concerto in A, HWV296 Preston (org), English Concert, Pinnock
◇ DG Archiv 435 037-2, 3 CDs [D] **M**

  6 Concerti Grossi, Op. 3; Alcina: Overture; Ariodante: Overture ASMF, Marriner
Decca 430 261-2 (US: London 430 261-2) [A] **M**

  6 Concerti Grossi, Op. 3 Brandenburg Consort, Goodman
◇ Hyperion CDA 66633 [D] **F**

  12 Concerti Grossi, Op. 6 I Musici
Philips 422 370-2, 3 CDs **F**

O *12 Concerti Grossi, Op. 6 Nos. 1–4* English Concert, Pinnock
◇ DG Archiv 410 897-2 [D] **F**

12 Concerti Grossi, Op. 6 Nos. 5–8 English Concert, Pinnock
◇ DG Archiv 410 898-2 [D] **F**

12 Concerti Grossi, Op. 6 Nos. 9–12 English Concert, Pinnock
◇ DG Archiv 410 899-2 [D] **F**

Music for the Royal Fireworks, HWV351 Cleveland Symphonic
Winds, Fennell
(+ Holst: *Suites for Military Band*)
Telarc CD 80038 [D] **F**

*Music for the Royal Fireworks, HWV351; The Water Music,
HWV348–50* Orpheus CO
DG 435 390-2 [D] **F**

Water Music (complete) EBS, Gardiner
◇ Philips 434 122-2 [D] **F**

Overtures: *Agrippina; Alceste; Il pastor fido; Samson; Saul (Acts I
& II); Teseo* English Concert, Pinnock
◇ DG Archiv 419 219-2 [D] **F**

C *The Complete Chamber Music* Various artists
◇ CRD 3373/8, 6 separate CDs [A] **F**

Recorder Sonatas Nos. 1–6 Petri (rec), Jarrett (hpd)
◇ RCA RD 60441 (US: 60441-2) [D] **F**

S *Harpsichord Suites Nos. 1–8; 6 Fugues or Voluntaries; Fugue in E;
Fugue in F* Nicholson (hpd)
Hyperion CDA 66931/2, 2 CDs [D] **F**

V *10 Duets* Fisher (sop), Bowman (alt), King's Consort, King
◇ Hyperion CDA 66440 [D] **F**

Aci, Galatea e Polifemo (dramatic cantata); **Recorder Sonatas
Nos. 3 & 5* Kirkby (sop), Watkinson (cont), Thomas (bs),
London Baroque, Medlam; *Piguet (rec), Toll (hpd),
Medlam (vcl)
◇ HM HMC90 1253/4, 2 CDs [D] **F**

Acis and Galatea (oratorio), *HWV49b; Look down, harmonious
Saint* (cantata), *HWV124* McFadden (sop), Ainsley (ten),
Covey-Crump (ten), George (bs), Harre-Jones (alt), King's
Consort, King
◇ Hyperion CDA 66361/2, 2 CDs [D] **F**

*Ah! che troppo ineguali, HWV 230; Donna, che in ciel di tanta luce
splendi, HWV 233; Haec est Regina virginum, HWV 235; Il pianto
di Maria: 'Giunta l'ora fatal', HWV 234* von Otter (mezzo),
Musica Antiqua Köln, Goebel
◇ DG Archiv 439 866-2 [D] **F**

Alceste (incidental music), *HWV45; Comus* (incidental music)
Nelson (sop), Kirkby (sop), Kwella (sop), Cable (mez), Elliot
(ten), Thomas (bs), AAM, Hogwood
◇ L'Oiseau-Lyre 443 183-2 [A] **M**

Alexander's Feast (ode for St. Cecilia's day), *HWV75 (interpolates
Harp Concerto in B♭, H294; Organ Concerto in G, HWV289)*
Argenta (sop), Partridge (ten), George (bs), Lawrence-King
(hpd), Nicholson (org), Tragicomedia, The Sixteen O & Ch,
Christophers
◇ Collins 70162, 2 CDs [D] **F**

V *L'Allegro, il penseroso ed il moderato* (oratorio), *HWV55* Ginn
(tbl), Kwella (sop), McLaughlin (sop), Smith (sop), Davies
(ten), Hill (ten), Varcoe (bar), Monteverdi Ch, EBS,
Gardiner
◊ Erato 2292 45377-2, 2 CDs [D] **F**

Cantatas: *Alpestre monte, HWV81; Mi palpita il cor, HWV132;
Tra le fiamme, HWV170; Tu fedel? Tu costante?, HWV171* Kirkby
(sop), AAM, Hogwood
◊ L'Oiseau-Lyre 414 473-2 [D] **F**

Aminta e Fillide Fisher (sop), Kwella (sop), London Handel O,
Darlow
◊ Hyperion CDA 66118 [A] **F**

*As pants the hart (Chandos Anthem No. 6), HWV251; I will magnify
thee (Chandos Anthem No. 5b), HWV250b; O Sing unto the Lord
(Chandos Anthem No. 4a), HWV249a* Dawson (sop), Partridge
(ten), The Sixteen, Christophers
◊ Chandos CHAN 0504 [D] **F**

Athalia (oratorio), *HWV52* Sutherland (sop), Kirkby (sop),
Jones (trb), Bowman (alt), Rolfe Johnson (ten), Thomas (bs),
New College Ch, AAM, Hogwood
◊ L'Oiseau-Lyre 417 126-2, 2 CDs [D] **F**

Belshazzar (oratorio), *HWV61* Auger (sop), Gooding (sop),
Robbin (mez), Bowman (alt), Short (alt), Rolfe Johnson (ten),
Robertson (ten), Wilson-Johnson (bar), Wistreich (bs), English
Concert O & Ch, Pinnock
◊ DG Archiv 431 793-2, 3 CDs [D] **F**

*Blessed are they that considereth the poor (Foundling Hospital
Anthem), HWV268; Eternal source of light divine (Ode for the
birthday of Queen Anne), HWV74* Nelson (sop), Kirkby (sop),
Minty (mez), Bowman (alt), Hill (ten), Thomas (bs), Christ
Church Cathedral Ch, AAM, Simon Preston
(+ Haydn: *Mass No. 2*)
◊ L'Oiseau-Lyre 421 654-2 [A] **F**

Cantatas: *Carco sempre di Gloria, HWV87; La Lucrezia; Mi
palpita il cor, HWV132; Splenda l'alba in Oriente; Trio Sonata in
G, HWV399* Lesne (alt), Seminario Musicale
◊ Virgin VC7 59059-2 (US: 59059) [D] **F**

Cecilia vogi un sguardo (cantata); *Silete venti* (motet) Smith
(sop), Elwes (ten), English Concert, Pinnock
◊ DG Archiv 419 736-2 [D] **F**

Chandos Anthems Nos. 1-11 (complete) Various soloists, The
Sixteen Ch & O, Christophers
◊ Chandos CHAN 0554/7, 4 CDs [D] **F**

Coronation Anthems: *The King shall rejoice, HWV260; Let Thy
hand be strengthened, HWV259; My heart is inditing, HWV261;
Zadok the Priest, HWV258* Westminster Abbey Ch, Pinnock
(org), English Concert, Preston
◊ DG Archiv 447 282-2 [D] **M**

Deborah (oratorio) Kenny (sop), Gritton (sop), Denley (mez),
Bowman (alt), George (bs), New College Ch, King's Consort,
King
◊ Hyperion CDA 66841/2, 2 CDs [D] **F**

*Dixit Dominus, HWV232; Nisi Dominus, HWV238; Salve Regina,
HWV241* Westminster Abbey Ch, English Concert, Preston
◊ DG Archiv 423 594-2 [D] **F**

Esther (oratorio), *HWV50* Kirkby (sop), Kwella (sop), Minter (alt), Rolfe Johnson (ten), Thomas (bs), Partridge (ten), Elliot (ten), King (ten), Westminster Cathedral Boys' Ch, AAM O & Ch, Hogwood
⋄ L'Oiseau-Lyre 414 423-2, 2 CDs [D] **F**

Have mercy upon me (Chandos Anthem No. 3), HWV248; In the Lord put I my trust (Chandos Anthem No. 2), HWV247; O be joyful in the Lord (Chandos Anthem No. 1), HWV246 Dawson (sop), Partridge (ten), The Sixteen O & Ch, Christophers
⋄ Chandos CHAN 8600 [D] **F**

Hercules (oratorio), *HWV60* Smith (sop), Walker (mez), Denley (mez), Rolfe Johnson (ten), Tomlinson (bs), Savidge (bar), Monteverdi Ch, EBS, Gardiner
⋄ DG Archiv 423 137-2, 3 CDs [D] **F**

Israel in Egypt (oratorio) Jenkin (sop), Dunkley (sop), Trevor (cont), MacKenzie (ten), Evans (bs), Birchall (bs), The Sixteen Ch & O, Christophers
⋄ Collins 70352, 2 CDs [D] **F**

Jephtha (oratorio), *HWV70* Dawson (sop), Holton (sop), von Otter (mez), Chance (alt), Robson (ten), Varcoe (bar), Monteverdi Ch, EBS, Gardiner
⋄ Philips 422 351-2, 3 CDs [D] **F**

Joshua (oratorio), *HWV64* Kirkby (sop), Bowman (alt), Ainsley (ten), George (bs), Oliver (trb), New College Ch, King's Consort, King
⋄ Hyperion, CDA 66461/2, 2 CDs [D] **F**

Judas Maccabeus, *HWV63* Kirkby (sop), Denley (mez), Bowman (alt), MacDougall (ten), George (bs), Birchall (bs), New College Ch, King's Consort, King
⋄ Hyperion CDA 66641/2, 2 CDs [D] **F**

The King shall Rejoice, HWV265; Te Deum in D (Dettingen), HWV283 Tipping (alt), Christophers (ten), Varcoe (bar), Pearce (bs), Westminster Abbey Ch, English Concert, Preston
⋄ DG Archiv 410 647-2 [D] **F**

Let God arise (Chandos Anthem No. 11), HWV256; The Lord is my light (Chandos Anthem No. 10), HWV255 Dawson (sop), Partridge (ten), The Sixteen Ch & O, Christophers
⋄ Chandos CHAN 0509 [D] **F**

Messiah (oratorio), *HWV56*
Rodgers (sop), Jones (mez), Robson (ten), Langridge (ten), Terfel (bs-bar), Collegium Musicum 90, Hickox
⋄ Chandos CHAN 0522/3, 2 CDs [D] **F**
Harwood (sop), Baker (mez), Esswood (alt), Tear (ten), Herincx (bs), Ambrosian Singers, ECO, Mackerras
EMI CZS7 62748-2 (US: CDMB 62748), 2 CDs **B**

My Song shall be alway (Chandos Anthem No. 7), HWV252; O come, let us sing (Chandos Anthem No. 8), HWV253; O praise the Lord with one consent (Chandos Anthem No. 9), HWV254 Kwella (sop), Bowman (alt), Partridge (ten), George (bs), The Sixteen Ch & O, Christophers
⋄ Chandos CHAN 0505 [D] **F**

Ode for St. Cecilia's Day, HWV76 Lott (sop), Rolfe Johnson (ten), English Concert Ch & O, Pinnock
⋄ DG Archiv 419 220-2 [D] **F**

V *La Resurrezione di Nostro Signor Gesú Cristo* (oratorio) Argenta (sop), Schlick (sop), Laurens (mez), de Mey (ten), Mertens (bs), Amsterdam Baroque O, Koopman
◇ Erato 2292 45617-2, 2 CDs [D] **F**

Samson (oratorio) Alexander (sop), Rolfe Johnson (ten), Prégardien (ten), Arnold Schoenberg Ch, VCM, Harnoncourt
◇ Teldec 9031 74871-2, 2 CDs [D] **F**

Saul (oratorio), *HWV53* Dawson (sop), Brown (sop), Ragin (alt), Ainsley (ten), Mackie (ten), Miles (bar), Monteverdi Ch, EBS, Gardiner
◇ Philips 426 265-2, 3 CDs [D] **F**

Semele (oratorio), *HWV58* Battle (sop), Horne (mez), McNair (sop), Chance (alt), Aler (ten), Mackie (ten), Ramey (bs-bar), Doss (bs), Ambrosian Opera Ch., Nelson
DG 435 782-2, 2 CDs [D] **F**

Solomon (oratorio), *HWV67* Watkinson (cont), Argenta (sop), Hendricks (sop), Rolfe Johnson (ten), Monteverdi Ch, EBS, Gardiner
◇ Philips 412 612-2, 2 CDs [D] **F**

Susanna (oratorio) Hunt (sop), Minter (alt), Feldman (sop), Parker (bar), J. Thomas (ten), D. Thomas (bs), U.C. Berkeley Chamber Ch, Philharmonia Baroque O, McGegan
◇ HM HMU90 7030/2, 3 CDs [D] **F**

Te Deum and Jubilate in D (Utrecht), HWV278-9 Kirkby (sop), Nelson (sop), Brett (alt), Elliot (ten), Covey-Crump (ten), Thomas (bs), Christ Church Cathedral Ch, AAM, Preston
◇ L'Oiseau-Lyre 443 178-2 [D] **M**

Theodora (oratorio), *HWV68* Hunt (sop), Minter (alt), Lane (mez), Thomas (bs), U.C. Berkeley Chamber Ch, Philharmonia Baroque O, McGegan
◇ HM HMU90 7060/2, 3 CDs [D] **F**

The Triumph of Time and Truth (oratorio), *HWV71* Fisher (sop), Kirkby (sop), Brett (alt), Partridge (ten), Varcoe (bar), London Handel O & Ch, Darlow
◇ Hyperion CDA 66071/2, 2 CDs [D] **F**

HANSON, Howard (1896–1981) USA

O *Symphonies: No. 1 in E min. (Nordic); No. 2 (Romantic); *Song o, Democracy* Eastman-Rochester O, *Eastman School of Music Ch, Hanson
Philips Mercury 432 008-2 [A] **M**

*Symphonies: No. 3; No. 6; *Fantasy-Variations on a Theme of Youth* *Rosenberger (pno), Seattle SO, Schwarz; New York Chamber SO, Schwarz
Delos DE 3092 [D] **F**

*Symphony No. 4; *Lament for Beowulf; Merry Mount: Suite; **Pastorale; **Serenade* Seattle SO & *Chorale, **New York Chamber SO, Schwarz
Delos DE 3105 [D] **F**

*Symphonies: No. 5 (Sinfonia sacra); *No. 7 (A Sea Symphony); Piano Concerto in G* Rosenberger (pno), Seattle SO & *Chorale, Schwarz
Delos DE 3130 [D] **F**

HARBISON, John (born 1938) USA

> *Symphony No.2; *Oboe Concerto* *Bennett (ob), SFSO, Blomstedt
> (+Sessions: *Symphony No.2*)
> Decca 443 376-2 (US: London 443 376-2) [D] **F**

HARRIS, Roy (1898–1979) USA

> *American Creed; When Johnny Comes Marching Home* (overture)
> Seattle SO, Schwarz
> (+Copland: *Lincoln Portrait*, etc.)
> Delos DE 3140 [D] **F**

> *Symphony No. 3* NYPO, Bernstein
> (+ Schumann: *Symphony No. 3*)
> DG 419 780-2 [D] **F**

: *Violin Sonata; Complete Piano Works* Ross (vln), Zimdars (pno)
> Albany TROY 105 [D] **F**

HARTMANN, Karl Amadeus (1905–1963) GERMANY

> *Concerto funèbre* Zehetmair (vln/dir), Deutsche
> Kammerphilharmonie
> (+Berg: *Violin Concerto;* Janáček: *Violin Concerto*)
> Teldec 2292 46449-2 [D] **F**

> *Symphonies Nos. *1–8; **Gesangsszene* *Soffel (mez), **Fischer-
> Dieskau (bar), Bavarian RSO, Rieger (No. 1), Kubelik (Nos. 2,
> 4–6 & 8), Leitner (No. 3), Macal (No. 7)
> Wergo WER 60187-50, 4 CDs [A] **F**

> *Symphony No. 2 (Adagio); *Gesangsszene; Sinfonia Tragica*
> *Nimsgern (bar), Bamberg SO, Rickenbacker
> Koch 3-1295-2 [D] **F**

MARTY, Sir Hamilton (1879–1941) IRELAND

● *A Comedy Overture; An Irish Symphony* Ulster O, Thomson
> Chandos CHAN 8314 [D] **F**

> *Piano Concerto in B min.; *In Ireland* (fantasy); *With the Wild
> Geese* (tone poem) Binns (pno), *Fleming (fl), Kelly (hp),
> Ulster O, Thomson
> Chandos CHAN 8321 [D] **F**

> *Violin Concerto in D min.; Variations on a Dublin Air* Holmes
> (vln), Ulster O, Thomson
> Chandos CHAN 8386 [A] **F**

> *With the Wild Geese* (tone poem) SNO, Gibson
> (+ German: *Welsh Rhapsody;* MacCunn: *Land of Mountain and
> Flood;* Smyth: *The Wreckers Overture*)
> Classics for Pleasure CD-CFP 4635 [A] **B**

> *The Children of Lir; Ode to a Nightingale* Harper (sop), Ulster O,
> Thomson
> Chandos CHAN 8387 [D] **F**

HARVEY, Jonathan (born 1939) ENGLAND

> *Song Offerings* Walmsley-Clark (sop), London Sinfonietta,
> Benjamin
> (+ Benjamin: *Antara;* Boulez: *Dérive; Mémoriale*)
> Nimbus NI 5167 [D] **F**

HAYDN, Franz Joseph (1732–1809) AUSTRIA

O   *Cello Concertos: No. 1 in C; No. 2 in D* Coin (vcl), AAM,
Hogwood
◇ L'Oiseau-Lyre 414 615-2 [D] **F**
Mørk (vcl), Norwegian CO, Brown
Virgin VC5 45014-2 (US: 45014) [D] **F**

**Horn Concertos Nos. 1 & 2; **Trumpet Concerto in Eb; ***Cello
Concerto No. 1 in C* *Tuckwell (hn), **Stringer (tpt), ASMF
Marriner; ***Rostropovich (vcl), ECO, Britten
Decca 430 633-2 (US: London 430 633-2) [A] **M**

Keyboard Concertos Nos. 3, 4 & 11 Ax (pno/dir), Franz Liszt
CO
Sony CD 48383 [D] **F**

Trumpet Concerto in Eb Stringer (tpt), ASMF, Marriner
(+ Albinoni: *Trumpet Concerto in C*; Hummel: *Trumpet Concerto
in Eb*; L. Mozart: *Trumpet Concerto in D*; Telemann: *2 Oboe and
Trumpet Concerto No. 1*)
Decca 417 761-2 (US: London 417 761-2) [A] **M**

*Violin Concertos: No. 1 in C; No, 3 in A; No. 4 in G; *Violin and
Harpsichord Concerto in F* Kussmaul (vln/dir), *Hill (hpd),
Amsterdam Bach Soloists
Olympia OCD 428 [D] **F**

*Symphonies Nos. 1–104; Symphonies A & B; *Sinfonia Concertante
in Bb* *Engl (vln), *Baranyi (vcl), *Ozim (ob), *Racz (bsn),
Philharmonia Hungarica, Dorati
Decca 430 100-2 (US: London 430 100-2), 32 CDs [A] **M**

Symphonies Nos. 1–16 Philharmonia Hungarica, Dorati
Decca 425 900-2 (US: London 425 900-2), 4 CDs [A] **M**

Symphonies Nos. 1–5 Hanover Band, Goodman
◇ Hyperion CDA 66524 [D] **F**

Symphonies Nos. 1, 2, 4, 5, 10, 11, 18, 27, 32, 37 & 107 AAM,
Hogwood
◇ L'Oiseau-Lyre 436 428-2, 3 CDs [D] **F**

*Symphonies Nos. 3, 14, 15, 17, 19, 20, 25, 33, 36, 36 & 108
(Partita)* AAM, Hogwood
◇ L'Oiseau-Lyre 436 592-2, 3 CDs [D] **F**

Symphonies Nos. 6–8 English Concert, Pinnock
◇ DG Archiv 423 098-2 [D] **F**

Symphonies Nos. 9–12 Hanover Band, Goodman
◇ Hyperion CDA 66529 [D] **F**

Symphonies: No. 9 in C; No. 12 in E; No. 13 in D; No. 40 in F
Austro-Hungarian Haydn O, Fischer
Nimbus NI 5321 [D] **F**

Symphonies Nos. 13-16 Hanover Band, Goodman
◇ Hyperion CDA 66534 [D] **F**

Symphonies Nos. 17–33 Philharmonia Hungarica, Dorati
Decca 425 905-2 (US: London 425 905-2), 4 CDs [A] **M**

Symphonies Nos. 17–21 Hanover Band, Goodman
◇ Hyperion CDA 66533 [D] **F**

Symphonies Nos. 21–24, 28–31 & 34 AAM, Hogwood
◇ L'Oiseau-Lyre 430 082-2, 3 CDs [D] **F**

○   *Symphonies Nos. 22–25* Hanover Band, Goodman
    ◇ Hyperion CDA 66536 [D] **F**

*Symphonies: No. 22 in E♭ (Der Philosoph); No. 63 in C; No. 80 in
D min.* Orpheus CO
DG 427 337-2 [D] **F**

Symphonies Nos. 26, 35, 38–9, 41–2, 43, 52, 58–9 English
Concert, Pinnock
    ◇ DG Archiv 435 001-2, 6 CDs [D] **M**

*Symphonies Nos. 26 (Lamentatione), 42, 43 (Merkur), 44 (Trauer),
48 (Maria Theresa) & 49 (La passione)* AAM, Hogwood
    ◇ L'Oiseau-Lyre 440 222-2, 3 CDs [D] **F**

*Symphonies: No. 26 in D min. (Lamentatione); No. 52 in C min.;
No. 53 in D (L'Impériale)* La Petite Bande, Kuijken
    ◇ Virgin VC7 59148-2 (US: 59148) [D] **F**

Symphonies Nos. 34–47 Philharmonia Hungarica, Dorati
Decca 425 910-2 (US: London 425 910-2), 4 CDs [A] **M**

Symphonies Nos. 35, 38–9, 41, 58–9 & 65 AAM, Hogwood
    ◇ L'Oiseau-Lyre 433 012-2, 3 CDs [D] **F**

Symphonies Nos. 41–43 Tafelmusik, Weil
    ◇ Sony CD 48370 [D] **F**

Symphonies Nos. 44, 51 & 52 Tafelmusik, Weil
    ◇ Sony CD 48371 [D] **F**

Symphonies Nos. 45 (Farewell), 46 & 47 Tafelmusik, Weil
    ◇ Sony CD 53986 [D] **F**

Symphonies Nos. 48–59 Philharmonia Hungarica, Dorati
Decca 425 915-2 (US: London 425 915-2), 4 CDs [A] **M**

Symphonies Nos. 48–50 Hanover Band, Goodman
    ◇ Hyperion CDA 66531 [D] **F**

Symphonies Nos. 50, 64 & 65 Tafelmusik, Weil
    ◇ Sony CD 53985 [D] **F**

Symphonies Nos. 50, 64 (Tempora mutantas) & 65 Tafelmusik,
Weil
    ◇ Sony CD 53985 [D] **F**

Symphonies Nos. 53 (L'Impériale), 73 (La Chasse) & 79 Orpheus
CO
DG 439 779-2 [D] **F**

Symphonies Nos. 60–71 Philharmonia Hungarica, Dorati
Decca 425 920-2 (US: London 425 920-2), 4 CDs [A] **M**

Symphonies: No. 60 in C (Il distratto); No. 70 in D; No. 90 in C
CBSO, Rattle
EMI CDC7 54297-2 (US: Angel CDC 54297) [D] **F**

Symphonies Nos. 70–72 Hanover Band, Goodman
    ◇ Hyperion CDA 66526 [D] **F**

Symphonies Nos. 72–83 Philharmonia Hungarica, Dorati
Decca 425 925-2 (US: London 425 925-2), 4CDs [A] **M**

Symphonies Nos. 73–75 Hanover Band, Goodman
    ◇ Hyperion CDA 66520 [D] **F**

Symphonies Nos. 76–78 Hanover Band, Goodman
    ◇ Hyperion CDA 66525 [D] **F**

O *Symphonies Nos. 82–87 (Paris)*
EDITORS' CHOICE: Tafelmusik, Weil
✧ Sony CD 66295; CD 662966, 2 separately available CDs [D] **F**

Symphonies: No. 82 in C (Bear); No. 84 in E♭ Saint Paul CO, Wolff
Teldec 9031 74005-2 [D] **F**

Symphonies Nos. 84–95 Philharmonia Hungarica, Dorati
Decca 425 930-2 (US: London 425 930-2), 4 CDs [A] **M**

Symphonies: No. 88 in G; No. 90 in C; No. 92 in G (Oxford)
Austro-Hungarian Haydn O, Fischer
Nimbus NI 5269 [D] **F**

Symphonies Nos. 90–92 Hanover Band, Goodman
✧ Hyperion CDA 66521 [D] **F**

Symphonies: No. 90 in C; No. 93 in D Eighteenth Century O, Brüggen
✧ Philips 422 022-2 [D] **F**

Symphonies: No. 92 in G (Oxford); No. 94 in G (Surprise); No. 96 (Miracle) Cleveland O, Szell
Sony CD 46332 [A] **B**

Symphonies Nos. 93–104 Concertgebouw O, C. Davis
Philips 442 611-2; 442 614-2, 2 separate 2CD sets [A] **B**

Symphonies Nos. 93–98 RPO, Beecham
EMI CMS7 64389-2 (US: CDMB 64389), 2 CDs [A] **M**

Symphonies: No. 94 in G (Surprise); No. 101 in D (Clock) LPO, Jochum
DG 423 883-2 [A] **M**

*Symphonies Nos. 96–104; Symphonies A & B; *Sinfonia Concertante* *Engl (vln), *Baranyi (vcl), *Ozim (ob), *Racz (bn), Philharmonia Hungarica, Dorati
Decca 425 935-2 (US: London 425 935-2), 4 CDs [A] **M**

Symphonies Nos. 96 (Miracle), 97 & 98 La Petite Bande, Kuijken
✧ DHM 05472 77294-2 [D] **F**

Symphonies Nos. 97 & 98 18th Century O, Bruggen
✧ Philips 434 921-2 [D] **F**

Symphonies Nos. 99–104 RPO, Beecham
EMI CMS7 64066-2 (US: CDMB 64066), 2 CDs [A] **M**

Symphonies Nos. 99 & 100 (Military); Overture to Dalomon's opera 'Windsor Castle' LCP, Norrington
✧ EMI CDC5 55192-2 (US: Angel CDC 55192) [D] **F**

Symphonies: No. 101 in D (Clock); No. 103 in E♭ (Drum Roll)
Eighteenth Century O, Bruggen
✧ Philips 422 240-2 [D] **F**

Symphonies: No. 101 (Clock) & 102 LCP, Norrington
✧ EMI CDC5 55111-2 (US: Angel CDC 55111) [D] **F**

Symphonies: No. 103 in E♭ (Drum Roll); No. 104 in D (London)
Royal Concertgebouw O, Harnoncourt
Teldec 2292 43526-2 [D] **F**

C *Baryton Trios Nos. 71, 96, 113 & 126* Hsu (baryton), Miller (vla), Arico (vcl)
✧ ASV CDGAU 109 [D] **F**

C *Baryton Trios Nos. 87, 97, 101 & 111* Hsu (baryton), Miller (vla), Arico (vcl)
◈ ASV CDGAU 104 [D] **F**

4 Flute Trios (London); Divertimenti: in G; in D Rampal (fl), Stern (vln), Rostropovich (vcl)
Sony CD 37786 [D] **F**

Piano Trios Nos. 1–41 (complete) Beaux Arts Trio
Philips 432 061-2, 9 CDs [A] **M**

Piano Trios Nos. 9–12 & 25 Mathot (hpd), Manze (vln), vasn der Linden (vcl)
◈ Erato 4509 91728-2 [D] F

Piano Trios Nos. 24–26 London Fortepiano Trio
◈ Hyperion CDA 66297 [D] **F**

Piano Trios Nos. 27–30 Beths (vln), Bylsma (vcl) Levin (fnpo)
◈ Sony CD 53120 [D] **F**

Piano Trios Nos. 28–31 Beaux Arts Trio
Philips 420 790-2 [A] **F**

Piano Trios Nos. 38–40 Cohen (fpno), Hobarth (vln), Coin (vcl)
Harmonia Mundi HMC 90514 [D] **F**

The Seven Last Words of Christ on the Cross (String Quartets Nos. 50–56, Op. 71) Lindsay Quartet
ASV CDDCA 853 [D] **F**

6 String Quartets, Op. 1, Nos. 1–4 Kodály Quartet
Naxos 8.550398 [D] **F**

String Quartets: Op. 1/0 & 6; Op. 2/1 & 2 Kodály Quartet
Naxos 8.550399 [D] **F**

String Quartets: Op. 2/4 & 6; Op. 42 Kodály Quartet
Naxos 8.550732 [D] **F**

6 String Quartets, Op. 9 Kodály Quartet
Naxos 8.550786 (Nos. 1, 3 & 4); 8.550787 (Nos. 2, 5 & 6), 2 separate CDs [D] **B**

6 String Quartets (Sun), Op. 20 Mosaïques Quartet
◈ Astrée Auvidis E8784, 2 CDs [D] **F**
Hagen Quartet
DG 439 920-2, 2 CDs [D] **F**

String Quartets: No. 32 in C, Op. 20/2; No. 44 in Bb, Op. 50/1; No. 76 in D min., Op. 76/2 Lindsay Quartet
ASV CDQS 6144 [D] **B**

6 String Quartets, Op. 33 Weller Quartet
Nos. 1–3 (+ Op. 1/3):
Decca 433 691-2 (US: London 433 691-2) [A] **M**
Nos. 4–6 (+ Op. 103):
Decca 433 692-2 (US: London 433 692-2) [A] **M**

6 String Quartets, Op. 50 (Prussian) Salomon Quartet
◈ Hyperion CDA 66821/2, 2 separate CDs [D] **F**

3 String Quartets, Op. 54 Lindsay Quartet
ASV CDDCA 582 [D] **F**

String Quartets: No. 58 in C, Op. 54/2; No. 67 in D (Lark), Op. 64/5 Gabrieli Quartet
Chandos CHAN 8531 [D] **F**

C *String Quartets Op. 55/1–3* Lindsay Quartet
ASV CDDCA 906 [D] **F**

6 String Quartets, Op. 64 Kodály Quartet
Naxos 8.550673/4, 2 separate CDs [D] **B**

3 String Quartets, Op. 71; 3 String Quartets, Op. 74 Salomon
Quartet
◇ Hyperion CDA 66065, 66098, 66124, 3 separate CDs [D] **F**

6 String Quartets, Op. 76 Kodály Quartet
Naxos 8.550314/5, 2 separate CDs [D] **B**

String Quartets Op. 76 Nos. 1–3 Carmina Quartet
Denon CO-75970 [D] **F**

String Quartets: Op.77/1 & 2; Op.103 Quatuor Festetics
Harmonia Mundi HMA190 3001 [D] **F**

S *Piano Sonatas: No. 11 in B; No. 31 in Ab; No. 39 in D; No. 47 in B
min.* Richter (pno)
Decca 436 455-2 (US: London 436 455-2) [D] **F**

Piano Sonatas Nos. 32, 47, 53 & 59 Ax (pno)
Sony CD 53635 [D] **F**

*Piano Sonatas: No. 32 in G min.; No. 54 in G; No. 55 in Bb; No. 58
in C; No. 62 in Eb* Richter (pno)
Decca 436 454-2 (US: London 436 454-2) [D] **F**

*Piano Sonatas Nos. 33, 47, 50, 53, 54, 56 & 58–62; Adagio in F;
Fantasia in C; Variations in F min.* Brendel (pno)
Philips 416 643-2, 4 CDs [D/A] **F**

*Piano Sonatas: No. 33 in C min.; No. 60 in C; No. 62 in Eb;
Andante and Variations in F min.* Pletnev (pno)
Virgin VC7 59258-2 (US: 59258) [D] **F**

*Piano Sonatas No. 34 & 53; Variations in Eb; Variations in F min.;
6 'Kaiser' Variations* Staier (fpno)
◇ DHM 05472 77285-2 [D] **F**

*Piano Sonatas: No. 47 in B min.; No. 53 in E min.; No. 56 in D;
Adagio in F; Fantasia in C* Brendel (pno)
Philips 412 228-2 [D] **F**

Piano Sonatas Nos. 58–62 Staier (fpno)
◇ DHM RD 77160 (US: 77160-2) [D] **F**

V *Die Jahreszeiten (The Seasons – oratorio)* Bonney (sop), Rolfe
Johnson (ten), Schmidt (bar), Monteverdi Ch, EBS, Gardiner
◇ DG Archiv 431 818-2, 2 CDs [D] **F**
Janowitz (sop), Schreier (ten), Talvela (bs), Vienna
Singverein, Vienna SO, Böhm
DG 423 933-2, 2 CDs [A] **M**

*Mass No. 1a in G (Rorate coeli desuper); Mass No. 5 in Eb (Missa
in honorem); Mass No. 6 in G (Missa Sancti Nikolai)* Nelson
(sop), Watkinson (cont), Minty (alt), Hill (ten), Covey-Crump
(ten), Thomas (bs), Christ Church Cathedral Ch, AAM,
Preston
◇ L'Oiseau-Lyre 421 478-2 [A] **F**

Mass No. 2 in F (Missa brevis) Nelson (sop), Kirkby (sop),
Christ Church Cathedral Ch, AAM, Preston
(+ Handel: *Blessed are they that considereth the poor; Eternal source
of light divine*)
◇ L'Oiseau-Lyre 421 654-2 [A] **F**

∨ *Mass No. 3 in C (Missa Cellensis in honorem)* Nelson (sop), Cable (mez), Hill (ten), Thomas (bs), Christ Church Cathedral Ch, AAM, Preston
◇ L'Oiseau-Lyre 417 125-2 [D] **F**

Masses: No. 6 in G (Missa Sancti Nikolai); No. 12 in B♭ (Theresienmesse) Argenta (sop), Robbin (mez), Scade (ten), Miles (bs), English Concert & Ch, Pinnock
◇ DG Archiv 437 807-2 [D] **F**

*Masses: No. 7 in B♭ (Missa brevis Sancti Joannis de Deo); No. 8 in C; *Organ Concerto No. 1 in C* Smith (sop), Watts (cont), Tear (ten), Luxon (bar), St. John's College Ch, ASMF, Guest; *Preston (org), ASMF, Marriner
Decca 430 160-2 (US: London 430 160-2) [A] **M**

Mass No.7 in B♭ (Missa brevis Sancti Joannis de Deo); Missa 'Sunt bona mixta malis' (fragment); Offertorium: 'Non nobis, Domine'; Ave Regina; Responsoria de Venerabili; Responsorium ad absolutionem 'Libera me' Vallin (sop), Monoyios (sop), Tolz Boys' Ch., L'Archibudelli, Weil
◇ Sony CD 53368 [D] **F**

Mass No. 9 in B♭ (Missa Sancti Bernardi von Offida) Cantelo (sop), Minty (mez), Partridge (ten), Keyte (bs), St. John's College Ch, ASMF, Guest
(+ Mozart: *Litaniae de venerabili*)
Decca 430 158-2 (US: London 430 158-2) [A] **M**

Mass No. 10 in C (Mass in Time of War) Cantelo (sop), Watts (cont), Tear (ten), McDaniel (bar), St. John's College Ch, ASMF, Guest
(+ Mozart: *Vesperae solennes de confessore, K339*)
Decca 430 157-2 (US: London 430 157-2) [A] **M**

Mass No. 11 in D min. (Nelson); Te Deum No. 2 in C Lott (sop), Watkinson (cont), Davies (ten), Wilson-Johnson (bar), English Concert O & Ch, Pinnock
◇ DG Archiv 423 097-2 [D] **F**

Mass No. 12 in B♭ (Theresienmesse) Spoorenberg (sop), Greevy (mez), Mitchinson (ten), Krause (bar), St. John's College Ch, ASMF, Guest
(+ M. Haydn: *Ave Regina;* Mozart: *Ave verum corpus*)
Decca 430 159-2 (US: London 430 159-2) [A] **M**

Mass No. 13 in B♭ (Creation) Cantelo (sop), Watts (cont), Tear (ten), Robinson (bs), St. John's College Ch, ASMF, Guest
(+ Mozart: *Mass No. 12*)
Decca 430 161-2 (US: London 430 161-2) [A] **M**

Mass No. 14 in B♭ (Harmonienmesse) Spoorenberg (sop), Watts (cont), Young (ten), Rouleau (bs), St. John's College Ch, ASMF, Guest
(+ Mozart: *Vesperae de dominica*)
Decca 430 162-2 (US: London 430 162-2) [A] **M**

Il ritorno di Tobia (oratorio) Hendricks (sop), Zoghby (sop), Jones (mezzo), Langridge (ten), Luxon (bar), Brughton Festival Ch., RPO, Dorati
Decca 440 038-2 (US: London 440 038-2), 3 CDs [A] **M**

Die Schöpfung (The Creation – oratorio*)* Janowitz (sop), Ludwig (mez), Wunderlich (ten), Krenn (ten), Berry (bs), Vienna Singverein, BPO, Karajan
DG 435 077-2, 2 CDs [A] **M**

V Monoyios (sop), Hering (ten), van der Kamp (bs), Tolz Boys'
Ch., Tafelmusik, Weil
◇ Sony CD 57965, 2 CDs [D] **F**

Stabat Mater Rozario (sop), Robbin (mez), Rolfe Johnson
(ten), Hauptmann (bs), English Concert & Ch, Pinnock
◇ DG Archiv 429 733-2 [D] **F**

HAYDN, Michael (1737–1806) AUSTRIA

O *Horn Concerto in D; Organ & Viola Concerto in C; 6 Minuets;
Divertimento in G Tuckwell (hn), Preston (org), Shingles
(vla), ASMF, Marriner; *Vienna Octet
Decca 436 222-2 (US: London 436 222-2) [A] **M**

*Symphony in G, P27; Divertimento in D; Sinfonia in C (Andromeda
e Perseo)* Oradea PO, Rimbu
Olympia OCD 485 [A] **F**

Symphonies: in C, P10; in D, P11/21; in D min., P20 Oradea PO,
Acel, Ratiu
Olympia OCD 407 [A] **F**

*Symphonies: in Eb, P26; in Bb, P28; in D, P29; in D, P52; in Bb,
P52; Pastorello in C, P91* Oradea PO, Acel
Olympia OCD 404 [A] **F**

V *Ave Regina* St. John's College Ch, Guest
(+ J. Haydn: *Mass No. 12;* Mozart: *Ave verum corpus*)
Decca 430 159-2 (US: London 430 159-2) [A] **M**

Missa Sancti Aloysii; Missa subtitulo St. Leopoldi; Vesperae pro festo
Trinity College Ch, Marlow
Conifer CDCF 220 [D] **F**

HEADINGTON, Christopher (born 1930) ENGLAND

O *Violin Concerto* Wei (vln), LPO, Glover
(+ R. Strauss: *Violin Concerto*)
ASV CDDCA 780 [D] **F**

HENSELT, Adolf (1814–1899) GERMANY

O *Piano Concerto in F min., Op.16; Variations de concert, Op.11*
Hamelin (pno), BBC Scottish SO, Brabbins
(+Alkan: *Concerti da camera, Op.10*)
Hyperion CDA 66717 [D] **F**

HENZE, Hans Werner (born 1926) GERMANY

Requiem (9 sacred concertos) Wiget (pno), Hardenberger (tpt),
Ensemble Modern, Metzmacher
Sony CD 58972 [D] **F**

O *Symphonies Nos. 1–*6* BPO, *LSO, Henze
DG 429 854-2, 2CDs [A] **M**

Symphony No. 7; Barcorola CBSO, Rattle
EMI CDC7 54762-2 (US: CDC 54762) [D] **F**

C *String Quartets Nos. 1–5* Arditti Quartet
Wergo WER 60114/5-50, 2 CDs [D] **F**

HERBERT, Victor (1859–1924) USA

O *Hero and Leander* (symphonic poem), *Op. 33; 10 miniatures*
(orch. Sanford) Pittsburgh SO, Maazel
(+Grofé: *Grand Canyon Suite*)
Sony CD 52491 [D] **F**

HÉROLD, Ferdinand (1791–1833) FRANCE

> *La Fille mal gardée* (ballet) ROHO, Lanchberry
> (+ Lecocq: *Mam'zelle Angot*)
> Decca 430 849-2 (US: London 430 849-2), 2CDs [A] **M**

HERRMANN, Bernard (1911–1975) USA

> *The Devil and Daniel Webster: Suite; Silent Noon: Idyll; For the Fallen: Berceuse; Currier & Ives: Suite* New Zealand SO, Sedares
> Koch 3-7224-2 [D] **F**

> *North by Northwest* (film score) London Studio SO, Johnson
> Unicorn-Kanchana UKCD 2040 [D] **M**

> *Psycho* (film score) National PO, Herrmann
> Unicorn-Kanchana UKCD 2021 [A] **M**

> *Symphony No. 1; The Fantasticks* (song cycle) Rippon (bs), Dickinson (cont), Amis (ten), Humphreys (sop), Thames Chamber Ch, National PO, Herrmann
> Unicorn-Kanchana UKCD 2063 [A] **M**

> *Clarinet Quintet; *String Quartet (Echoes)* Hill (cl), Ariel Quartet; *Amici Quartet
> Unicorn-Kanchana UKCD 2069 [A] **M**

> *Moby Dick* (cantata); *For the Fallen* Amis (ten), Kelly (bs), R. Bowman (ten), Rippon (bs), Aeolian Singers, LPO, *National PO, Herrmann
> Unicorn-Kanchana UKCD 2061 [A] **M**

HILDEGARD OF BINGEN (1098–1179) GERMANY

> *Ave generosa; Columba aspexit; O ecclesia oculi tui; O euchari; O ignis spiritus; O Jerusalem aure civitas; O presul vere; O viridissima virga* Kirkby (sop), Gothic Voices, Muskett (symphony), White (bagpipes), Page (hp)
> Hyperion CDA 66039 [A] **F**

HINDEMITH, Paul (1895–1963) GERMANY

> *Cello Concerto; **Theme and Variations (The Four Temperaments)* *Wallfisch (vcl), **Shelley (pno), BBC PO, Tortelier
> Chandos CHAN 9124 [D] **F**

> *Concerto for Orchestra* CSO, Järvi
> (+ Schmidt: *Symphony No. 3*)
> Chandos CHAN 9000 [D] **F**

> *Violin Concerto; *Mathis der Maler (Symphony); **Symphonic Metamorphosis on Themes of Weber* D. Oistrakh, LSO, Hindemith; *OSR, Kletzki; **LSO, Abbado
> Decca 433 081-2 (US: London 433 081-2) [A] **M**

> *Kammermusik Nos. 1–7; Kleine Kammermusik No. 1, Op. 24* Royal Concertgebouw O, Chailly
> Decca 433 816-2 (US: London 433 816-2), 2 CDs [D] **F**

> *Mathis der Maler (Symphony); Symphonic Metamorphosis on Themes of Weber; *Trauermusik* *Walther (vla), SFSO, Blomstedt
> Decca 421 523-2 (US: London 421 523-2) [D] **F**

> *Nobilissima visione Concert Music, Op. 50; *Der Schwanendreher* *Walther (vla), SFSO, Blomstedt
> Decca 433 809-2 (US: London 433 809-2) [D] **F**

O   *Symphony in E♭; Nobilissima visione; Neues vom Tage*   BBC PO, Tortelier
Chandos CHAN 9060 [D] **F**

     Symphonia Serena; Symphony 'Die Harmonie der Welt'   BBC PO, Tortelier
Chandos CHAN 9217 [D] **F**

C   *A Frog he went a-courting; Kleine Sonata; 3 Leichte Stücke; Cello Sonata* (1948) Berger (vcl), Mauser (pno)
Wergo WER 60145-50 [D] **F**

     Sonatas: Bass Tuba; Horn; Horn in E♭; Trombone; Trumpet Torchinsky (bs tuba), Jones (hn/E♭ hn), Smith (tbn), Johnson (tpt), Gould (pno)
Sony CD 52671, 2 CDs [A] **M**

     Cello Sonata, Op. 11/3; 3 Pieces, Op. 8 Berger (vcl), Mauser (pno)
Wergo WER 60144-50 [D] **F**

     Viola Sonatas Nos. 1–3; Meditation Imai (vla), Pöntenen (pno)
BIS BIS-CD 651 [D] **F**

S   *Organ Sonatas Nos. 1–3* Kee (org)
(+ Reger: *Organ works*)
Chandos CHAN 9097 [D] **F**

     Solo Viola Sonatas Nos. 1–4 Imai (vla)
BIS BIS-CD 57 [D] **F**

     In einer Nacht, Op. 15; Suite '1922', Op. 26 Mauser (pno)
Wergo WER 6181-2 [D] **F**

     Piano Sonatas Nos. 1–3 Gould (pno)
Sony CD 52670 [A] **M**

V   *20 Lieder* Fischer-Dieskau (bar), Reimann (pno)
Orfeo C15686 1A [D] **F**

     When lilacs last in the door-yard bloom'd (Requiem for those we love) De Gaetani (mez), Stone (bar), Atlanta SO & Ch, Shaw
Telarc CD 80132 [D] **F**

HODDINOTT, Alun (born 1929) WALES

O   *Doubles; The Heaventree of Stars; Passaggio; Star Children* BBC Welsh SO, Otaka
Nimbus NI 5357 [D] **F**

     Noctis Equi, Op. 132 Rostropovich (vcl), LSO, Nagano
(+ Honegger: *Cello Concerto;* Milhaud: *Cello Concerto*)
Erato 2292 45489-2 [D] **F**

S   *Piano Sonatas Nos. 1–5* Jones (pno)
Nimbus NI 5369 [D] **F**

     Piano Sonatas Nos. 6-10 Jones (pno)
Nimbus NI 5370 [D] **F**

HOLBROOKE, Joseph (1879–1958) ENGLAND

C   *Eilen Shona* King (cl), Britten Quartet
(+ Cooke; Frankel; Maconchy: *Clarinet Quintets*)
Hyperion CDA 66428 [D] **F**

HOLLOWAY, Robin (born 1943) ENGLAND

O   *Violin Concerto, Op. 70; Horn Concerto, Op. 43* Kovacic (vln), Tuckwell (hn), Scottish CO, Bamert
Collins 14392 [D] **F**

O *Second Concerto for Orchestra* BBC SO, Knussen
NMC CD 015 [D] **M**

V *Sea-Surface Full of Clouds, Op. 31; *Romanze, Op. 31* Walmsley-Clarke (sop), Cable (cont), Hill (ten), Brett (alt), *Gruenberg (vln), R Hickox Singers., City of London Sinfonia, Hickox
Chandos CHAN 9228 [D] **F**

Since I Believe in God the Father Almighty Kendall (ten), Harvey (bs), Gonville & Caius College Ch, Webber
(+ C. Wood: *St. Mark Passion*)
ASV CDDCA 854 [D] **F**

HOLMBOE, Vagn (born 1909) DENMARK

O *Symphonies Nos. 1, 3 & 10* Aarhus SO, Hughes
BIS BIS-CD 605 [D] **F**

Symphony No. 4 (Sinfonia sacra), Op. 29; Symphony No. 5, Op. 35
Aarhus SO, Hughes
BIS BIS-CD 572 [D] **F**

Symphony No. 6, Op. 43; Symphony No. 7 (in one movement), Op. 50 Aarhus SO, Hughes
BIS BIS-CD 573 [D] **F**

HOLST, Gustav (1874–1934) ENGLAND

O *Beni Mora (Oriental Suite); Brook Green Suite; Egdon Heath (Homage to Hardy); The Perfect Fool (opera): Ballet Suite; St. Paul's Suite; Short Festival Te Deum; Psalm 86* Various artists
EMI CDC7 49784-2 (US: Angel CDC 49784) [A] **F**

Beni Mora (Oriental Suite); Fugal Overture; Hammersmith; Japanese Suite; Scherzo; Somerset Rhapsody LPO, LSO, Boult
Lyrita SRCD 222 [A] **F**

Brook Green Suite; St. Paul's Suite; Double Violin Concerto, Op. 49; Fugal Concerto Op. 49/2; 2 Songs without Words, Op. 22; Lyric Movement Various artists, City of London Sinfonia, Hickox
Chandos CHAN 9270 [D] **F**

The Planets (suite) CSO & Ch, Levine
DG 429 730-2 [D] **F**

Suites for Military Band: No. 1 in E♭; No. 2 in F Cleveland Symphonic Winds, Fennell
(+ Handel: *Music for the Royal Fireworks*)
Telarc CD 80038 [D] **F**

C *Air and Variations; 3 Pieces for Oboe and String Quartet* Francis (ob), English Quartet
(+ Bax: *Oboe Quintet;* Jacob: *Oboe Quartet;* Moeran: *Fantasy Quartet*)
Chandos CHAN 8392 [D] **F**

V *A Choral Fantasia, H177; Choral Symphony No. 1, H155* Dawson (sop), Birch (org), Guildford Choral Society, RPO, Davan Wetton
Hyperion CDA 66660 [D] **F**

6 Choral Folk Songs; 2 Eastern Pictures; 13 Partsongs; Songs from 'The Princess' Theodore (ob), Truman (vcl), Williams (hp), Holst Singers, Layton
Hyperion CDA 66705 [D] **F**

The Cloud Messenger; The Hymn of Jesus Jones (mez), LSO & Ch, Hickox
Chandos CHAN 8901 [D] **F**

V *2 Eastern Pictures; Hymn to Dionysus; Choral Hymns from the Rig
Veda: Groups 1–4* *Ellis (hp), RCM Chamber Ch, RPO,
Willcocks
Unicorn-Kanchana DKPCD 9046 [D] **F**

*The Evening Watch; 6 Male Choruses; Nunc Dimittis; 7 Partsongs;
Psalm 86; Psalm 148* Holst Singers & O, Davan Wetton
Hyperion CDA 66329 [D] **F**

HONEGGER, Arthur (1892–1955) FRANCE/SWITZERLAND

O *Cello Concerto* Rostropovich (vcl), LSO, Nagano
(+ Hoddinott: *Noctis Equi*; Milhaud: *Cello Concerto*)
Erato 2292 45489-2 [D] **F**

*3 Symphonic Movements: Pacific 231; Rugby; Horace victorieux;
Pastorale d'été; La Tempête: Prélude; La Traversée des Andes: Suite;
Le Vol sur l'Atlantique* Toulouse Capitole O, Plasson
DG 435 438-2 [D] **F**

*Symphony No. 1; Pastorale d'été; 3 Symphonic Movements: Pacific
231; Rugby; No. 3* Bavarian RSO, Dutoit
Erato 2292 45242-2 [D] **F**

Symphonies Nos. 2 & 3 (Liturgique) BPO, Karajan
DG 423 242-2 [A] **M**

*Symphonies: No. 4 (Deliciae basiliensis); No. 5 (Di tre re); Pacific
231* Toulouse Capitole O, Plasson
EMI CDM7 64275-2 (US: Angel CDM 64275) [A] **M**

V *Jeanne d'Arc au bûcher* (stage oratorio) Keller (narr), Wilson
(narr), Escourrou (narr), Pollet (sop), Command (sop),
Stützman (cont), French Radio Ch, FNO, Ozawa
DG 429 412-2 [D] **F**

Le Roi David (dramatic psalm) Audel (narr), Danco (sop), De
Montmollin (mez), Hamel (ten), Martin (pno), SRO & Ch,
Ansermet
Decca 425 621-2 (US: London 425 621-2) [A] **M**

HOVHANESS, Alan (born 1911) USA

O *Mysterious Mountain (Symphony No. 2); Prayer of St. Gregory;
Prelude and Quadruple Fugue; And God Created Whales; Alleluia
and Fugue; Celestial Fantasy* Seattle SO, Hovhaness, Schwarz
Delos DE 3157 [D] **F**

*Symphony No. 6 (The Celestial Gate); *Prayer of St Gregory;
*Haroutian: Aria; Mountains and Rivers Without End (chamber
symphony); *Return and Rebuild the Desolate Places* *Gekker
(tpt), Manhattan CO, Auldon Clark
Koch 3-7221-2 [D] **F**

*Symphony No. 22 (City of Light); *Symphony No. 50 (Mount St.
Helens)* Seattle SO, Hovhaness, *Schwarz
Delos DE 3137 [D] **F**

*Symphonies Nos. *29 & 53 (Star Dawn); The Flowering Peach
(incidental music); Symphony No. 2: Grand Final Processional*
*Lindberg (tbn), Ohio State Concert Band, Brion
Delos DE 3158 [D] **F**

*Symphonies Nos. *39 & 46 (To the Green Mountains)* *Long (gtr),
KBS SO, Jordania
(+Trad [arr. Hee-jo] : *Milyang Arirang*)
Koch 3-7208-2 [D] **F**

C *Quartets Nos. 1 (Jupiter), 3 (Reflections on My Childhood) & 4 (The Ancient Tree); 4 Bagatelles; String Quartet No. 2: Suite (Gamelan; Spirit Murmur; Hymn)* Shanghai Quartet
Delos DE 3162 [D] **F**

S *14 Piano Works* M. Rosen (pno)
Koch 3-7288-2 [D] **F**

HOWELLS, Herbert (1892–1983) ENGLAND

O *Piano Concerto No. 2; *Concerto for Strings; 3 Dances* Stott (pno), *Stewart (vln), RLPO, Handley
Hyperion CDA 66610 [D] **F**

Concerto for Strings; Elegy; Serenade; Suite for Strings City of London Sinfonia, Hickox
Chandos CHAN 9161 [D] **F**

C *String Quartet (In Gloucestershire)* Divertimenti
(+ Dyson: *3 Rhapsodies*)
Hyperion CDA 66139 [D] **F**

Violin Sonatas: No. 1 in E, Op. 18; No. 2 in E♭, Op. 26; No. 3 in E min., Op. 38; Cradle Song, Op. 9/1; 3 Pieces, Op. 28 Barritt (vln), Edwards (pno)
Hyperion CDA 66665 [D] **F**

S *Gadabout; Sarum Sketches, 3 Pieces; Slow Dance; Cobbler's Hornpipe; Snapshots, Op, 30; The Chosen Tune; 4 Pieces from Lambert's Clavichord; Musica Sine Nomine; Sonatina* Fingerhut (pno)
Chandos CHAN 9273 [D] **F**

Howells's Clavichord; Lambert's Clavichord McCabe (pno)
Hyperion CDA 66689 [D] **F**

Three Psalm Preludes – Sets 1 & 2; 3 Rhapsodies, Op. 17 Dearnley (org)
Hyperion CDA 66394 [D] **F**

V *2 South African Settings; 3 Folksongs; A Garland for de la Mare; Peacock Pie, Op. 33; 4 French Chansons, Op. 29; In Green Ways, Op. 43; 3 Children's Songs; 4 Songs, Op. 22; 6 unpublished songs; 12 published songs* Dawson (sop), Pierard (sop), Ainsley (ten), Luxon (bar), Drake (pno)
Chandos CHAN 9185/6, 2 CDs [D] **F**

*Behold, O God our Defender; Collegium Regale: Te deum; Jubilate; Like as the Hart; St. Paul's Service; Take Him, Earth, for Cherishing; *6 Pieces: No. 3; *Psalm-Preludes Set 2: No. 1* *Dearnley (org), Scott (org), St. Paul's Cathedral Ch, Dearnley
Hyperion CDA 66260 [D] **F**

*Flourish for a Bidding; *Howells's Clavichord: Walton's Toye; Jacob's Brawl; *Lambert's Clavichord: de la Mare's Pavane; *St. Louis Comes to Clifton; House of the Mind; A Hymn for St. Cecilia; King of Glory; New College Service; O Pray for the Peace of Jerusalem; A Sequence for St. Michael *Higginbottom (org), Burchell (org), New College Ch, Higginbottom
CRD 3454 [D] **F**

Hymnus Paradisi; An English Mass Kennard (sop), Ainsley (ten), RLPO & Ch, Handley
Hyperion CDA 66488 [D] **F**

Mass in the Dorian Mode; Come, my soul; Nunc dimittis; O salutaris Hostia; Regina caeli; Salve Regina; Sweetest of Sweets Finzi Singers, Spicer

(+ Stevens: *Mass for Double Choir*)
Chandos CHAN 9021 [D] **F**

V *Requiem; The House of the Mind; A Sequence for St. Michael* Finzi
Singers, Spicer
(+ Vaughan Williams: *Lord, Thou hast been our refuge*, etc.)
Chandos CHAN 9019 [D] **F**

Requiem Corydon Singers, Best
(+ Vaughan Williams: *Mass; Te Deum*)
Hyperion CDA 66076 [A] **F**

Stabat Mater Archer (ten), LSO & Ch., Rozhdestvensky
Chandos CHAN 9314 [D] **F**

HUMMEL, Johann (1778–1837) AUSTRIA

O *Bassoon Concerto in F* Thunemann (bsn), ASMF, Marriner
(+ Weber: *Andante e rondo ungarese; Bassoon Concerto*)
Philips 432 081-2 [D] **F**

Piano Concertos: in A min., Op. 85; in B min., Op. 89 Hough
(pno), ECO, Thomson
Chandos CHAN 8507 [D] **F**

Trumpet Concerto in E♭ Wilbraham (tpt), ASMF, Marriner
(+ Albinoni: *Trumpet Concerto in C*; Haydn: *Trumpet Concerto in
E♭*; L. Mozart: *Trumpet Concerto in D*; Telemann: *2 Oboe and
Trumpet Concerto No. 1*)
Decca 417 761-2 (US: London 417 761-2) [A] **M**

C *Nocturne, Op. 99; Violin Sonatas in E♭, Op. 5/3, & D, Op. 50*
Holmes (vln), Burnett (fpno)
✧ Amon Ra CD-SAR 12 [A] **F**

Piano Quintet, Op. 87 Hausmusik
(+ Schubert: *Piano Quintet in A*)
✧ EMI CDC7 54264-2 (US: Angel CDC 54264) [D] **F**

3 String Quartets, Op. 30 Delmé Quartet
Hyperion CDA 66568 [D] **F**

Septet in C (Septet Militaire), Op. 114 Nash Ensemble
(+ C. Kreutzer: *Septet in E♭, Op. 62*)
CRD 3390 [A] **F**

Septet in D min., Op. 74 Nash Ensemble
(+ Berwald: *Grand Septet in B♭*)
CRD 3344 [A] **F**

HUMPERDINCK, Engelbert (1854–1921) GERMANY

O *Hansel und Gretel: Overture; The Bluebird: Prelude & Star Dance;
Königskinder: Overture; Preludes to Acts II & III; The Sleeping
Beauty: Suite (Nos. 1-5)* Bamberg SO, Rickenbacher
Virgin VC7 59067-2 (US: 59067) [D] **F**

HURLSTONE, William (1876–1906) ENGLAND

O *The Magic Mirror Suite; Variations on an Original Theme;
Variations on an Hungarian Air* LPO, Braithwaite
Lyrita SRCD 208 [D] **F**

C *4 Characteristic Pieces* King (cl), Benson (pno)
(+ Finzi: *Five Bagatelles*; Ferguson: *4 Short Pieces, Op. 6*;
Stanford: *Clarinet Sonata, Op. 129*)
Hyperion CDA 66014 [D] **F**

IBERT, Jacques (1890–1962) FRANCE

○ *Bacchanale; Bostoniana; Escales; *Flute Concerto; Louisville Concerto; Suite symphonique (Paris); Hommage à Mozart* *Hutchins (fl), Montreal SO, Dutoit
Decca 440 332-2 (US: London 440 332-2) [D] **F**

Divertissement Ulster O, Tortelier
(+ Milhaud: *Le Boeuf sur le toit*, etc.; Poulenc: *Les Biches*)
Chandos CHAN 9023 [D] **F**

Flute Concerto Milan (fl), City of London Sinfonia, Hickox
Chandos CHAN 8840 [D] **F** (see collections – *Works for Flute and Orchestra*)

Symphonie Concertante de Lancie (ob), LSO, Previn
(+ Françaix: *L'Horloge de flore;* Satie: *Gymnopédies Nos. 1 & 3;* R. Strauss: *Oboe Concerto*)
RCA GD 87989 (US: 7989-2) [A] **M**

d'INDIA, Sigismondo (c.1582–1629) ITALY

∨ *Amico hai vint'io; Diana; Misera me; Piangono al pianger mio; Sfere fermate; Torna il sereno zefiro* Kirkby (sop), Rooley (chitarrone)
(+ Monteverdi: *Lamento d'Olympia*, etc.)
Hyperion CDA 66106 [D] **F**

D'INDY, Vincent (1851–1931) FRANCE

○ *Jour d'été à la montagne, Op. 61; Tableaux de voyage, Op. 36* Loire PO, Dervaux
EMI CDM7 64364-2 (US: CDM 64364) [A] **M**

Symphonie sur un chant montagnard français, Op. 25 Henriot-Schweitzer (pno), Boston SO, Monteux
(+ Berlioz: *Overture: Béatrice et Bénédict;* Franck: *Symphony in D min.*)
RCA GD 86805 (US: 6805-2) [A] **M**

PPOLITOV-IVANOV, Mikhail (1859–1935) RUSSIA

○ *Caucasian Sketches* BBC PO, Glushchenko
(+Khachaturian: *Symphony No. 3*, etc.)
Chandos CHAN 9321 [D] **F**

√ *Liturgy of St. John Chrysostom, Op. 37; Vespers, Op. 43* Chamber Choir 'Lege Artis', Abalyan
Sony CD 64091 [D] **M**

RELAND, John (1879–1962) ENGLAND

○ *Piano Concerto in E♭* Stott (pno), RPO, Handley
(+ Bridge: *Phantasm;* Walton: *Sinfonia Concertante*)
Conifer CDCF 175 [D] **F**

*Piano Concerto; *Legend; Mai-Dun (symphonic rhapsody)
*Parkin (pno), LPO, Thomson
Chandos CHAN 8461 [D] **F**

A Downland Suite; The Holy Boy; Meditation on John Keble's Rogation Hymn Garforth
(+ Bridge: *Suite for Strings*)
Chandos CHAN 8390 [D] **F**

Epic March; The Holy Boy; A London Overture; Greater Love Hath No Man (motet); *These Things Shall Be; Vexilla Regis (Hymn for Passion Sunday)* Terfel (bs-bar), LSO & Ch, Hickox
Chandos CHAN 8879 [D] **F**

C *Cello Sonata* Lloyd Webber (vcl), McCabe (pno)
(+ Bridge: *Elegy; Scherzetto;* Stanford: *Cello Sonata No. 2*)
ASV CDDCA 807 [D] **F**

Phantasie Trio in A min. Hartley Piano Trio
(+ Bridge: *Phantasie Trio in C min.;* Clarke: *Piano Trio*)
Gamut GAMCD 518 [D] **F**

S *Ballade; The Darkened Valley; Equinox; Greenways; In those Days;
Leaves from a Child's Sketchbook; London Pieces; 2 Pieces; Prelude
in Eb* Parkin (pno)
Chandos CHAN 9140 [D] **F**

*Piano Sonata; The Almond Tree; Decorations; Merry Andrew;
Preludes; Rhapsody; Summer Evening; The Towing-Path*
Parkin (pno)
Chandos CHAN 9056 [D] **F**

*A Sea Idyll; On a Birthday Morning; Soliloquy; 2 Pieces, Sets I &
II; Spring Will Not Wait; Ballade of London Nights; Month's Mind;
3 Pastels; Columbine; Sarnia* Parkin (pno)
Chandos CHAN 9250 [D] **F**

ISAAC, Heinrich (c.1450–1517) NETHERLANDS

V *Missa de apostolis; Optime... pastor; Regina caeli laetare; Resurrexi
et adhuc tecum sum; Tota pulchra es; Virgo prudentissima* Tallis
Scholars, Phillips
Gimell CDGIM 023 [D] **F**

IVES, Charles (1874–1954) USA

O *Calcium Light Night; Country Band March; Largo Cantabile: Hymn*
(from *A Set of 3 Short Pieces for String Quartet*); *Orchestral Set No.
1 (Three Places in New England); Postlude in F; 4 Ragtime Dances;
Set for Theatre Orchestra; Yale-Princetown Football Game* New
England O, Sinclair
Koch 3-7025-2 [D] **F**

*Central Park in the Dark; Holidays Symphony; The Unanswered
Question* (original and revised versions) CSO & Ch, Tilson
Thomas
Sony CD 42381 [D] **F**

Symphony No. 1 Detroit SO, Järvi
(+ Barber: *Essays for Orchestra Nos. 1–3*)
Chandos CHAN 9053 [D] **F**

Symphonies Nos. 1 & 4 CSO, Tilson Thomas
Sony CD 44939 [D] **F**

*Symphony No. 2; Central Park in the Dark; The Gong on the Hook
and Ladder; Tone Roads: No. 1; A Set of 3 Short Pieces; The
Unanswered Question* NYPO, Bernstein
DG 429 220-2 [D] **F**

Symphony No. 3; Three Places in New England Eastman-
Rochester O, Hanson
(+ Mennin: *Symphony No. 5;* Schuman: *New England
Triptych*)
Philips Mercury 432 755-2 [A] **M**

*Symphony No. 3; Three Places in New England; Central Park in th
Dark; The Unanswered Question; March III with the Air 'Old
Kentucky Home'; Fugue in 4 keys (The Shining Shore)* St. Louis
SO, Slatkin
RCA 09026 61222-2 [D] **F**

Three Places in New England; The Unanswered Question; *A Set of Pieces; Symphony No. 3 (The Camp Meeting); Set No. 1 *Kalish, Orpheus CO
DG 439 869-2 [D] **F**

Variations on 'America' (arr. Schuman) St. Louis SO, Slatkin
(+ Schuman: *Symphony No. 10, etc.*)
RCA 09026 61282-2 [D] **F**

String Quartets Nos. 1 & 2; Scherzo (Holding your own) Emerson Quartet
(+ Barber: *String Quartet*)
DG 435 864-2 [D] **F**

Piano Sonata No. 1 Lawson (pno)
(+ Griffes: *Piano Sonata;* Sessions: *Piano Sonata No. 2*)
Virgin VC7 59316-2 (US: 59316) [D] **F**

Piano Sonata No. 2 'Concord Mass' Hamelin (pno)
(+ Wright: *Piano Sonata*)
New World NW378-2 [D] **F**

Three-page Sonata Lawson (pno)
(+ Barber: *Piano Sonata;* Carter: *Piano Sonata;* Copland: *Piano Sonata*)
Virgin VC7 59008-2 (US: 59008) [D] **F**

26 Songs Alexander (sop), Crone (pno)
Etcetera KTC 1020 [D] **F**

13 Songs Hampson (bar), Guzelimian (pno)
(+Songs by Griffes & MacDowell)
Teldec 9031 72168-2 [D] **F**

ACOB, Gordon (1895–1984) ENGLAND

5 Pieces Reilly (harmonica), ASMF, Marriner
(+ Moody: *Little Suite;* Tausky: *Concertino;* Vaughan Williams: *Romance*)
Chandos CHAN 8617 [D] **F**

Divertimento Reilly (harmonica), Hindar Quartet
(+ Moody: *Harmonica Quintet; Suite dans le style français*)
Chandos CHAN 8802 [D] **F**

Oboe Quartet Francis (ob), Members of the English Quartet
(+ Bax: *Oboe Quintet;* Holst: *Air and Variations; 3 Pieces;* Moeran: *Fantasy Quartet*)
Chandos CHAN 8392 [D] **F**

ANÁČEK, Leoš (1854–1928) MORAVIA

Capriccio; Concertino Firkušný (pno), Czech PO, Neumann
(Dvořák: *Piano Concerto*)
RCA RD 60781 (US: 09026 60781-2) [D] **F**

Violin Concerto Zehetmair (vln), Philharmonia O, Holliger
(+Berg: *Violin Concerto;* Hartmann: *Concerto funèbre*)
Teldec 2292 46449-2 [D] **F**

Sinfonietta; Taras Bulba VPO, Mackerras
(+ Shostakovich: *Age of Gold: Suite*)
Decca 430 727-2 (US: London 430 727-2) [D] **M**

Sinfonietta; Taras Bulba; *In the Mists Bavarian RSO, Kubelik; *Rudolf Firkušný (pno)
DG 439 437-2 [A] **B**

O *Sinfonietta* Bavarian RSO, Kubelik
   (+ Smetana: *Hakon Jarl; Prague Carnival; Richard III;*
   Wallenstein's Camp)
   DG 437 254-2 [A] **M**

C *Violin Sonata* Kremer (vln), Argerich (pno)
   (+ Bartók: *Violin Sonata No. 1;* Messiaen: *Theme et Variations*)
   DG 427 351-2 [D] **F**

   String Quartets Nos. 1 & 2 Vanburgh Quartet
   (+ Dvořák: *String Quartet No. 10*)
   Collins 13812 [D] **F**

S *Along an Overgrown Path; In the Mist; Reminiscence; Piano Sonata*
   (1.X.1905); Theme and Variations (Zdenka) Firkušný (pno)
   DG 429 857-2 [A] **M**

V *Diary of One Who Disappeared* (song cycle); *Sinfonietta*
   *Balleys (cont), *Langridge (ten), *Women of RIAS Chamber
   Ch, BPO, Abbado
   DG 427 313-2 [D] **F**

   Glagolitic Mass Söderström (sop), Drobková (cont), Livora
   (ten), Novák (bs), CPO & Ch, Mackerras
   Supraphon C37-7448 [D] **F**

   Glagolitic Mass (original version) Kiberg (sop), Stene (cont),
   Svensson (ten), Cold (bs), Salo (org), Danish National Radio
   Ch & SO, Mackerras
   (+Kodály: *Psalmus Hungaricus*)
   Chandos CHAN 9310 [D] **F**

JANEQUIN, Clément (c.1485–1558) FRANCE

V *20 Chansons* Clément Janequin Ensemble
   HM HMC90 1099 [A] **F**

JOPLIN, Scott (1868–1917) USA

S Rags: *A Breeze from Alabama; The Cascades; The Crysanthemum;*
   The Easy Winners; Elite Syncopations; The Entertainer; Maple leaf
   Rag; Original Rags; Palm leaf Rag; Peacherine Rag; Something
   Doing; The Strenuous Life; Sunflower Slow Drag; Swipesy; The
   Sycamore; Weeping Willow Hyman (pno)
   RCA GD 87993 (US: 7993-2) [D] **F**

JOSQUIN DESPREZ (c.1440–1521) FRANCE

V *Ave maria, virgo serena; Ave nobilissima creatura; Miserere mei,*
   Deus; O bone et dulcissime Jesu; Salve regina; Stabat mater
   dolorosa; Usquequo, Domine Paris Chapelle Royale Ch,
   Herreweghe
   HM HMC90 1243 [D] **F**

   Benedicta es Tallis Scholars, Phillips
   (+ Palestrina: *Missa Benedictus es*)
   Gimell CDGIM 001 [D] **F**

   Missa La sol fa re mi; Missa Pange Lingua Tallis Scholars,
   Phillips
   Gimell CDGIM 009 [D] **F**

   Missa L'homme armé sexti toni; Missa L'homme armé super voces
   musicales Tallis Scholars, Phillips
   Gimell CDGIM 019 [D] **F**

KABALEVSKY, Dmitri (1904–1987) RUSSIA

O *Cello Concertos: No. 1 in G min., Op. 49; No. 2 in C min., Op. 77;*
*Improvisato; *Rondo Tarasova (vcl), Russian SO, Dudurova;
*Likhopol (vln), Kuritskaya (pno)
Olympia OCD 292 [D] **F**

Violin Concerto in C, Op. 48 Mordkovitch (vln), SNO, Järvi
(+ Khachaturian: *Violin Concerto*)
Chandos CHAN 8918 [D] **F**

Symphonies: No. 1 in C♯ min., Op. 18; No. 2 in C min., Op. 19
Szeged SO, Acel
Olympia OCD 268 [D] **F**

Symphony No. 4, Op. 54; *Requiem, Op. 72 Leningrad
PO/Kabalevsky; *Soloists, Moscow SO & Ch, Kabalevsky
Olympia OCD 290, 2 CDs [A] **F**

C *Cello Sonata in B♭, Op. 71; Scherzo, Op. 27/14; Novelette,*
Op. 27/25; Round-Dance Op. 60/2; Étude, Op. 27/3; Major-Minor
Studies for Solo Cello, Op. 68; In Memory of Sergei Prokoviev,
Op. 79; *6 Preludes and Fugues, Op. 61 Tarasova (vcl),
Polezhaev (pno); *McLachlan (pno)
Olympia OCD 294 [D] **F**

String Quartets: No. 1, Op. 8; No. 2 in G min., Op. 44 Glazunov
Quartet
Olympia OCD 293 [D] **F**

S *Piano Sonatas Nos. 1 & 2; Sonatina No. 2; 4 Preludes, Op. 5;*
Rondo in A min., Op. 59 McLachlan (pno)
Olympia OCD 267 [D] **F**

Piano Sonata No. 3 in F, Op. 46; 24 Preludes; Sonatina in C,
Op. 13 No. 1 McLachlan (pno)
Olympia OCD 266 [D] **F**

KALINNIKOV, Vasily (1866–1901) RUSSIA

O *Symphony No. 1 in G min.* SNO, Järvi
(+ Glazunov: *The Sea; Spring*)
Chandos CHAN 8611 [D] **F**

Symphony No. 2 in A; The Cedar and the Palm; Tsar Boris (opera):
Overture SNO, Järvi
Chandos CHAN 8805 [D] **F**

KANCHELI, Giya (born 1935) GEORGIA

O *Symphonies Nos. 1 & 7; Liturgy for Viola and Orchestra*
*Belonogov (vla), Moscow State SO, Glushchenko
Olympia OCD 424 [D] **F**

Symphonies Nos. 3 & *6 Gonashvili (ten), *Kharadze (vla),
*Chaduneli (vla), Georgia State SO, Kakhidze
Olympia OCD 401 [A] **F**

Symphonies Nos. 4 & 5 Georgia State SO, Kakhidze
Olympia OCD 403 [A] **F**

KETELBEY, Albert (1875–1959) ENGLAND

O *Bank Holiday ('Appy 'Ampstead); Bells across the Meadows; The*
Clock and the Dresden Figures; Dance of the Merry Mascots; In a
Chinese Temple Garden; In a Monastery Garden; In a Persian
Market; In the Mystic Land of Egypt; Sanctuary of the Heart; With
Honour crowned London Promenade O, Faris
Philips 400 011-2 [D] **F**

KHACHATURIAN, Aram (1903–1978) ARMENIA

O *Cello Concerto; Concerto Rhapsody* Tarasova (vcl), Moscow SO,
   Dudarova
   Olympia OCD 539 [D] **F**

   Piano Concerto; Gayeneh (ballet): *Suite; Masquerade* (incidental
   music): *Suite* Orbelian (pno), SNO, Järvi
   Chandos CHAN 8542 [D] **F**

   Violin Concerto in D min.
   Szeryng (vln), LSO, Dorati
   (+ Brahms: *Violin Concerto*)
   Philips Mercury 434 318-2 [A] **M**
   Mordkovitch (vln), SNO, Järvi
   (+ Kabalevsky: *Violin Concerto in C*)
   Chandos CHAN 8918 [D] **F**

   Gayeneh (ballet in 3 acts) USSR Radio and TV Large SO,
   Kakhidze
   Russian Disc RDCD 11029, 2 CDs [A] **F**

   Spartacus: Ballet Suites Nos. 1–3 SNO, Järvi
   Chandos CHAN 8927 [D] **F**

   Symphony No. 2; Gayeneh (ballet): *Suite* SNO, Järvi
   Chandos CHAN 8945 [D] **F**

   Symphony No. 3 (Simfoniya-poema); Triumphal Poem BBC PO,
   Glushchenko
   (+Ippolitov-Ivanov: *Caucasian Sketches*)
   Chandos CHAN 9321 [D] **F**

S *10 Children's Pieces; Poem; Sonata; Sonatina; Toccata; Valse from
   Masquerade* McLachlan (pno)
   Olympia OCD 423 [D] **F**

KNUSSEN, Oliver (born 1952) ENGLAND

O *Coursing, Op. 17; Ophelia Dances, Book 1, Op. 13; Symphonies
   Nos. 2 & 3; Cantata, Op. 15; Trumpets, Op. 12* Various artists,
   Knussen
   Unicorn-Kanchana UKCD 2010 [D] **M**

V *Songs without Voices, Op. 26; *Sonya's Lullaby, Op. 16;
   *Variations, Op. 24; **Hums and Songs of Winnie-the-Pooh, Op. 6;
   **4 Late Poems and an Epigram of Rainer Maria Rilke, Op. 23;
   ***Ocean de terre, Op. 10; ****Whitman Settings, Op. 25*
   Saffer (sop), */****Shelton (sop), Lincoln Centre
   Chamber Music Society O, Knussen; */****Serkin (pno)
   Virgin VC7 59308-2 (US: 59308) [D] **F**

KODÁLY, Zoltán (1882–1967) HUNGARY

O *Dances from Galánta; Dances from Marosszék; *Háry János Suite*
   *Philharmonia Hungarica, Minneapolis SO, Dorati
   (+ Bartók: *Hungarian Sketches; Romanian Folkdances*)
   Philips Mercury 432 005-2 [A] **M**

   Háry János; Peacock Variations; Psalmus Hungaricus Ustinov
   (narr), Edinburgh Festival Ch., Kertesz
   Decca 443 488-2 (US: London 443 488-2), 2 CDs [A] **B**

   Háry János Suite Cleveland O, Szell
   (+ Mussorgsky: *Pictures at an Exhibition;* Prokofiev: *Lieutenant
   Kijé Suite*)
   Sony CD 48162 [A] **B**

C *Duo, Op. 7; Solo Cello Sonata, Op. 4* *Gingold (vln), Starker (vcl)
Delos DE 1015 [A] **F**

  String Quartets Nos. 1 & 2 Kontra Quartet
BIS BIS-CD 564 [D] **F**

V *Psalmus Hungaricus* Svensson (ten), Danish National Radio
Ch & SO, Mackerras
(+Janacek: *Glagolitic Mass*)
Chandos CHAN 9310 [D] **F**

  *Hymn of Zrinyi; *Psalmus Hungaricus, Op. 13* Luxon (bar),
Brighton Festival Ch, Heltay; *Kozma (ten), Brighton Festival
Ch, Wandsworth School Boys' Ch, LSO, Kertész
(+ Dvořák: *Requiem*)
Decca 421 810-2 (US: London 421 810-2), 2CDs [A] **M**

KOECHLIN, Charles (1867–1950) FRANCE

O *The Jungle Book* Berlin RSO, Zinman
RCA 09026 61955-2, 2 CDs [D] **M**

  **The Seven Stars Symphony, Op. 132;* **Ballade, Op. 50* *Pellie
(ondes martenot), **Rigutto (pno), Monte-Carlo PO, Myrat
EMI CDM7 64369-2 (US: CDM 64369) [D] **M**

C *14 Chants, Op. 157b; Morceau de lecture pour la flûte, Op. 218;
Flute Sonata, Op. 52; Sonata for Two Flutes, Op. 75; Premier
album de Lilian* (from film score), *Op. 139; Deuxième album de
Lilian, Op. 149* Smith (fl), Buyse (fl), West (sop), Amlin (pno)
Hyperion CDA 66414 [D] **M**

  *Morceau de lecture, Op. 218; *15 Pièces, Op. 180; *Horn Sonata,
Op. 70; 20 Sonneries, Op. 123: Nos. 1, 3, 10, 13 & 20; 20
Sonneries, Op. 142: Nos. 2 & 5; 10 Sonneries, Op. 153/2: Nos. 2, 3,
5 & 11* Tuckwell (hn), *Blumenthal (pno)
ASV CDDCA 716 [D] **F**

V *7 Chansons pour Gladys, Op. 151; 16 chansons and rondels*
Leblanc (sop), Sharon (pno)
Hyperion CDA 66243 [D] **F**

KOKKONEN, Joonas (born 1921) FINLAND

O *Cello Concerto; Symphonic Sketches; Symphony No. 4* Thedéen
(vcl), Lahti SO, Vänskä
BIS BIS-CD 468 [D] **F**

  *Symphony No. 1; Music for Strings; *The Hades of the Birds* (song
cycle) *Groop (mez), Lahti SO, Söderblom
BIS BIS-CD 485 [D] **F**

  *Symphony No. 2; Inauguratio; *Erekhthion* (cantata); *The Last
Temptations* (opera): *Interludes* *Vihavainen (sop), Groenroos
(bar), Lahti SO, Vänskä
BIS BIS-CD 498 [D] **F**

  *Symphony No. 3; *Opus Sonorum; **Requiem* *Sivonen (pno),
**Isokoski (sop), **Groenroos (bar), Savonlinna Opera
Festival Ch, Lahti SO, Söderblom
BIS BIS-CD 508 [D] **F**

KORNGOLD, Erich (1897–1957) AUSTRO-HUNGARY/USA

O *Cello Concerto; Film Scores* (excerpts): *Another Dawn; Anthony
Adverse; Of Human Bondage; The Prince and the Pauper; The
Private Lives of Elizabeth and Essex; The Sea Wolf* Gabarro (vcl),
National PO, Gerhardt
RCA GD 80185 (US: 80185-2) [A] **M**

o *Violin Concerto; Much Ado about Nothing: Suite*
   EDITORS' CHOICE: Shaham (vln), LSO, Previn
   (+Barber: *Violin Concerto*)
   DG 429 886-2 [D] **F**

   Sinfonietta; Symphonic Overture: Sursum Corda BBC PO,
   Bamert
   Chandos CHAN 9317 [D] **F**

   *Symphony in F♯, Op. 40; *Abschiedslieder* *Finnie (sop), BBC
   PO, Downes
   Chandos CHAN 9171 [D] **F**

c *Piano Trio in D, Op. 1* Beaux Arts Trio
   (+ Zemlinsky: *Piano Trio*)
   Philips 434 072-2 [D] **F**

   String Sextet in D, Op. 10 Raphael Ensemble
   (+ Schoenberg: *Verklärte Nacht*)
   Hyperion CDA 66425 [D] **F**

s *Der Schneemann (ballet in 2 acts); Potpourri from 'Der Ring des
   Polykrates'* Wolley (pno)
   Koch 3-7277-2 [D] **F**

KRAMAŘ František (1759–1831) BOHEMIA

o *Clarinet Concerto in E♭, Op. 36; Clarinet Concerto in E min.,
   Op. 86; *Double Clarinet Concerto in E♭, Op. 35* Friedli (cl), *Pay
   (cl), ECO, Pay
   Claves CD-50 8602 [D] **F**

   *Flute Concerto No. 1 in G, Op. 30; Flute and Oboe Concertino,
   Op. 65; Oboe Concerto in F, Op. 52* Graf (fl/dir), Holliger
   (ob/dir), ECO
   Claves CD 50-8203 [D] **F**

   Symphonies: No. 2 in D, Op. 40; No. 4 in C min., Op. 102 London
   Mozart Players, Bamert
   Chandos CHAN 9275 [D] **F**

c *Octet Partitas in B♭, Op. 67 & E♭, Op. 79* Nash Ensemble
   (+ Dvořák: *Serenade for Wind in D min., Op. 44*)
   CRD 3410 [A] **F**

KRASA, Hans (1899-1944) CZECHOSLOVAKIA

c *String Quartet* Hawthorne Quartet
   (+ Haas: *String Quartets Nos. 1 & 2*)
   Decca 440 853-2 (US: London 440 853-2) [D] **F**

KREISLER, Fritz (1875–1962) AUSTRIA/USA

c *Allegretto in the style of Boccherini; Allegretto in the style of Porpora;
   Caprice viennois; Cavatina; La Chasse in the style of Cartier; La
   Gitana; Grave in the style of W.F. Bach; Gypsy caprice; Liebesfreud;
   Liebesleid; Praeludium and Allegro in the style of Pugnani;
   Recitativo and scherzo-caprice; Schön Rosmarin; Shepherd's
   Madrigal; Sicilienne et Rigaudon in the style of Francoeur; Toy
   Soldiers' march; Viennese rhapsodic fantasia* Shumsky (vln),
   Kaye (pno)
   ASV CDQS 6039 [A] **B**

   *Caprice in E♭ (Wieniawski); Caprice viennois; Danse espagnole
   (Granados); La Gitana; Larghetto (Weber); Liebesfreud; Liebesleid;
   Polichinelle; La Précieuse; Recitativo and scherzo-caprice; Rondo on
   a theme of Beethoven; Sérénade espagnole (Glazunov); Slavonic
   dance No. 10 in E min. (Dvořák); Syncopation; Tambourin chinois;*

Tango (Albéniz); Zigeuner Mintz (vln), Benson (pno)
DG 423 876-2 [A] **M**

KREUTZER, Conradin (1780–1849) GERMANY

C *Septet in E♭, Op. 62* Nash Ensemble
(+ Hummel: *Septet in C, Op. 114*)
CRD 3390 [A] **F**

LALO, Édouard (1823–1892) FRANCE

O *Cello Concerto in D min.* Haimowitz (vcl), CSO, Levine
(+ Bruch: *Kol Nidrei, Op. 47;* Saint-Saëns: *Cello Concerto No. 1*)
DG 427 323-2 [D] **F**

Symphonie espagnole, Op. 21 Perlman (vln), Paris O, Barenboim
(+ Saint-Saëns: *Violin Concerto No. 3*)
DG 445 549-2 [D] **M**

C *Piano Trios Nos. 1–3* Barbican Piano Trio
ASV CDDCA 899 [D] **F**

LAMBERT, Constant (1905–1951) ENGLAND

O *Horoscope* (ballet): *Suite* English Northern PO, Lloyd-Jones
(+ Bliss: *Checkmate;* Walton: *Façade*)
Hyperion CDA 66436 [D] **F**

V **Rio Grande; **Summer's Last Will and Testament; Aubade
héroïque* *Burgess (mez), *Gibbons (pno), **Shimell (bar),
*Opera North Ch, **Leeds Festival Ch, English Northern
PO, Lloyd-Jones
Hyperion CDA 66565 [D] **F**

LANGGAARD, Rued (1893–1952) DENMARK

O *Symphonies No. 1 (Klippepastoraler);* Fra Dybet Danish
National Radio Ch & SO, Segerstam
Chandos CHAN 9249 [D] **F**

Symphonies Nos. 4–6 Danish National RSO, Järvi
Chandos CHAN 9064 [D] **F**

LANGLAIS, Jean (1907–1991) FRANCE

S *Symphonie No. 1; Symphonie No. 2 (alla Webern); Suite Brève;
Nazard; Poem of Happiness; Suite Française: Arabesque sur les
flûtes* Bowyer (org)
Nimbus NI 5408 [D] **F**

LASSUS, Orlando de (1532–1594) NETHERLANDS/GERMANY

V *Alma redemptoris mater; Ave Maria gratia plena; Magnificat
Praeter rerum seriem; Misa pro defunctis; O bone Jesu* Pro
Cantione Antiqua, Hamburg Early Music Wind Ensemble,
Collegium Aureum, Turner
DHM GD 77066 (US: Editio Classica 77066-2) [A] **M**

*Alma redemptoris mater; Ave regina caelorum; Hodie completi
sunt; Missa Osculetur me; Osculetur me; Regina coeli; Salve regina
mater; Timor et tremor* Tallis Scholars, Phillips
Gimmell CDGIM 018 [D] **F**

*Exaltabo te Domine; Missa Qual donna attende; Missa Venatorum;
Psalmi Davidis poenitentales: De profundis; Tristis est anima mea*
Christ Church Cathedral Ch, Darlington
Nimbus NI 5150 [D] **F**

Lagrime di San Pietro Ensemble Vocal Européen, Herreweghe
HM HMC90 1483 [D] **F**

V *9 Lamentationes Hieremiae; Motets: Aurora lucis rutilat; Christus resurgens; Magnificat Aurora lucis rutilat; Missa Pro defunctis; Regina coeli; Surgens Jesu* Pro Cantione Antiqua, Turner
Hyperion CDA 66321/2, 2 CDs [D] **F**

Missa super Bell'Amfitrit'alterna; Psalmi Davidis penitentialis: Domine exaudi; Motets: *Alma redemptoris Mater; Omnes de Saba venient; Salve regina; Tui sunt coeli* Christ Church Cathedral Ch. Preston
Decca 433 679-2 (US: London 433 679-2) [A] **M**

LAWES, Henry (1596–1662) ENGLAND

V Songs: *Amintor's welladay; Come, sad turtle; Farewell, despairing hopes; Hark, shepherd swains; I laid me down; I prithee send me; In quel gelato core; The Lark; Man's life is but vain; My soul the great God's praises sing; Orpheus's Hymn; Sing fair Clorinda; Sitting by the streams; Slide soft you silver floods; Sweet, stay awhile; Thee and thy wondrous deeds; This mossy bank* Consort of Musicke, Rooley
◇ Hyperion CDA 66135 [D] **F**

LAWES, William (1602–1645) ENGLAND

C *Airs; Consort Setts: a 5 in C min.; a 5 in F; a 6 in C min.; a 6 in F; Divisions in G min.* Fretwork, Nicholson
◇ Virgin VC7 59021-2 (US: 59021) [D] **F**

LECLAIR, Jean-Marie (1697–1764) FRANCE

O *Violin Concertos: Op. 7 Nos. 2 in D & 5 in Amin.; Op. 10 Nos. 1 in B♭ & 5 in E min.* Standage (vln/dir), Collegium Musicum 90
◇ Chandos CHAN 0551 [D] **F**

Violin Concertos: Op. 7 Nos. 3, 4 & 6; Op. 10 No. 2 Standage (vln/dir), Collegium Musicum 90
◇ Chandos CHAN 0564 [D] **F**

C *Quatrième livre de sonates, Op. 9: Nos. 7 & 9; Troisième livre de sonates, Op. 5: No. 6* Trio Sonnerie
◇ ASV CDGAU 106 [D] **F**

6 Ouvertures et Sonates, Op. 13 Purcell Quartet
◇ Chandos CHAN 0542 [D] **F**

6 Sonatas for Strings, Op. 4 Purcell Quartet
◇ Chandos CHAN 0536 [D] **F**

6 Sonatas, Op. 3 Holloway (vln), Banchini (vln)
◇ Erato 2292 45013-2 [D] **F**

6 Sonatas, Op. 12 Holloway (vln), Banchini (vln)
◇ Erato 2292 45519-2 [D] **F**

LECOCQ, Charles (1832–1918) FRANCE

O *Mam'zelle Angot* (ballet) National PO, Bonynge
(+ Hérold: *La Fille mal gardée*)
Decca 430 849-2 (US: London 430 849-2), 2 CDs [A] **M**

LEIGHTON, Kenneth (1929–1988) ENGLAND

O *Cello Concerto, Op. 31; *Symphony No. 3* R. Wallfisch (vcl), *Mackie (ten), SNO, Thomson
Chandos CHAN 8741 [D] **F**

Veris gratia, Op. 9 R. Wallfisch (vcl), Caird (ob), RLPO, Handley
(+ Finzi: *Cello Concerto*)
Chandos CHAN 8471 [D] **F**

Missa Brevis; Crucifixus pro nobis; An Evening Hymn; Let all the World; Lully, Lulla (Coventry Carol); Magnificat and Nunc Dmittis (Second Service); Te Deum Mackie (ten), St. Paul's Cathedral Ch, Scott
Hyperion CDA 66489 [D] **F**

IGETI, György (born 1923) HUNGARY/AUSTRIA

Cello Concerto; Piano Concerto; Violin Concerto Queyras (vcl), Aimard (pno), S. Gawriloff (vln), Ensemble Intercontemporain, Boulez
DG 439 808-2 [D] **F**

Chamber Concerto; Ramifications; Aventures; *String Quartet No. 2; **Lux aeterna Ensemble Intercontemporain, Boulez; *LaSalle Quartet; **North German Radio Ch, Franz
DG 423 244-2 [A/D] **M**

String Quartet No. 1 Hagen Quartet
(+ Lutoslawski: *String Quartet*; Schnittke: *Kanon in memoriam I: Stravinsky*)
DG 431 686-2 [D] **F**

ISZT, Franz (1811–1886) HUNGARY

Piano Concertos: No. 1 in Eb; No. 2 in A; Fantasia on Hungarian Folk Themes; Fantasy on a Theme from Beethoven's 'Ruins of Athens'; Grand Symphonic Fantasy on Themes from Berlioz's 'Lelio'; Malediction; Polonaise brillante; Totentanz; Wandererfantasie (Schubert arr.) Béroff (pno), LGO, Masur
EMI CZS7 67214-2 (US: CDMB 67214), 2 CDs [A] **B**

Piano Concertos: No. 1 in Eb; No. 2 in A; Fantasia on Hungarian Folk Themes; Totentanz Thibaudet (pno), Montreal SO, Dutoit
Decca 433 075-2 (US: London 433 075-2) [D] **F**

Piano Concerto No. 3 in Eb; De profundis; Totentanz (1853 version) Mayer (pno), LSO, Vásáry
ASV CDDCA 778 [D] **F**

Dante Symphony; *Dante Sonata BPO, Barenboim; *Barenboim (pno)
Teldec 9031 77340-2 [D] **F**

Fantasia on Hungarian Folk Themes
Bolet (pno), LSO, Fischer
(+ Addinsell: *Warsaw Concerto*; Gershwin: *Rhapsody in Blue*; Gottschalk: *Grande fantaisie*; Litolff: *Concerto symphonique No. 4*)
Decca 430 726-2 (US: London 430 726-2) [D] **M**

A Faust Symphony
EDITORS' CHOICE: Seiffert (ten), Prague Philharmonic Male Ch., BPO, Rattle
EMI CDC5 55220-2 (US: CDC 55220) [D] F

Hungarian Rhapsodies Nos. 1–6 LSO, Dorati
(+ Enescu: *Romanian Rhapsody No. 1*)
Philips Mercury 432 015-2 [A] **M**

The Complete Symphonic Poems LPO, Haitink
Volume 1: Ce qu'on entend sur la montagne; Tasso; Les Préludes; Orpheus; Prometheus; Mazeppa; Festklänge
Philips 438 751-2, 2 CDs [A] **B**
Volume 2: Héroïde funèbre; Ideale; Episodes from Faust; Hungaria; Hamlet; Hunnenschlacht; Von der Wiege bis zum Grabe
Philips 438 754-2, 2 CDs [A] **B**

O *Les Préludes; Mazeppa; Tasso, lamento e trionfo; Mephisto Waltz No. 2; Hungarian Rhapsodies Nos. 2, 4 & 5; *Fantasia on Hungarian Folk Themes* *Cherkassky (pno), BPO, Karajan
DG 415 967-2, 2 CDs [A] **F**

C *Grand Duo Concertante; Rhapsodie hongroise; Valse-Caprice (arr. Oistrakh); Consolation No. 3 (arr. Milstein); Mephisto Waltz No. 1 (arr. Milstein); Duo (Sonata) in C♯ Min.; Epithalum; Valse oubliée (arr. Hubay)* Nicholls (vln), Ayerst (pno)
Hyperion CDA 66743 [D] **F**

S *À la chapelle sixtine; Fantasia and Fugue in G min. (Bach arr.); 6 Preludes and Fugues (Bach arr.)* Howard (pno)
Hyperion CDA 66438 [D] **F**

Abschied; Am Grabe Richard Wagners; Dem Andenken Petőfis; Der Bilde Sänger; Carousel de Mme. Pelet-Narbonne; Epithalum zu Edward Reményis Vermählungsfeier; 5 Kleine Klavierstücke; Lugubre gondola; Mosonyis Grabgeleit; Nuages gris; Piano piece in F♯; 2 Piano Pieces; R.W.– Venezia; Recueillement; Resignazione; Romance oubliée; Schlaflos, Frage und Antwort (two versions); Toccata; Ungarische Königslied; Ungarns Gott; Unstern: sinistre, disastro; Wiegenlied Howard (pno)
Hyperion CDA 66445 [D] **F**

Transcriptions: Auber: *3 pièces;* Bellini: *Réminiscences de Norma;* Berlioz: *Benvenuto Cellini: Bénédiction et serment;* Donizetti: *Réminiscences de Lucia di Lammermoor; Lucia di Lammermoor, funeral march and cavatina;* Duke Ernst of Saxe-Coburg-Gotha: *Tony: Hunting Chorus;* Glinka: *Ruslan and Ludmilla march;* Gounod: *Faust: Waltz;* Handel: *Almira sarabande and chaconne;* Meyerbeer: *Africaine illustrations;* Mozart: *Réminiscences de Don Juan;* Tchaikovsky: *Eugene Onegin Polonaise;* Verdi: *Aida: Danza sacra e duetto finale;* Wagner: *Tristan und Isolde: Liebestod;* Weber: *Der Freischütz Overture* Howard (pno)
Hyperion CDA 66371/2, 2 CDs [D] **F**

Album d'un Voyageur; Chanson du Béarn; Fantaisie romantique sur deux melodies suisses; Faribolo Pastour Howard (pno)
Hyperion CDA 66601/2, 2 CDs [D] **F**

Albumblatt in Walzerform; Bagatelle sans tonalité; 3 Caprices-valses: Nos. 1 & 2; Ländler in A♭; Mephisto Waltzes Nos. 1–4; Valse-impromptu; 4 Valses oubliées Howard (pno)
Hyperion CDA 66201 [D] **F**

Alleluja and Ave Maria (Arcadelt arr.); Ave Maria (Die Glocken von Rom); Ave Maria (versions II–IV); Ave maris stella; Harmonies poétiques et religieuses; L'hymne du Pape; 2 Hymns; In festo transfigurationis Domine nostri Jesu Christe; Invocation; O Roma nobilis; 2 Pieces from the Hungarian Coronation Mass; Sancta Dorothea; Slavimo slavno slaveni!; Stabat mater; Urbi et orbi, bénédiction papale; Vexilla regis prodeunt; Zum Haus des Herrn ziehen wir Howard (pno)
Hyperion CDA 66421/2, 2 CDs [D] **F**

Années de pèlerinage (complete) Berman (pno)
DG 437 206-2, 3 CDs [A] **M**

Années de pèlerinage (année 1): Suisse Bolet (pno)
Decca 410 160-2 (US: London 410 160-2) [D] **F**

Années de pèlerinage (année 2): Italie Bolet (pno)
Decca 410 161-2 (US: London 410 161-2) [D] **F**

S *Années de pèlerinage (année 2) Supplément: Venezia e Napoli;*
Années de pèlerinage (année 3) Bolet (pno)
Decca 411 803-2 (US: London 411 803-2) [D] **F**

Schubert transcriptions: *Auf dem Wasser zu singen; Aufenthalt;*
Erlkönig; Die Forelle (second version)*; Horch, horch die Lerch;*
Lebewohl; Der Lindenbaum; Lob der Tränen; Der Müller und der
Bach; Die Post; Das Wandern; Wohin? Bolet (pno)
Decca 414 575-2 (US: London 414 575-2) [D] **F**

Ballades: No. 1 in D♭; No. 2 in B min.; Berceuse; Impromptu in F♯;
Klavierstück in A♭; 2 Légendes; 2 Polonaises Howard (pno)
Hyperion CDA 66301 [D] **F**

6 Chants polonais (Chopin arr.)*; Danse macabre* (Saint-Saëns arr.)*;*
Berlioz transcriptions: *Les Francs-juges Overture; Idée fixe*
(Symphonie Fantastique); Marche des pèlerins (Harold en Italie); Le
Roi Lear Overture; Valses des Sylphes (La Damnation de Faust)
Howard (pno)
Hyperion CDA 66346 [D] **F**

3 Concert Studies; 2 Concert Studies; 6 Consolations; Réminiscences
de Don Juan (Mozart arr.) Bolet (pno)
Decca 417 523-2 (US: London 417 523-2) [A] **F**

11 Chorales: Crux ave benedicte; Jesus Christe; Meine Seele; Nun
danket alle Gott; Nun ruhen alle Wälder; O Haupt; O Lamm Gottes;
O Traurigkeit; Vexilla Regis; Was Gott tut; Wer nur den Lieben; Via
crucis; Weihnachtsbaum Howard (pno)
Hyperion CDA 66388 [D] **F**

Deuxième fantaisie sur des motifs des Soirées musicales; Grande
fantaisie sur des motifs des Soirées musicales; Nuits d'été à
Pausilippe; Soirées italiennes; Soirées musicales; Tre Sonetti di
Petrarca; Venezia e Napoli Howard (pno)
Hyperion CDA 66661/2, 2 CDs [D] **F**

12 Études d'exécution transcendante (1838 version) Weber (pno)
Pickwick MCD 10 [D] **B**

12 Études d'exécution transcendante (1851 version) Arrau (pno)
Philips 416 458-2 [A] **F**

Fantasia and Fugue on the Name B-A-C-H; Funeral odes; Grosses
Konzertsolo; Variations on 'Weinen, Klagen, Sorgen, Zagen';
Weinen, Klagen, Sorgen, Zagen (Prelude after Bach) Howard (pno)
Hyperion CDA 66302 [D] **F**

Hungarian Rhapsodies Nos. 1–19
Szidon (pno)
DG 423 925-2, 2 CDs [A] **M**

Hungarian Rhapsodies Nos. 1–15; Rhapsodie espagnole Cziffra
(pno)
EMI CZS 67888-2 (US: CDMB 67888), 2 CDs [A] **B**

Liszt at the Opera, Vol. 3 Howard (pno)
Hyperion CDA 66861-2, 2 CDs [D] **F**

National Songs and Anthems (paraphrases, fantasies and
transcriptions) Howard (pno)
Hyperion CDA 66787 [D] **F**

3 Orchestral movements from 'Christus' 4 Pieces from 'Elisabeth';
2 Polonaises from 'Stanislaus'; Salve Polonia Howard (pno)
Hyperion CDA 66466 [D] **F**

S *Polonaise brillante: Introduction* Milne (pno)
(+ Weber: *Piano Sonatas Nos. 3 & 4; Polacca brillante*)
CRD 3486 [D] **F**

Piano Sonata in B min.; 2 Légendes; Scherzo and March
Demidenko (pno)
Hyperion CDA 66616 [D] **F**

Piano Sonata in B min.; Funérailles; La lugubre gondola II; La Notte; Nuages gris Zimerman (pno)
DG 431 780-2 [D] **F**

Symphonies Nos. 1–9 (Beethoven arr.) Katsaris (pno)
Teldec 9031 71619-2, 6 CDs [D] **M**

Transcriptions of songs by Beethoven, Mendelssohn, Franz, Dessauer, Schumann & Rubinstein Howard (pno)
Hyperion CDA 66481/2, 2 CDs [D] **F**

Transcriptions of theatre music by Beethoven, Mendelssohn, Liszt, Weber & Lassen Howard (pno)
Hyperion CDA 66575 [D] **F**

The Major Piano Works Arrau (pno)
Philips 432 305-2, 5 CDs [A] **M**

Organ Music: Évocation à la Chapelle Sixtine; Fantasia and Fugue on 'Ad nos, ad salutarem undam'; Prelude and Fugue on the name BACH (first version, 1855); Variations on 'Weinen, Klagen, Sorgen, Zagen' Trotter (org)
Argo 440 283-2 [D] **F**

'The Young Liszt': The Complete Juvenilia Howard (pno)
Hyperion CDA 66771/2, 2 CDs [D] **F**

V *18 Lieder* Fassbaender (cont), Thibaudet (pno)
Decca 430 512-2 (US: London 430 512-2) [D] **F**

Missa choralis Atkinson (trb), Tinkler (trb), Royall (alt), Kendall (ten), Suart (bs), St. John's College Ch, Cleobury (org), Guest
(+ Dvořák: *Mass in D*)
Decca 430 364-2 (US: London 430 364-2) [A] **M**

LITOLFF, Henry (1818–1891) ENGLAND/FRANCE

O *Concerto symphonique No. 4 in D min., Op. 112: Scherzo* Ortiz (pno), RPO, Atzmon
(+ Addinsell: *Warsaw Concerto;* Gershwin: *Rhapsody in Blue;* Gottschalk: *Grande fantaisie;* Liszt: *Fantasia on Hungarian Folk Themes*)
Decca 430 726-2 (US: London 430 726-2) [D] **M**

LLOYD, George (born 1913) ENGLAND

O *Piano Concertos Nos. 1 & 2* Roscoe (pno), BBC PO, Lloyd
Albany TROY 037-2 [D] **F**

Piano Concerto No. 3 Stott (pno), BBC PO, Lloyd
Albany TROY 019-2 [D] **F**

*Piano Concerto No. 4; The Lily-leaf and the Grasshopper; The Transformation of the Naked Ape Stott (pno), *LSO, *Lloyd
Albany AR 004 [D] **F**

Symphonies Nos. 1 & 12 Albany SO, Lloyd
Albany TROY 032-2 [D] **F**

Symphonies Nos. 2 & 9 BBC PO, Lloyd
Albany TROY 005-2 [D] **F**

O   *Symphony No. 4 in B* Albany SO, Lloyd
Albany AR 002 [D] **F**

Symphony No. 5 BBC PO, Lloyd
Albany TROY 022-2 [D] **F**

*Symphonies Nos. 6 & *10 (Winter Journeys); John Socman* (opera):
Overture BBC PO, *BBC PO Brass, Lloyd
Albany TROY 015-2 [D] **F**

Symphony No. 7 BBC PO, Lloyd
Albany TROY 057-2 [D] **F**

Symphony No. 11 Albany SO, Lloyd
Albany TROY 060-2 [D] **F**

V   *A Symphonic Mass* Brighton Festival Ch, Bournemouth SO, Lloyd
Albany TROY 100 [D] **F**

LLOYD WEBBER, Andrew (born 1948) ENGLAND

O   *Variations* J. Lloyd Webber (vcl), LPO, Maazel
(+ W. Lloyd Webber: *Aurora*)
Philips 420 342-2 [D] **F**

V   *Requiem* Brightman (sop), Domingo (ten), Miles-Kingston
(trb), Drew (trb), Lancelot (org), Winchester Cathedral Ch,
ECO, Maazel
EMI CDC7 47146-2 (US: Angel CDC 47146) [D] **F**

LLOYD WEBBER, William (1914–1982) ENGLAND

O   *Aurora* LPO, Maazel
(+ A. Lloyd Webber: *Variations*)
Philips 420 342-2 [D] **F**

C   *Air varié; In the half-light; Arabesque; Badinage de Noël; Presto for
Perseus; Romantic Evening; Scherzo in G min.; Song without words;
The Divine Compassion: Thou art the King; Over the bridge; The
pretty washer-maiden; A Rent for love; The Sœviour: The King of
Love; So lovely the rose; Utopia, Missa Sanctae Mariae Magdalenae*
J. Lloyd Webber (vcl), Lill (pno); Graham-Hall (ten), Ledger
(pno); Richard Hickox Singers, Watson (hpd), Hickox
ASV CDDCA 584 [D] **F**

LOCATELLI, Pietro (1695–1764) ITALY

O   *12 Violin Concertos, Op. 3 (L'Arte del violino)* E. Wallfisch (vln),
Raglan Baroque Players, Kraemer
◇ Hyperion CDA 66721/3, 3 CDs [D] **F**

C   *12 Flute Sonatas, Op. 2* Stephen Preston (fl), Hogwood (hpd)
◇ L'Oiseau-Lyre 436 191-2, 2 CDs [A] **F**

12 Sonate da camera, Op. 6: Nos. 1, 6, 11 & 12 Locatelli Trio
◇ Hyperion CDA 66363 [D] **F**

LOCKE, Matthew (1621/2–1677) ENGLAND

V   *Audi, Domine; Be Thou Exalted; Descende caelo cincta sororibus;
How doth the city sit solitary; Jesu auctor clementiae; Lord, let me
know mine end; O be joyful; Super flumina Babylonis* New
College Ch, Parley of Instruments, Higginbottom
◇ Hyperion CDA 66373 [D] **F**

LUDFORD, Nicholas (c.1485–c.1557) ENGLAND

V   *Missa Benedicta; Magnificat Benedicta* Cardinall's Musick,
Carwood
ASV CDGAU 132 [D] **F**

V *Missa Christi Virgo Dilectissima; Domina Ihesu Christe* The
Cardinall's Musick, Carwood
ASV CDGAU 133 [D] **F**

Missa Lapidaverunt Stephanum; Ave Maria ancilla trinitatis
Cardinall's Musick, Carwood
ASV CDGAU 140 [D] **F**

Missa Videte miraculum; Ave cuius conceptio Cardinall's Musick,
Carwood
ASV CDGAU 131 [D] **F**

LULLY, Jean-Baptiste (1632–1687) FRANCE

V *Le Bourgeois Gentilhomme; Les Noces de Village; Cadmus et
Hermione* London Oboe Band, Petit (perc), Goodwin(ob/dir)
(+Philidor: *Le Mariage de la Grosse Cathos*)
◊ Harmonia Mundi HMU90 7122 [D] **F**

*Anima Christe; Ave coeli; Dixit Dominus; Dimine salvum; Exaudi
Deus; Laudate pueri; O dulcissime; O sapientia; Omnes gentes;
Regina coeli; Salve regina* Les Arts Florissants Vocal &
Instrumental Ensembles, Christie
◊ HM HMC90 1274 [D] **F**

Divertissements Nos. I–III (arr. Sempé) Laurens (mez),
Capriccio Stravagante, Sempé
◊ DHM RD 77218 (US: 77218-2) [D] **F**

LUMBYE, Hans Christian (1810–1874) DENMARK

O *15 Galops, Polkas and Waltzes* Odense SO, Guth
Unicorn-Kanchana DKPCD 9089 [D] **F**

LUTOSLAWSKI, Witold (1913–1994) POLAND

O *Chain 2; Partita* Mutter (vln), BBC SO, Lutoslawski
(+ Stravinsky: *Violin Concerto*)
DG 423 696-2 [D] **F**

Cello Concerto Rostropovich (vcl), Paris O, Lutoslawski
(+ Dutilleux: *Cello Concerto*)
EMI CDC7 49304-2 (US: Angel CDC 49304) [A] **F**

Piano Concerto; Chain 3; Novelette Zimerman (pno), BBC SO,
Lutoslawski
DG 431 664-2 [D] **F**

*Concerto for Orchestra; Jeux vénitiens; Livre pour orchestre; Mi-
parti* Polish National RSO, Lutoslawski
EMI CDM5 65305-2 (US: CDM 65305) [A] **M**

Dance Preludes King (cl), ECO, Litton
(+ Blake: *Clarinet Concerto;* Seiber: *Clarinet Concertino*)
Hyperion CDA 66215 [D] **F**

*Symphonies Nos. 1 & 2; Symphonic Variations; Music funèbre for
Strings* Polish National RSO, Lutoslawski
EMI CDM5 65076-2 (US: CDM 65076) [A] **M**

Symphonies Nos. 3 & 4; Les Espaces du sommeil Shirley-Quirk
(bar), LAPO, Salonen
Sony CD 66280 [D] **F**

C *String Quartet* (1964)
LaSalle Quartet
(+ Cage: *String Quartet;* Mayuzumi: *Prelude;* Penderecki: *String
Quartet*)
DG 423 245-2 [A] **M**

Varsovia Quartet
(+ Penderecki: *String Quartet No. 2;* Szymanowski: *String Quartets Nos. 1 & 2*)
Olympia OCD 328 [A] **F**

Hagen Quartet
(+ Ligeti: *String Quartet No. 1;* Schnittke: *Kanon in memoriam I: Igor Stravinsky*)
DG 431 686-2 [D] **F**

.UYTENS, Elizabeth (1906–1983) ENGLAND

> *6 Tempi; Chamber Concerto No. 1; Triolets Nos. I & II; Requiescat 'in memoriam Igor Stravinsky'; The Valley of Hatsu-seIsis and Osiris: Lament* Jane's Minstrels, Montgomery
NMC NMCD 011 [D] **F**

.YADOV, Anatole (1855–1914) RUSSIA

> *About Olden Times* (ballad), *Op. 21b; Baba-Yaga, Op. 56; The Enchanted Lake, Op. 62; 3 Fanfares; Kikimora, Op. 63; A Musical Snuff-box, Op. 32; Polonaise (in memory of Pushkin), Op. 49; Polonaise in D (for the unveiling of the statue of Anton Rubinstein), Op. 55; 8 Russian Folksongs, Op. 58* Mexico City SO, Bátiz
ASV CDDCA 657 [D] **F**

.YAPUNOV, Sergey (1859–1924) RUSSIA

> *Symphony No. 1; Ballade* Moscow State SO, Glushchenko
Olympia OCD 519 [D] **F**

> *12 Transcendental Studies, Op. 11* Binns (pno)
Pearl SHE 9624 [D] **F**

MacCUNN, Hamish (1868–1916) SCOTLAND

> *Land of Mountain and Flood* (overture), *Op. 3* SNO, Gibson
(+ German: *Welsh Rhapsody;* Harty: *With the Wild Geese;* Smyth: *The Wreckers Overture*)
Classics for Pleasure CD-CFP 4635 [A] **B**

MacDOWELL, Edward (1860–1908) USA

> *Piano Concertos: No. 1 in A min., Op. 15; No. 2 in D min., Op. 23* Amato (pno), LPO, Freeman
Olympia OCD 353 [D] **F**

> *Piano Sonatas Nos. 1–3* Tocco (pno)
Kingdom KCLCD 2009 [D] **F**

> *Piano Sonata No. 4 in E min. (Keltic), Op. 59* Landes (pno)
(+ Griffes: *3 Fantasy Pieces; Piano Sonata; 3 Tone Pictures*)
Koch 3-7045-2 [D] **F**

> *3 Lieder, Op. 11; 2 Lieder, Op. 12* Hampson (bar), Guzelimian (pno)
(+Songs by Griffes & Ives)
Teldec 9031 72168-2 [D] **F**

MACHAUT, Guillaume de (c.1300–1377) FRANCE

> *Amours me fait désirer; Biaute que toutes autes père; Dame, à qui m'ottri; Dame, à vous sans retollir; Dame, de qui toute ma joie vient; Dame, je sui cilz; Dame, mon cuer en vous remaint; Douce dame jolie, pour Dieu; Felix virgo; Foy porter; Je vivroie liement; Rose, liz, printemps, verdure; Tuit mi penser sont* Kirkby (sop), Van Evera (sop), Covey-Crump (ten), Gothic Voices, Page
Hyperion CDA 66087 [D] **F**

V *Messe de Nostre Dame; Je ne cesse de prier; Pas de tor en thies pais*
Hilliard Ensemble, Hillier
Hyperion CDA 66358 [D] **F**

MACKENZIE, Alexander (1847–1935) SCOTLAND

O *The Cricket on the Hearth: Overture, Op. 62; Twelfth Night, Op. 40,
Benedictus, Op. 37/3; Scottish Rhapsody No. 2 (Burns), Op. 24;
Coriolanus: Incidental Music, Op. 61* BBC Scottish SO, Brabbins
Hyperion CDA 66764 [D] **F**

MACMILLAN, James (born 1959) SCOTLAND

O **Busqueda; Visitatio sepulchri*
EDITORS' CHOICE: Scottish CO, Bolton, *MacMillan
RCA Catalyst 09026 62669-2 [D] **F**

**Veni, Veni Emmanuel; **After the Tryst; 3 Dawn Rituals;
. . . 'others see us . . .'; Untold* *Glennie (perc), Scottish CO,
MacMillan, *Saraste; **Crouch (vln), **Evans (pno)
RCA Catalyst 09026 61916-2 [D] **F**

MACONCHY, Elizabeth (born 1907) ENGLAND

C *Clarinet Quintet* King (cl), Britten Quartet
(+ Cooke: *Clarinet Quintet;* Frankel: *Clarinet Quintet;*
Holbrooke: *Eilen Shona*)
Hyperion CDA 66428 [D] **F**

String Quartets Nos. 1–4 Hanson Quartet
Unicorn-Kanchana DKPCD 9080 [D] **F**

String Quartets Nos. 5–8 Bingham Quartet
Unicorn-Kanchana DKPCD 9081 [D] **F**

String Quartets Nos. 9–13 Mistry Quartet
Unicorn-Kanchana DKPCD 9082 [D] **F**

MADERNA, Bruno (1920–1973) ITALY

O *Oboe Concertos Nos. 1–3* Holliger (ob), Köln RSO, Bertini
Philips 442 015-2 [D] **F**

MADETOJA, Leevi (1887–1947) FINLAND

O *Symphonies: No. 1, Op. 29; No. 2, Op. 35* Iceland SO, Sakari
Chandos CHAN 9115 [D] **F**

*Symphony No. 3 in A min.; The Ostrobothnians (opera): Suite,
Op. 45; Huvonaytelmaalku (comedy overture), Op. 53; Okon
Fuoco (ballet): Suite No. 1, Op. 58* Iceland SO, Sakari
Chandos CHAN 9036 [D] **F**

MAHLER, Gustav (1860–1911) AUSTRIA

O *Symphonies Nos. 1–10* Various soloists, Bavarian RSO & Ch,
Kubelik
DG 429 042-2, 10 CDs [A] **M**

Symphony No. 1 in D; *Lieder eines fahrenden Gesellen *Fischer-
Dieskau (bar), Bavarian RSO, Kubelik
DG 439 410-2 [A] **B**

Symphony No. 2 in C min. (Resurrection) McNair (sop), Van Nes
(cont), Ernst-Senff Ch., BPO, Haitink
Philips 438 935-2, 2 CDs [D] **F**

Symphony No. 3 in D min.
Van Nes (cont), Tölz Boys' Ch, Ernst-Senff Ch, BPO, Haitink
Philips 432 162-2, 2 CDs [D] **F**

*Symphony No. 4 in G; *Lieder eines fahrenden Gesellen* Raskin (sop), Cleveland O, Szell; *von Stade (sop), LPO, Davis
Sony CD 46535 [A] **B**

Symphony No. 5 in C♯ min. VPO, Bernstein
DG 423 608-2 [D] **F**

*Symphony No. 6 in A min.; *5 Rückert Lieder* *Ludwig (mez), BPO, Karajan
DG 415 099-2, 2 CDs [A] **F**

Symphony No. 7; Symphony No. 10 (Adagio) BPO, Haitink
Philips 434 997-2, 2 CDs [D] **F**

Symphony No. 8 in E♭ Connell (sop), Wiens (sop), Lott (sop), Schmidt (sop), Denize (sop), Versalle (ten), Hynninen (bar), Sotin (bs), Tiffin Boys' Ch, LPO & Ch, Tennstedt
EMI CDS7 47625-8 (US: Angel CDCB 47625), 2 CDs [D] **F**

*Symphony No. 9; *Kindertotenlieder; *Rückert Lieder* Ludwig (mez), BPO, Karajan
DG 439 678-2, 2 CDs [A] **B**

Symphony No. 10 (ed. Cooke) Bournemouth SO, Rattle
EMI CDC7 54406-2 (US: Angel CDC 54406) [D] **F**

Im Lenz; Lieder eines fahrenden Gesellen; Lieder und Gesänge; Winterlied Baker (mez), Parsons (pno)
Hyperion CDA 66100 [D] **F**

*Kindertotenlieder; *Lieder eines fahrenden Gesellen; Rückert Lieder Nos. 1 & 3–5* Fischer-Dieskau (bar), BPO, Böhm; *Bavarian RSO, Kubelik
DG 415 191-2 [A] **F**

Das klagende Lied Dunn (sop), Fassbaender (mez), Hollweg (ten), Baur (trb), Schmidt (bar), Bavarian RSO & Ch, Chailly
Decca 425 719-2 (US: London 425 719-2) [D] **F**

Des knaben Wunderhorn Hampson (bar), Parsons (pno)
Teldec 9031 74726-2 [D] **F**

Des Knaben Wunderhorn Nos. 1–10, 13 & 14 Schwarzkopf (sop), Fischer-Dieskau (bar), LSO, Szell
EMI CDC7 47277-2 (US: Angel CDC 47277) [A] **F**

Das Lied von der Erde Baker (mez), King (ten), Concertgebouw O, Haitink
Philips 432 279-2 [A] **M**

*Lieder eines fahrenden Gesellen; 7 Early Lieder; *11 Early Lieder; (orch. Berio)* Hampson (bar), Lutz (pno), *Philharmonia O, Berio
Teldec 9031 74002-2 [D] **F**

Lieder eines fahrenden Gesellen; Rückert Lieder; Lieder from Des Knaben Wunderhorn; Lieder from Aus der Jugendzeit Ludwig (mez), Fischer-Dieskau (bar), Berry (bs), Bernstein (pno)
Sony CD 47170, 2 CDs [A] **M**

Lieder eines fahrenden Gesellen; Kindertotenlieder; 5 Rückert Lieder; 3 Lieder aus 'Des Knaben Wunderhorn' Fassbaender (mez), Berlin RSO, Chailly
Decca 425 790-2 (US: London 425 790-2) [D] **F**

Lieder selection von Otter (mez), Gothoni (pno)
(+ Wolf: *9 Lieder*)
DG 423 666-2 [D] **F**

MALIPIERO, Gian Francesco (1882–1973) ITALY

C *String Quartets Nos. 1–8* Orpheus Quartet
ASV CDDCD 457, 2 CDs [D] **F**

MARAIS, Marin (1656–1728) FRANCE

C *Pièces de viole: Livre 1, Part 1* (complete) Smithsonian
Chamber Players
✧ DHM RD 77146 (US: 77146-2) [D] **F**

*Pièces de viole: Livre 2, Part 1: No. 20; Livre 3, Part 1: Nos. 40–2,
55 & 58; Pièces en trio: Nos. 1–4, 6, 7, 9, 58, 61–3, 66 & 67*
Purcell Quartet
✧ Hyperion CDA 66310 [D] **F**

MARCELLO, Alessandro (1684–1750) ITALY

O *6 Oboe Concertos (La Cetra)* Holliger (ob), Berne Camerata,
Füri
DG 427 137-2 [A] **M**

6 Violin Concertos (La Cetra); Violin Concerto in B♭ Standage
(vln/dir), Collegium Musicum 90
✧ Chandos CHAN 0563 [D] **F**

MARTIN, Frank (1890–1974) SWITZERLAND

O *Trombone Ballade; Piano Ballade; Harpsichord Concerto* Rosin
(tbn), Benda (pno), Jaccotet (hpd), Lausanne CO, Martin
Jecklin-Disco JD 529-2 [A] **F**

*Concerto for 7 Wind Instruments, Percussion & Strings; Studies for
String Orchestra; Erasmi monumentum* LPO, Bamert
Chandos CHAN 9283 [D] **F**

Symphonie; Symphonie Concertante; Passacaglia
EDITORS' CHOICE: LPO, Bamert
Chandos CHAN 9312 [D] **F**

C *Piano Trio on Popular Irish Folk Tunes* Borodin Trio
(+ Debussy: *Piano Trio;* Turina: *Piano Trio No. 1*)
Chandos CHAN 9016 [D] **F**

V *Der Cornet* Lipovšek (cont), Austrian RSO, Zagrosek
Orfeo C 164881A [D] **F**

Golgotha (oratorio); **Messe pour double choeur* Staempfli,
Montmollin, Tappy, Huttenlocher, Orchestre Symphonique,
Faller; **Midi Chamber Ch, Martin
Erato 2292 45779-2 [D] **F**

MARTINŮ, Bohuslav (1890–1959) BOHEMIA

O *Cello Concertos Nos. 1 & 2; Cello Concertino* R. Wallfisch (vcl),
Czech PO, Bělohlávek
Chandos CHAN 9015 [D] **F**

*Double Concerto for 2 String Orchestras, Piano and Timpani;
Concerto for String Quartet and Orchestra; Sinfonia Concertante for
Oboe, Bassoon, Violin, Cello Soli & Orchestra* Endellion Quartet,
City of London Sinfonia, Hickox
Virgin VC7 59575-2 (US: 59575) [D] **F**

Violin Concertos Nos. 1 & 2 Suk (vln), Czech PO, Neumann
Supraphon 11 0702-2 [A] **F**

3 Estampes; Overture; The Parables; La Rhapsodie Czech PO,
Bělohlávek
Supraphon 10 4140-2 [D] **F**

O *La Revue de Cuisine; Sinfonietta la Jolla; Tre Ricercari* St. Paul
CO, Hogwood
Decca 433 660-2 (US: London 433 660-2) [D] **F**

Serenades Nos. 1–5 Prague CO
Supraphon 11 0098-2 [D] **F**

Symphonies Nos. 1–6 Czech PO, Neumann
Supraphon 11 0382-2, 3 CDs [A] **M**

Symphonies Nos. 1 & 2 Berlin SO, Flor
RCA RD 60154 (US: 60154-2) [D] **F**

Symphonies Nos. 3 & 4 Bamberg SO, Järvi
BIS BIS-CD 363 [D] **F**

Symphonies Nos. 5 & 6 Bamberg SO, Järvi
BIS BIS-CD 402 [D] **F**

C *4 Madrigals for Oboe, Clarinet and Bassoon; 3 Madrigals for
Violin and Viola; Madrigal Sonata for Piano, Flute and Violin;
5 Madrigal Stanzas for Violin and Piano* Dartington Ensemble
Hyperion CDA 66133 [D] **F**

Nonet; La Revue de cuisine; Trio in F Dartington Ensemble
Hyperion CDA 66084 [D] **F**

Piano Quartet (1942) Domus
(+ Dvořák: *Bagatelles;* Suk: *Piano Quartet*)
Virgin VC7 59245-2 (US: CDC 59245) [D] **F**

Piano Quintet (1944) Frankl (pno), Lindsay Quartet
(+Dvorak: *Piano Quintet*)
ASV CDDCA 889 [D] **F**

Cello Sonatas Nos. 1-3 Isserlis (vcl), Evans (pno)
Hyperion CDA 66296 [D] **F**

S *3 Czech Dances; 7 Czech Dances; 12 Esquisses; 4 Movements; Les
Ritournelles; Window onto the Garden* Kvapil (pno)
Unicorn-Kanchana DKPCD 9140 [D] **F**

*Études and Polkas; Fantasy and Toccata; Julietta (opera):
Moderato (arr. Firkušný); Les Ritournelles; Piano Sonata*
Firkušný (pno)
RCA RD 87987 (US: 7987-2) [D] **F**

MARTUCCI, Giuseppe (1856–1909) ITALY

O *Piano Concerto No. 1 in D min.; *Canzone dei ricordi* (lyric poem)
Caramiello (pno), *Yakar (sop), Philharmonia O, d'Avalos
ASV CDDCA 690 [D] **F**

**Piano Concerto No. 2 in B♭ min., Op. 66; Canzonetta, Op. 55/1;
Giga, Op. 61/3; Minuetto, Op. 57/2; Momento musicale, Op. 57/3;
Serenata, Op. 57/1; Tempo di gavotta, Op. 55/2 *Caramiello
(pno), Philharmonia O, d'Avalos
ASV CDDCA 691 [D] **F**

Giga, Op. 61/3; Notturno, Op. 70/1; Novelette, Op. 82/2 La Scala
PO, Muti
(+ Busoni: *Turandot Suite;* Casella: *Paganiniana*)
Sony CD 53280 [D] **F**

*Symphony No. 1 in D min., Op. 75; Notturno in G♭, Op. 70/1;
Noveletta, Op. 82/2; Tarantella, Op. 44/6* Philharmonia O,
d'Avalos
ASV CDDCA 675 [D] **F**

O *Symphony No. 2 in F, Op. 81;* **Andante, Op. 69/2; Colore orientale, Op. 44/3* *Ives (vcl), Philharmonia O, d'Avalos
ASV CDDCA 689 [D] **F**

MASSENET, Jules (1842–1912) FRANCE

O **Piano Concerto in E♭;* Solo Piano Works: *Devant la Madonne; 2 Impromptus; Musique pour bercer les petits enfants; 2 Pièces; 10 Pièces de genre; Toccata in B♭; Valse folle; Valse très lente* Ciccolini (pno), *Monte Carlo PO, *Cambreling
EMI CDM7 64277-2 (US: CDM 64277) [A] **M**

Le Cid (opera): *Ballet music* National PO, Bonynge
(+ Delibes: *Sylvia*)
Decca 425 475-2 (US: London 425 475-2), 2 CDs [A] **M**

Cigale (ballet) Hartle (sop), National PO, Bonynge
(+ Tchaikovsky: *Swan Lake*)
Decca 425 413-2 (US: London 425 413-2), 3 CDs [A] **M**

Scènes alsaciennes; Scènes pittoresques; Don Quichotte Monte-Carlo Opera O, Gardiner
Erato 2292 45859-2 [D] **F**

Scènes dramatiques; Scènes de Féerie; Le dernier Sommeil de la Vierge Monte-Carlo Opera O, Gardiner
Erato 2292 45858-2 [D] **F**

MATHIAS, William (1934–1992) WALES

O *Symphonies: No. 1, Op. 31; No. 2 (Summer Night), Op. 90* BBC Welsh SO, Mathias
Nimbus NI 5260 [D] **F**

Symphony No. 3; Helios; *Oboe Concerto; Requiescat *Cowley (ob), BBC Welsh SO, Llewellyn Nimbus NI 5343 [D] **F**

S *Complete Organ Music* Scott (org)
Nimbus NI 5367 [D] **F**

V *As truly as God is our Father; Ave Rex, Op. 45; A Grace, Op. 89/3; I will celebrate; Jesus College Service, Op. 53; Let the people praise thee* (royal wedding anthem), *Op. 87; Missa Aedis Christi, Op. 92; O how amiable, Op. 90/3; Rex gloriae, Op. 83* Christ Church Cathedral Ch, Lawford (org), Darlington
Nimbus NI 5243 [D] **F**

Lux aeterna Lott (sop), Cable (mez), Walker (mez), Bach Ch, St. George's Chapel Ch, LSO, Willcocks
Chandos CHAN 8695 [D] **F**

MATTHEWS, David (born 1942) ENGLAND

O *Symphony No. 4, Op. 52* East of England O, Nabarro
Collins 20082 [D] **F**

MAW, Nicholas (born 1935) ENGLAND

O *Odyssey* CBSO, Rattle
EMI CDS7 54277-2 (US: Angel CDCB 54277), 2 CDs [D] **F**

MAXWELL DAVIES, Peter (born 1934) ENGLAND

O *The Bairns of Brough; Vesalii icones; Runes from a Holy Island* Fires of London, Maxwell Davies
Unicorn-Kanchana UKCD 2068 [A/D] **M**

Film scores: *The Boyfriend; The Devils: Suites; *Seven in nomine* *Thomas (sop), Aquarius, N. Cleobury
Collins 10952 [D] **F**

o *Trumpet Concerto; *Symphony No. 4* Wallace (tpt), SNO,
*Scottish CO, Maxwell Davies
Collins 11812 [D] **F**

Violin Concerto Stern (vln), RPO, Previn
(+Britten: *Cello Symphony*)
Sony CD 58928 [D] **M**

*Jimmack the Postie; Kinlochie, his Fantasia; An Orkney wedding,
with Sunrise; Renaissance Scottish dances; *Farewell to Stromness;
*Yesnaby Ground; **Lullaby for Lucy; **Seven Songs Home*
Scottish CO, **St. Mary's Edinburgh Ch, Maxwell Davies;
*Maxwell Davies (pno)
Unicorn-Kanchana DKPCD 9070 [D] **F**

*Sinfonia; *Sinfonia Concertante* *Nicholson (fl), *Miller (ob),
*Morrison (cl), *Newman (bsn), *Cooke (hn), *Fry (perc)
Scottish CO, Maxwell Davies
Unicorn-Kanchana UKCD 2026 [D] **M**

*Sinfonietta Accademica; *Into the Labyrinth* (cantata) *Mackie
(ten), Scottish CO, Maxwell Davies
Unicorn-Kanchana UKCD 2022 [A] **M**

*Sir Charles: His Pavan; The Turn of the Tide; *Worldes Blis*
BBC PO, *RPO, Maxwell Davies
Collins 13902 [D] **F**

*Strathclyde Concertos Nos. *1 & **2* *Miller (ob), **Conway
(vcl), Scottish CO, Maxwell Davies
Unicorn-Kanchana DKPCD 9085 [D] **F**

*Strathclyde Concertos Nos. *3 & **4* *Cook (ob), *Franks (tpt),
**Morrison (cl), Scottish CO, Maxwell Davies
Collins 12392 [D] **F**

*Strathclyde Concertos Nos. *5 & **6* *Clark (vln),*Marwood
(vla), **Nicholson (fl), Scottish CO, Maxwell Davies
Collins 13032 [D] **F**

*Strathclyde Concertos Nos. *7 & **8; A Spell for Green Corn: The
Macdonald Dances* *McTier (db), **Leveaux (bsn), Scottish
CO, Maxwell Davies
Collins 13862 [D] **F**

Symphony No. 2 BBC PO, Maxwell Davies
Collins 14032 [D] **F**

Symphony No. 3 BBC PO, Maxwell Davies
Collins 14162 [D] **F**

v *Black Pentecost; Stone Litany* Jones (mez), Wilson-Johnson
(bar), BBC PO, Maxwell Davies
Collins 13662 [D] **F**

MAYERL, Billy (1902–1959) ENGLAND

s *April's Fool; Evening Primrose; Four Aces –suite: Nos. 2 & 3;
From a Spanish lattice; The Harp of the Winds; 3 Japanese Pictures:
Almond Blossom; The Joker; The Legends of King Arthur: prelude;
Guinevere; Lady of the Lake; The Passing of Arthur; Marigold;
Nimble-fingered Gentleman; Railroad rhythm; Shallow waters; Song
of the Fir-Tree* Parkin (pno)
Chandos CHAN 8560 [D] **F**

*Aquarium Suite; Autumn Crocus; Bats in the Belfry; 3 Dances in
syncopation; Four Aces – suite: Nos. 1 & 4; Green tulips;
Hollyhock; Hop-'o-my-thumb; Jill all alone; Mistletoe; The Parade*

of the Sandwich-board Men; Sweet William; White heather
Parkin (pno)
Chandos CHAN 8848 [D] **F**

MAYUZAMI, Toshiro (born 1929) JAPAN

C   *Prelude* LaSalle Quartet
(+ Cage: *String Quartet;* Lutoslawski: *String Quartet;*
Penderecki: *String Quartet*)
DG 423 245-2 [A] **M**

McEWEN, John (1869–1948) SCOTLAND

O   *A Solway Symphony; *Hills o' Heather; Where the Wild Thyme*
Blows *Welsh (vcl), LPO, Mitchell
Chandos CHAN 9345 [D] **F**

MEDTNER, Nikolay (1880–1951) RUSSIA

O   *Piano Concerto No. 1 in C min., Op. 33; *Piano Quintet* Alexeev
(pno), BBC SO, Lazarev; *New Budapest Quartet
Hyperion CDA 66744 [D] **F**

Piano Concertos: No. 2 in C min., Op. 50; No. 3 in E min., Op. 60
Demidenko (pno), BBC Scottish SO, Maksymiuk
Hyperion CDA 66580 [D] **F**

C   *Violin Sonatas: No. 1 in B min., Op. 21; No. 3 in E min. (Epic),*
Op. 57; Nocturne No. 3 in C min., Op. 16/3 Labko (vln),
Svetlanov (pno)
Russian Disc RDCD 11017 [A] **F**

Violin Sonata No. 2 in G, Op. 44; Piano Quintet in C, Op. Posth.
Labko (vln), Svetlanov (pno), Borodin Quartet
Russian Disc RDCD 11019 [A] **F**

S   *3 Dithyrambs, Op. 10/2; 2 Elegies, Op. 59/2; Fairy Tale in D min.;*
3 Fairy Tales, Op. 9/3; 2 Fairy Tales, Op. 14; 4 Fairy Tales,
Op. 26/2; 4 Fairy Tales, Op. 35/4; 5 Forgotten Melodies, Op. 39
(Set 2): Nos. 1 & 3; 3 Hymns, Op. 49 Milne (pno)
CRD 3338 [A] **F**

Piano Sonata in F min.; Improvisation No. 2, Op. 47 Milne
(pno)
CRD 3461 [D] **F**

Piano Sonata in E min, Op. 25/2; Sonata Triad, Op.11 Milne (pno)
CRD CRD 3339 [A] **F**

Improvisation No. 2, Op. 47; Sonate-idylle, Op. 56; Forgotten
Melodies, Op. 39 Wild (pno)
Chesky AD1 [D] **F**

Piano Sonata in G min., Op. 22; Sonata Reminiscenza in A min.,
Op. 38/1; Dancing Fairy Tale, Op. 48/1; 5 Fairy Tales; Funeral
March, Op. 31/2; The Organ Grinder, Op. 54/3; Russian Fairy
Tale, Op. 42/1 Tozer (pno)
Chandos CHAN 9050 [D] **F**

Sonata Elegia, Op. 11/2; Sonata Reminiscenza, Op. 38/1; Sonata
Tragica, Op. 39/5; Canzona Matinata, Op. 39/4; Canzona
Serenata, Op. 38/6; Dithyrambe, Op. 10/2; Fairy Tale, Op. 20/1;
Theme and Variations, Op. 55 Demidenko (pno)
Hyperion CDA 66636 [D] **F**

MÉHUL, Nicolas (1763–1817) FRANCE

O   *Symphonies Nos. 1–4; La Chasse du jeune Henri* (opera): *Overture;*
Le trésor supposé (opera): *Overture* Gulbenkian Foundation O,

Swierczewski
Nimbus NI 5184/5, 2 CDs [D] F

MENDELSSOHN, Fanny (1805–1847) GERMANY

C *3 Pieces for piano duet* Duo Tal & Groethuysen
(+ Felix Mendelssohn: *Piano duets*)
Sony CD 48494 [D] F

Piano Trio in G min., Op. 11 Dartington Piano Trio
(+ C. Schumann: *Piano Trio in G min., Op. 17*)
Hyperion CDA 66331 [D] F

MENDELSSOHN, Felix (1809–1847) GERMANY

O Overtures: *Athalia, Op. 74; Calm Sea and Prosperous Voyage,
Op. 27; The Hebrides, Op. 26; The Marriage of Camacho, Op. 10;
A Midsummer Night's Dream, Op. 17; Ruy Blas, Op. 95* Bamberg
SO, Flor
RCA 07863 57905-2 (US: 7905-2) [D] F

*Piano Concertos: No. 1 in G min., Op. 25; No. 2 in D min., Op. 40;
Capriccio brillant, Op. 22* Shelley (pno/dir), LMP
Chandos CHAN 9215 [D] F

Double Piano Concertos: in A♭; in E Coombs (pno), Munro
(pno), BBC Scottish SO, Maksymiuk
Hyperion CDA 66567 [D] F

*Violin Concerto in D min.; *Violin and Piano Concerto in D min.*
Kremer (vln), *Argerich (pno), Orpheus CO
DG 427 338-2 [D] F

Violin Concerto in E min., Op. 64 Lin (vln), Chicago SO, Tilson Thomas
(+Bruch: *Violin Concerto No.1;* Vieuxtemps: *Violin Concerto No. 5*)
Sony CD 64250 [D] M
Szeryng, LSO, Dorati
(+Schumann: *Violin Concerto*)
Philips Mercury 434 339-2 [A] M

*A Midsummer Night's Dream (Overture and Incidental Music,
Opp. 21 & 61)* Wiens (sop), Walker (mez), LPO & Ch, Litton
Classics for Pleasure CD-CFP 4593 [D] B

String Symphonies Nos. 1–12 London Festival O, Pople
Hyperion CDA 66561/3, 3 CDs [D] F

String Symphonies Nos. 8–10 Orpheus CO
DG 437 528-2 [D] F

Symphonies Nos. 1–5 Mathis (sop), Rebmann (sop), Hollweg
(ten), German Opera Ch, BPO, Karajan
DG 429 664-2, 3 CDs [A] M

Symphonies Nos. 1 & 5 Bamberg SO, Flor
RCA 09026 60391-2 [D] F

Symphony No. 2 in B♭ (Hymn of Praise) Mathis (sop),
Rebmann (sop), Hollweg (ten), German Opera Ch, BPO,
Karajan
DG 431 471-2 [A] M

*Symphonies: No. 3 in A min. (Scottish), Op. 56; No. 4 in A
(Italian), Op. 90*
LCP, Norrington
✧ **EMI CDC7 54000-2 (US: Angel CDC 54000) [D] F**
SFSO, Blomstedt
Decca 433 811-2 (US: London 433 811-2) [D] F

C *Andante & Variations Op. 83a; Andante and Allegro brillant, Op. 92; Piano Trio, Op. 66 (arr.)* Duo Tal & Groethuysen (pno duo) (+ Fanny Mendelssohn: *Piano duets*)
Sony CD 48494 [D] **F**

Cello Sonatas: No. 1 in B♭, Op. 45; No. 2 in D, Op. 58; Songs without Words, Opp. 19/1, & 109; Variations concertantes, Op. 17 Harrell (vcl), Canino (pno)
Decca 430 198-2 (US: London 430 198-2) [D] **F**

Piano Quartets Nos. 1–3 Domus
Virgin CUV5 61203-2 (US: 61203) [D] **M**

Piano Trios: No. 1 in D min., Op. 49; No. 2 in C min., Op. 66 Trio Fontenay
Teldec 2292 44947-2 [D] **F**

String Octet in E♭, Op. 20; String Quintet No. 1 in A, Op. 18 Hausmusik
✧ **EMI CDC7 49958-2 (US: Angel CDC 49958)** [D] **F**

String Quartets Nos. 1–6; String Quartet in E♭; 4 Movements, Op. 81 Melos Quartet
DG 415 883-2, 3 CDs [A] **M**

String Quartet No. 2 in A min., Op. 13; String Quintet No. 2 in B♭, Op. 87 Hausmusik
✧ **Virgin VC5 45104-2 (US: 45104)** [D] **F**

Violin Sonata in F min., Op. 4; Violin Sonata in F Mintz (vln), Ostrovsky (pno)
DG 419 244-2 [D] **F**

S *Andante and rondo capriccioso, Op. 14; Andante cantabile and presto agitato in B; Capriccio, Op. 5; Capriccio, Op. 118; 3 Caprices, Op. 33; 2 Klavierstücke; Perpetuum mobile in C, Op. 119; Scherzo in B min.; Scherzo a capriccio in F♯ min.* Jones (pno)
Nimbus NI 5069 [A] **F**

3 Fantasias, Op. 16; Fantasia on 'The Last Rose of Summer'; Fantasy in F♯ min., Op. 28; Variations in B♭, Op. 83; Variations in E♭, Op. 82; Variations sérieuses, Op. 54 Jones (pno)
Nimbus NI 5072 [A] **F**

Kinderstücke, Op. 72; Piano Sonata in E, Op. 6; Piano Sonata in G min., Op. 105; Piano Sonata in B♭, Op. 106 Jones (pno)
Nimbus NI 5070 [A] **F**

Prelude and Fugue in E min.; 3 Preludes, Op. 104a; 6 Preludes and Fugues, Op. 35; 3 Studies, Op. 104b; Study in F min. Jones (pno)
Nimbus NI 5071 [A] **F**

Songs without Words: Book 1, Op. 19; Book 2, Op. 30; Book 3, Op. 38; Book 4, Op. 53; Book 5, Op. 62; Book 6, Op. 67; Book 7, Op. 85; Book 8, Op. 102; Albumblatt, Op. 117; Gondellied in A; Kinderstücke, Op. 72; 2 Klavierstücke Barenboim (pno)
DG 437 470-2, 2 CDs [A] **B**

Allegro maestoso in C; Allegro in B♭; Allegro, Chorale and Fugue in D; Andante in D; Andante in F; 2 Fugues; 3 Preludes and Fugues, Op. 37; 6 Organ Sonatas, Op. 65 Scott (org)
Hyperion CDA 66491-2, 2 CDs [D] **F**

V *6 Anthems, Op. 79; Ehre sei Gott in der Hohe; Hear my Prayer; Heilig heilig ist Gott, der Herr Zabaoth; Kyrie eleison in A; 3 Psalms, Op. 78; 3 Sacred Pieces, Op. 23/2: Ave Maria; No. 3: Mitten wir im*

Leben sind; Verleih uns frieden Corydon Singers, Best
Hyperion CDA 66359 [D] **F**

V *Elijah* (oratorio) Ameling (sop), Burmeister (mez), Adam
(bs-bar), Leipzig Radio Ch, LGO, Sawallisch
Philips 438 368-2, 2 CDs [A] **B**

27 Lieder Bonney (sop), Parsons (pno)
Teldec 2292 44946-2 [D] **F**

40 Lieder Fischer-Dieskau (bar), Sawallisch (pno)
EMI CMS7 64827-2 (US: CDMB 64827), 2 CDs [A] **M**

Paulus (oratorio), *Op. 36* Janowitz (sop), Lang (cont),
Blochwitz (ten), Adam (bs), LGO & Radio Ch, Masur
Philips 420 212-2, 2 CDs [A] **F**

MENNIN, Peter (1923–1983) USA

O *Symphony No. 5* Eastman-Rochester O, Hanson
(+ Ives: *Symphony No. 3; Three Places in New England;* Schuman:
New England Triptych)
Philips Mercury 432 755-2 [A] **M**

MESSAGER, André (1853–1929) FRANCE

O *Les Deux Pigeons* Welsh National Opera O, Bonynge
Decca 433 700-2 (US: London 433 700-2) [D] **F**

MESSIAEN, Olivier (1908–1992) FRANCE

O *Éclairs sur l'Au-Delà* . . . Bastille Opera O, Chung
DG 439 929-2 [D] **F**

*Et Exspecto Resurrectionem Mortuorum; Chronochromie; La Ville
d'en Haut* Cleveland O, Boulez
DG 445 827-2 [D] **F**

*Oiseaux exotiques; Sept Haïkaï; Couleurs de la cité céleste; Un vitrail
et des oiseaux; La Ville d'en Haut; Et expecto resurrectionem
Mortuorum* Donohoe (pno), Netherlands Wind Ensemble, de
Leeuw
Chandos CHAN 9301-2, 2 CDs [D] **F**

Turangalîla Symphony Y. Loriod (pno), J. Loriod (ondes
martenot), Paris Bastille O, M-W. Chung
DG 431 781-2 [D] **F**

C *Quartet for the End of Time; *Le Merle noir* *Zoller (fl), Aloys
Kontarsky (pno); Gruenberg (vln), de Peyer (cl), Pleeth (vcl),
Beroff (pno)
EMI CDM7 63947-2 (US: Angel CDM 63947) [A] **M**

Thème et Variations Kremer (vln), Argerich (pno)
(+ Bartók: *Sonata No. 1;* Janáček: *Sonata*)
DG 427 351-2 [D] **F**

Cantéjodoyâ; 4 Études de rhythme; Fantaisie burlesque; Rondeau
Hill (pno)
Unicorn-Kanchana DKPCD 9078 [D] **F**

Catalogues d'oiseaux (complete); *Fauvettes des Jardins* Ugorski
(pno)
DG 439 214-2, 3 CDs [D] **F**

Catalogue d'oiseaux 1–6 Hill (pno)
Unicorn-Kanchana DKPCD 9062 [D] **F**

Catalogue d'oiseaux 7–10 Hill (pno)
Unicorn-Kanchana DKPCD 9075 [D] **F**

S   *Catalogue d'oiseaux 11–13; La Fauvette des Jardins* Hill (pno)
Unicorn-Kanchana DKPCD 9090 [D] **F**

Pièce pour le tombeau de Paul Dukas; Huit Préludes Hill (pno)
Unicorn-Kanchana DKPCD 9144 [D] **F**

Vingt regards sur l'enfant Jésus Hill (pno)
Unicorn-Kanchana DKP 9122/3, 2 CDs [D] **F**

*Vingt regards sur l'enfant Jésus; Petites esquisses d'oiseaux; Huit
Préludes; Quatre Études de rythme* Loriod (pno)
Erato 4509 96222-2, 3 CDs [A] **M**

*Visions de l'Amen; Fantaisie Burlesque; Petites esquisses d'oiseaux;
Pièce pour le tombeau de Paul Dukas; Rondeau* Hill (pno),
*Frith (pno)
Unicorn-Kanchana DKPCD 9144 [D] **F**

Complete Organ Works
EDITORS' CHOICE: Weir (org)
Collins 70312, 7 CDs [D] **M**

*Apparition de l'église éternelle; Livre d'orgue; Verset pour la fête de
la dédicace* Bate (org)
Unicorn-Kanchana DKPCD 9028 [D] **F**

*L'Ascension; 9 Méditations sur le mystère de la Sainte Trinité; Messe
de la Pentecôte* Bate (org)
Unicorn-Kanchana DKPCD 9024/5, 2 CDs [D] **F**

Le Banquet céleste; La Nativité du Seigneur Bate (org)
Unicorn-Kanchana DKPCD 9005 [D] **F**

Les Corps glorieux; Diptyque Bate (org)
Unicorn-Kanchana DKPCD 9004 [D] **F**

Le Livre du Saint Sacrement Bate (org)
Unicorn-Kanchana DKPCD 9067/8, 2 CDs [D] **F**

V   *O sacrum convivium; 3 Petites liturgies de la présence divine;
5 Rechants* London Sinfonietta Ch, London Sinfonietta,
Edwards
Virgin VC7 59051-2 (US: 59051) [D] **F**

O sacrum convivium BBC Symphony Ch., Jackson
(+Daniel-Lesur: *Le cantique des cantiques*, etc.)
ASV CDDCA 900 [D] **F**

*La Transfiguration de Notre Seigneur Jésus Christ; *La Nativité du
Seigneur* Sylvester (ten), Aquino (bar), Westminster
Symphonic Ch, National SO, Dorati; *Preston (org)
Decca 425 616-2 (US: London 425 616-2), 2 CDs [A] **M**

MEYERBEER, Giacomo (1791–1864) GERMANY

O   *Les Patineurs* (ballet; arr. Lambert) National PO, Bonynge
(+ Tchaikovsky: *Sleeping Beauty*)
Decca 425 468-2 (US: London 425 468-2), 3 CDs [A] **M**

V   *12 Songs* Hampson (bar), Parsons (pno)
(+ Rossini: *7 Songs*)
EMI CDC7 54436-2 (US: Angel CDC 54436) [D] **F**

MIASKOVSKY, Nikolay (1881–1950) RUSSIA

O   *Cello Concerto in C min., Op. 66; *Cello Sonatas: No. 1 in D,
Op. 12; No. 2 in A min., Op. 81* Tarasova (vcl), Moscow New
Opera O, Samoilov; *Ploezhaev (pno)
Olympia OCD 530 [D] **F**

O *Serenade in E♭, Op. 32/1; Sinfonietta, in B min. Op. 32/2; Lyric Concertino in G, Op. 32/3; Salutation Overture* Moscow New Opera O, Samoilov
Olympia OCD 528 [D] **F**

Symphonies: No. 1 in C min., Op. 3; No. 19 in E♭, Op. 46 USSR Ministry of Culture SO, Rozhdestvensky
Russian Disc RDCD 11 007 [A] **F**

Symphonies: No. 5 in D, Op. 18; No. 9 in E min. BBC PO, Downes
Marco Polo 8. 2323499 [D] **F**

Symphony No. 8 in A, Op. 26 Czech RSO, Stankowsky
Marco Polo 8.223297 [D] **F**

Symphony No. 12 in G min., Op. 35; Silence, Op. 9 Slovak RSO (Bratislava), Stankowsky
Marco Polo 8.223302 [D] **F**

C *String Quartets: No. 1 in A min., Op. 33/1; No. 4 in F min., Op. 33/4* Taneyev Quartet
Russian Disc RDCD 11013 [A] **F**

String Quartets: No. 3 in D min., Op. 33/3; No 10 in F, Op. 67/1; No. 13 in A min., Op. 86 Leningrad Taneiev Quartet
Olympia OCD 148 [A] **F**

S *Piano Sonatas Nos. 1–3 & 6* McLachlan (pno)
Olympia OCD 214 [D] **F**

Piano Sonatas Nos. 4 & 5; Sonatina in E min., Op. 57; Prelude, Op. 58 McLachlan (pno)
Olympia OCD 217 [D] **F**

Piano Sonatas Nos. 7–9; Reminiscences, Op. 29; Rondo-Sonata in B♭ min.; Scherzo; Yellowed Leaves, Op. 31 McLachlan (pno)
Olympia OCD 252 [D] **F**

MILHAUD, Darius (1892–1974) FRANCE

O *Le Boeuf sur le toit* (ballet), *Op. 58; *Le Printemps, Op. 18* Kremer (vln), LSO, Chailly; *Kremer (vln), Bashkirova (pno)
(+ Chausson: *Poème;* Satie: *Choses vues à droite et à gauche;* Vieuxtemps: *Fantasia appassionata*)
Philips 432 513-2 [A] **M**

Le Boeuf sur le toit, Op. 58; La Création du Monde (ballet), *Op. 81* Ulster O, Tortelier
(+ Ibert: *Divertissement;* Poulenc: *Les Biches*)
Chandos CHAN 9023 [D] **F**

Le carnaval d'Aix, Op. 83b; Piano Concertos: No.1, Op. 127; No. 4, Op. 295; Ballade, Op. 61; 5 Études, Op. 63 Helffer (pno), FNO, Robertson
Erato 2292 45992-2 [D] **F**

Cello Concerto No. 1, Op. 136 Rostropovich (vcl), LSO, Nagano
(+ Hoddinott: *Noctis Equi;* Honegger: *Cello Concerto*)
Erato 2292 45489-2 [D] **F**

Symphonies Nos. 1 & 2, Opp. 210 & 247; Suite provençale Toulouse Capitole O, Plasson
DG 435 437-2 [D] **F**

Symphonies Nos. 4 & 8 (Rhodanienne), Opp. 281 & 362 FNRO, Milhaud
Erato 2292 45841-2 [A] **F**

O   *Symphonies Nos. 6 & 7, Opp. 343 & 344; Ouverture*
Méditerranéenne, Op. 330 Toulouse Capitol O, Plasson
DG 439 939-2 [D] **F**

C   *La Cheminée du roi René, Op. 205; Divertimento, Op. 229b;*
Pastorale, Op. 147; 2 Sketches, Op. 227b; Suite d'après Corrette,
Op. 161b Athena Ensemble
Chandos CHAN 6536 [A] **M**

  Clarinet Sonatina, Op. 127; Flute Sonatina, Op. 76; Oboe
Sonatina, Op. 337; Sonata for Flute, Oboe, Clarinet and Piano,
Op. 47 Brunner (cl), Nicolet (fl), Holliger (ob),
Maisenberg (pno)
Orfeo CO 60831A [D] **F**

  Scaramouche, Op. 165b K. & M. Labèque (pno duo)
(+ Poulenc: *Double Piano Concerto; Capriccio; Élégie;*
Embarquement pour Cythère; Sonata for 4 Hands)
Philips 426 284-2 [D] **F**

V   *Alissa; L'amour chante; Poèmes juifs* Farley (sop),
Constable (pno)
ASV CDDCA 810 [D] **F**

MOERAN, Ernest J. (1894–1950) ENGLAND

O   *Cello Concerto; Sinfonietta* R. Wallfisch (vcl), Bournemouth
Sinfonietta, del Mar
Chandos CHAN 8456 [D] **F**

  *Violin Concerto; Lonely Waters; Whythorne's Shadow
**Mordkovitch (vln), Ulster O, Handley
Chandos CHAN 8807 [D] **F**

  In the Mountain Country; *Rhapsody in F♯; Rhapsodies Nos. 1 & 2
**Fingerhut (pno), Ulster O, Handley
Chandos CHAN 8639 [D] **F**

  Serenade in G; *Nocturne *Mackey (bar), *Renaissance Singers,
Ulster O, Handley
(+ Warlock: *Capriol Suite; Serenade for Strings*)
Chandos CHAN 8808 [D] **F**

  Symphony in G min.; Overture to a Masque Ulster O, Handley
Chandos CHAN 8577 [D] **F**

C   *Fantasy Quartet* Francis (ob), Members of the English Quartet
(+ Bax: *Oboe Quintet;* Holst: *Air and Variations; 3 Pieces;* Jacob:
Oboe Quartet)
Chandos CHAN 8392 [D] **F**

  String Quartet in A min.; *Violin Sonata in E min. Melbourne
Quartet; *Scotts (vln), Talbot (pno)
Chandos CHAN 8465 [D] **F**

MONTEVERDI, Claudio (1567–1643) ITALY

V   *Ab aeterno ordinata sum; Confitebor tibi, Domine I, II, and III;*
Deus tuorum militum; Iste confessor; Laudate Dominum II; Nisi
Dominus aedificaverit domum; Su le penne de' venti Kirkby (sop),
Partridge (ten), Thomas (bs), Parley of Instruments
◊ Hyperion CDA 66021 [D] **F**

  Adoramus te, Christe; Beatus vir; Chi vol che m'innamore;
Confitebor tibi, Domine II & V; E questa vita un lampo; Gloria in
excelsis Deo; Laudate Dominum, O omnes gentes I; O ciechi il tanto
affaticar Les Arts Florissants Vocal & Instrumental

Ensembles, Christie
✧ HM HMC90 1250 [D] **F**

V *Cantata domino; Domine, ne in furore; Missa de cappella a 4; Missa in illo tempore* Phillips (org), The Sixteen, Christophers
✧ Hyperion CDA 66214 [D] **F**

Chiome d'oro; Come dolci hoggi l'auretta; Con che soavità; Mentre vaga Angioletta; Ogni amante e guerrier; Ohimè, dov'è il mio ben?; Parlo miser' taccio; S'el vostro cor, Madonna; Tempro la cetra; Vorrei baciarti o Filli Kirkby (sop), Nelson (sop), Holden (sop), Elliot (ten), King (ten), Thomas (bs), Consort of Musicke, Rooley
✧ L'Oiseau-Lyre 421 480-2 [D] **F**

Lamento d'Olympia; Maladetto sia l'aspetto; Ohimè ch'io cado; Quel sguardo sdegnosetto; Voglio di vita uscia Kirkby (sop), Rooley (chitarrone)
(+ d'India: *Amico hai vint'io, etc.*)
✧ Hyperion CDA 66106 [D] **F**

Madrigals, Book 2 (complete) Consort of Musicke, Rooley
✧ Virgin VC7 59282-2 (US: CDC 59282) [D] **F**

Madrigals, Book 3 (complete) Consort of Musicke, Rooley
✧ Virgin VC7 59283-2 (US: CDC 59283) [D] **F**

Madrigals, Book 4 (complete) Consort of Musicke, Rooley
✧ L'Oiseau-Lyre 414 148-2 [D] **F**

Madrigals, Book 5 (complete) Consort of Musicke, Rooley
✧ L'Oiseau-Lyre 410 291-2 [D] **F**

Madrigals, Book 6 (complete) Consort of Musicke, Rooley
✧ Virgin VC7 59605-2 (US: 59605) [D] **F**

Madrigals, Book 8: Madrigali amorosi Consort of Musicke, Rooley
✧ Virgin VC7 59621-2 (US: 59621) [D] **F**

Madrigals, Book 8: (Balletti): Il ballo delle ingrate; Il combattimento di Tancredi e Clorinda; Volgendo il ciel; Armato il cor Consort of Musicke, Rooley
✧ Virgin VC7 59620-2 (US: 59620) [D] **F**

Vespro della Beata Vergine (vespers) Monoyios (sop), Pennichi (sop), Chance (alt), Tucker (ten), Robson (alt), Naglia (ten), Terfel (bs-bar), Miles (bar), His Majesties Sackbutts & Cornetts, Monteverdi Ch, London Oratory Ch, EBS, Gardiner
✧ DG Archiv 429 565-2, 2 CDs [D] **F**

MOODY, James (born 1907) ENGLAND

O *Little Suite* Reilly (harmonica), ASMF, Marriner
(+ Jacob: *5 Pieces;* Tausky: *Concertino;*
Vaughan Williams: *Romance*)
Chandos CHAN 8617 [D] **F**

C *Harmonica Quintet; *Suite dans le style français* Reilly (harmonica), *Kanga (hp), Hindar Quartet
(+ Jacob: *Divertimento*)
Chandos CHAN 8802 [D] **F**

MORLEY, Thomas (1557/8–1602) ENGLAND

V *12 Ayres/Canzonets & 2 Madrigals* Consort of Musicke, Rooley
✧ L'Oiseau-Lyre 436 862-2 [D] **F**

MOSZKOWSKI, Moritz (1854–1925) POLAND/GERMANY

O   *Piano Concerto in E, Op. 59* Lane (pno), BBC Scottish SO,
     Maksymiuk
     (+ Paderewski: *Piano Concerto in A min.*)
     Hyperion CDA 66452 [D] **F**

S   *17 Piano Miniatures* Tanyel (pno)
     Collins 14122 [D] **F**

MOZART, Leopold (1719–1787) GERMANY/AUSTRIA

O   *Trumpet Concerto in D*
     Wilbraham (tpt), ASMF, Marriner
     (+ Albinoni: *Trumpet Concerto in C*; Haydn: *Trumpet Concerto in
     Eb*; Hummel: *Trumpet Concerto in Eb*; Telemann: *2 Oboe and
     Trumpet Concerto No. 1*)
     Decca 417 761-2 (US: London 417 761-2) [A] **M**

MOZART, Wolfgang Amadeus (1756–1791) AUSTRIA

O   *Bassoon Concerto in Bb, K191; Clarinet Concerto in A, K622; Flute
     Concerto No. 1 in G, K313; Flute and Harp Concerto in C, K299;
     Horn Concertos Nos. 1–4; Oboe Concerto in C, K314; Sinfonia
     Concertante in Eb, K297b; Andante for Flute and Orchestra in C,
     K315* Various artists, Orpheus CO
     DG 431 665-2, 3 CDs [D] **B**

     *Bassoon Concerto in Bb, K191; Clarinet Concerto in A, K622; *Duo
     in Bb, K292* Thunemann (bsn), Leister (cl), Orton (vcl),
     ASMF, Marriner
     Philips 422 390-2 [D] **F**

     Clarinet Concerto in A, K622 Ottensamer (cl), VPO, Colin
     Davis
     (+ Spohr: *Clarinet Concerto No.1*; Weber: *Clarinet Concerto No. 2*)
     Philips 438 868-2 [D] **F**

     *Flute Concertos: No. 1 in G, K313; No. 2 in C, K314; Flute and
     Harp Concerto in C, K299; Andante in C, K315; Rondo, K373;
     Eine kleine Nachtmusik, K525* Galway (fl), Robles (hp), COE
     RCA RD 87861 (US: 7861-2), 2 CDs [D] **F**

     Horn Concertos Nos. 1–4; Rondo in Eb, K371
     Civil (hn), ASMF, Marriner
     Philips 442 397-2 [A] **M**
     Brown (hn), Age of Enlightenment O, Kuijken
     ✧ Virgin VC7 59558-2 (US: 59558-2) [D] **F**

     Piano Concertos (after J.C. Bach), K103 Nos. 1–3 Perahia
     (pno/dir), ECO
     (+ Schröter: *Piano Concerto in C, Op. 3 No. 3*)
     Sony CD 39222 [D] **F**

     Piano Concertos Nos. 1–6, 9, & 11–27 Anda (pno), Salzburg
     Mozarteum Camerata Academica
     DG 429 001-2, 10 CDs [A] **M**

     *Piano Concertos Nos. 5, 6, 8, 9 & 11–27; *Double Piano Concerto
     in Eb, K365; **Triple Piano Concerto in F, K242*
     Bilson (fpno), */**Levin (fpno), **Tan (fpno), EBS,
     Gardiner
     ✧ DG Archiv 431 211-2, 9 CDs [D] **M**

     Piano Concertos Nos. 1–4 Perahia (pno/dir), ECO
     Sony CD 39225 [D] **F**

Piano Concertos: No. 5 in D, K175; No. 6 in Bb, K238; Rondo in D, K382 Schiff (pno), Salzburg Camerata Academica, Végh
Decca 430 517-2 (US: London 430 517-2) [D] **F**

Piano Concertos: No. 6 in Bb, K238; No. 13 in C, K415 Perahia (pno/dir), ECO
Sony CD 39223 [A] **F**

Piano Concertos: No. 8 in C, K246; No. 11 in F, K413; Concert Rondo in A Schiff (pno), Salzburg Mozarteum, Végh
Decca 433 042-2 (US: London 433 042-2) [D] **F**

Piano Concertos Nos. 8, 23, 24 & 27 Kempff (pno), BPO, Bamberg SO, Leitner
DG 439 699-2, 2 CDs [A] **B**

Piano Concertos Nos. 9, 15, 22, 25 & 27 Brendel (pno), ASMF, Marriner
Philips 442 571-2, 2 CDs [A] **B**

Piano Concertos: No. 9 in Eb, K271; No. 17 in G, K453 Shelley (pno/dir), London Mozart Players
Chandos CHAN 9068 [D] **F**

Piano Concertos: No. 9 in Eb, K271; No.27 in Bb, K595 Tan (fpno/dir), New Mozart Ensemble
✧ Virgin VC7 45012-2 (US: 45012) [D] **F**

Piano Concertos: No. 12 in A, K414; No. 19 in F, K459 Shelley (pno/dir), London Mozart Players
Chandos CHAN 9256 [D] **F**

Piano Concertos: No. 13 in C, K415; No. 24 in C min., K491 Shelley (pno/dir), LMP
Chandos CHAN 9326 [D] **F**

Piano Concertos Nos. 14–16 Barenboim (pno/dir), ECO
EMI CDM7 69124-2 (US: Angel CDM 69124) [A] **M**

Piano Concertos: No. 15 in Bb, K450; No. 16 in D, K451 Perahia (pno/dir), ECO
Sony CD 37824 [D] **F**

Piano Concertos: No. 17 in G, K453; No. 18 in Bb, K456 Perahia (pno/dir), ECO
Sony CD 36686 [D] **F**

Piano Concertos Nos. 19–21, 23 & 24; Rondos K382 & 386 Brendel (pno), ASMF, Marriner
Philips 442 269-2, 2 CDs [A] **B**

Piano Concertos: No. 19 in F, K459; No. 23 in A, K488 Pollini (pno), VPO, Böhm
DG 413 793-2 [A] **F**

Piano Concertos: No. 19 in F, K459; No. 27 in Bb, K595 Schiff (pno), Salzburg Camerata Academica, Vegh
Decca 421 259-2 (US: London 421 259-2) [D] **F**

Piano Concertos: No. 20 in D min., K466; No. 23 in A, K488 Tan (fpno), LCP, Norrington
✧ EMI CDC7 54366-2 (US: Angel CDC 54366) [D] **F**
Shelley (pno/dir), London Mozart Players
Chandos CHAN 8992 [D] **F**

Piano Concertos: No. 20 in D min., K466; No. 21 in C, K467 Schiff (pno), Salzburg Mozarteum Camerata Academica, Végh
Decca 430 510-2 (US: London 430 510-2) [D] **F**

○ *Piano Concertos: No. 21 in C, K467; No. 25 in C, K503*
Kovacevich (pno), LSO, C. Davis
Philips 426 077-2 [A] **B**

Piano Concertos: No. 23 in A, K488; No. 24 in C min., K491
Kempff (pno), Bamberg SO, Leitner
DG 423 885-2 [A] **M**

*Piano Concertos: No. 23 in A, K488; No. 26 in D (Coronation),
K537* Casadesus (pno), Cleveland O, Szell
Sony/CBS CD 45884 [A] **M**

Piano Concertos: No. 24 in C min., K491; No. 25 in C, K503 Tan
(fpno), LCP, Norrington
◇ EMI CDC7 54295-2 (US: Angel CDC 54295) [D] **F**

*Piano Concertos: No. 25 in C, K503; No. 26 in D (Coronation),
K537* Ashkenazy (pno/dir), Philharmonia O
Decca 411 810-2 (US: London 411 810-2) [D] **F**

*Piano Concerto No. 27 in B♭, K595; *Double Piano Concerto in
E♭, K365* Emil Gilels (pno), *Elena Gilels (pno), VPO, Böhm
DG 419 059-2 [A] **M**

*Double Piano Concerto in E♭, K365; Triple Piano Concerto in F,
K242 (2-piano version); Andante & 5 Variations in G, K501;
Fantasia in F min., K608* Perahia (pno/dir), Lupu (pno), ECO
Sony CD 44915 [D] **F**

*Violin Concertos Nos. 1–5 & 7; Adagio in E, K261; Violin and
Piano Concerto in D, K315f; Concertone in C, K190; Rondo in B♭,
K269; Rondo in C, K373; Sinfonia Concertante in A, K320e;
Sinfonia Concertante in E♭, K364* Szeryng (vln), Poulet (vln),
Giurrana (vla) etc., ASMF, Marriner, NPO, Gibson
Philips 422 508-2, 4 CDs [D/A] **M**

*Violin Concertos: No. 1 in B♭, K207; No. 2 in D, K211; No. 5 in A
K219 (Turkish)* Huggett (vln/dir), Age of Enlightenment O
◇ Virgin VC5 45010-2 (US: 45010) [D] **F**

*Violin Concerto No. 2 in D, K211; Violin Concerto in D, K271a
(spurious); Rondo in C, K373* Lin (vln), ECO, Leppard
Sony CD 44913 [D] **F**

*Violin Concertos Nos. 3 & 4; Adagio in E, K261; Rondo in B♭,
K269* Hugget (vln), Age of Enlightenment O
◇ Virgin VC5 45060-2 (US: 45060) [D] **F**

Violin Concertos: No. 3 in G, K216; No. 5 in A (Turkish), K219
Mutter (vln), BPO, Karajan
DG 415 327-2 [D] **F**

Violin Concertos: No. 4 in D, K218; No. 5 in A (Turkish), K219
Shumsky (vln), Scottish CO, Tortelier
Nimbus NI 5009 [A] **F**

Violin Concerto No. 5 in A (Turkish), K219 Schneiderhan
(vln/dir), BPO
(+Beethoven: *Violin Concerto in D*)
DG 447 403-2 [A] **M**

Complete Dance Music Vienna Mozart Ensemble, Boskovsky
Philips 422 506-2, 6 CDs [A] **M**

*Divertimenti for Strings Nos. 1–3, K136–8; Divertimenti: No. 1 in
E♭, K113; No. 7 in D, K205; No. 10 in F, K247; No. 11 in D,
K251; No. 15 in B♭, K287; No. 17 in D, K334; March in D, K290;
March in F, K248; March in D, K445; Ein Musikalischer Spass*

(A Musical Joke), K522; Serenade No. 13 in G (Eine kleine Nachtmusik), K525 ASMF Chamber Ensemble
Philips 422 504-2, 5 CDs **M**

Divertimenti: No. 10 in F, K247; No. 17 in D, K334
L'Archibudelli
⬥ Sony CD 46494 [D] **F**

Complete Divertimenti and Serenades for Wind Holliger Wind Ensemble; Netherlands Wind Ensemble, de Waart; ASMF, Marriner
Philips 422 505-2, 6 CDs [D/A] **M**

6 German Dances, K509; 6 German Dances, K536; 6 German Dances, K 567; 6 German Dances, K571; 12 German Dances, K586
Tafelmusik, Weil
⬥ Sony CD 46696 [D] **F**

Organ (Epistle) Sonatas Nos. 1–17 Watson (org), King's Consort Classical O, King
⬥ Hyperion CDA 66377 [D] **F**

Overtures: *La Clemenza di Tito; Così fan Tutte; Don Giovanni; Die Entführung aus dem Serail; Idomeneo; Le Nozze di Figaro; Der Schauspieldirektor; Die Zauberflöte; Serenade No. 13 in G (Eine kleine Nachtmusik), K525* Tafelmusik, Weil
⬥ Sony CD 46695 [D] **F**

Serenades: No. 1 in D, K100; No. 3 in D, K185; No. 4 in D (Colloredo), K203; No. 5 in D, K204; No. 6 in D (Serenata notturna), K239; No. 7 in D (Haffner), K250; No. 8 in D (Notturno for 4 Orchestras), K286; No. 9 in D (Posthorn), K320; No. 13 in G (Eine kleine Nachtmusik), K525; Cassations: No. 1 in G (Final-Musik), K63; No. 2 in Bb, K99; Divertimento No. 2 in D, K131; Gallimathias musicum, K32; Marches: in D, K62; in D, K189; in D, K237; in D, K215; in D, K249; in D, K335 Nos. 1 & 2 ASMF, Marriner
Philips 422 503-2, 7 CDs [D] **M**

Serenades: No. 6 in D (Serenata notturna), K239; No. 13 in G (Eine kleine Nachtmusik), K525; Symphony in F, K76; March in D, K290 Amsterdam Baroque O, Koopman
⬥ Erato 2292 45713-2 [D] **F**

Serenade No. 7 in D (Haffner), K250; March in D, K249
Amsterdam Baroque O, Koopman
⬥ Erato 2292 45436-2 [D] **F**

Serenade No. 10 (for 13 wind instruments) in Bb, K361 COE Wind Soloists, Schneider
ASV CDCOE 804 [D] **F**

Serenades (for wind): No. 11 in Eb, K375; No. 12 in C min., K388
Orpheus CO
DG 431 683-2 [D] **F**

Serenade No. 13 in G (Eine kleine Nachtmusik), K525; Divertimenti for Strings, K136–8 Moscow Virtuosi, Spivakov
RCA RD 60066 (US: 60066-2) [D] **F**

*Sinfonia concertante in Eb, K364; *Concertone in C, K190*
Perlman (vln), Zukerman (vla/*vln), Israel PO, Mehta
DG 415 486-2 [D] **F**

Complete Symphonies AAM, Hogwood
Volume 1
⬥ L'Oiseau-Lyre 417 140-2, 2 CDs [A] **F**

o *Volume 2*
   ◇ L'Oiseau-Lyre 417 518-2, 2 CDs [A] **F**
   Volume 3
   ◇ L'Oiseau-Lyre 417 592-2, 3 CDs [A] **F**
   Volume 4
   ◇ L'Oiseau-Lyre 417 841-2, 3 CDs [A] **F**
   Volume 5
   ◇ L'Oiseau-Lyre 421 104-2, 3 CDs [A] **F**
   Volume 6
   ◇ L'Oiseau-Lyre 421 085-2, 3 CDs [D] **F**
   Volume 7
   ◇ L'Oiseau-Lyre 421 135-2, 3 CDs [D/A] **F**

*Symphonies: Nos. 1–41; in B♭, K55b; in F, K75; in D, K81; in C,
K96; in D, K97; in A, KAnh223* Prague CO, Mackerras
Telarc CD 80300, 10 CDs [D] **M**

23 Early Symphonies, Nos. 16–30 English Concert, Pinnock
◇ DG 439 915-2, 4 CDs [D] **F**

Symphonies Nos. 17–19, 22 & 32 Amsterdam Baroque O,
Koopman
◇ Erato 2292 45714-2 [D] **F**

*Symphonies: No. 21 in A, K134; No. 23 in D, K181; No. 24 in B♭,
K182, No. 27 in G, K199* Amsterdam Baroque O, Koopman
◇ Erato 2292 45544-2 [D] **F**

*Symphonies: No. 25 in G min., K183; No. 29 in A, K201; No. 33 in
B♭* Amsterdam Baroque O, Koopman
◇ Erato 2292 45431-2 [D] **F**

*Symphonies Nos. 28, 33, 35 (Haffner), 39, 40 & 41 (Jupiter);
Serenade No. 13 in G (Eine kleine Nachtmusik), K525; Serenade
No. 9 in D (Posthorn) K320; *Exsultate jubilate, K165; Marriage
of Figaro: Overture* *Raskin (sop), Cleveland O, Szell
Sony CD 46515, 3 CDs [A] **F**

Symphonies: No. 29 in A, K201; No. 33 in B♭, K319 EBS, Gardiner
◇ Philips 412 736-2 [D] **F**

Symphonies: Nos. 31, 34, 35, 36, 38 & 41 Amsterdam Baroque
O, Koopman
◇ Erato 2292 45857-2, 2 CDs [D] **F**

*Symphonies: No. 31 in D (Paris), K297 (first version); No. 34 in C,
K338* EBS, Gardiner
◇ Philips 420 937-2 [D] **F**

*Symphonies: No. 35 in D (Haffner), K385; No. 38 in D (Prague),
K504; No. 39 in E♭, K543* ECO, Barenboim
EMI Eminence CD-EMX 2097 (US: Classics for Pleasure CDEMX
2097) [A] **M**

*Symphonies: No. 35 in D (Haffner), K385; No. 40 in G min., K550;
No. 41 in C (Jupiter), K551* Cleveland O, Szell
Sony CD 46333 [A] **B**

Symphonies: No. 36 in C (Linz), K425; No. 38 in D (Prague), K504
Prague CO, Mackerras
Telarc CD-80148 [D] **F**

Symphonies: No. 38 in D (Prague), K504; No. 39 in E♭, K543
COE, Harnoncourt
Teldec 4509 90866-2 [D] **F**

O *Symphonies: No. 38 in D (Prague), K504; No. 40 in G min., K550*
LCP, Norrington
◇ EMI CDC7 54336-2 (US: Angel CDC 54336) [D] **F**

Symphonies: No. 39 in Eb, K543; No. 41 in C (Jupiter), K551
LCP, Norrington
◇ EMI CDC7 54090-2 (US: Angel CDC 54090) [D] **F**

6 Symphonies after Serenades: in D, K100; in D, K185; in D, K203; in D, K204; in D, K250; in D, K320 Tafelmusik, Weil
◇ Sony CD 47260, 2 CDs [D] **F**

C *Clarinet Quintet in A, K581; Flute Quartets Nos. 1–4; Oboe Quartet in F, K370; Horn Quintet in Eb, K407; Bassoon and Cello Duo, K292; various completed fragments* Pay (cl), Bennett (fl), Grumiaux Trio, Brown (hn), Black (ob), Thunemann (bsn), Orton (vcl), ASMF Chamber Ensemble
Philips 422 510-2, 3 CDs [A/D] **M**

Clarinet Quintet in A, K581 de Peyer (cl), Melos Ensemble
(+ Brahms: *Clarinet Quintet*)
EMI CDM7 63116-2 (US: Angel CDM 63116) [A] **M**

*Divertimento in Eb for String Trio, K563; *Duos Nos. 1 & 2 for Violin and Viola, K423–4; **6 Preludes and Fugues for String Trio, K404a; String Trio in Bb, K266* Grumiaux Trio;
*Grumiaux (vln), Pellicia (vla); **ASMF Chamber Ensemble
Philips 422 513-2, 2 CDs [A/D] **M**

Divertimento in Eb for String Trio, K563; 6 Preludes and Fugues, K404a L'Archibudelli
◇ Sony 46497 [D] **F**

Flute Quartets Nos. 1–4 Bennett (fl), Grumiaux Trio
Philips 422 835-2 [A] **M**

*Grande Sestetto Concertante (after the Sinfonia Concertante, K364); *Duos Nos. 1, K423 & 2, K424* L'Archibudelli; *V. Beths (vln), Kussmaul (vla)
◇ Sony CD 46631 [D] **F**

Piano Trios Nos. 1–6; Piano Trio in D min., K442; Piano Quartets Nos. 1, K478, & 2, K493; Piano and Wind Quintet in Eb, K452; Adagio and Rondo in C min., K617; Divertimento in Bb for Piano Trio, K254 Beaux Arts Trio, Giurrana (vla), Hoffman (glass harmonica), Nicolet (fl), Schouten (vla), Decross (vcl), Brendel (pno), Holliger (ob)
Philips 422 514-2, 5 CDs [A/D] **M**

Piano Quartets Nos. 1, K478, & 2, K493 Beaux Arts Trio, Giurrana (vla)
Philips 410 391-2 [D] **F**

Piano and Wind Quintet, K452 Perahia (pno), Black (ob), King (cl), Halstead (hn), Sheen (bsn)
(+ Beethoven: *Piano and Wind Quintet*)
Sony/CBS CD 42099 [D] **F**

Piano Trios Nos. 1–6 London Fortepiano Trio
◇ Hyperion CDS 44021/3, 3 CDs [D] **F**
Trio Fonteney
Teldec 2292 46439-2, 2 CDs [D] **F**

String Quartets Nos. 1–23 Italian Quartet
Philips 422 512-2, 8 CDs [A] **M**

String Quartets Nos. 14–23 Alban Berg Quartet
Teldec 4509-95495-2, 4 CDs [A] **M**

C *String Quartets: No. 14 in G, K387; No. 23 in F, K590* Brandis Quartet
Orfeo C041831A [D] **F**

String Quartets: No. 17 in Bb, K458 (Hunt); No. 19 in C, K465 (Dissonance); No. 23 in F, K590 Musikverein Quartet
Decca 433 694-2 (US: London 433 694-2) [A] **M**

String Quintets Nos. 1–6 Grumiaux Ensemble
Philips 422 511-2, 3 CDs [A] **M**

String Quintets: No. 3 in C, K515; No. 4 in G min., K516 Hausmusik
✧ EMI CDC7 54482-2 (US: Angel CDC 54482) [D] **F**

String Quintets: No. 5 in D, K593; No. 6 in Eb, K614 Hausmusik
✧ EMI CDC7 54876-2 (US: Angel CDC 54876) [D] **F**

Violin Sonatas Nos. 1–36; Adagio in C min., K396; Allegro in Bb, K372; Andante and Allegretto in C, K404; Andante and Fugue, K402; Sonatina in C, K46d; Sonatina in F, K46e; 6 Variations on 'Hélas, j'ai perdu mon amant'; 12 Variations on 'La bergère Célimène' Poulet (vln), Verlet (fpno); Grumiaux (vln), Klien (pno); van Keulen (vln), Brautigam (pno)
Philips 422 515-2, 7 CDs [A/D] **M**

Violin Sonatas Nos. 17–28 & 32–36 Perlman (vln), Barenboim (pno)
DG 431 784-2, 4 CDs [D] **M**

Violin Sonatas: No. 17 in C, K296; No. 32 in Bb, K454; No. 35 in A, K526 Stern (vln), Bronfman (pno)
Sony CD 53972 [D] **F**

Sonatas: in C for Piano Duet, K19d; in Bb for Piano Duet, K358; in D for Piano Duet, K381; in F for Piano Duet, K497; in C for Piano Duet, K521; in D for Two Pianos, K448; Adagio and Allegro in F min., K594; Andante with 5 Variations in G, K501; Fantasia in F min., K608 Eschenbach (pno), Frantz (pno)
DG 435 042-2, 2 CDs [A] **M**

S *Complete solo keyboard works* (excluding sonatas) Uchida (pno), Haebler (pno), Koopman (hpd), Mathot (hpd)
Philips 422 518-2, 5 CDs [D/A] **M**

Piano Sonatas Nos. 1–18 Eschenbach (pno)
DG 419 445-2, 5 CDs [A] **M**

Piano Sonatas Nos. 3, 10 & 13; Rondo, K485; Adagio, K540 Horowitz (pno)
DG 445 517-2 [D] **M**

V *Complete Religious Works* (excluding Masses) Various artists and orchestras conducted by C. Davis, Kegel, Winkler
Philips 422 520-2, 5 CDs [A/D] **M**

Complete Concert Arias Various artists and orchestras conducted by Hager, C. Davis, Schreier, Marriner, Harrer
Philips 422 523-2, 8 CDs [D/A] **M**

Complete Shorter Vocal Works Various artists and orchestras conducted by Marriner, Hager, Schreier
Philips 422 522-2, 6 CDs [A/D] **M**

Complete Lieder Ameling (sop), Baldwin (pno), etc.
Philips 422 524-2, 2 CDs [D] **M**

V *Lieder* (selection) Schreier (ten), Schiff (pno)
Decca 430 514-2 (US: London 430 514-2) [D] **F**

Ave verum corpus St. John's College Ch, Guest
(+ M. Haydn: *Ave Regina;* J. Haydn: *Mass No. 12*)
Decca 430 159-2 (US: London 430 159-2) [A] **M**

Litaniae de venerabili Marshall (sop), Cable (mez), Evans (ten),
Roberts (bs), St. John's College Ch, Wren O, Guest
(+ Haydn: *Mass No. 9*)
Decca 430 158-2 (US: London 430 158-2) [A] **M**

Masses Nos. 1–19 Various artists and orchestras conducted by
C. Davis, Kegel, Harrer, Gardiner and Schreier
Philips 422 519-2, 9 CDs [A/D] **M**

*Masses: No. 11 in C (Credo), K257; No. 12 in C (Spauermesse),
K258; No. 13 in C (Organ Solo), K259* Monoyios (sop), Schlick
(sop), Graf (cont), Groenewald (cont), Pfaff (ten), Schafer
(ten), Mertens (bs), Selig (bs), Köln Chamber Ch, Collegium
Cartusianum, Neumann
✧ EMI CDC7 54037-2 (US: CDC 54037) [D] **F**

Mass No. 12 in C, K258 Palmer (sop), Cable (mez), Langridge
(ten), Roberts (bs), St. John's College Ch, Wren O, Guest
(+ Haydn: *Mass No. 13 in B♭*)
Decca 430 161-2 (US: London 430 161-2) [A] **M**

Mass No. 16 in C (Coronation), K317 Tomova-Sintow (sop),
Baltsa (mez), Krenn (ten), van Dam (bs), Vienna Singverein,
BPO, Karajan
(+ Beethoven: *Missa Solemnis*)
DG 423 913-2, 2 CDs [A] **M**

*Mass No. 16 in C, K317 (Coronation); Vesperae solennes de
confessore, K339; Ave verum corpus, K618* Pennecchi (sop),
Patriasz (cont), Vendersteene (ten), Draijer (bs), Netherlands
Chamber Ch., Bruggen
✧ Philips 434 799-2 [D] **F**

Mass No. 18 in C min. (Great), K427 Hendricks (sop), Perry
(sop), Schreier (ten), Luxon (bar), Vienna Singverein, BPO,
Karajan
DG 439 012-2 [D] **M**

*Mass No. 18 in C min., K427 (Great); Exsultate jubilate, K165;
Vespers, K339* Bonney (sop), Rogers (alt), McDougall (ten),
Gadd (bs), English Concert & Ch., Pinnock
✧ DG Archiv 445 353-2 [D] **F**

Mass No. 19 in D min. (Requiem), K626 Schlick (sop),
Watkinson (cont), Prégardien (ten), van der Kamp (bs),
Netherlands Bach Society Ch, Amsterdam Baroque O,
Koopman
✧ Erato 2292 45472-2 [D] **F**

Vesperae de Dominica, K321 Marshall (sop), Cable (mez), Evans
(ten), Roberts (bs), St. John's College Ch, Wren O, Guest
(+ Haydn: *Mass No. 14 in B♭*)
Decca 430 162-2 (US: London 430 162-2) [A] **M**

Vesperae solennes de confessore, K339 Palmer (sop), Cable (mez),
Langridge (ten), Roberts (bar), St. John's College Ch, Wren
O, Guest
(+ Haydn: *Mass No. 10 in C*)
Decca 430 157-2 (US: London 430 157-2) [A] **M**

MUNDY, William (c.1529–1591) ENGLAND

V *Adolescentulus sum ego; Ah, helpless wretch; Beatus et sanctus;*
Evening service; Kyrie; O Lord, the maker of all things; O Lord, the
world's saviour; The secret sins; Sive vigilem; Videte miraculum; Vox
patris caelestis The Sixteen, Christophers
Hyperion CDA 66319 [A] **F**

Vox patris caelestis Tallis Scholars, Phillips
(+ Allegri: *Miserere mei;* Palestrina: *Missa Papae Marcelli*)
Gimell CDGIM 339 [A] **F**

MUSSORGSKY, Modest (1839–1881) RUSSIA

O *Chorus of Priestesses (Salammbo); The Destruction of Sennacherib;*
Calitsin's Journey; Joshua; Night on a Bare Mountain (original
version); *Oedipus in Athens; Prelude (Khovanshchina); Scherzo in*
Bb; Triumphal March LSO, Abbado
RCA 09026 61354-2 [A] **M**

Pictures at an Exhibition (orch. Ravel); *Night on a Bare Mountain*
Chicago SO, Reiner
(+Works by Glinka, Borodin, Tchaikovsky & Kabalevsky)
RCA 09026 61958-2 [A] **M**

Pictures at an Exhibition (orch. Ravel) Cleveland O, Szell
(+ Kodály: *Háry János Suite;* Prokofiev: *Lieutenant Kijé Suite*)
Sony CD 48162 [A] **B**

S *Pictures at an Exhibition* Pletnev (pno)
(+ Tchaikovsky: *Sleeping Beauty: Suite* [arr. Pletnev])
Virgin VC7 59611-2 (US: 59611) [D] **F**

Songs and Dances of Death; The Nursery; The Peep-Show;
Forgotten; The Seminarist; Darling Savishna; The He-Goat; A
Worldly Story; Mephistopheles's Song of the Flea Leiferkus (bar),
Skigin (pno)
Conifer CDCF 229 [D] **F**

NANCARROW, Conlon (born 1912) USA/MEXICO

S *Studies for Player Piano* (complete) Nancarrow (player piano)
Wergo WER 6168-2, 2 CDs [D] **F**; WER 60166/7-50, 2 CDs [D]
F; WER 60165-50 [D] **F**

NIELSEN, Carl (1865–1931) DENMARK

O *Aladdin* (complete) Ejsing (cont), Paevatalu (bar), Danish
National Radio SO & Ch, Rozhdestvensky
Chandos CHAN 9135 [D] **F**

*Aladdin (suite); *Springtime in Fünen* *Nielsen (sop), *von
Binzer (ten), *Klint (bs), *Muko University Ch, *St. Klemens
Children's Ch, Odense SO, Veto
Unicorn-Kanchana DKPCD 9054 [D] **F**

Clarinet Concerto; Flute Concerto; Violin Concerto Thomsen (cl),
Christiansen (fl), Sjøgren (vln), Danish RSO, Schønwandt
Chandos CHAN 8894 [D] **F**

Violin Concerto Lin (vln), Swedish RSO, Salonen
(+ Sibelius: *Violin Concerto*)
Sony/CBS CD44548 [D] **F**

Helios Overture; Symphonic Rhapsody; Dream of Gunnar; An
Evening at Giske; Paraphrase on 'Nearer my God to Thee' for
Windband; Bohemian-Danish Folktune; Rhapsody Overture; Pan &
Syrinx Danish National RSO, Rozhdestvensky
Chandos CHAN 9287 [D] **F**

O *Symphonies Nos. 1–6* SFSO, Blomstedt
Decca 443 117-2 (US: London 443 117-2), 3 CDs [D] **F**

Symphonies: No. 1 in G min.; No. 6 (Sinfonia Semplice) SFSO,
Blomstedt
Decca 425 607-2 (US: London 425 607-2) [D] **F**

*Symphonies: No. 2 (The Four Temperaments); No. 3 (Sinfonia
espansiva)* SFSO, Blomstedt
Decca 430 280-2 (US: London 430 280-2) [D] **F**

Symphonies: No. 4 (Inextinguishable); No. 5 SFSO, Blomstedt
Decca 421 524-2 (US: London 421 524-2) [D] **F**

Symphony No. 4 (Inextinguishable) BPO, Karajan
(+Sibelius: *Tapiola*)
DG 445 518-2 [D] **M**

C *Violin Sonatas: No. 1 in A; No. 2* Mordkovitch (vln), Benson
(pno)
Chandos CHAN 8598 [D] **F**

S *Complete Solo Piano Music* Westenholz (pno)
BIS BIS-CD 167/8 [A] **F**

*Commotio; 29 Little Preludes; 2 Preludes; *3 Motets* Westenholz
(org); *Camarata Chamber Ch, Enewold
BIS BIS-CD 131 [A] **F**

NONO, Luigi (1924–1990) ITALY

O *La Lontananza nostalgica utopica futura; 'Hay que caminar'
sognando* Kremer (vln), Grindenko (vln), Tonband
DG 435 870-2 [D] **F**

*. . . sofferte onde serene . . . for piano and magnetic tape; *Como una
ola de fuerza y luz for soprano, piano, orchestra and magnetic tape;
**Contrappunto dialettico alla mente for voices through magnetic
tape* Pollini (pno); *Taskova (sop), Pollini (pno), Bavarian
RSO, Abbado; **Various artists, RAI Chamber Ch,
Antonellini
DG 423 248-2 [A] **M**

NOSKOWSKI, Zygmunt (1846–1909) POLAND

C *Piano Quartet in D min., Op. 8* Polish Piano Quartet
(+ Zelinski: Piano Quartet)
Olympia OCD 381 [D] **F**

NYMAN, Michael (born 1948) ENGLAND

O *Piano Concerto; *MGV* Stott (pno), RLPO, Nyman; *Michael
Nyman Band & O, Nyman
Argo 443 382-2 [D] **F**

Prospero's Books (film score) Michael Nyman Band, Nyman
Argo 425 224-2 [D] **F**

C *String Quartets Nos. 1–3* Balanescu Quartet
Argo 433 093-2 [D] **F**

V *Songbook* Lemper (sop), Michael Nyman Band, Nyman
Decca 425 227-2 (US: London 425 227-2) [D] **F**

*Time Will Pronounce; Self-Laudatory Hymn of Inanna & her
Omnipotence; The Convertibility of Lute Strings; For John Cage*
Various artists
Argo 440 282-2 [D] **F**

OFFENBACH, Jacques (1819–1880) GERMANY/FRANCE

O Overtures: *Barbe-Bleue; La belle Hélène; La Grande-duchesse de Gérolstein; Orpheus in the Underworld; Vert-Vert; Barcarolle (Tales of Hoffmann)* BPO, Karajan
DG 400 044-2 [D] **F**

ONSLOW, Georges (1784–1853) ENGLAND/FRANCE

C *String Quartets: in C min., Op. 56; in F♯ min., Op. 46/1; Variations on 'God Save the Queen', Op. 9/1* Coull Quartet
ASV CDDCA 808 [D] **F**

ORFF, Carl (1895–1982) GERMANY

V *Carmina Burana* McNair (sop), Aler (ten), Hagegard (bar), St Louis SO & Ch., Slatkin
RCA 09026 61673-2 [D] **F**

De temporum fine comoedia (symbolic drama) Tomowa-Sintow (sop), Ludwig (mez), Schreier (ten), Greindl (bs), Boysen (spkr), RIAS Chamber Ch, etc., Köln RSO, Karajan
DG 429 859-2 [A] **M**

PACHELBEL, Johann (1653–1706) GERMANY

O *Canon and Gigue in D* Orpheus CO
DG 492 390-2 [D] **F** (see collections – *Popular Baroque*)

S *Praeludium, Fugue and Chaconne in D min.; Chaconne in F min.; Prelude and Fugue in C min.; Toccata in F; Toccata and Ricercare in C min.; 10 Chorale Preludes* Jacob (org)
Virgin VC7 59197-2 (US: 59197) [D] **F**

PADEREWSKI, Jan (1860–1941) POLAND

O *Piano Concerto in A min., Op. 17* Lane (pno), BBC Scottish SO, Maksymiuk
(+ Moszkowski: *Piano Concerto in E, Op. 59*)
Hyperion CDA 66452 [D] **F**

PAGANINI, Niccolò (1782–1840) ITALY

O *Violin Concertos Nos. 1–6* Accardo (vln), LPO, Dutoit
DG 437 210-2, 3 CDs [A] **B**

Violin Concerto No. 1 in D, Op. 6; Sonate Napoleone; I Palpitti, Op. 13; Moto perpetuo, Op. 11 Accardo (vln), LPO, Dutoit
DG 439 981-2 [A] **M**

Violin Concerto No. 1 in D, Op. 6 Perlman (vln), RPO, Foster
(+Sarasate: *Carmen Fantasy*)
EMI CDC7 47101-2 (US: Angel CDC 47101) [A] **F**

Violin Concerto No. 2 in B min. (trans. Hall) Hall (gtr), London Mozart Players, Litton
(+ Castelnuovo-Tedesco: *Guitar Concerto No. 1;* Sarasate: *Zigeunerweisen*)
Decca 440 293-2 (US: London 440 293-2) [D] **F**

C *Complete Music for Violin and Guitar* Shaham (vln), Sollscher (gtr)
DG 437 837-2 [D] **F**

S *24 Caprices, Op. 1* Perlman (vln)
EMI CDC7 47171-2 (US: Angel CDC 47171) [A] **F**

PAINE, John Knowles (1839–1906) USA

○ *Symphony No. 1 in C min., Op. 23; As You Like It (overture),*
   Op. 28 NYPO, Mehta
   New World NW 374-2 [D] **F**

   Symphony No. 2 in A (In the Spring), Op. 34 NYPO, Mehta
   New World NW 350-2 [D] **F**

PAISIELLO, Giovanni (1740–1816) ITALY

○ *Piano Concertos: No. 1 in C; No. 5 in D; No. 7 in A; No. 8 in C*
   Monetti (pno), ECO, Gonley
   ASV CDDCA 873 [D] **F**

   Piano Concertos: No. 2 in F; No. 3 in A; No. 4 in G min.; No. 6
   in B♭ Monetti (pno), ECO, Gonley
   ASV CDDCA 872 [D] **F**

PALESTRINA, Giovanni da (1525/6–1594) ITALY

✓ *Assumpta est Maria; Missa Assumpta est Maria; Missa Sicut*
   lilium inter spinas; Sicut lilium inter spinas I Tallis Scholars,
   Phillips
   Gimell CDGIM 020 [D] **F**

   Ave Maria (offertory); *Canite tuba; Hodie Christus natus est;*
   Jubilate Deo omnis terra; Missa Hodie Christus natus est; O
   magnum mysterium; Tui sunt caeli King's College Ch,
   Ledger
   EMI Eminence CD-EMX 2098 (US: Classics for Pleasure CDEMX
   2098) [A] **M**

   Duo ubera tua; Magnificat Primi Toni; Missa Aeterna Christi
   munera; Nigra sum, sed formosa; Quae est ista; Sicut cervus; Super
   flumina Babylonis; Surge, amica mea; Vidi turbam magnam
   Westminster Cathedral Ch, O'Donnell
   Hyperion CDA 66490 [D] **F**

   Missa Ave Maria; Missa De beata Virgine Westminster Cathedral
   Ch, O'Donnell
   Hyperion CDA 66364 [D] **F**

   Missa Benedicta es Tallis Scholars, Phillips
   (+ Josquin: *Benedicta es*)
   Gimell CDGIM 001 [D] **F**

   Missa brevis; Missa Nasce la gioia mia Tallis Scholars, Phillips
   (+ Primavera: *Nasce la gioia mia*)
   Gimell CDGIM 008 [D] **F**

   Missa Dum complerentur; 5 Motets Christ Church Cathedral Ch,
   Dartington
   Nimbus NI 5100 [D] **F**

   Missa Nigra sum Tallis Scholars, Phillips
   (+ De Silva: *Nigra sum;* Lhéritier: *Nigra sum;* Victoria: *Nigra*
   sum)
   Gimell CDGIM 003 [D] **F**

   Missa O Rex gloriae; Missa Viri Galilaei; O Rex gloriae; Viri
   Galilaei Westminster Cathedral Ch, O'Donnell
   Hyperion CDA 66316 [D] **F**

   Missa Papae Marcelli Tallis Scholars, Phillips
   (+ Allegri: *Miserere mei;* Mundy: *Vox Patris caelestis*)
   Gimell CDGIM 339 [A] **F**

PANUFNIK, Andrzej (1914–1991) POLAND/BRITAIN

O *Autumn Music; Heroic Overture; Nocturne; *Sinfonia Rustica; Tragic Overture* Peebles (pno), LSO, Horenstein; *Monte Carlo Opera O, Panufnik
Unicorn-Kanchana UKCD 2016 [A] **M**

*Bassoon Concerto; Violin Concerto; *Hommage à Chopin* Thompson (bsn), Smietana (vln), *Jones (fl), London Musici, Stephenson
Conifer CDCF 182 [D] **F**

*Concerto festivo; Concerto for Timpani, Percussion and Strings; Katyń Epitaph; Landscape; **Sinfonia sacra* Goedicke (timpani), Frye (perc), LSO, **Monte Carlo Opera O, Panufnik
Unicorn-Kanchana UKCD 2020 [A] **M**

Cello Concerto Rostropovich (vcl), LSO, Wolff
NMC NMCD 010S [D] **M**

Sinfonia Concertante for Flute, Harp & Strings; Concertino for Timpani, Percussion & Strings; Harmony Jones (fl), Masters (hp), Benjafield (perc), Cole (timp), London Musici, Stephenson
Conifer CDCF 217 [D] **F**

*Sinfonia sacra; *Arbor cosmica* Royal Concertgebouw O, *NY Chamber Symphony, Panufnik
Elektra-Nonesuch 7559 79228-2 (US: 79228-2) [D] **F**

Symphony No. 8 Boston SO, Ozawa
(+ Sessions: *Concerto for Orchestra*)
Hyperion CDA 66050 [D] **F**

Symphony No. 9; Piano Concerto Poblocka (pno), LSO, Panufnik
Conifer CDCF 206 [D] **F**

C *String Quartets Nos. 1–3; String Sextet; Song to the Virgin Mary* Chilingirian String Quartet, Chase (vla), Orton (vcl)
Conifer CDCF 218 [D] **F**

PARRY, Hubert (1848–1918) ENGLAND

O *The Birds: Bridal March; An English Suite; Overture to an Unwritten Tragedy; Lady Radnor's Suite; Symphonic Variations* LSO, LPO, Boult
Lyrita SRCD 220 [A] **F**

English Suite English String O, Boughton
(+Bridge: *Cherry Ripe*, etc.; Finzi: *Eclogue*)
Nimbus NI 5366 [D] **F**

Lady Radnor's Suite English String O, Boughton
(+ Bridge: *Suite;* Butterworth: *The Banks of Green Willow*, etc.)
Nimbus NI 5068 [D] **F**

Symphonies Nos. 1–5; Symphonic Variations LPO, Bamert
Chandos CHAN 9120/2, 3 CDs [D] **F**

Symphony No. 1 in G min.; Concertstück in G min. LPO, Bamert
Chandos CHAN 9062 [D] **F**

Symphony No. 2 in F (Cambridge); Symphonic Variations LPO, Bamert
Chandos CHAN 8961 [D] **F**

Symphonies: No. 3 in C (English); No. 4 in E min. LPO, Bamert
Chandos CHAN 8896 [D] **F**

O *Symphony No. 5 in B min.* (symphonic fantasia); *Elegy for Brahms; From Death to Life* (symphonic poem) LPO, Bamert
Chandos CHAN 8955 [D] **F**

C *Violin Sonata in D, Op. 103; Fantasie-Sonata in B min., Op. 78; 12 Short Pieces* Gruenberg (vln), Vignoles (pno)
Hyperion CDA 66157 **F**

Nonet in B♭ Capricorn
(+ Stanford: *Serenade*)
Hyperion CDA 66291 [D] **F**

V *Evening Service in D; Hear my words, ye people; I was glad; Jerusalem; 6 Songs of Farewell* Judd (org), St. George's Chapel Ch, Windsor, Robinson
Hyperion CDA 66273 [D] **F**

Invocation to Music Dawson (sop), Davies (ten), Rayner Cook (bar), LPO & Ch, Bamert
Chandos CHAN 9025 [D] **F**

The Soul's Ransom; Choric Song from Tennyson's 'The Lotus Eaters' Jones (sop), Wilson-Johnson (bar), LPO & Ch, Bamert
Chandos CHAN 8990 [D] **F**

PÄRT, Arvo (born 1935) ESTONIA/AUSTRIA

O *Arbos; Pari intervalli; An den Wassern zu Babel; De Profundis; Es sang vor langen Jahren; Stabat Mater; Summa* Stuttgart State O Brass Ensemble, Davies; Bowers-Broadbent (org); Hilliard Ensemble; Bickley (sop), Kremer (vln), Mendelssohn (vla); Dawson (sop), Covey-Crump (ten)
ECM 831 959-2 [D] **F**

Cantus in Memory of Benjamin Britten; Festina Lente; Fratres; Spiegel im Spiegel; Summa; Tabula Rasa Little (vln), Roscoe (pno), Bournemouth Sinfonietta, Studt
EMI Eminence CD-EMX 2221 (US: Classics for Pleasure CDEMX 2221) [D] **M**

Cello Concerto; Perpetuum mobile; Symphonies Nos. 1–3 Helmerson (vcl), Bamberg SO, Järvi
BIS BIS-CD 434 [D] **F**

*Symphony No. 2; Collage; *Credo; Festina lente; Fratres; Summa; Wenn Bach Bienen gesuchet hatte* *Berman (pno), Philharmonia O & Ch, Järvi
Chandos CHAN 9134

*Festina lente; *Miserere; **Sarah was ninety years old* Bonn Beethovenhalle O, Davies; *Western Wind Chamber Ch, Hilliard Ensemble, Hillier
ECM 847 539-2 [D] **F**

C *Fratres for 12 cellos; *Tabula rasa; **Fratres for violin and piano* 12 Cellos of the BPO, *Kremer (vln), Grindenko (vln); Schnittke (prepared pno), Lithuanian CO, Sondeckis; **Kremer (vln), Jarrett (pno)
ECM 817 764-2 [D] **F**

Fratres; Summa Chilingirian Quartet
(Tavener: *The Last Sleep of the Virgin*, etc.)
Virgin VC5 45023-2 (US: 45023) [D] **F**

V *Passio Domini nostri Jesu Christe secundum Johannem* George (bs), Potter (ten), Dawson (sop), Covey-Crump (ten), Layton (vln), Maxwell (ob), Wilson (vcl), Ducket (bsn), Bowers-

Broadbent (org), Western Wind Chamber Ch, Hillier
ECM 837 109-2 [D] **F**

PENDERECKI, Krzysztof (born 1933) POLAND

O *Anaklasis; Canticum Canticorum Salomonis;*Capriccio; De Natura
Sonoris Nos. 1 & 2; The Dream of Jacob; Fonogrammi; Threnody
for the Victims of Hiroshima* Wilkomirska (vln), Polish National
RSO, LSO, Penderecki
EMI CDM5 65077-2 (US: CDM 65077) [A] **F**

*Cello Concerto No. 2; Viola Concerto; The Dream of Jacob; Paradise
Lost* (opera): *Adagietto* Monighetti (vcl), Kamasa (vla), Polish
NRO, Wit
Polski Nagrania PNCD 020 [A] **F**

Violin Concerto; *Symphony No. 2 Kulka (vln), Polish NRO,
Penderecki; *Polish NRO, Kaspszyk
Polski Nagrania PNCD 019 [A] **F**

C *String Quartet No. 1* LaSalle Quartet
(+ Cage: *String Quartet;* Lutoslawski: *String Quartet;* Mayuzumi:
Prelude)
DG 423 245-2 [A] **M**

String Quartet No. 2 Varsovia Quartet
(+ Lutoslawski: *String Quartet;* Szymanowski: *String Quartets
Nos. 1 & 2*)
Olympia OCD 328 [A] **F**

V *Polish Requiem* Haubold (sop), Wingrodska (mez), Terzakis
(ten), Smith (bs), North German & Bavarian Radio Chs, North
German RSO, Penderecki
DG 429 720-2, 2 CDs [D] **F**

St. Luke Passion von Osten (sop), Roberts (bar), Rydl (bs),
Lubaszenko (narr), Crakow Boys' Ch, Polish National PO &
Ch, Penderecki
Argo 430 328-2 [D] **F**

PERGOLESI, Giovanni (1710–1736) ITALY

V *Magnificat* Vaughan (sop), Baker (mez), Partridge (ten), Keyte
(bs), King's College Ch, ASMF, Willcocks
(+ Vivaldi: *Gloria, RV 589; Magnificat, RV611*)
Decca 425 724-2 (US: London 425 724-2) [A] **M**

Stabat Mater; *In coelestibus regnis; Salve regina in A min. Fisher
(sop), *Chance (bs), King's Consort, King
Hyperion CDA 66294 [D] **F**

PERSICHETTI, Vincent (1915–1987) USA

O *Divertimento for Band, Op. 42; Psalm for Band, Op. 53; Choral
Prelude: O God Unseen, Op. 160; Pageant, Op. 59; Masquerade for
Band , Op. 102; O Cool is the Valley, Op. 118; Parable for Band
(Poem for Band), Op. 121* LSO Winds, Amos
HM HMU90 7092 [D] **F**

PFITZNER, Hans (1869–1949) GERMANY

O *Das Käthchen von Heilbronn* (incidental music), *Op. 17: Overture;
Palestrina* (opera): *Preludes to Acts I–III; Die Rose vom
Liebesgarten* (opera): *Miracle of the Blossoms; Funeral March*
Bavarian RSO, Sawallisch
Orfeo C168881A [D] **F**

C *Piano Quintet in C, Op. 23; Clarinet and Piano Sextet in G min.,*
Op. 55 Consortium Classicum
Orfeo C281931A [D] **F**

V *18 Lieder* Fischer-Dieskau (bar), Höll (pno)
Orfeo C036821A [D] **F**

Von deutscher Seele (cantata) Giebel (sop), Topper (mez),
Wunderlich (ten), Wiener (bs), Bavarian RSO & Ch, Keilberth
(+ Schoeck: *Lebendig begraben*)
DG 437 033-2, 2 CDs [A] **M**

PHILIDOR, André (c. 1646–1730) FRANCE

O *Le Mariage de la Grosse Cathos* London Oboe Band, Petit
(perc), Goodwin(ob/dir)
(+Lully: *Le Bourgeois Gentilhomme*, etc.)
Harmonia Mundi HMU90 7122 [D] **F**

PHILIPS, Peter (1560/1–1628) ENGLAND

S *Almand (Tregian); Aria a 5; Aria del Gran Duca Ferdinando;*
Balla d'amore; Galliard (Coranto); Galliard a 5; Pavan
(Passamezzo); Pavan a 2; Pavan and Galliard; Pavan and
Galliard (Dolorosa); Pavan and Galliard (after Morley); Pavan
and Galliard (Paget); Pavan and Galliard (1580); Pavan and
Galliard in F Parley of Instruments
Hyperion CDA 66240 [D] **F**

16 Motets Winchester Cathedral Ch, Parley of Instruments, Hill
Hyperion CDA 66643 [D] **F**

PIERNÉ, Gabriel (1863–1937) FRANCE

O *Piano Concerto in C min., Op. 42; Ramuntcho* (ballet): *Suites Nos.*
1 & 2 Aschatz (pno), Lorraine PO, Houtmann
BIS BIS-CD 381 [D] **F**

Cydalise et le Chèvre-pied; Ramuntcho (complete) Paris National
Opéra O, Mari
EMI CDM7 64278-2 (US: CDM 64278) [A] **M**

PISTON, Walter (1894–1976) USA

O **Incredible Flutist: Suite; **Fantasy for English Horn, Harp &*
Strings ; Concerto for String Quartet, Wind Instruments and
Percussion; ***Psalm and Prayer of David *Goff (fl),
**Danielson (Eng hn), **Wunrow (hp), Juilliard Quartet,
Seattle Symphony & ***Chorale, Schwarz
Delos DE 3126 [D] **F**

Symphony No. 4; *Capriccio for Harp and Strings; Three New
England Sketches; **Serenata *Wunrow (hp), Seattle SO,
**New York Chamber SO, Schwarz
Delos DE 3106 [D] **F**

Symphonies Nos. *5, 7 & 8 Louisville O, *Whitney, Mester
Albany AR 011 [A] **F**

Symphony No. 6; The Incredible Flutist (ballet): *Suite; Three New*
England Sketches St. Louis SO, Slatkin
RCA RD 60798 (US: 60798-2) [D] **F**

PIZZETTI, Ildebrando (1880–1968) ITALY

V *Messe di requiem; 3 Composizione corali; 2 Composizione corali*
Danish National Radio Chamber Ch, Parkman
Chandos CHAN 8964 [D] **F**

PONCE, Manuel (1882–1948) MEXICO

S *Mazurkas Nos. 1–7 & 19; 9 Piano Pieces* Osorio (pno)
ASV CDDCA 874 [D] **F**

POTTER, Cipriani (1792–1871) ENGLAND

O *Symphonies: No. 8 in E♭; No. 10 in G min.* Milton Keynes CO,
Wetton
Unicorn-Kanchana DKPCD 9091 [D] **F**

POULENC, Francis (1899–1963) FRANCE

O *Les animaux modèles* (ballet music); *Les Biches* (ballet); *Concert
champêtre; Double Piano Concerto; 2 Marches et un intermède; Les
mariés de la tour Eiffel* (ballet): *La baigneuse de Trouville;
Discourse du Génal; Matelote provençale; Pastourelle; Sinfonietta;
Suite française* Various artists, Paris Conservatoire O,
Philharmonia O, Paris O, Cluytens
EMI CZS7 62690-2 (US: CDMB 62690), 2 CDs [D/A] **B**

Aubade; Sinfonietta Evans (pno), New London O, Corp
(+ Hahn: *Le bal de Béatrice d'Este: Suite*)
Hyperion CDA 66347 [D] **F**

Les Biches (ballet) Ulster O, Tortelier
(+ Milhaud: *Le Boeuf sur le toit*, etc.; Ibert: *Divertissement*)
Chandos CHAN 9023 [D] **M**

Organ Concerto; Piano Concerto; Double Piano Concerto Hurford
(org), Rogé (pno), Deferne (pno), Philharmonia O, Dutoit
Decca 436 546-2 (US: London 436 546-2) [D] **F**

*Double Piano Concerto; Capriccio; Élégie; Embarquement pour
Cythère; Sonata for 4 hands* K. & M. Labèque (pno duo/2 pnos)
(+ Milhaud: *Scaramouche*)
Philips 426 284-2 [D] **F**

C *Sextuor; Trio; Clarinet Sonata; Flute Sonata; Oboe Sonata*
Various artists, Rogé (pno)
Decca 421 581-2 (US: London 421 581-2) [D] **F**

S *Humoresque; Improvisations Nos. 4, 5, 9–11 & 14; 3 Intermezzi;
8 Nocturnes; Presto in B♭; Suite in C; Thème varié; Villageoises*
Rogé (pno)
Decca 425 862-2 (US: London 425 862-2) [D] **F**

*Improvisations Nos. 1–3, 6–8, 12, 13 & 15; 3 Mouvements
perpétuels; 2 Novelettes; Novelette sur un thème de Falla in E min.;
Pastourelle; 3 Pièces; Les soirées de Nazelles; Valse* Rogé (pno)
Decca 417 438-2 (US: London 417 438-2) [D] **F**

V *Ave verum corpus; Exultate deo; Laudes de Saint Antoine de
Padoue; Mass in G; 4 Motets pour le temps de Noël; 4 Motets pour
un temps de pénitence; 4 Petites prières de Saint François d'Assise;
Salve regina* Trinity College Ch, Marlow
Conifer CDCF 151 [D] **F**

Gloria; Litanies à la Vierge; Stabat mater Dubosc (sop),
Westminster Singers, City of London Sinfonia, Hickox
Virgin VC7 59286-2 (US: CDC 59286) [D] **F**

*Mass in G; Quatre Motets I & II; Litanies; Quatre Petites Prières;
Exultate Deo; Salve Regina*
Westminster Cathedral Ch, O'Donnell
Hyperion CDA 66664 [D] **F**

39 Melodies Dubosc (sop), Cachemille (bar), Rogé (pno)
Decca 436 991-2 (US: London 436 991-2) [D] **F**

PRAETORIUS, Michael (c.1571–1621) GERMANY

✔ *Magnificat; Aus tiefer Not; Peccavi fateor; Psalms of David: CXVI; Der Tag vertreibt die finster Nacht; Venite exultemus Domino* Huelgas Ensemble, van Nevel
Sony CD 48039 [D]

Terpsichore (excerpts); *Allein Gott in der Höh; Aus tiefer Not; Christus, der uns selig macht; Erhalt uns, Herr; Gott der Vater; Resonet in laudibus* Boys of the Cathedral & Abbey Church, St. Albans, Early Music Consort of London, Munrow
EMI CDM7 69024-2 (US: CDM 69024) [A] **M**

Terpsichore: Nos. 1, 283–5 & 310; Musae Sioniae VI, No. 53: Es ist ein Ros' entsprungen; Polyhymnia caduceatrix et panegyrica Nos. 9–10, 12 & 17; Puericinium Nos. 2, 4 & 5 Westminster Cathedral Ch, Parley of Instruments, Hill
Hyperion CDA 66200 [D] **F**

PRIMAVERA, Giovanni (c.1540/45–after 1585) ITALY

✔ *Nasce la gioia mia* Tallis Scholars, Phillips
(+ Palestrina: *Missa brevis; Missa Nasce la gioia mia*)
Gimell CDGIM 008 [D] **F**

PROKOFIEV, Sergey (1891–1953) RUSSIA

❍ *Boris Godunov* (incidental music), *Op. 70b: Fountain Scene; Polonaise; Dreams* (symphonic tableau), *Op. 6; Eugene Onegin* (incidental music), *Op. 71: Minuet; Polka; Mazurka; 2 Pushkin Waltzes, Op. 120; Romeo and Juliet* (ballet): *Suite No. 2, Op. 64c* SNO, Järvi
Chandos CHAN 8472 [D] **F**

Cinderella (ballet), *Op. 87* Cleveland O, Ashkenazy
Decca 410 162-2 (US: London 410 162-2), 2 CDs [D] **F**

Piano Concertos Nos. 1–5; Overture on Hebrew Themes, Op. 34; Visions fugitives, Op. 22 Beroff (pno), LGO, Masur
EMI CMS7 62542-2 (US: CDZB 62542), 2 CDs [A] **M**

Piano Concertos: No. 1 in Db, Op. 10; No. 3 in C, Op. 26 Kissin (pno), BPO, Abbado
DG 439 898-2 [D] **F**

Piano Concerto No. 1 in Db, Op. 10; Suggestion diabolique Op. 4/4 Gavrilov (pno), LSO, Rattle
(+ Balakirev: *Islamey;* Tchaikovsky: *Piano Concerto No.1*, etc.)
EMI CDM7 64329-2 (US: CDM 64329) [A] **F**

Piano Concertos: No. 2 in G min., Op. 16; No. 3 in C, Op. 26 Gutierrez (pno), Royal Concertgebouw O, Järvi
Chandos CHAN 8889 [D] **F**

Piano Concerto No. 3 in C, Op. 26 Janis (pno), Moscow PO, Kondrashin
(+Rachmaninov: *Piano Concerto No. 1*; solo piano works by Prokofiev, Schumann, Mendelssohn & Pinto)
Philips Mercury 434 333-2 [A] **M**

Piano Concerto No. 4, Op. 53 Fleisher (pno), Boston SO, Ozawa
(+ Britten: *Diversions;* Ravel: *Piano Concerto for the Left Hand*)
Sony CD 47188 [D] **F**

Piano Concerto No. 5 in G min., Op. 55 Richter (pno), Warsaw National PO, Wislocki
(+ Rachmaninov: *Piano Concerto No. 2*)
DG 415 119-2 [A] **F**

○ *Violin Concertos: No. 1 in D, Op. 19; No. 2 in G min., Op. 63* Lin (vln), LAPO, Salonen
(+Stravinsky: *Violin Concerto*)
Sony CD 53969 [D] **F**

Violin Concerto No. 1 in D, Op. 19
EDITORS' CHOICE: Vengarov (vln), LSO, Rostropovich
(+Shostakovich: *Violin Concerto No. 1*)
Teldec 4509 98143-2 [D] **F**

Violin Concerto No. 2 in G min., Op. 63 Heifetz (vln), Boston SO, Munch
(+ Glazunov: *Violin Concerto;* Sibelius: *Violin Concerto*)
RCA RD 87019 (US: RCDI 7019) [A] **F**

The Gambler (opera), *Op. 49: 4 Portraits and Dénouement; Semyon Kotko* (symphonic suite), *Op. 81b* SNO, Järvi
Chandos CHAN 8803 [D] **F**

Lieutenant Kijé Suite, Op. 60 Cleveland O, Szell
(+ Kodály: *Háry János Suite;* Mussorgsky: *Pictures at an Exhibition*)
Sony CD 48162 [A] **B**

Lieutenant Kijé Suite, Op. 60; *Alexander Nevsky (cantata), *Op. 78*
*Elias (mez), CSO & *Ch, Reiner
(+ Glinka: *Ruslan and Lyudmila Overture*)
RCA GD60176 (US: 60176-2) [A] **M**

Peter and the Wolf, Op. 67 Gielgud (narr), Academy of London, Stamp
(+Saint-Saëns: *Carnival of the Animals*)
Virgin CUV5 61137-2 (US: 61137) [D] **F**

Prodigal Son (ballet), *Op. 46; Andante, Op. 29b; Divertissement, Op. 43; Symphonic Song, Op. 57* SNO, Järvi
Chandos CHAN 8728 [D] **F**

Romeo and Juliet (ballet), *Op. 64* Cleveland O, Maazel
Decca 417 510-2 (US: London 417 510-2), 2 CDs [A] **F**

Romeo and Juliet, Op. 64 (highlights) Royal Concertgebouw O, M-W Chung
DG 439 870-2 [D] **F**

Symphonies Nos. 1–7; Russian Overture, Op. 72; Scythian Suite, Op. 20 LSO, LPO, Weller
Decca 430 782-2 (US: London 430 782-2), 4 CDs [A] **M**

Symphonies: No. 1 in D, Op. 25 (Classical); No. 7 in C♯ min., Op. 131; Love of Three Oranges (opera): *Suite* Philharmonia O, Malko
Classics for Pleasure CD-CFP 4523 [A] **B**

Symphony No. 1 in D, Op. 25 (Classical) ASMF, Marriner
(+ Bizet: *Symphony in C;* Stravinsky: *Pulcinella Suite*)
Decca 417 734-2 (US: London 417 734-2) [A] **M**

Symphony No. 2 in D min., Op. 40; Romeo and Juliet (ballet): *Suite No. 1, Op. 64b* SNO, Järvi
Chandos CHAN 8368 [D] **F**

Symphonies: No. 3 in C min., Op. 44; No. 4 in C, Op. 112 (revised version) Moscow SO, Kitaenko
Olympia OCD 260 [D] **F**

O *Symphonies: No. 5 in B♭, Op. 100; No. 1 in D, Op. 25 (Classical)*
BPO, Karajan
DG 437 253-2 [A] M

 *Symphony No. 6 in E♭, Op. 111; Waltz Suite, Op. 110: Nos. 1, 5
& 6* SNO, Järvi
Chandos CHAN 8359 [D] F

C *Cello Sonata in C, Op. 119* Harrell (vcl), Ashkenazy (pno)
(+ Shostakovich: *Moderato; Cello Sonata*)
Decca 421 774-2 (US: London 421 774-2) [D] F

 String Quartets: No. 1 in B min., Op. 50; No. 2 in F, Op. 92
American Quartet
Olympia OCD 340 [D] F

 *Violin Sonatas: No. 1 in F min., Op. 80; No. 2 in D, Op. 94a;
5 Melodies, Op. 35b* Kremer (vln), Argerich (pno)
DG 431 803-2 [D] F

S *Piano Sonatas Nos. 1–9; 3 Pieces, Op. 59 Nos. 2 & 3; 2 Sonatinas,
Op. 54; Visions fugitives, Op. 22* Lill (pno)
ASV CDDCS 314, 3 CDs [D] F

 Piano Sonatas Nos. 1, 4, 5 & 10 McLachlan (pno)
Olympia OCD 255 [D] F

 *Piano Sonatas: No. 1 in F min., Op. 1; No. 4 in C min., Op. 29;
No. 6 in A, Op. 82* Bronfman (pno)
Sony CD 52484 [D] F

 *Piano Sonata No. 3 in A min., Op. 28; 10 Pieces, Op. 12; 3 Pieces
from 'Cinderella', Op. 95; Thoughts, Op. 62* Berman (pno)
Chandos CHAN 9069 [D] F

 *Piano Sonata No. 4 in C min., Op. 29; Music for Children, Op. 65;
6 Pieces, Op. 52* Berman (pno)
Chandos CHAN 8926 [D] F

 *Piano Sonata No. 5 in C, Op. 38 (rev. Op. 135); 10 Pieces from
'Romeo and Juliet', Op. 75; 4 Pieces, Op. 32; Love of Three Oranges
(opera): March and Scherzo (arr.)* Berman (pno)
Chandos CHAN 8851 [D] F

 Piano Sonatas Nos. 6–8 Donohoe (pno)
EMI CDC7 54281-2 (US: Angel CDC 54281) [D] F

 Piano Sonata No. 7 in B♭, Op. 83 Pollini (pno)
(+ Boulez: *Piano Sonata No. 2;* Stravinsky: *3 Movements from
Petrushka;* Webern: *Variations*)
DG 447 431-2 [A] M

 *Piano Sonata No. 9 in C, Op. 103; Chose en soi, Op. 45 (A & B);
Divertissement, Op. 43b; Studies, Op. 2* Berman (pno)
Chandos CHAN 9211 [D] F

 Visions fugitives, Op. 22 Demidenko (pno)
(+ Scriabin: *Piano works*)
Conifer CDCF 204 [D] F

V *5 Akhmatova Poems, Op. 27; 2 Poems, Op. 9; 5 Poems, Op. 36;
3 Romances, Op. 73* Farley (sop), Aronov (pno)
Chandos CHAN 8509 [D] F

 *Alexander Nevsky; Lieutenant Kijé: Suite; Scythian Suite
*Obraztsova (mez), *LSO, Chicago SO, Abbado
DG 447 419-2 [A] M

V *Alexander Nevsky* (cantata), *Op. 78* Reynolds (mez), LSO &
Ch, Previn
(+ Rachmaninov: *The Bells*)
EMI CDM7 63114-2 (US: CDM 63114) [A] **M**

*Cantata for the 20th Anniversary of the October Revolution; The
Stone Flower: Excerpts* Rozhdestvensky (narr), Philharmonia
O & Ch, Järvi
Chandos CHAN 9095 [D] **F**

*3 Children's Songs, Op. 68; 5 Poems, Op. 23; 12 Russian Folksongs,
Op. 104: Nos. 1 & 2; 5 Songs without Words, Op. 35; The Ugly
Duckling, Op. 18* Farley (sop), Vignoles (pno)
ASV CDDCA 669 [D] **F**

Ivan the Terrible (ed. Palmer) Finnie (cont), Storojev (bs-bar),
Philharmonia O & Chorus, Järvi
Chandos CHAN 8977 [D] **F**

PUCCINI, Giacomo (1858–1924) ITALY

O *Complete Orchestral Works* Berlin RSO, Chailly
Decca 444 154-2 (US: London 444 154-2) [D] **M**

C *Crisantemi; 3 Minuets; Scherzo in A min.; String Quartet in D;
*Foglio d'album; *Piccolo tango; **Avanti! Urania!; **E
l'uccellino; **Inno a Diana; **Menti all'avviso; **Morire?;
**Salve del ciel regina; **Sole e amore; **Storiella d'amore;
**Terra e mare* Raphael Quartet, *Crone (pno), **Alexander
(sop), Crone (pno)
Etcetera KTC 1050 [D] **F**

V *Messa di Gloria* Carreras (ten), Prey (bar), Ambrosian Singers,
Philharmonia O, Scimone
Erato 2292 45197-2 [D] **F**

PURCELL, Henry (1659–1695) ENGLAND

O *Excerpts from 45 stage works; Chaconne in G min.; Overture in D
min.; Overture in G min.; Pavan in G min.; 4 Pavans; Trio sonata
in G min.* Various artists, Taverner Ch, AAM, Hogwood
◇ L'Oiseau-Lyre 425 893-2, 6 CDs [A] **M**

C *Chaconne in G min.; Fantasia upon a Ground; 4 Pavans: Nos. 1 &
4; 10 Sonatas: Nos. 1 & 2; 12 Sonatas: Nos. 8–12* Purcell
Quartet
◇ Chandos CHAN 8663 [D] **F**

*12 Fantazias in 3 & 4 Parts; Fantazia in A min.; Fantazia 'upon
one note'; In nomine in 6 Parts; In nomine in 7 Parts* Fretwork
◇ Virgin VC5 45062-2 (US: 45062) [D] **F**

Complete Sonatas in 3 & 4 Parts; Complete Pavans Purcell
Quartet
◇ Chandos CHAN 0572-3, 2 CDs [D] **F**

S *Harpsichord Suites Nos. 1–8; A New Ground; Hornpipe* Gilbert
(hpd)
Harmonia Mundi HMC 90146 [D] **F**

*The Purcell Manuscript: Suite in A min.; 12 miscellaneous pieces;
Suite in C* Moroney (virg/hpd)
(+pieces by Gibbons & Draghi)
Virgin VC5 45166-2 (US: 45166) [D] **F**

V *March and Canzona in C min.; Come ye sons of art, away; Funeral
Music for Queen Mary* Lott (sop), Brett (alt), Williams (alt),

Allen (bar), Equale Brass, Monteverdi O & Ch, Gardiner
✧ Erato 2292 45123-2 [A] **F**

V *Complete Odes and Welcome Songs* Various artists, Ch of New
College Oxford, King's Consort, King
✧ Hyperion CDS 44031/8, 8 CDs [D] **M**

*Arise, my muse (Ode for the birthday of Queen Mary); Now does the
glorious day appear (Ode for the birthday of Queen Mary); Welcome
to all the pleasures (Ode for St. Cecilia's Day)* Fisher (sop),
Bonner (sop), Bowman (alt), Chance (alt), Daniels (ten),
Ainsley (ten), George (bs), Pott (bs), King's Consort, King
✧ Hyperion CDA 66314 [D] **F**

The Complete Anthems & Services Various artists, King's Consort,
King
✧ CDA 66585, 66609, 66623, 66644, 66656, 66663, 66677,
66686, 66693, 66707 & 66716, 11 separate CDs [D] **F**

Anthems: *Blow up the trumpet in Sion; Hear my prayer, O Lord;
I will sing unto the Lord; Jubilate in D; Lord, how long wilt thou be
angry; O God, Thou art my God; O God, Thou hast cast us out;
O Lord God of Hosts; Remember not, Lord, our offences; Save me,
O God; Morning Service; Coronation Music for King James II;
Funeral Music for Queen Mary* Jackson (org), Trinity College
Ch, Marlow
Conifer CDCF 152 [D] **F**

*Celebrate this Festival (Ode for the birthday of Queen Mary); Fly,
bold rebellion (Welcome ode for King Charles II); Sound the Trumpet
(Welcome ode for King James II)* Fisher (sop), Bonner (sop),
Bowman (alt), Kenny (alt), Covey-Crump (ten), Muller (ten),
George (bs), Pott (bs), King's Consort, King
✧ Hyperion CDA 66412 [D] **F**

*Celestial music did the gods inspire (ode); From hardy climes and
desperate toils of war (Welcome song); Ye Tuneful Muses (Welcome
ode for King James II)* Fisher (sop), Bonner (sop), Bowman
(alt), Daniels (alt), Covey-Crump (ten), George (bs), Pott (bs),
King's Consort, King
✧ Hyperion CDA 66456 [D] **F**

*Great Parent Hail (Welcome song); Summer's Abscence unconcerned
we bear (Welcome song for King Charles II); Welcome, welcome,
glorious morn (Welcome song for the birthday of Queen Mary)*
Fisher (sop), Tubb (sop), Bowman (alt), Short (alt), Covey-
Crump (ten), Ainsley (ten), George (bs), Pott (bs), King's
Consort, King
✧ Hyperion CDA 66476 [D] **F**

*Hail Bright Cecilia (Ode for St. Cecilia's Day); Who can from Joy
refrain? (Ode for the birthday of the Duke of Gloucester)* Fisher
(sop), Bowman (alt), Covey-Crump (ten), Ainsley (ten),
George (bs), Keenlyside (trb), New College Ch, King's
Consort, King
✧ Hyperion CDA 66349 [D] **F**

My heart is inditing (verse anthem), *Z30; O Sing Unto the Lord*
(verse anthem) *Praise the Lord, O Jerusalem* (verse anthem),
Z46; They that go down to the sea in Ships (verse anthem), *Z57;
Te Deum and Jubilate Deo in D* Christ Church Cathedral Ch,
English Concert, Pinnock
✧ DG Archiv 427 124-2 [A] **M**

Secular Solo Songs Bonney (sop), Gritton (sop), Bowman (c-ten), Covey-Crump (ten), Daniles (ten), George (bs), Caudle (bs viol), Miller (archlute, theorbo), King (chbr org, hpd)
Volume 1
✧ Hyperion CDA 66710 [D] **F**
Volume 2
✧ Hyperion CDA 66720 [D] **F**
Volume 3
✧ Hyperion CDA 66730 [D] **F**

QUILTER, Roger (1877–1953) ENGLAND

V *Arab love song; At close of day; 7 Elizabethan Lyrics; Go, lovely rose; I arise from dreams of thee; In the bud of the morning-o; Love's philosophy; Music when soft voices die; Now sleeps the crimson petal; 3 Shakespeare Songs, Op. 6; 4 Songs, Op. 14; 3 Songs of William Blake, Op. 20; To Julia: 6 Songs, Op. 8* Luxon (bar), Willison (pno)
Chandos CHAN 8782 [D] **F**

RACHMANINOV, Sergey (1873–1943) RUSSIA/USA

O *Concerto Élégiaque* (orch. of Piano Trio No. 2); *Corelli Variations* (orch.); *Vocalise* Detroit SO, Järvi
Chandos CHAN 9261 [D] **F**

Piano Concertos Nos. 1–4
Collard (pno), Toulouse Capitole O, Plasson
EMI CZS7 67419-2 (US: CDMB 67419), 2 CDs [A] **B**

Piano Concertos: No. 1 in F♯ min., Op. 1; No. 4 in G min., Op. 40; Rhapsody on a Theme of Paganini, Op. 43 Wild (pno), RPO, Horenstein
Chesky CD 41 [A] **F**

Piano Concerto No. 1 in F♯ min., Op. 1; Rhapsody on a Theme of Paganini, Op. 43 Pletnev (pno), Philharmonia O, Pesek
Virgin VC7 59506-2 (US: 59506) [D] **F**

Piano Concerto No.1 in F# min., Op.1 Janis (pno), Moscow PO, Kondrashin
(+Prokoviev: *Piano Concerto No. 3*; solo piano works by Prokofiev, Schumann, Mendelssohn & Pinto)
Philips Mercury 434 333-2 [A] **M**

Piano Concerto No. 2 in C min., Op. 18 Richter (pno), Warsaw National PO, Wislocki
(+ Prokofiev: *Piano Concerto No. 5*)
DG 415 119-2 [A] **F**

*Piano Concertos: No. 2 in C min., Op. 18; *No. 3 in D min., Op. 30; Preludes: Op. 3/2 in C♯ min.; Op. 23/6 in E♭* Janis (pno), Minneapolis SO, *LSO, Dorati
Philips Mercury 432 759-2 [A] **M**

Piano Concerto No. 3 in D min., Op. 30 Horowitz (pno), NYPO, Ormandy
RCA 09026 61564-2 [A] **F**

Piano Concerto No. 4 in G min., Op. 40 Michelangeli (pno), Philharmonia O, Gracis
(+ Ravel: *Piano Concerto in G*)
EMI CDC7 49326-2 (US: Angel CDC 49326) [A] **F**

*Piano Concerto No. 4 in G min., Op. 40 (original version); *Monna Vanna* (opera) *Black (pno), Walker (sop), McCoy

(ten), Thorsteinsson (ten), Milnes (bar), Karousatos (bar),
Iceland, Opera Ch, Iceland SO, Buketoff
Chandos CHAN 8987 [D] **F**

O *Rhapsody on a Theme of Paganini, Op. 43; *Piano Concerto No. 3
in D min., Op. 30* Pennario, Boston Pops O, Fiedler;
*Ashkenazy (pno), Philadelphia O, Ormandy
RCA GD 86524 (US: 6524-2) [A] **M**

The Rock (fantasy), *Op. 7* LSO, Previn
(+ Shostakovich: *Symphony No. 5*)
RCA GD 86801 (US: 6801-2) [A] **M**

Symphonies Nos. 1–3
Philadelphia O, Ormandy
(+ *Vocalise, Op. 34/14*)
Sony/CBS CD 45678, 2 CDs [A] **M**
LSO, Previn
(+ *Isle of the Dead; Symphonic Dances; Aleko: excerpts; Vocalise*)
EMI CMS7 64530-2 (US: ZDMC 64530), 3 CDs [A] **M**

Symphony No. 1 in D min., Op. 13; Isle of the Dead, Op. 29
Concertgebouw O, Ashkenazy
Decca 436 479-2 (US: London 436 479-2) [D] **M**

Symphony No. 2 in E min., Op. 27; Vocalise, Op. 34/14 Baltimore
SO, Zinman
Telarc CD 80312 [D] **F**

Symphony No. 3 in A min., Op. 44; Symphonic Dances, Op. 45
Baltimore SO, Zinman
Telarc CD 80331 [D] **F**

Symphony No. 3 in A min., Op. 44 LSO, Previn
(+ Shostakovich: *Symphony No. 6*)
EMI CDM7 69564-2 (US: Angel CDM 69564) [A] **M**

C *6 Morceaux, Op. 11; 2 Pieces; Polka italienne; Romance in G;
Russian Rhapsody; Suites Nos. 1 & 2; Symphonic Dances* Engerer
(pno), Maisenberg (pno)
HM HMC90 1301/2, 2 CDs [D] **F**

*Cello Sonata in G min.; Prelude, Op. 2/1; Oriental Dance, Op. 2/2;
Romance; Vocalise, Op. 34/14* Harrell (vcl), Ashkenazy (pno)
(+Altschuler: *Melodie on a Theme by Rachmaninov*)
Decca 414 340-2 (US: London 414 340-2) [D] **F**

*Suites for 2 Pianos: *No. 1, Op. 5; *No. 2, Op. 17; Études-
Tableaux, Op. 33* Ashkenazy (pno), *Previn (pno)
Decca 425 029-2 (US: London 425 029-2) [A] **M**

Trios élégiaques: No. 1 in G min.; No.2 in D min., Borodin Trio
Chandos CHAN 8341 [D] **F**

S *Complete transcriptions* Shelley (pno)
Hyperion CDA 66486 [D] **F**

Complete Solo Piano Music Shelley (pno)
Hyperion CDS 44041/8, 8 CDs [D/A] **M**

Études-Tableaux, Opp. 33 & 39 Fergus-Thompson (pno)
ASV CDDCA 789 [D] **F**

9 Études-Tableaux from Opp. 33/39; 13 Preludes from Opp. 23/32
Richter (pno)
Olympia OCD 337 [A/D] **F**

s *Fragments in Ab; Fughetta in F; 4 Pieces; Morceaux de Fantaisie in G min.; 3 Nocturnes; Oriental Sketch in Bb; Piece in D min.; Piano Sonata No. 2 (original version); Song without Words in D min.* Shelley (pno)
Hyperion CDA 66198 [D] **F**

6 Moments Musicaux, Op. 16; 7 Morceaux de Salon, Op. 10 Shelley (pno)
Hyperion CDA 66184 [D] **F**

24 Preludes, Opp. 23 & 32; Piano Sonata No. 2 in Bb min., Op. 36 Ashkenazy (pno)
Decca 443 841-2 (US: London 443 841-2), 2 CDs [A/D] **B**

24 Preludes, Opp. 23 & 32; Prelude in F; Prelude in D min.; 5 Morceaux de Fantaisie, Op. 3 Shelley (pno)
Hyperion CDA 66081/2, 2 separate CDs [D] **F**

Piano Sonatas: No. 1 in D min., Op. 28; No. 2 in Bb min. (original version), Op. 36 Fergus-Thompson (pno)
Kingdom KCLCD 2007 [D] **F**

Variations on a Theme of Chopin, Op. 22; Variations on a Theme of Corelli, Op. 42; Mélodie in E, Op. 3/3 (revised version); Scherzo from 'A Midsummer Night's Dream' (Mendelssohn) Shelley (pno)
Hyperion CDA 66009 [A] **F**

Piano Recital Rachmaninov (pno rolls)
Decca 440 066-2 (US: London 440 066-2) [A] **M**

v *The Bells* (choral symphony), *Op. 35* Armstrong (sop), Tear (ten), Shirley-Quirk (bar), LSO & Ch, Previn
(+ Prokofiev: *Alexander Nevsky*)
EMI CDM7 63114-2 (US: CDM 63114) [A] **M**

The Complete Songs Söderström (sop), Ashkenazy (pno)
Decca 436 920-2 (US: London 436 920-2), 3 CDs [A] **M**

Liturgy of St John Chrysostom, Op. 31 Corydon Singers, Best
Hyperion CDA 66703 [D] **F**

Songs: Op. 4 Nos. 1, 3 & 4; Op. 8 No. 5; Op. 14 No. 9; Op. 21 No. 6; Op. 26 Nos. 2, 6 & 13 Hvorostovsky (bar), Boshniakovich (pno)
(+ Tchaikovsky: *Songs*)
Philips 432 119-2 [D] **F**

Vespers (All-night Vigil), Op. 37 Corydon Singers, Best
Hyperion CDA 66460 [D] **F**

RAFF, Joachim (1822–1882) GERMANY

o *Symphonies: No. 3 in F (Im Walde), Op. 153; No. 4 in G min., Op. 167* Milton Keynes City O, Wetton
Hyperion CDA 66628 [D] **F**

Symphony No. 5 in E (Leonore), Op. 177 LPO, Herrmann
Unicorn-Kanchana UKCD 2031 [A] **M**

RAMEAU, Jean-Philippe (1683–1764) FRANCE

o *Abaris (Les Boréades – tragédie lyrique): Suite; Dardanus (tragédie en musique): Suite* Eighteenth Century O, Brüggen
✧ **Philips 420 240-2** [D] **F**

Hippolyte et Aricie (tragédie en musique): Suite La Petite Bande, Kuijken
✧ **DHM GD77009 (US: Editio Classica 77009-2)** [A] **M**

Les Indes Galantes: Suite 18th Century O, Bruggen
✧ **Philips 438 946-2** [D] **F**

Complete Harpsichord Music
Gilbert (hpd)
DG Archiv 427 176-2, 2 CDs [A] M
Rousset (hpd)
L'Oiseau-Lyre 425 886-2, 2 CDs [D] F

Les Indes Galantes (trans. Rameau) Gilbert (hpd)
HM HMC90 1028 [A] F

Deus noster refugiam; In convertendo; Quam dilecta Daneman
(sop), Rime (sop), Agnew (cont), Rivenq (ten), Cavallier (bs),
Les Arts Florissants, Christie
✧ **Erato 4509 96967-2 [D] F**

In convertendo; Laboravi; Quam dilecta Gari (sop), Monbaliu
(sop), Ledroit (alto), de Mey (ten), Kooy (bs), Varcoe (bar),
Jansen (org), Ghent Collegium Vocale, Paris Chapelle Royale
O & Ch, Herreweghe
✧ **HM HMC90 1078 [A] F**

RAVEL, Maurice (1875–1937) FRANCE

Complete Orchestral Music Various artists, Montreal SO, Dutoit
Decca 421 458-2 (US: London 421 458-2), 4 CDs [D] M

*Alborada del gracioso; Une Barque sur l'Océan; Boléro; Ma mère
l'oye; Rapsodie espagnole* BPO, Boulez
DG 439 859-2 [D] F

*Alborada del gracioso; L'éventail de Jeanne: Fanfare; Ma mère
l'oye; *Shéhérazade; La vallée des cloches; La valse* *Ewing (sop),
CBSO, Rattle
EMI CDC7 54204-2 (US: Angel CDC 54204) [D] M

*Alborada del gracioso; Pavane pour une infante défunte; Rapsodie
espagnole* CSO, Reiner
(+ Debussy: *Images: Iberia*)
RCA GD 60179 (US: 60179-2) [A] M

Boléro; Daphnis et Chloé: Suite No. 2 BPO, Karajan
(+ Debussy: *La Mer; Prélude à l'après-midi d'un faune*)
DG 427 250-2 [A] M

*Boléro; L'éventail de Jeanne: Fanfare; Ma mère l'oye; Pièce en forme
de habañera; Rapsodie espagnole* LSO, Tilson Thomas
Sony CD 44800 [D] F

Boléro; Rapsodie espagnole; La Valse Boston SO, Munch
(+Debussy: *Images*)
RCA 09026 61956 2 [A] M

Piano Concerto in G Michelangeli (pno), Philharmonia O,
Gracis
(+ Rachmaninov: *Piano Concerto No. 4*)
EMI CDC7 49326-2 (US: Angel CDC 49326) [A] F

*Piano Concerto in G; Piano Concerto for the Left Hand; Une Barque
sur l'océan; L'Éventail de Jeanne: Fanfare; Menuet antique* Rogé
(pno), Montreal SO, Dutoit
Decca 410 230-2 (US: London 410 230-2) [D] F

**Piano Concerto in G; Gaspard de la nuit; **Ma mere l'oye*
Argerich (pno), *BPO, Abbado; **Kontarsky Brothers (pno
duet)
DG 439 450-2 [A] B

Piano Concerto for the Left Hand Fleisher (pno), Boston SO,
Ozawa

(+ Britten: *Diversions;* Prokofiev: *Piano Concerto No. 4*)
Sony CD 47188 [D] **F**

O *Daphnis et Chloé* (ballet) Montreal SO, Dutoit
Decca 400 055-2 (US: London 400 055-2) [D] **F**

Ma mère l'oye Ulster O, Tortelier
(+ Debussy: *La Boîte à Joujoux*)
Chandos CHAN 8711 [D] **F**

Le Tombeau de Couperin; Valses nobles et sentimentales Ulster O,
Tortelier
(+ Debussy: *Petite Suite*, etc.)
Chandos CHAN 8756 [D] **F**

Tzigane Perlman (vln), Paris O, Martinon
(+ Chausson: *Poème;* Saint-Saëns: *Havanaise; Introduction and
rondo capriccioso*)
EMI CDC7 47725-2 (US: Angel CDC 47725) [A] **F**

C *Berceuse sur le nom de Fauré; Piano Trio; Violin Sonata (1928);
Violin and Cello Sonata* Kantorow (vln), Muller (vcl),
Rouvier (pno)
Erato 2292 45920-2 [A] **F**

*Boléro; Introduction and Allegro; Ma mère l'oye; Rapsodie
espagnole; La Valse* Lortie (pno), Mercier (pno)
Chandos CHAN 8905 [D] **F**

Entre cloches; Frontispiece; Ma mère l'oye; Rapsodie espagnole
Alfons & Aloys Kontarsky (pno)
(+ Debussy: *Piano duet works*)
DG 427 259-2, 2 CDs [A] **M**

*Frontispiece; Introduction and Allegro; Rapsodie espagnole;
Shéhérazade (Ouverture de féerie); Sites auriculaires: Entre cloches;
La valse* Coombs (pno), Scott (pno)
Gamut GAMCD 517 [D] **F**

Rapsodie espagnole; Ma mere l'oye Argerich (pno), Freire (pno)
(+Bartok: *Sonata for 2 Pianos and Percussion*)
DG 439 867-2 [D] **F**

String Quartet in F
Britten Quartet
(+ Vaughan Williams: *String Quartet No. 1; On Wenlock Edge*)
EMI CDC7 54346-2 (US: Angel CDC 54346) [D] **F**
Carmina Quartet
(+ Debussy: *String Quartet*)
Denon CO-75164 [D] **F**

Violin Sonata (1827) Takezawa (vln), de Silva (pno)
(+ Debussy: *Violin Sonata;* Saint-Saëns: *Violin Sonata No. 1*)
RCA 09026 61386-2 [D] **F**

S *Complete Solo Piano Works* Thibaudet (pno)
Decca 433 515-2 (US: London 433 515-2), 2 CDs [D] **F**

*À la manière de Borodine; À la manière de Chabrier; Menuet
antique; Menuet sur le nom de Haydn; Prélude; Sonatine; Le
Tombeau de Couperin* Perlemuter (pno)
Nimbus NI 5011 [A] **F**

*À la manière de Borodine; À la manière de Chabrier; Menuet
antique; Menuet sur le nom de Haydn; Pavane pour une infante
défunte; Prelude; Sérénade grotesque; Sonatine*
Fergus-Thompson (pno)
ASV CDDCA 809 [D] **F**

Gaspard de la nuit; Jeux d'eau; Le Tombeau de Couperin; Valses nobles et sentimentales Fergus-Thompson (pno)
ASV CDDCA 805 [D] **F**

Histoires naturelles Stutzmann (cont), C. Collard (pno)
(+ Debussy: *Ariettes oubliées*, etc.)
RCA RD 60899 (US: 09026 60899-2) [D] **F**

*Trois Poèmes de Stéphane Mallarmé; **Chansons madécasses; ***Don Quichotte à Dulcinée; ***Cinq Mélodies populaires grecques *Gomez (sop), **Norman (sop), ***van Dam (bar), */***BBC SO, **Ensemble InterContemporain, Boulez
(+Roussel: *Symphony No. 3*)
Sony CD 64107 [A] **M**

RAWSTHORNE, Alan (1905–1971) ENGLAND

Piano Concertos Nos. 1 & 2; *Concerto for 2 Pianos Tozer (pno), *Cislowski (pno), LPO, Bamert
Chandos CHAN 9125 [D] **F**

REGER, Max (1873–1916) GERMANY

*2 Romanzen, Op. 50; Symphonische Prolog, Op. 108 *Maile (vln), Berlin RSO, Albrecht
Schwann 311076 [A] **F**

4 Symphonic Poems after Böcklin, Op. 128; Variations and Fugue on a Theme of Hiller, Op. 100 Concertgebouw O, Järvi
Chandos CHAN 8794 [D] **F**

Variations and Fugue on a Theme of Beethoven, Op. 86; Eine Ballettsuite, Op. 130; 4 Tone Pictures after Böcklin, Op. 128 Norrköping SO, Segerstam
BIS BIS-CD601 [D] **F**

Serenades for Flute Trio, Opp.77a & 141a; Suites for Solo Viola Nos. 1–3 Serenata of London (mbrs)
ASV CDDCA 875 [D] **F**

6 Burlesques, Op. 58; Introduction and Passacaglia; 12 Walzer-Capricen, Op. 9; Variations and Fugue, Op. 132a Tal (pno), Groethuysen (pno)
Sony CD 47671 [D] **F**

Preludes and Fugues for solo violin, Opp. 117 & 131a (complete)
Marinkovic (vln)
ASV CDDCA 876, 2 CDs [D] **F**

Aus Tiefer Not, Op. 67/3; Herr, wie du willst; Introduction, Passacaglia and Fugue in E min., Op. 127; Nun freut euch lieben Christen, Op. 67/28; Straf mich nicht in deinem Zorn, Op. 40/2; Vom Himmel hoch, Op. 67/40; Wer weiss, wie nahe, Op. 6/48 Barber (org)
Hyperion CDA 66223 [D] **F**

Aus Tiefer Not, Op. 67/3; Intermezzo in F min., Op. 129/7; Introduction and Passacaglia in D min., Op. Posth.; Prelude in D min., Op. 65/7 Kee (org)
(+ Hindemith: *Organ Sonatas Nos. 1–3*)
Chandos CHAN 9097 [D] **F**

3 Six-Part Choruses, Op. 39; 3 Five-Part Motets, Op. 110 Danish National Radio Ch., Parkman
Chandos CHAN 9298 [D] **F**

REICH, Steve (born 1936) USA

O *Six Pianos; Music for Mallet Instruments and Organ; *Variations for Winds, Strings and Keyboards* Steve Reich and Musicians; *San Francisco SO, de Waart
DG 439 431-2 [A] **B**

Variations SFSO, De Waart
(+ Adams: *Shaker Loops*)
Philips 412 214-2 [A] **F**

C *Music for 18 Musicians* Ensemble, Reich
ECM 821 417-2 [A] **F**

*Clapping Music; *Piano Phase; **Come out; **It's gonna Rain* Hartenberger, Reich; *Tiles (pno), *Nieman (pno); **Reich (pno)
Elektra-Nonesuch 7559 79169-2 (US: 79169-2) [D] **F**

*Different Trains; *Electric Counterpoint* Kronos Quartet; *Metheny (gtr)
Elektra-Nonesuch 7559 79176-2 (US: 79176-2) [D] **F**

6 Marimbas; Sextet Steve Reich & Musicians
Elektra-Nonesuch 7559 79138-2 (US: 79138-2) [D] **F**

Drumming Steve Reich & Musicians
Elektra-Nonesuch 7559 79170-2 (US: 79170-2) [D] **F**

Music for Mallet Instruments, Voices and Organ; Four Sections Steve Reich & Musicians
Elektra-Nonesuch 7559 79220-2 (US: 79220-2) [D] **F**

V *The Desert Music* Brooklyn PO & Ch, Tilson Thomas
Elektra-Nonesuch 7559 79101-2 (US: 79101-2) [D] **F**

*Tehillin for Voices and Ensemble; *Three Movements for Orchestra* Schonberg Ensemble, Percussion Group The Hague, de Leeuw; *LSO Tilson Thomas
Elektra-Nonesuch 7559 79295-2 (US: 79295-2) [D] **F**

REICHA, Antonín (1770–1836) BOHEMIA/FRANCE

C *String Quintets Nos. 1–3* L'Archibudelli
✧ Sony CD 53118 [D] **F**

Wind Quintet in B♭, Op. 88/5; Wind Quintet in A, Op. 91/5 Prague Academic Wind Quintet
Hyperion CDA 66379 [D] **F**

RESPIGHI, Ottorino (1879–1936) ITALY

O *Ancient Airs and Dances: Suites Nos. 1–3* Boston SO, Ozawa
DG 419 868-2 [A] **M**

*Belfagor Overture; *Fantasia Slava; *Toccata; Tre Corali* *Toze (pno), BBC PO, Downes
Chandos CHAN 9311 [D] **F**

Belkis, Queen of Sheba (ballet): *Suite; Metamorphosen modi XII* Philharmonia O, Simon
Chandos CHAN 8405 [D] **F**

*The Birds; 3 Botticelli Pictures; *Il Tramonto; **Adagio con variazioni* *Finnie (sop), **R. Wallfisch (vcl), Bournemouth Sinfonietta, Vasary
Chandos CHAN 8913 [D] **F**

◡ *La Boutique fantasque* (ballet) National PO, Bonynge
(+ Chopin: *Les Sylphides*)
Decca 430 723-2 (US: London 430 723-2) [D] **M**

Brazilian Impressions; Church Windows; Roman Festivals
Cincinnati SO, López-Cobos
Telarc CD-80356 [D] **F**

Piano Concerto; Concerto in modo misolidio Tozer (pno)
BBC PO, Downes
Chandos CHAN 9285 [d] **F**

*Concerto gregoriano; Poema autunnale; Ballata delle Gnomidi
*Mordkovitch (vln), BBC PO, Downes
Chandos CHAN 9232 [D] **F**

Fountains of Rome; Pines of Rome; Roman Festivals Montreal
SO, Dutoit
Decca 430 729-2 (US: London 430 729-2) [D] **M**

*Fountains of Rome; Pines of Rome; Ancient Airs and Dances: Suite
No. 3* BPO, Karajan
DG 413 822-2 [A] **F**

Sinfonia dramatica BBC PO, Downes
Chandos CHAN 9213 [D] **F**

◡ *Violin Sonata in B min.* Chung (vln), Zimerman (pno)
(+ R. Strauss: *Violin Sonata*)
DG 427 617-2 [D] **F**

*Aretusa; *Il Tramonto; Lauda per la Natività del Signore;
3 Botticelli Pictures* *Baker (mez), City of London Sinfonia,
Hickox
Collins 13492 [D] **F**

EUBKE, Julius (1834–1858) GERMANY

Sonata in B♭ min.; Sonata on the 94th Psalm Bowyer (org)
(+ Schumann: *6 Fugues*)
Nimbus NI 5361 [D] **F**

EVUELTAS, Silvestre (1899–1940) MEXICO

◡ *Caminos; Música para charlar; Ventanas* RPO, Bátiz
(+ Chavez: *Symphonies Nos. 1 & 4*)
ASV CDDCA 653 [D] **F**

*Homenaje a Federico García Lorca; Sensemaya; *Ocho X Radio;
*Toccata; *Alcancias; *Pianos; **La noche de los Mayas* NPO,
Mata; *London Sinfonietta, Atherton; **Jalapa SO, de la
Fuente
RCA 09026 62672-2 [D] **F**

HEINBERGER, Joseph (1839–1901) GERMANY

Organ Concerto No. 1 in F, Op. 137 Murray (org), RPO, Ling
(+ Dupré: *Organ Symphony, Op. 25*)
Telarc CD 80136 [D] **F**

ILEY, Terry (born 1935) USA

Salome Dances for Peace Kronos Quartet
Elektra-Nonesuch 7559 79217-2 (US: 79217-2), 2 CDs [D] **F**

IMSKY-KORSAKOV, Nikolay (1844–1908) RUSSIA

Capriccio espagnol, Op. 34; Golden Cockerel (opera): *Suite; Russian
Easter Festival Overture, Op. 36* LSO, Dorati

(+ Borodin: *Prince Igor: Polovtsian Dances*)
Philips Mercury 434 308-2 [A] **M**

O *Piano Concerto No. 1 in C♯ min., Op. 30* Binns (pno), English Northern PO, Lloyd-Jones
(+ Balakirev: *Piano Concertos Nos. 1 & 2*)
Hyperion CDA 66640 [D] **F**

Opera excerpts: *Christmas Eve; Le Coq d'or; Legend of the Invisible City of Kitezh; May Night; Mlada; The Snow Maiden; The Tale of Tsar Saltan* SNO, Järvi
Chandos CHAN 8327/9, 3 CDs [D] **F**

Scheherazade; Capriccio espagnol LSO, Mackerras
Telarc CD 80208 [D] **F**

Scheherazade (symphonic suite), *Op. 35* CSO, Reiner
(+ Debussy: *La Mer*)
RCA GD 60875 (US: 09026 60875-2) [A] **M**

Symphonies Nos. 1–3; Capriccio espagnol, Op. 34; Russian Easter Festival Overture, Op. 36 Gothenburg SO, Järvi
DG 423 604-2, 2 CDs [D] **F**

Symphonies: No. 1 in E min., Op. 1; No. 2, Op. 9 (Antar) Russian State SO, Svetlanov
RCA 09026 62558-2 [D] **F**

C *Capriccio espagnol, Op. 34; Neapolitan song, Op. 63; Scheherazade* (symphonic suite), *Op. 35* Goldstone, Clemmow (pno duo)
Gamut GAMCD 521 [D] **F**

Piano and Wind Quintet in B♭ Capricorn
(+ Glinka: *Grand Sextet in E♭*)
Hyperion CDA 66163 [A] **F**

RODRIGO, Joaquín (born 1902) Spain

O *Concierto Andaluz for 4 guitars; Concierto de Aranjuez; Concierto madrigal; Concierto para una fiesta; Fantasia para un gentilhombre; Bajando de la Meseta; En los trigales; Junto al Generalife; 3 Piezas españolas; Romance de Durandarte; Sonata a la española; Tiento antiguo; 3 Petites Pièces* P. Romero (gtr), Los Romeros (gtrs), ASMF, Marriner
Philips 432 581-2, 3 CDs [A] **M**

Concierto de Aranjuez
Bream (gtr), Melos Ensemble, C Davis
(+Arnold: *Guitar Concerto*; Bennett: *Guitar Concerto*)
RCA 09026 61598-2 [A] **M**
Bream (gtr), Monteverdi O, Gardiner
(+L. Berkeley: *Guitar Concerto*; Brouwer: *Guitar Concerto No. 3*)
RCA 09026 61605-2 [A] **M**

Concierto de Aranjuez; Fantasia para un gentilhombre; Canzoneta; Invocation et danse; Trois petites pièces P. Romero (gtr), ASMF, Marriner
Philips 438 016-2 [D] **F**

S *Cinco Piezas del Siglo XVI; Tres Evocaciones; Cuatro Piezas para Piano; Deux Berceuses; Cuatro Estampas Andaluzas; À l'ombre de Torre Bermeja* Pizzaro (pno)
Collins 14342 [D] **F**

ROSETTI, Antonio (1746–1792) BOHEMIA

O *Horn Concerto in E, K3: 42; Horn Concerto in E, K3: 44; Horn
Concerto in E♭, K3: 39* Tuckwell (hn/dir) ECO
Classics for Pleasure CD-CFP 4578 [D] **B**

ROSLAVETS, Nikolay (1881–1944) RUSSIA

C *Viola Sonata No. 1* Bashmet (vla), Muntian (pno)
(+ Glinka: *Viola Sonata;* Shostakovich: *Viola Sonata*)
RCA 09026 61273-2 [D] **F**

ROSSINI, Gioachino (1792–1868) ITALY

O *Introduction, Theme and Variations* Neidich (cl), Orpheus CO
(+ Weber: *Clarinet Concertino; Clarinet Concertos Nos. 1 & 2*)
DG 435 875-2 [D] **F**

Complete Overtures ASMF, Marriner
Philips 434 016-2, 3 CDs [A] **M**

Overtures: *Il barbiere di Siviglia; La gazza ladra; Guillaume Tell;
L'Italiana in Algeri; La scala di seta; Il signor Bruschino;
Semiramide* LCP, Norrington
◇ EMI CDC7 54091-2 (US: Angel CDC 54091) [D] **F**

Overtures: *Il barbiere di Siviglia; La Cenerentola; La gazza ladra;
Guillaume Tell; L'Italiana in Algeri; La scala di seta; Il signor
Bruschino* CSO, Reiner
RCA GD 60387 (US: 60387-2) [A] **M**

String Sonatas Nos. 1–6 ASMF, Marriner
(+ Bellini: *Oboe Concerto;* Cherubini: *Horn Sonata;* Donizetti:
String Quartet)
Decca 443 838-2 (US: London 443 838-2), 2 CDs [A] **B**

S *Sins of Old Age* (14 piano pieces) Portugheis (pno)
ASV CDDCA 901 [D] **F**

V *L'âme délaissée; Ariette à l'ancienne; Beltà crudele; Canzonetta
spagnuola; Giovanna d'Arco; Mi lagnerò tacendo* (6 settings);
*Nizza; L'Orpheline du Tyrol; La Pastorella; Pompadour, la grande
coquette; La regata veneziana; Il Trovatore* Bartoli (mez),
Spencer (pno)
Decca 430 518-2 (US: London 430 518-2) [D] **F**

Petite messe solenelle Schalzi (mez), Sabbatini (ten), Petusi (bs),
Bologna Teatro Communale O & Ch., Chailly
Decca 444 134-2 (US: London 444 134-2), 2 CDs [D] **M**

7 Songs Hampson (bar), Parsons (pno)
(+ Meyerbeer: *12 Songs*)
EMI CDC7 54436-2 (US: Angel CDC 54436) [D] **F**

Stabat Mater Field (sop), Jones (mez), Davies (ten), Earle (bs),
LSO Ch, City of London Sinfonia, Hickox
Chandos CHAN 8780 [D] **F**

ROUSSEL, Albert (1869–1937) FRANCE

O *Bacchus et Ariane* (ballet), *Op. 43: Suite No. 2; Suite in F,
Op. 33* Paris O, Dutoit
Erato 2292 45278-2 [D] **F**

Suite in F, Op. 33 Detroit SO, Paray
(+ Chabrier: *Orchestral works*)
Philips Mercury 434 303-2 [A] **M**

O   *Symphony No. 3 in G min., Op. 42* NYPO, Boulez
(+Ravel: *Trois Poèmes de Stéphane Mallarmé*, etc.)
Sony CD 64107 [A] **M**

S   *Doute; 3 Pieces, Op. 5; Prelude and Fugue, Op. 29; Rustiques,*
Op. 16; Segovia, Op. 49; Sonatine, Op. 46; Suite in F♯ min., Op. 14
Parkin (pno)
Chandos CHAN 8887 [D] **F**

RUBBRA, Edmund (1901–1986) ENGLAND

O   *Violin Concerto, Op. 103; *Viola Concerto, Op. 75* Little (vln),
*Golani (vla), RPO, Handley
Conifer CDCF 225 [D] **F**

  Improvisations on Virginal Pieces by Giles Farnaby, Op. 50;
Symphony No. 10 (Sinfonia da camera), Op. 145; A Tribute (for
RVW on his 70th birthday), Op. 56 Bournemouth Sinfonietta,
Schönzeler
Chandos CHAN 6599 [A] **M**

  Symphonies Nos. 2 & *7; Festive Overture NPO, Handley;
*LPO, Boult
Lyrita SRCD 235 [A] **F**

  Symphonies Nos. 3 & 4; Resurgam; A Tribute Philharmonia O,
Del Mar
Lyrita SRCD 202 [D] **F**

  Symphonies Nos. 6 & 8; *Soliloquy Philharmonia O, Del Mar;
*de Saram (vcl), LSO, Handley
Lyrita SRCD 234 [A] **F**

V   *Missa in honorem sancti domini, Op. 66; 3 Hymn Tunes, Op. 114;*
Magnificat and Nunc Dimittis, Op. 65; 3 Motets, Op. 76 Gonville
& Caius College Ch, Webber
(+ Hadley: *Choral works*)
ASV CDDCA 881 [D] **F**

RUBINSTEIN, Anton (1829–1894) RUSSIA

S   *Piano Sonatas No. 1 in E min., Op. 12; No. 3 in F, Op. 41*
Howard (pno)
Hyperion CDA 66017 [D] **F**

  Piano Sonatas: No. 2 in C min., Op. 20; No. 4 in A min., Op. 100
Howard (pno)
Hyperion CDA 66105 [D] **F**

RUTTER, John (born 1945) ENGLAND

V   *All things bright and beautiful; For the beauty of the earth; A Gaelic*
blessing; Gloria; God be in my head; The Lord bless you and keep
you; The Lord is my shepherd; O clap your hands; Open thou mine
eyes; Praise ye the Lord; A prayer of St. Patrick Cambridge
Singers, Philips Jones Brass Ensemble, City of London
Sinfonia, Rutter
Collegium COLCD 100 [D] **F**

  Requiem; I will lift up mine eyes Ashton (sop), Dean (sop),
Cambridge Singers, City of London Sinfonia, Rutter
Collegium COLCD 103 [D] **F**

SAINT-SAËNS, Camille (1835–1921) FRANCE

O   *Carnival of the Animals* Nel (pno), Snell (pno), Academy of
London, Stamp
(+ Prokofiev: *Peter and the Wolf*)
Virgin CUV5 61137-2 (US: 61137) [D] **M**

Cello Concerto No. 1 in A min., Op. 33; *Allegro appassionato, Op. 43; *Chant saphique, Op. 91; *Gavotte, Op. posth.; ***Prière, Op. 158; *Romances Nos. 1 & 2, Opp. 36/51; *Cello Sonata No. 1 in C min., Op. 32; **The Swan Isserlis (vcl), LSO, Tilson Thomas; *Devoyon (pno); **Tilson Thomas, Moore (pnos); ***Grier (org)
RCA 09026 61678-2 [D] F

Cello Concerto No. 1 in A min., Op. 33 Haimowitz (vcl), CSO, Levine
(+ Bruch: *Kol Nidrei, Op. 47*; Lalo: *Cello Concerto*)
DG 427 323-2 [D] F

Piano Concertos Nos. 1–5 Rogé (pno), Philharmonia, RPO, LPO, Dutoit
Decca 443 865-2 (US: London 443 865-2), 2 CDs [A] B

Piano Concertos: No. 2 in G min., Op. 22; No. 4 Collard (pno), RPO, Previn
EMI CDC7 47816-2 (US: Angel CDC 47816) [D] F

Violin Concertos Nos. 1–3; Caprice andalous, Op. 122; Le Déluge: Prélude; Étude, Op. 52/6: Étude en forme de valse; Havanaise, Op. 83; Introduction & rondo capriccioso, Op. 28; Morceau de concert, Op. 62; *La Muse et le poète, Op. 132; Romance in Db, Op. 37; Romance in C, Op. 48 Hoelscher (vln), *Kirschbaum (vcl), NPO, Dervaux
EMI CMS7 64790-2 (US: Angel CDMB 64790), 2 CDs [A] M

Violin Concerto No. 3 in B min., Op. 61 Perlman (vln), Paris O, Barenboim
(+ Lalo: *Symphonie espagnole*)
DG 445 549-2 [D] M

Danse macabre, Op. 40; *Le Déluge (oratorio), Op. 45: Prélude; *Samson et Dalila (opera): Bacchanale; *Symphony No. 3 in C min., Op. 78 Litaize (org), CSO, *Paris O, Barenboim
DG 415 847-2 [A] M

Havanaise, Op. 83; Introduction & Rondo capriccioso, Op. 28 Perlman (vln), Paris O, Martinon
(+ Chausson: *Poème*; Ravel: *Tzigane*)
EMI CDC7 47725-2 (US: Angel CDC 47725) [A] F

Introduction & Rondo capriccioso, Op. 28 Oistrakh (vln), Boston SO, Munch
(+ Chausson: *Symphony in Bb; Poème*)
RCA GD 60683 (US: 09026 60683-2) [A] M

Le rouet d'Omphale Op. 31 Boston SO, Munch
(+ Berlioz: *Orchestral works*)
RCA 09026 61400-2 [A] M

Symphonies: Nos. 1–*3; in A; in F *Gavoty (org), FNRO, Martinon
EMI CZS7 62643-2 (US: Angel CDMB 62643), 2 CDs [A] B

Symphony No. 3 in C min. (Organ), Op. 78 Preston (org), BPO, Levine
(+ Dukas: *L'apprenti sorcier*)
DG 419 617-2 [D] F

Berceuse, Op. 38; Élégie, Op. 120; Élégie, Op. 143; Romance in Db, Op. 37; Violin Sonatas: No. 1 in D min., Op. 75; No. 2 in Eb, Op. 102 Charlier (vln), Hubeau (pno)
Erato 2292 45017-2 [A] F

C *Romance, Op. 67* Tuckwell (hn), Ashkenazy (pno)
(+ Brahms: *Horn Trio;* Franck: *Violin Sonata;* Schumann:
Adagio and Allegro)
Decca 433 695-2 (US: London 433 695-2) [A] **F**

Violin Sonata No. 1 in D min., Op. 75 Takezawa (vln),
de Silva (pno)
(+ Debussy: *Violin Sonata;* Ravel: *Violin Sonata [1927]*)
RCA 09026 61386-2 [D] **F**

SALLINEN, Aulis (born 1935) FINLAND

O *Symphonies Nos. 4 & 5; Shadows, Op. 52* Malmö SO, DePriest
BIS BIS-CD 607 [D] **F**

SARASATE, Pablo (1844–1908) SPAIN

O *Carmen Fantasy* Perlman (vln), RPO, Foster
(+ Paganini: *Violin Concerto No. 1*)
EMI CDC7 47101-2 (US: Angel CDC 47101) [A] F

Zigeunerweisen, Op. 20 Shaham (vln), LSO, Foster
(+ Wieniawski: *Violin Concertos Nos. 1 & 2; Légende*)
DG 431 815-2 [D] **F**

Zigeunerweisen (trans. Hall) Hall (gtr), LMP, Litton
(+ Castelnuovo-Tedesco: *Guitar Concerto No. 1;* Paganini:
Violin Concerto No. 2)
Decca 440 293-2 (US: London 440 293-2) [D] **F**

SATIE, Erik (1866–1925) FRANCE

O *Les Aventures de Mercure; La belle excentrique; 5 Grimaces for
'A Midsummer Night's Dream'; Gymnopédies Nos. 1 & 3* (orch.
Debussy); *Jack-in-the-box* (orch. Milhaud); *Morceaux en forme
de poire; Parade; Relâche* Utah SO, Abravanel
Vanguard 08.4030.71 (US: OUC 4030) [A] **M**

Choses vues à droite et à gauche Kremer (vln), LSO, Chailly
(+ Chausson: *Poème;* Milhaud: *Le Boeuf sur le toit; Le printemps;*
Vieuxtemps: *Fantasia appassionata*)
Philips 432 513-2 [A] **M**

Gymnopédies Nos. 1 & 3 de Lancie (ob), LSO, Previn
(+ Ibert: *Symphonie Concertante;* Françaix: *L'horloge de flore;*
R. Strauss: *Oboe Concerto*)
RCA GD 87989 (US: 7989-2) [A] **M**

S *Avant-dernières pensées; Embryons desséchés; 6 Gnossiennes; 3
Gymnopédies; Heures séculaires et instantanées; Je te veux; Parade*
(excerpt); *Pièces froides; Prélude de la porte héroïque du ciel; Sport
et divertissements; Valses du précieux degoûté; Véritables préludes
flasques; Vieux séquins et vieilles cuirasses* MacGregor (pno)
Collins 10532 [D] **F**

*Avant-dernières pensées; Chapitres tournés en tous sens; Croquis et
agaceries d'un gros bonhomme en bois; Descriptions automatiques;
2 rêveries nocturnes; Heures séculaires et instantanées; Nocturnes
Nos. 1–3 & 5; Nouvelles pièces froides; Pièces froides; Prélude de la
porte héroïque du ciel; Les trois valses distinguées d'un précieux
dégoûté; Véritables préludes flasques* Rogé (pno)
Decca 421 713-2 (US: London 421 713-2) [D] **F**

*Embryons desséchés; 6 Gnossiennes; 3 Gymnopédies; Je te veux;
Nocturne No. 4; Le Picadilly; 4 préludes flasques; Prélude en
tapisserie; Sonatine bureaucratique; Vieux séquins et vieilles cuirasses*
Rogé (pno)
Decca 410 220-2 (US: London 410 220-2) [D] **F**

SAXTON, Robert (born 1953) ENGLAND

⊃ *Violin Concerto; In the Beginning; *I will Awake the Dawn* Little (vln), BBC SO, Bamert; *BBC Singers, Poole
Collins 12832 [D] **F**

SCARLATTI, Alessandro (1660–1725) ITALY

✔ *Dixit Dominus II* Argenta (sop), Attrot (sop), Denley (mez), Stafford (ten), Varcoe (bar), English Concert O & Ch, Pinnock
(+ Vivaldi: *Gloria in D, RV 589*)
♦ DG Archiv 423 386-2 [D] **F**

Cantatas: *Correa nel seno amato; *Già lusingato appieno;
Variations on 'La Folia' *Dawson (sop), Purcell Quartet
♦ Hyperion CDA 66254 [D] **F**

SCARLATTI, Domenico (1685–1757) ITALY

§ *Keyboard Sonatas Nos. 1–555* Ross (hpd)
Erato 2292 45309-2, 34 CDs [A] **M**

Keyboard Sonatas Nos. 1, 9, 30, 69, 113, 127, 132, 133, 141, 144, 159, 175, 215, 380, 430, 481, 492 & 502 MacGregor (pno)
Collins 13222 [D] **F**

Keyboard Sonatas Nos. 3, 52, 184, 185, 191–3, 208, 209, 227, 238, 239, 252 & 253 Leonhardt (hpd)
RCA GD 71955 (US: 71955-2) [A] **M**

Keyboard Sonatas Nos. 33, 39, 54, 55, 96, 146, 162, 198, 322, 380, 455, 466, 474, 481, 491, 525 & 531 Horowitz (pno)
Sony CD 53460 [A] **M**

Keyboard Sonatas Nos. 46, 87, 95, 99, 124, 201, 204, 490–2, 513, 520 & 521 Pinnock (hpd)
CRD 3368 [A] **F**

14 Unpublished Sonatas Sone (hpd)
Erato 4509 94806-2 [D] **F**

SCHARWENKA, Xaver (1850–1924) POLAND

⊃ *Piano Quartet in F, Op. 37; Piano Trio in A min, Op. 45* Tanyel (pno), Chilingirian (vln), Der Werff (vla), Atmacayan (vcl)
Collins 14192 [D] **F**

§ *Piano Sonata No. 1, Op. 6; Eglantine Waltz, Op. 84; Impromptu, Op. 17; Polish Dances, Op. 3; Polonaise, Op. 12; Polonaise, Op. 42; Valse-caprice, Op. 31* Tanyel (pno)
Collins 13252 [D] **F**

Piano Sonata No. 2 in E♭, Op. 36; 2 Dances Polonaises, Op. 29; Romanzero, Op. 33; Sonatina, Op. 52/1 Tanyel (pno)
Collins 13522 [D] **F**

Theme & Variations, Op. 48, Barcarolle, Op. 14; Novellete & Melodie, Op. 22; 4 Polish Dances, Op. 58; Scherzo, Op. 4 Tanyel (pno)
Collins 13652 [D] **F**

SCHMIDT, Franz (1874–1939) AUSTRIA

⊃ *Symphony No. 2 in E♭* CSO, Järvi
Chandos CHAN 8779 [D] **F**

Symphony No. 3 in A CSO, Järvi
(+ Hindemith: *Concerto for Orchestra*)
Chandos CHAN 9000 [D] **F**

SCHMITT, Florent (1870–1958) FRANCE

O   *La tragédie de Salomé; *Psalm 47* *Sweet (sop), *Gil (org),
*French Radio Ch, French Radio New PO, Janowski
Erato 2292 45029-2 [D] **F**

SCHNITTKE, Alfred (born 1934) RUSSIA

O   *Cello Concerto No. 1; *4 Hymns; Klingende Buchstaben* (solo cello)
Thedéen (vcl), Danish National RSO, Segerstam; *Radoukanov,
Davidsson, Fredlund, Kamata, Holdar, Loguin (vcls)
BIS BIS-CD 507 [D] **F**

*Cello Concerto No. 2; *In memoriam...* Rostropovich (vcl), LSO,
Ozawa; *LSO, Rostropovich
Sony CD 48241 [D] **F**

*Concerto Grosso No. 1; A Paganini; Quasi una Sonata; Moz-art à
la Haydn* Kremer (vln), Grindenko (vln), Smirnov (pno),
COE, Schiff
DG 445 520-2 [D] **M**

*Oboe and Harp Concerto; Piano Concerto No. 3; *Concerto grosso
No. 1* Jahren (ob), Lier (hp), Pöntinen (pno), *Bergqvist (vln),
*Swedrup (vln), *Pöntinen (hpd), New Stockholm CO,
Markiz
BIS BIS-CD 377 [D] **F**

Concerti grossi: No. 3; No. 4 (Symphony No. 5) Royal
Concertgebouw O, Chailly
Decca 430 698-2 (US: London 430 698-2) [D] **F**

Concerto grosso No. 5 Kremer (vln), VPO, von Dohnányi
(+ Glass: *Violin Concerto*)
DG 437 091-2 [D] **F**

*Viola Concerto; *Trio Sonata* (arr. Bashmet) Bashmet (vla),
LSO, Rostropovich; *Moscow Soloists, Bashmet
RCA RD 60446 (US: 60446-2) [D] **F**

Violin Concertos Nos. 1 & 2 Lubotsky (vln), Malmö SO, Klas
BIS BIS-CD 487 [D] **F**

*Violin Concertos Nos. 2 & 3; *Stille Nacht; *Gratulationsrondo*
Kremer (vln), COE, Eschenbach (cond/*pno)
Teldec 4509 94540-2 [D] **F**

Violin Concertos Nos. 3 & 4 Krysa (vln), Malmö SO, Klas
BIS BIS-CD 517 [D] **F**

*Klein Sommernachtstraum; Passacaglia; Ritual; *Seid nüchtern und
wachet (Faust Cantata)* Malmö SO, Segerstam; *Blom (cont),
Bellini (alt), Devos (ten), Cold (bs), Malmö SO & Ch,
De Priest
BIS BIS-CD 437 [D] **F**

Quasi una Sonata; Piano Trio; Piano Sonata No. 2 Rostropovitch
(vcl/cond), Lubotsky (vln), I. Schnittke (pno), ECO
Sony CD 53271 [D] **F**

Symphony No. 1 Dominique (pno), Kallenberg (vln),
Lannerholm (trb), Royal Stockholm PO, Segerstam
BIS BIS-CD 577 [D] **F**

Symphony No. 3 Stockholm PO, Klee
BIS BIS-CD 477 [D] **F**

*Symphony No. 4; *Requiem* Bellini (alt), Parkman (ten),
Uppsala Academic Chamber Ch, Stockholm Sinfonietta,

Kamu; *Salomonsson (sop), Sjöberg (sop), Lindholm (sop), Eker (cont), Högman (ten), Uppsala Academic Chamber Ch, Stockholm Sinfonietta, Parkman
BIS BIS-CD 497 [D] **F**

C *Kanon in memoriam I: Igor Stravinsky* Hagen Quartet
(+ Ligeti: *String Quartet No. 1;* Lutoslawski: *String Quartet*)
DG 431 686-2 [D] **F**

Piano Quintet; Canon for Solo Violin and Strings; Gratulationsrondo; Sonata No. 1 for Violin & Chamber Orchestra Various artists
Sony CD 53357 [D] **F**

Suite in the Olden Style; Moz-Art; Praeludium in Memoriam Dmitri Shostakovich; A Paganini; Stille Musik; Stille Nacht; Madrigal in Memoriam Oleg Kagan; Gratulationsrondo Marinkovic (vln), Hendry (pno), Bowes (vln), Hugh (vcl)
ASV CDDCA 877 [D] **F**

Violin Sonatas Nos. 1 & 2; String Trio Marinkovic (vln), Hendry (pno), Silverthorne (vla), Hugh (vcl)
ASV CDDCA 868 [D] **F**

String Quartets Nos. 1–3 Tale Quartet
BIS BIS-CD 467 [D] **F**

V *Choral Concerto* Russian State Symphonic Cappella, Polyansky
Chandos CHAN 9332 [D] **F**

SCHOECK, Othmar (1886–1957) SWITZERLAND

O *Cello Concerto No. 1 in A, Op. 61; Sommernacht, Op. 58* Goritzki (vcl/dir), Neusse German Chamber Academy
Claves CD50-8502 [D] **F**

V *Lebendig begraben* (song cycle), *Op. 40* Fischer-Dieskau (bar), Berlin RSO, Rieger
(+ Pfitzner: *Von deutscher Seele*)
DG 437 033-2, 2 CDs [A] **M**

Das Stille Leuchten (song cycle), *Op. 60* Fischer-Dieskau (bar), Höll (pno)
Claves CD50-8910 [D] **F**

Unter Sternen (song cycle), *Op. 55* Fischer-Dieskau (bar), Höll (pno)
Claves CD50-8606 [D] **F**

SCHOENBERG, Arnold (1874–1951) AUSTRIA/USA

O *Chamber Symphonies Nos. 1, Op. 9 & 2, Op. 38; Verklärte Nacht* Orpheus CO
DG 429 233-2 [D] **F**

*Chamber Symphony No. 1, Op. 9; **Erwartung, Op. 17; Variations for Orchestra, Op. 31* *Birmingham Contemporary Music Group, **Bryn-Julson (sop), CBSO, Rattle
EMI CDC5 55212-2 (US: 55212) [D] **F**

Piano Concerto, Op. 42; Violin Concerto, Op. 36 Brendel (pno), Zeitlin (vln), Bavarian RSO, Kubelik
(+ Berg: *Violin Concerto*)
DG 431 740-2 [A] **M**

Pelleas und Melisande (symphonic poem), *Op. 5; Variations for Orchestra, Op. 31; Verklärte Nacht, Op. 4* BPO, Karajan

(+ Berg: *Lyric Suite*, etc.; Webern: *5 Movements*, etc.)
DG 427 424-2, 3 CDs [A] **M**

O *5 Orchestral Pieces, Op. 16* LSO, Dorati
(+ Berg: *3 Orchestral Pieces; Lulu: Symphonic Suite;* Webern:
5 Pieces)
Philips Mercury 432 006-2 [A] **M**

C *String Quartet in D; String Quartets Nos. 1–4* LaSalle Quartet
(+ Berg: *Lyric Suite; String Quartet, Op. 3;* Webern: *6 Bagatelles*,
etc.)
DG 419 994-2, 4 CDs [A] **M**

String Trio, Op. 45; Verklärte Nacht, Op. 4 LaSalle Quartet,
McInnes (vla), Pegis (vcl)
DG 423 250-2 [A] **M**

Suite, Op. 29; Wind Quintet, Op. 26 London Sinfonietta, Atherton
Decca 433 083-2 (US: London 433 083-2) [A] **M**

Verklärte Nacht, Op. 4 Raphael Ensemble
(+ Korngold: *String Sextet*)
Hyperion CDA 66425 [D] **F**

S *Piano Pieces, Opp. 33a & b; 3 Piano Pieces, Op. 11; 6 Piano Pieces,
Op. 19; 5 Piano Pieces, Op. 23; Suite, Op. 25* Pollini (pno)
DG 423 249-2 [A] **M**

V *3 Deutsche Volkslieder; Dreimal Tausend Jahre, Op. 50a; Friede auf
Erden, Op. 13; Kol Nidre, Op. 39; Moderner Psalm, Op. 50c; O daß
der Sinnen doch so viele sind; Psalm 130, Op. 50b; 3 Satiren, Op.
28; 4 Stücke, Op. 27; 6 Stücke, Op. 35; A Survivor from Warsaw,
Op. 46; 3 Volkslieder, Op. 49; Wenn der schwer Gedruckte klagt*
Shirley-Quirk (bar), Reich (narr), BBC SO & Singers, Boulez
Sony CD 44571, 2 CDs [A/D] **M**

*Gurrelieder; *8 Lieder* Borkh (sop), Topper (mezzo), Engen
(bs), Bavarian RSO & Ch, Kubelik; *Fischer-Dieskau (bar),
Reimann (pno)
(+ Berg: *4 Lieder, Op. 2;* Webern: *Lieder*)
DG 431 744-2, 2 CDs [A] **M**

Pierrot Lunaire, Op. 21; Erwartung, Op. 17; Lied der Waldtaube
Various artists, Boulez
Sony CD 48466 [A] **M**

Ode to Napoleon Bonaparte, Op. 41 Griffiths (spkr), Litwin
(pno), LaSalle Quartet
(+ Webern: *String Trio*, etc.)
DG 437 036-2 [A] **M**

SCHOENFIELD, Paul (born 1947) USA

O *4 Parables; Vaudeville; Klezmer Rondos* Wincenc (fl), Basch
(picc tpt), Kahane (pno), New World Symphony, Nelson
Argo 440 212-2 [D] **F**

SCHUBERT, Franz (1797–1828) AUSTRIA

O *Konzertstück in D, D345; Polonaise in Bb, D580; Rondo in A, D438*
Kremer (vln), LSO, Tchakarov
(+ Beethoven: *Concerto movement*, etc.)
DG 431 168-2 [A] **M**

*Rosamunde (Die Zauberharfe): Overture, D644, and Incidental
Music, D797* (complete) von Otter (mez), Ernst-Senff Ch,
COE, Abbado
DG 431 655-2 [D] **F**

O *Symphonies Nos. 1–6 & 8–9; Grand Duo in C, D812 (orch. Joachim); Rosamunde (Die Zauberharfe) Overture, D644* COE, Abbado
DG 423 651-2, 5 CDs [D] **F**

Symphonies: No. 1 in D, D82; No. 2 in B♭, D125 COE, Abbado
DG 423 652-2 [D] **F**

Symphonies: No. 3 in D, D200; No. 5 in B♭, D485; No. 6 in C, D589 RPO, Beecham
EMI CDM7 69750-2 (US: Angel CDM 69750) [A] **M**

Symphonies: No. 3 in D, D200; No. 8 in B min. (Unfinished), D759 VPO, Kleiber
DG 415 601-2 [A] **F**

Symphonies: No. 4 in C min. (Tragic), D417; No. 6 in C, D589 LCP, Norrington
✧ EMI CDC7 54210-2 (US: Angel CDC 54210) [D] **F**

Symphonies: No. 5 in B♭, D485; No. 6 in C, D589 Classical Band, Weil
✧ Sony CD 46697 [D] **F**

Symphonies: No. 5 in B♭, D485; No. 8 in B min. (Unfinished), D759 LCP, Norrington
✧ EMI CDC7 49968-2 (US: Angel CDC 49968) [D] **F**

Symphonies: No. 8 in B min. (Unfinished), D759; No. 9 in C (Great), D944
Classical Band, Weil
✧ Sony CD 48132 [D] **F**
Cleveland O, Szell
Sony CD 48268 [A] **B**

Symphony No. 9 in C (Great), D944 LCP, Norrington
✧ EMI CDC7 49949-2 (US: Angel CDC 49949) [D] **F**

C *Fantaisie in F min., D940; Rondo in A, D951; Rondo in D, D608; Sonata in B♭, D617* Eden, Tamir (pno duo)
CRD 3465 [D] **F**

Fantasy in C, D934; Rondo brillant in B min., D895; Sonata (Duo) in A, D574 Kremer (vln), Afanassiev (pno)
DG 431 654-2 [D] **F**

Octet in F, D803
AAM Chamber Ensemble
✧ L'Oiseau-Lyre 425 519-2 [D] **F**
Berlin Philharmonic Ensemble
Denon CO-75671 [D] **F**

Overture in F, D675; 8 Variations on a Theme from Herold's 'Marie', D908; Rondo in D, D608; 3 Marches Héroïques, D602; Fantaisie in F min., D940; Introduction, 4 Variations on an Original Theme & Finale, D603; Divertissement a l'hongroise, D818; 6 Polonaises, D824 Tal & Groethuysen (pno duo)
Sony CD 58955, 2 CDs [D] **F**

Piano Quintet in A, D667 (Trout) Hausmusik
(+ Hummel: *Piano Quintet, Op. 87*)
✧ EMI CDC7 54264-2 (US: Angel CDC 54264) [D] **F**

*Piano Quintet in A, D667 (Trout); *String Quartet No. 14 in D min. (Death and the Maiden), D810* Curzon (pno), Vienna Octet;

*VPO Quartet
Decca 417 459-2 (US: London 417 459-2) [A] **M**

C *Piano Quintet in A, D667 (Trout); String Trios: in Bb, D581; in Bb, D28* *Haebler (pno), *Cazauran (db), Grumiaux Trio
Philips 422 838-2 [A] **M**

Piano Trio No. 1 in Bb, D898 Szeryng (vln), Fournier (vcl), Rubinstein (pno)
(+Schumann: *Piano Trio No. 1*)
RCA GD 86262 (US: 6262-2) [A] **M**

Piano Trio No. 2 in Eb, D929; Sonatensatz, D28 Castle Trio
Virgin VC7 59303-2 (US: CDC 59303) [D] **F**
Beaux Arts Trio
Philips 426 096-2 [A] **M**

Sonata in A min. (Arpeggione), D821 Rostropovich (vcl), Britten (pno)
(+ Debussy: *Cello Sonata;* Schumann: *5 Stücke in Volkston*)
Decca 417 833-2 (US: London 417 833-2) [A] **M**

Sonatinas Nos. 1–3; Fantasy in C, D934; Sonata (Duo) in A, D574 Stern (vln), Barenboim (pno)
Sony CD 44504, 2 CDs [D] **F**

String Quartets Nos. 1–15 Melos Quartet
DG 419 879-2, 6 CDs [A] **M**

String Quartets: No. 8 in Bb, D112; No. 13 in A min., D804 Lindsay Quartet
ASV CDDCA 593 [D] **F**

String Quartets: No. 10 in Eb, D87; No. 14 in D min. (Death and the Maiden), D810 Britten Quartet
EMI CDC7 54345-2 (US: Angel 54345) [D] **F**

String Quartet No.10 in Eb, D87; String Trio in Eb (fragment), D471; String Trio in Bb, D581 (revised version) L'Archibudelli
✧ Sony CD 53982 [D] **F**

String Quartets: No. 12 in C min. (Quartettsatz), D703; No. 14 in D min. (Death and the Maiden), D810 Lindsay Quartet
ASV CDDCA 560 [D] **F**

String Quartets: No. 13 in A min., D804; No. 14 in D min. (Death and the Maiden), D810 Italian Quartet
Philips 426 383-2 [A] **M**

String Quartet No. 15 in G, D887 Lindsay Quartet
ASV CDDCA 661 [D] **F**

String Quintet in C, D956 Hagen Quartet, Schiff (vcl)
(+Beethoven: *Grosse Fuge*)
DG 439 774-2 [D] **F**

*String Quintet in C, D956; *Rondo, D438* *Beths (vln), L'Archibudelli
✧ Sony CD 46669 [D] **F**

S *Fantasy in C (Wanderer), D760; Piano Sonata No. 16 in A min., D845* Pollini (pno)
DG 419 672-2 [A] **F**

8 Impromptus, D899 & 935; 12 Waltzes D145 Brendel (pno)
Philips 411 711-2 [D] **F**

6 Moments musicaux, D780; Piano Sonata No. 19 in C min., D958
Lupu (pno)
Decca 417 785-2 (US: London 417 785-2) [A] **M**

Piano Sonatas Nos. 1–21 Kempff (pno)
DG 423 496-2, 7 CDs [A] **M**

*Piano Sonatas: No. 1 in E, D157; No. 14 in A min., D784; No. 20
in A, D959* Lupu (pno)
Decca 425 033-2 (US: London 425 033-2) [A] **M**

*Piano Sonatas: No. 2 in C, D279; No. 21 in Bb, D960; in F min.,
D261* Schiff (pno)
Decca 440 310-2 (US: London 440 310-2) [D] **F**

Piano Sonatas: No. 4 in A min., D537; No. 20 in A, D959 Schiff
(pno)
Decca 440 309-2 (US: London 440 309-2) [D] **F**

*Piano Sonatas: No. 5 in Ab, D557; No. 9 in B, D575; No. 18 in G,
D894* Schiff (pno)
Decca 440 307-2 (US: London 440 307-2) [D] **F**

*Piano Sonatas: No. 6 in E min., D566; No. 14 in A min., D784;
No. 17 in D, D850* Schiff (pno)
Decca 440 306-2 (US: London 440 306-2) [D] **F**

Piano Sonatas: No. 7 in Eb, D568; No. 19 in C min., D958 Schiff
(pno)
Decca 440 308-2 (US: London 440 308-2) [D] **F**

*Piano Sonatas: No. 8 in F# min., D571; No. 15 in C (Relique),
D840; No. 16 in A min., D845* Schiff (pno)
Decca 440 305-2 (US: London 440 305-2) [D] **F**

*Piano Sonatas: No. 9 in B, D575; No. 11 in F min., D625;
6 Moments musicaux, D780* Richter (pno)
Olympia OCD 286 [A] **F**

*Piano Sonatas: No. 13 in A, D664; No. 14 in A min., D784;
Impromptus, D899/2&4* Richter (pno)
Olympia OCD 288 [D] **F**

Piano Sonatas: No. 13 in A, D664; No. 21 in Bb, D960 Lupu
(pno)
Decca 440 295-2 (US: London 440 295-2) [D] **F**

Piano Sonatas: No. 14 in A min., D784; No. 17 in D, D850
Brendel (pno)
Philips 422 063-2 [D] **F**

*Piano Sonatas: No. 14 in A min., D784; No. 18 in G, D894;
Waltzes, D145* Ashkenazy (pno)
Decca 425 017-2 (US: London 425 017-2) [A] **M**

Piano Sonatas: No. 16 in A min., D845; No. 18 in G, D894
Lupu (pno)
Decca 417 640-2 (US: London 417 640-2) [A] **F**

Piano Sonatas: No. 19 in C min., D958; No. 20 in A, D959
Pollini (pno)
DG 427 327-2 [D] **F**

Piano Sonatas: No. 19 in C min., D958; No. 21 in Bb, D960
Richter (pno)
Olympia OCD 335 [D] **F**

S *Piano Sonata No. 21; 3 Impromptus; 2 Moments Musicaux*
Kempff (pno)
DG 439 462-2 [A] **B**

V *Vocal Duets, Trios and Quartets* Ameling (sop), Baker (mez),
Schreier (ten), Laubenthal (ten), Fischer-Dieskau (bar),
Moore (pno)
DG 435 596-2, 2 CDs [A] **M**

Lieder (near-complete) Fischer-Dieskau (bar), Moore (pno)
DG 437 214-2, 21 CDs [A] **B**

Lieder: Volume 1 (1811–17) Fischer-Dieskau (bar),
Moore (pno)
DG 437 215-2, 9 CDs [A] **B**

Lieder: Volume 2 (1817–28) Fischer-Dieskau (bar),
Moore (pno)
DG 437 225-2, 9 CDs [A] **B**

*Lieder Edition Volume 1: Der Alpenjäger, D588; Amalia, D195;
An den Frühlen (second version), D587; An den Mond (second
version), D296; Erster Verlust, D226; Die Erwartung, D159; Der
Fischer, D225; Der Flüchtling, D402; Das Geheimnis (first version
D250; Der Jüngling am Bache, D30; Lied, D284; Meeres Stille
(second version), D216; Nähe des Geliebten, D162; Der Pilgrim,
D794; Schäfers Klagelied D121; Sehnsucht (second version), D636,
Thekla (first version), D73; Wanderers Nachtlied I, D224; Wonne
der Wehmut, D260* Baker (mez), Johnson (pno)
Hyperion CDJ 33001 [D] **F**

*Lieder Edition Volume 2: Am Bach im Frühling, D361; Am Flusse
(second version), D766; Auf der Donau, D553; Fahrt zum Hades,
D526; Fischerlied (I & II), D351/562; Fischerweise, D881; Der
Schiffer, D536; Selige Welt, D743; Der Strom, D565; Der Taucher,
D77; Widerschein (first version), D639; Wie Ulfru fischt, D525*
Varcoe (bar), Johnson (pno)
Hyperion CDJ 33002 [D] **F**

*Lieder Edition Volume 3: Abschied, D475; An die Freunde, D654;
Augenlied, D297; Iphigenia, D573; Der Jüngling und der Tod,
D545; Lieb Minna, D222; Liedesend, D473; Nacht und Träume,
D827; Namenstagslied, D695; Pax vobiscum, D551; Rückweg,
D476; Trost im Liede, D546; Viola, D786; Der Zwerg, D771*
Murray (mez), Johnson (pno)
Hyperion CDJ 33003 [D] **F**

*Lieder Edition Volume 4: Alte Liebe rostet nie, D477; Am See, D12
Am Strome, D539; An Herrn Josef von Spaun (Epistel), D749; Au
der Riesenkoppe, D611; Das war ich, D174; Das gestörte Glück,
D309; Liebeslauschen, D698; Liebesrausch, D179; Liebeständelei,
D206; Der Liedler, D209; Nachtstück, D672; Sängers Morgenlied
(I & II), D163/ 165; Sehnsucht der Liebe, D180* Langridge (ten)
Johnson (pno)
Hyperion CDJ 33004 [D] **F**

*Lieder Edition Volume 5: Die Allmacht, D852; An die Natur, D37
Die Erde, D989; Ganymed, D544; Klage der Ceres, D323; Das Lie
im Grünen, D917; Morgenlied, D381; Die Mutter Erde, D788; Die
Sternenwelten, D307; Täglich zu singen, D533; Wehmut, D772*
Connell (sop), Johnson (pno)
Hyperion CDJ 33005 [D] **F**

*Lieder Edition Volume 6: Abendlied für die Entfernte, D856; Aben.
unter der Linde (I & II), D235/237; Abendstern, D806; Alinde,
D904; An die Laute, D905; Des Fischers Liebesglück, D933;*

Jagdlied, D521; Der Knabe in der Wieg (Wiegenlied), D529; Die Nacht, D534; Die Sterne, D939; Der Vater mit dem Kind, D906; Vor meiner Wiege, D927; Wilkommen und Abschied, D767; Zur guten Nacht, D903 Rolfe Johnson (ten), Johnson (pno)
Hyperion CDJ 33006 [D] **F**

Lieder Edition Volume 7: An den Frühling (first version), D283; An die Nachtigall, D196; An den Mond, D193; Idens Nachtgesang, D227; Idens Schwanenlied, D317; Der Jüngling am Bache (second version), D192; Kennst du das Land?, D321; Liane, D298; Die Liebe, D210; Luisens Antwort, D319; Das Mädchens Klage (second version), D191; Meeres Stille (first version), D215a; Mein Grüss an den Mai, D305; Minona oder die Kunde der Dogge, D152; Naturgenuss, D188; Das Rosenband, D280; Das Sehen, D231; Sehnsucht, D879; Die Spinnerin, D247; Die Sterbende, D186; Stimme der Liebe, D187; Von Ida, D228; Wer kauft Liebesgötter?, D261 Ameling (sop), Johnson (pno)
Hyperion CDJ 33007 [D] **F**

Lieder Edition Volume 8: Abendlied der Fürstin, D495; An den Mond in einer Herbstnacht, D614; Berthas Lied in der Nacht, D653; Erlkönig, D328; Die frühen Gräber, D290; Hochzeitlied, D463; In der Mitternacht, D464; Die Mondnacht, D238; Die Nonne (first version), D208; Romanze, D114; Die Sommernacht, D289; Ständchen, D920; Stimme der Liebe (second version), D418; Trauer der Liebe, D465; Wiegenlied, D498 Walker (mez), Johnson (pno)
Hyperion CDJ 33008 [D] **F**

Lieder Edition Volume 9: Blanka, D631; 4 Canzonen, D688; Daphne am Bach, D411; Didone abbandonata, D510; Der gute Hirt, D449; *Der Hirt auf dem Felsen, D965; Lambertine, D301; Liebe schwärmt auf allen Wegen; Lilla an die Morgenröte, D273; Misero pargoletto, D42; La pastorella al prato, D513; Der Sänger am Felsen, D482; Thekla (second version), D595; Der Vollmond strahlt (Romanze), D797 Auger (sop), *King (cl), Johnson (pno)
Hyperion CDJ 33009 [D] **F**

Lieder Edition Volume 10: Adelwold und Emma, D211; Am Flusse (first version), D160; An die Apfelbäume, D197; An die Geliebte, D303; An Mignon, D161; Auf den Tod einer Nachtigall, D201; Auf einen Kirchhof, D151; Harfenspieler (I); Labetrank der Liebe, D302; Die Laube, D214; Die Liebende, D207; Der Sänger, D149; Seufzer, D198; Der Traum, D213; Vergebliche Liebe, D177; Der Weiberfreund, D271 Hill (ten), Johnson (pno)
Hyperion CDJ 33010 [D] **F**

Lieder Edition Volume 11: An den Tod, D518; Auf dem Wasser zu singen, D774; Auflösung, D807; Aus 'Heliopolis' (I & II), D753/754; Dithyrambe, D801; Elysium, D584; Der Geistertanz, D116; Der König in Thule, D367; Lied des Orpheus, D474; Nachtstück, D672; Schwanengesang, D744; Seligkeit, D433; So lasst mich scheinen (first version), D727; Der Tod und das Mädchen, D531; Verklärung, D59; Vollendung, D989; Das Zügenglöcklein, D871 Fassbaender (mez), Johnson (pno)
Hyperion CDJ 33011 [D] **F**

Lieder Edition Volume 12: Adelaide, D95; Advokaten, D37; Andenken, D99; Lied aus der Ferne, D107; Ballade, D134; Betende, D102; Don Gayseros, D93; Geistertanz, D50; Jugendlicher Maienschwung, D61; An Laura, D115; Lied der Liebe, D109; Nachtgesang, D119; Schatten, D50; Sehnsucht, D123; Trost, An Elisa, D97; Trost in Tränen, D120; Vatermörder, D10; Verschwunden sind die Schmerzen, D88 Thompson (ten), Argenta

(sop), Ainsley (ten), Jackson (bs), Johnson (pno)
Hyperion CDJ 33012 [D] **F**

V *Lieder Edition Volume 13: Altschottische Ballade, D923; Ave Maria, D839; Gesang der Norna, D831; Gretchen am Spinnrade, D118; Gretchens Bitte, D564; Jäger, ruhe von der Jagd, D838; Lied der Anne Lyle, D830; Marie, D658; Marienbild, D623; Normans Gesang, D846; Raste Kreiger!, D837; Refrainlieder, D866 Nos. 1 & 3; Shilrik und Vinvela, D293; Szene aus Faust, D126*
McLaughlin (sop), Johnson (pno)
Hyperion CDJ 33013 [D] **F**

Lieder Edition Volume 14: Amphiaraos, D166; An die Leier, D737; Antigone und Oedipe, D542; Entsühnte Orest, D699; Fragment auf dem Aeschylus, D450; Freiwilliges Versinken, D700; Die Götter Griechenlands, D677; Gruppe aus dem Tartarus, D583; Hektors Abschied, D312; Hippolits Lied, D890; Lied eines Schiffers an die Dioskuren, D360; Memnon, D541; Orest auf Taurus, D548; Philioktet, D540; Uraniens Flucht, D554; Zurnenden Diana, D707
Hampson (bar), Johnson (pno)
Hyperion CDJ 33014 [D] **F**

Lieder Edition Volume 15: An die untergehende Sonne, D457; Am Fenster, D878; Binde Knabe, D833; Im Freien, D880; Junge Nonne, D828; Klage an den Mond, D436; Kolmas Klage, D217; Lied, D403; Mainacht, D194; Mondabend, D141; Morgenkuss, D264; Unglückliche, D713; Wanderer an den Mond, D870; Winterabend, D938 Price (sop), Johnson (pno)
Hyperion CDJ 33015 [D] **F**

Lieder Edition Volume 16: An Emma, D113; An die Freude, D654; Die Bürgschaft, D246; Die Entzuckung an Laura I & II, D390 & D577; Das Geheimnis, D793; Der Jüngling am Bache, D638; Laura am Klavier, D388; Leichenfantasie, D7; Das Mädchen aus der Fremde, D252; Der Pilgrim, D794; Sehnsucht, D52; Die vier Weltalter, D391 Allen (bar), Johnson (pno)
Hyperion CDJ 33016 [D] **F**

Lieder Edition Volume 17: Am Grabe Anselmos, D504; An den Mond, D468; An die Nachtigall, D497; An meinen Klavier, D342; Aus 'Diego Manazares' (Ilmerine), D458; Der Einsiedelei, D393; Frühlingslied, D938; Geheimnis, D491; Der Herbstabend, D405; Herbstlied, D501; Der Herbstnacht, D404; Klage, D371; Klage um Ali Bey, D496a; Lebenslied, D508; Leiden der Trennung, D509; Lied, D373; Lied in der Abwesenheit, D416; Litanei, D343; Lodas Gespenst, D150; Lorma, D376; Minnelied, D429; Pflicht und Liebe, D467; Phidile, D500; Winterlied, D401 Popp (sop), Johnson (pno)
Hyperion CDJ 33017 [D] **F**

Lieder Edition Volume 18: Abendlied, D499; An den Schlaf, D447; An die Entfernte, D765; An die Harmonie, D394; An mein Herz, D860; Auf den Tod eine Nachtigall, D399; Auf der Brucke, D853; Das Blume und der Quell, D874; Blumenlied, D431; Drang in die Ferne, D770; Emtelied, D399; Das Finden, D219; Das Heimweh, D456 & 851; Im Frühling, D882; Im Walde, D834; Lebensmut, D883; Der Liebliche Stern, D861; Die Nacht, D358; Tiefes Leid, D876; Über Wildermann, D884; Um Mitternacht, D862 Schreier (ten), Johnson (pno)
Hyperion CDJ 33018 [D] **F**

Lieder Edition Volume 19: Abendlied, D276; Auf dem See, D543; Auf dem Wasser zu singen, D774; Beim Winde, D669; Der Blumen Schmerz, D731; Die Blumensprache, D519; Gott im Frühling,

D448; Im Heine, D738; Im See, D476; Der liebliche Stern, D861; Nach einem Gewitter, D561; Nachtviolen, D752; Die Rose, D745; Die Sterne, D176; Die Sternennächte, D670; Suleika I & II, D720 & 717; Vergissmeinnicht, D792 Lott (sop), Johnson (pno)
Hyperion CDJ 33019 [D] **F**

Lieder Edition, Volume 20: 'An 1815 Schubertiad' (32 Lieder) Rozario (sop), Ainsley (ten), Bostridge (ten), George, (bs), Johnson (pno)
Hyperion CDJ 33020 [D] **F**

Lieder Edition Volume 21: Abschied von einem Freunde, D578; An die Musik, D547; An eine Quelle, D530; Die abgeblühte Linde, D514; Blondel zu Marien, D626; Der Blumenbrief, D622; Erlafsee, D586; Evangelium Johannes, D607; Der Flug der Zeit, D515; Die Forelle, D550; Grablied für die Mutter, D616; Hänflings Liebeswerbung, D552; Die Liebe, D522; Liebhaber in allen Gestalten, D558; Lied eines Kindes, D596; Das Lied von Reifen, D532; Lob der Tränen, D711; Nur wer die Liebe kennt, D513a; Der Schäfer und die Reiter, D517; Schlaflied, D527; Schweizerlied, D559; Sehnsucht, D516; Vom Mitleiden Maria, D632 Mathis (sop), Johnson (pno)
Hyperion CDJ 33021 [D] **F**

38 Lieder Fischer-Dieskau (bar), Moore (pno)
EMI CMS7 63566-2 (US: Angel CDMB 63566), 2 CDs [A] **M**

74 Lieder Ameling (sop), Baldwin (pno), Jansen (pno)
Philips 438 528-2, 4 CDs [A] **M**

21 Lieder Bär (bar), Parsons (pno)
EMI CDC7 54773-2 (US: Angel CDC 54773) [D] **F**

24 Goethe Settings Fassbaender (mez), Garben (pno)
Sony CD 53104 [D] **F**

33 Lieder Hendricks (sop), Lupu (pno)
EMI CDS7 54908-2 (US: Angel CDCB 54908), 2 CDs [D] F

17 Lieder Bonney (sop), Parsons (pno)
Teldec 4509 90873-2 [D] **F**

19 Lieder Blochwitz (ten), Jansen (pno)
Philips 438 932 [D] **F**

Complete Sacred Music, Vol. 1 (incl. the complete Masses) Donath (sop), Popp (sop), Fischer-Dieskau (bar), Fassbaender (mez), Schreier (ten), Araiza (ten), Protschka (ten), Dallapozza (ten), Bavarian RSO & Ch, Sawallisch
EMI CMS7 64778-2 (US: Angel CDMB 64778), 3 CDs [A/D] **M**

Complete Sacred Music, Vol. 2 (shorter choral works) Donath (sop), Popp (sop), Fischer-Dieskau (bar), Fassbaender (mez), Protschka (ten), Dallapozza (ten), Tear (ten), Bavarian RSO & Ch, Sawallisch
EMI CMS7 64783-2 (US: Angel CDMB 64783), 3 CDs [A/D] **M**

Mass No.5 in A♭, D678 (second version); *Deutsche Messe, D872* Vienna Boys' Ch., Chorus Viennensis, Age of Enlightenment O, Weil
✧ Sony CD 53984 [D] **F**

Mass No. 6 in E♭, D950 Mattila (sop), Lipovšek (cont), Hadley (ten), Pita (ten), Höll (bs), Vienna State O Ch, VPO, Abbado
DG 423 088-2 [D] **F**

Die schöne Müllerin (song cycle), *D795; Schwanengesang* (Lieder collection), *D957; Die Winterreise* (song cycle), *D911*

Fischer-Dieskau (bar), Moore (pno)
DG 437 235-2, 3 CDs [A] **B**

V *Die schöne Müllerin* (song cycle), *D795*
Hagegard (bar), Ax (pno)
RCA 09026 61705-2 [D] **F**
Prégardien (ten), Staier (fpno)
◇ DHM 05472 77273-2 [D] **F**

Schwanengesang (Lieder collection), *D957; An die Musik, D547;
An Sylvia, D891; Die Forelle, D550; Heidenröslein, D257; Im
Abendrot, D799; Der Musensohn, D764; Der Tod und das Mädchen
D531* Fischer-Dieskau (bar), Moore (pno)
DG 415 188-2 [A] **F**

Schwanengesang (Lieder collection), *D957; Am Fenster, D878;
Herbst, D945; Sehnsucht, D879; Der Wanderer an den Mond,
D870; Wiegenlied, D867* Fassbaender (mez), Reimann
(pno)
DG 429 766-2 [D] **F**

Die Winterreise (song cycle), *D911*
Fischer-Dieskau (bar), Demus (pno)
DG 447 421-2 [A] **M**
Schreier (ten), Schiff (pno)
Decca 436 122-2 (US: London 436 122-2) [D] **F**
Fassbaender (mez), Reimann (pno)
EMI CDC7 49846-2 (US: Angel CDC 49846) [D] **F**

SCHUMAN, William (born 1910) USA

O *Judith* (ballet); *New England Triptych; Symphony for Strings;
Variations on 'America'* Seattle SO, Schwarz
Delos DE 3115 [D] **F**

New England Triptych Eastman-Rochester O, Hanson
(+ Ives: *Symphony No. 3; Three Places in New England;* Mennin:
Symphony No. 5)
Philips Mercury 432 755-2 [A] **M**

Symphony No. 3 NYPO, Bernstein
(+ Harris: *Symphony No. 3*)
DG 419 780-2 [D] **F**

*Symphony No. 10 (American Muse); American Festival Overture;
New England Triptych* St. Louis SO, Slatkin
(+ Ives: *Variations on 'America'*)
RCA 09026 61282-2 [D] **F**

String Quartets Nos. 2, 3 & 5
Lydian Quartet
HM HMU 907114 [D] **F**

SCHUMANN, Clara (1819–1896) GERMANY

C *Piano Trio in G min., Op. 17* Dartington Piano Trio
(+ F. Mendelssohn: *Piano Trio in D, Op. 11*)
Hyperion CDA 66331 [D] **F**

SCHUMANN, Robert (1810–1856) GERMANY

O *Cello Concerto in A min., Op. 129;* *Adagio and Allegro, Op. 70;*
**5 Stücke im Volkston, Op. 102;* *Fantasiestücke, Op. 73* Ma (vcl)
Bavarian RSO, C. Davis; *Ax (pno)
Sony CD 42663 [D] **F**

Piano Concerto in A min., Op. 54 Kovacevich (pno), BBC SO,
C. Davis

(+ Grieg: *Piano Concerto*)
Philips 412 923-2 [A] **F**

Piano Concerto in A min., Op. 54; Arabeske; Symphonische Etüden Pollini (pno), *BPO, Abbado
DG 445 522-2 [D] **M**

Violin Concerto in D min., Op. posth Szeryng (vln), LSO, Dorati
(+ Mendelssohn: *Violin Concerto in E min.*)
Philips Mercury 434 339-2 [A] **M**

Overtures: *Genoveva, Op. 81; Julius Caesar, Op. 128; Manfred, Op. 115; Overture, Scherzo & Finale, Op. 52* LSO, Järvi
Chandos CHAN 6548 [D] **M**

Symphonies Nos. 1–4; Genoveva Overture; Manfred Overture BPO, Kubelik
DG 437 395-2, 2 CDs [A] **B**

Symphonies Nos. 1–4; Overture, Scherzo & Finale, Op. 52
Hanover Band, Goodman
✧ RCA 09026 61931-2, 2 CDs [D] **F**

Symphonies: No. 1 in B♭, Op. 38 (Spring); No. 4 in D min., Op. 120; Overture, Scherzo and Finale, Op. 52 Dresden State O, Sawallisch
EMI CDM7 69471-2 (US: Angel CDM 69471) [A] **M**

Symphonies: No. 2 in C, Op. 61; No. 3 in E♭ (Rhenish), Op. 97
Dresden State O, Sawallisch
EMI CDM7 69472-2 (US: Angel CDM 69472) [A] **M**

Symphonies: No. 3 in E♭ (Rhenish), Op. 97; No. 4 in D min., Op. 120 LCP, Norrington
✧ EMI CDC7 54025-2 (US: Angel CDC 54025) [D] **F**

Adagio and Allegro, Op. 70 Tuckwell (hn), Ashkenazy (pno)
(+ Brahms: *Horn Trio;* Franck: *Violin Sonata;* Saint-Saëns: *Romance, Op. 67*)
Decca 433 695-2 (US: London 433 695-2) [A] **F**

Adagio and Allegro, Op. 70; Fantasiestück, Op. 73; Romanzen, Op. 94; 5 Stücke in Volkston, Op. 102 Holliger (ob), Brendel (pno)
Philips 426 386-2 [A] **M**

Piano Quartet in E♭, Op. 47 Ax (pno), Stern (vln), Laredo (vla), Ma (vcl)
(+ Beethoven: *Piano Quartet*)
Sony CD 53339 [D] **F**

*Piano Quartet in E♭, Op. 47; *Piano Quintet in E♭, Op. 44* Gould (pno), *Bernstein (pno), Juilliard Quartet
Sony/CBS CD44848 [A] **M**

Piano Quintet in E♭, Op.44 Vladar (pno), Artis Quartet
(+Brahms: *Piano Quintet*)
Sony CD 58954 [D] **F**

Piano Trios Nos. 1–3; Fantasiestücke, Op. 88 Beaux Arts Trio
Philips 432 165-2, 2 CDs [D] **F**

Piano Trio No. 1 in D min., Op. 63 Szeryng (vln), Fournier (vcl), Rubinstein (pno)
(+Schubert: *Piano Trio No. 1*)
RCA GD 86262 (US: 6262-2) [A] **M**

Piano Trios: No. 2 in F, Op. 80; No. 3 in G min., Op. 110; Fantasiestücke, Op. 88 Israel Piano Trio
CRD 3458 [A] **F**

C *String Quartets Nos. 1–3* Melos Quartet
(+ Brahms: *String Quartets Nos. 1–3*)
DG 423 670-2, 3 CDs [D] **F**

Violin Sonatas: No. 1 in A min., Op. 105; No. 2 in D min., Op. 12
Kremer (vln), Argerich (pno)
DG 419 235-2 [D] **F**

5 Stücke in Volkston, Op. 102 Rostropovich (vcl), Britten (pno)
(+ Debussy: *Cello Sonata*; Schubert: *Arpeggione Sonata*)
Decca 417 833-2 (US: London 417 833-2) [A] **M**

S *Album für die Jugend, Op. 68* Brownridge (pno)
Hyperion CDH 88039 [D] **M**

*Arabeske, Op. 18; Blumenstück, Op. 19; Carnaval, Op. 9;
Davidsbündlertänze, Op. 6; Fantasie in C, Op. 17; 8 Fantasiestücke,
Op. 12; 3 Fantasiestücke, Op. 111; Faschingsschwank aus Wien,
Op. 26; Humoreske, Op. 20; Kinderszenen, Op. 15; Kreisleriana,
Op. 16; 4 Nachtstücke, Op. 23; 8 Novelletten, Op. 21; Papillons,
Op. 2; 3 Romances, Op. 28; Piano Sonatas: No. 1 in F♯ min.,
Op. 11; No. 2 in G min., Op. 22; Waldszenen, Op. 82* Arrau (pno)
Philips 432 308-2, 7 CDs [A] **M**

*Blumenstück, Op. 19; 4 Fugues, Op. 72; March in G min., Op. 76/2
Nachtstücke, Op. 23; Toccata, Op. 7* Richter (pno)
Decca 436 456-2 (US: London 436 456-2) [D] **F**

Carnaval, Op. 9; Papillons, Op. 2; Toccata, Op. 7 Licad (pno)
Sony CD 45742 [D] **F**

*Davidsbündlertänze, Op. 6; Fantasiestücke, Op. 12; Blumenstück,
Op. 19* Ashkenazy (pno)
Decca 425 109-2 (US: London 425 109-2) [D] **F**

*Fantasie in C, Op. 17; Faschingsschwank aus Wien, Op. 26;
Papillons, Op. 2* Richter (pno)
EMI CDM7 64625-2 (US: CDM 64625) [A] **M**

Fantasie in C, Op. 17; Piano Sonata No. 1 in F♯ min., Op. 11
Pollini (pno)
DG 423 134-2 [A] **F**

Kreisleriana, Op. 16; Kinderszenen, Op. 15 Argerich (pno)
DG 410 653-2 [D] **F**

*8 Novelletten, Op. 21; Allegro, Op. 8; 3 Fantasiestücke, Op. 111;
Gesänge der Frühe, Op. 133* Brautigam (pno)
Olympia OCD 436 [D] **F**

*Piano Sonata No. 2 in G min., Op. 22; Intermezzi, Op. 4;
Symphonic Studies, Op. 13; Toccata, Op. 7* Kazakevich (pno)
Conifer CDCF 227 [D] **F**

*Piano Sonata No. 3, Op. 14; Humoreske, Op. 20; Fantasiestücke,
Op. 12* Horowitz (pno)
RCA GD 86680 (US: 6680-2) [A] **M**

Complete Organ Music Latry (org)
Sony CD 57490 [D] **F**

6 Fugues on B-A-C-H, Op. 60 Bowyer (org)
(+ Reubke; *Sonata in B♭ min.*, etc.)
Nimbus NI 5361 [D] **F**

V *Dichterliebe (song cycle), Op. 48; Liederkreis (song cycle), Op. 39;
Myrthen Lieder, Op. 25 Nos. 1, 2, 3, 7, 8, 13 & 24* Fischer-
Dieskau (bar), Moore (pno)
DG 415 190-2 [A] **F**

Dichterliebe, Op. 48; Liederkreis, Op. 39 I. Partridge (ten),
J. Partridge (pno)
Classics for Pleasure CD-CFP 4651 [A] **F**

Dichterliebe, Op. 48 Prégardien (ten), Staier (fpno)
(+ Songs by Mendelssohn & Schubert)
RCA 05472 77319-2 [D] **F**

Frauenliebe und Leben (song cycle), *Op. 42; Liederkreis, Op. 24*
(song collection); *Abends am Strand, Op. 45/3; Lehn deine Wang,
Op. 142/2; Mein Wagen rollet langsam, Op. 142/4* Fassbaender
(mez), Gage (pno)
DG 415 519-2 [D] **F**

12 Kerner Lieder, Op. 35; Liederkreis (song collection), *Op. 24*
Bär (bar), Parsons (pno)
EMI CDC7 54027-2 (US: Angel CDC 54027) [D] **F**

12 Kerner Lieder, Op. 35; Liederkreis, Op. 39 Price (sop),
Johnson (pno)
Hyperion CDA 66596 [D] **F**

*5 Andersen Lieder, Op. 40; 12 Kerner Lieder, Op. 35; 5 Lieder,
Op. posth.; Sängers Trost, Op. 127/1; Trost im Gesang, Op. 142/1*
Hampson (bar), Parsons (pno)
Teldec 2292 44935-2 [D] **F**

*Liederkreis, Op. 39; 7 Lieder, Op. 90; 4 Lieder from Op. 40; 3
Lieder from Op. 98a; Nachtlied, Op. 96/1* Holl (bar), Schiff (pno)
Decca 436 123-2 (US: London 436 123-2) [D] **F**

Lieder Recital Walker (mez), Vignoles (pno)
CRD 3401 [A] **F**

Liederkreis, Op. 39 Fassbaender (mez), Leonskeya (pno)
(+ Brahms: *4 Last Songs, Op. 121; 10 Lieder*)
Teldec 9031 74872-2 [D] **F**

*Myrthen, Op. 25; Lieder und Gesänge, Op. 27; Die Löwenbraut,
Op. 31/1* Dawson (pno), Partridge (ten), Drake (pno)
Chandos CHAN 9307 [D] **F**

Manfred, Op. 115 Sieber (sop), Schreckenbach (cont), Ramirez
(ten), Stamm (bs), Various speakers, RIAS Chamber Ch,
Berlin RSO, Albrecht
Koch Schwann 31089-2 [D] **F**

Scenes from Goethe's Faust Blochwitz, Bonney, Graham,
Mattila, Peeters, Poschner-Klebel; Terfel, Vermillion,
Wottrich, BPO, Abbado
Sony CD 66308, 2 CDs [D] **F**

CHÜTZ, Heinrich (1585–1672) GERMANY

*Ach Herr, du Schöpfer aller Ding; Erbarm dich; Magnificat; Meine
Seele erhebt; Quemadmodum desiderat cervus; Die Sieben Worte;
Symphoniae sacrae: Anima mea; Adjuro vos* Clément Janequin
Ensemble, Saqueboutiers de Toulouse, Junghänel (lte), Cable
(gmba), Jansen
◇ HM HMC90 1255 [D] **F**

*Ach Herr, straf mich nicht; Cantate Domino; Christmas Story;
Deutsches Magnificat; Herr, unser Herrscher; Ich freu mich des;
Unser Herr Christus* Heinrich Schütz Ch, Symphoniae Sacrae
Chamber Ensemble, Norrington
◇ Decca 430 632-2 (US: London 430 632-2) [A] **M**

V *Auf dem Gebirge; Freue dich des Weibes deiner Jugend; List nicht Ephraim mein teurer Sohn; Musicalische Exequien; Saul, Saul, was verfolgst du mich* Monteverdi Ch, EBS, His Majesties Sagbutts & Cornets, Gardiner
◇ DG Archiv 423 405-2 [D] **F**

Bone Jesu; Bringt her dem Hernn; Eile, mich Gott; Habe deine Lust, Herzlich lieb hab ich dich; Ihr Heiligen; O Jesu, nomen dulce; O süsser; Was betrübst; Was hast du verwirket; Wie ein Rubin; Wohl dem, der nicht wandelt Concerto Vocale
◇ HM HMC90 1097 [D] **F**

Christmas Oratorio; Easter Oratorio Stuttgart Chamber Ch, Musica Fiata Köln, Stuttgart Baroque O, Bernius
◇ Sony CD 45943 [D] **F**

Psalms of David (complete) Stuttgart Chamber Ch, Musica Fiata Köln, Bernius
◇ Sony CD 48042, 2 CDs [D] **F**

Symphoniae Sacrae, Op. 10 Kirkby (sop I), Le Blanc (sop II), Bowman (alt), Rogers (ten I, Daniels (ten II), Varcoe (bs I), Wistreich (bs II), Purcell Quartet
◇ Chandos CHAN 0566-7, 2 CDs [D] **F**

SCOTT, Francis (1880–1958) SCOTLAND

S *Scottish Lyrics: Vol. 1 Nos. 1 & 2; Vol. 2/1; Vol. 3/1; Vol. 5 Nos. 1–3; There's News* McLachlan (pno)
(+ works by Center, Stevenson)
Olympia OCD 264 [D] **F**

SCRIABIN, Alexander (1872–1915) RUSSIA

O *Piano Concerto in F♯ min., Op. 20; *Poem of Ecstasy, Op. 54; Prometheus (Poem of Fire), Op. 60* Ashkenazy (pno), LPO, *Cleveland O, Maazel
Decca 417 252-2 (US: London 417 252-2) [A] **F**

*Poem of Ecstasy, Op. 54; *Prometheus (Poem of Fire), Op. 60; Symphonies Nos. **1–3* *Alexeev (pno), **Toczyska (mez), **Myers (ten), Philadelphia O, Muti
EMI CDS7 54251-2 (US: CDC 54251), 3 CDs [D] **F**

Poem of Ecstasy, Op. 54 NYPO, Boulez
(+Bartok: *Dance Suite*, etc.)
Sony CD 64100, 2 CDs [A] **M**

Symphony No. 2 in C min., Op. 29 SNO, Järvi
Chandos CHAN 8642 [D] **F**

Symphony No. 3 in C min. (Divine Poem), Op. 43 Danish National RSO, Järvi
(+ Arensky: *Silhouettes*)
Chandos CHAN 8898 [D] **F**

S *Mazurkas, Opp. 3, 25 & 40* Pizarro (pno)
Collins 1394-2 [D] **F**

Preludes: Op. 2/2; Op. 9/1; Opp. 11, 13, 15, 16 & 17
EDITORS' CHOICE: Fergus-Thompson (pno)
ASV CDDCA 919 [D] **F**

Piano Sonatas Nos. 1–10 Ashkenazy (pno)
Decca 425 579-2 (US: London 425 579-2), 2 CDs [A] **M**

Piano Sonatas: No. 2 in G♯ min., Op. 19 (Sonata-fantasy); No. 9 in F, Op. 68 (Black Mass); Études, Op. 8 Nos. 2, 4 & 5; Études, Op. 42 Nos. 3, 4 & 7; 4 Pieces, Op. 51; Vers la flamme, Op. 72

Demidenko (pno)
(+ Prokofiev: *Visions fugitives*)
Conifer CDCF 204 [D] **F**

Piano Sonatas Nos. 2 & 3; 12 Etudes, Op. 8; 2 Nocturnes, Op. 5
Fergus-Thompson (pno)
ASV CDDCA 882 [D] **F**

*Piano Sonata No. 3 in F♯ min., Op. 23; 2 Poems, Op. 32; Vers la
flamme, Op. 72* Fergus-Thompson (pno)
(+ Balakirev: *The Lark; Piano Sonata*)
Kingdom KCLCD 2001 [D] **F**

*Piano Sonatas: No. 3 in F♯ min., Op. 23; No. 5, Op. 53; Preludes:
Op. 11 Nos. 1, 3, 9, 10, 13, 14 & 16; Op. 15/2; Op. 16 Nos. 1 & 4;
Études: Op. 8 Nos. 7 & 12; Op. 42/5* Horowitz (pno)
RCA GD 86215 (US: 6215-2) [A] **mono/stereo M**

*Piano Sonatas Nos. 4, 5, 9 & 10; 8 Études, Op. 42; 3 Pieces, Op.
2/1 (Étude in C♯ min.)* Fergus-Thompson (pno)
ASV CDDCA 776 [D] **F**

CULTHORPE, Peter (born 1929) AUSTRALIA

*Nourlangie; From Kakadu; Into the Dreaming Williams (gtr),
*Australian CO, Hickox
(+Westlake: *Antarctica*)
Sony CD 53361 [D] **F**

EIBER, Matyas (1905–1960) HUNGARY/ENGLAND

Clarinet Concertino King (cl), ECO, Litton
(+ Blake: *Clarinet Concerto;* Lutoslawski: *Dance Preludes*)
Hyperion CDA 66215 [D] **F**

EREBRIER, José (born 1938) URUGUAY

Momento psicológico; Poema elegíaca RPO, Serebrier
(+ Bloch: *Violin Concerto; Baal Shem*)
ASV CDDCA 785 [D] **F**

ESSIONS, Roger (1896–1985) USA

Concerto for Orchestra Boston SO, Ozawa
(+ Panufnik: *Symphony No. 8*)
Hyperion CDA 66050 [D] **F**

Rhapsody for Orchestra; Symphonies Nos. 4 & 5 Columbus SO,
Badea
New World NW 345-2 [D] **F**

Symphony No. 2 SFSO, Blomstedt
(+Harbison: *Symphony No. 2*, etc.)
Decca 443 376-2 (US: London 443 376-2) [D] **F**

*Duo for Violin and Cello; Six Pieces for Cello; Duo for Violin and
Piano; Sonata for Violin* Macomber (vln), Krosnick (vcl),
Salwen (pno)
Koch 3-7153-2 [D] **F**

Piano Sonata No. 2 Lawson (pno)
(+ Griffes: *Piano Sonata;* Ives: *Piano Sonata No. 1*)
Virgin VC7 59316-2 (US: 59316) [D] **F**

When Lilacs last in the dooryard bloom'd Hinds (sop), Quivar
(mez), Cossa (bar), Tanglewood Festival Ch, Boston SO, Ozawa
New World NW 296-2 [D] **F**

SHAPERO, Harold (born 1920) USA

O   *Nine-minute Overture; Symphony for Classical Orchestra* LAPO,
Previn
New World NW 373-2 [D] **F**

SHCHEDRIN, Rodion (born 1932) RUSSIA

S   *24 Preludes & Fugues; 25 Preludes* McLaughlin (pno)
Olympia OCD 438, 2 CDs [D] **F**

SHEPPARD, John (c.1515–c.1559) ENGLAND

V   *Christe Redemptor omnium; In manus tuas I–III; Media vita; Rege
Tharsis; Sacris solemniis; Verbum caro* Tallis Scholars, Phillips
Gimell CDGIM 016 [D] **F**

*Filiae Hierusalem venite; Haec dies; In manus tuas I; In pace in
idipsum; Justi in perpetuum vivent; Laudem dicite Deo; Libera nos,
salva nos I; Paschal Kyrie; Reges Tharsis et insulae; Spiritus sanctu
procedens I; Verbo caro factum est* The Sixteen, Christophers
Hyperion CDA 66259 [D] **F**

*Gaude, gaude, gaude Maria; In manus tuas I; In pace; Laudem
dicite Deo; Verbo caro* Clerkes of Oxenford, Wulstan
(+ Tallis: *Spem in alium*, etc.)
Classics for Pleasure CD-CFP 4638 [A] **B**

*Mass 'The Western Wynde'; Aeterne Rex altissime; Christe virgo
dilectissima; Dum transisset sabbatum II; Hostes Herodes impie; In
manus tuas III; Te deum* The Sixteen, Christophers
Hyperion CDA 66603 [D] **F**

*Missa Cantate; Ave maris stella; Deus tuorum militum II; Jesu
salvator saeculi I & II; Salvator mundi Domine* The Sixteen,
Christophers
Hyperion CDA 66418 [D] **F**

SHOSTAKOVICH, Dmitry (1906–1975) RUSSIA

O   *Age of Gold* (ballet): *Suite, Op. 22a* LPO, Haitink
(+ Janáček: *Sinfonietta; Taras Bulba*)
Decca 430 727-2 (US: London 430 727-2) [D] **M**

*Ballet Suites Nos. 1–5; Festive Overture, Op. 96; Katerina
Ismailova (opera): Suite* SNO, Järvi
Chandos CHAN 7000/1, 2 CDs [D] **M**

The Bolt (ballet) Royal Stockholm PO, Rozhdestvensky
Chandos CHAN 9343/4, 2 CDs [D] **F**

Chamber Symphony, Op. 110a (arr. Barshai); *Symphony for
Strings, Op. 118a* (arr. Barshai) COE, Barshai
DG 429 229-2 [D] **F**

*Cello Concerto No. 1 in E♭, Op. 107; Piano Concertos: *No. 1 in C
min., Op. 35; **No. 2 in F, Op. 102* Rostropovich (vcl),
Philadelphia O, Ormandy; *Previn (pno), *Tachinno (tpt),
NYPO, Bernstein; **Bernstein (pno/dir), NYPO
Sony/CBS CD44850 [A] **M**

Cello Concertos: No. 1 in E♭, Op. 107; No. 2 in F, Op. 126 Maisk
(vcl), LSO, Tilson Thomas
DG 445 821-2 [D] **F**

Violin Concertos: No. 1 in A min., Op. 99; No. 2 in C♯ min., Op. 12
Sitkovetsky (vln), BBC SO, A. Davis
Virgin VC7 59601-2 (US: CDC 59601) [D] **F**

○ *Violin Concerto No. 1 in A min., Op. 77*
EDITORS' CHOICE: Vengarov (vln), LSO, Rostropovich
(+Prokofiev: *Violin Concerto No. 1*)
Teldec 4509 98143-2 [D] **F**

The Gadfly (film score): *Suite, Op. 97a* USSR Cinema SO,
Khachaturian
Classics for Pleasure CD-CFP4463 [A] **B**

The Golden Age (ballet) Royal Stockholm PO, Rozhdestvensky
Chandos CHAN 9251/2, 2 CDs [A] **F**

*Jazz Suites Nos. 1 & 2; Piano Concerto No. 1 in E♭, Op. 107; Tahiti
Trot., Op. 16* Brautigan (pno), Royal Concertgebouw O,
Chailly
Decca 433 702-2 (US: London 433 702-2) [D] **F**

Symphonies Nos. 1–15 Various artists, Moscow PO, Kondrashin
Melodiya/BMG 74321 19952-2, 10 CDs [A] **M**

*Symphonies: No. 1 in F min., Op. 10; No. 7 in C (Leningrad),
Op. 60* CSO, Bernstein
DG 427 632-2, 2 CDs [D] **F**

*Symphonies: No. 2 in B (To October), Op. 14; No. 3 in E♭ (First of
May), Op. 20* London Voices, LSO, Rostropovich
Teldec 4509 90853-2 [D] **F**

Symphony No. 4 in C min., Op. 43 SNO, Järvi
Chandos CHAN 8640 [D] **F**

Symphonies: No. 5 in D min., Op. 47; No. 9 in E♭, Op. 70 NYPO,
Bernstein
Sony CD 47615 [A] **M**

Symphony No. 5 in D min., Op. 47 LSO, Previn
(+ Rachmaninov: *The Rock*)
RCA GD 86801 (US: 6801-2) [A] **M**

Symphony No. 6 in B min., Op. 54 LSO, Previn
(+ Rachmaninov: *Symphony No. 3*)
EMI CDM7 69564-2 (US: Angel CDM 69564) [A] **M**

Symphony No. 7 in C (Leningrad), Op. 60 Moscow PO,
Kondrashin
Melodiya/BMG 74321 19839-2 [A] **M**

Symphony No. 8 in C min., Op. 65 Washington National SO,
Rostropovich
Teldec 9031 74719-2 [D] **F**

Symphony No. 10 in E min., Op. 93 BPO, Karajan
DG 429 716-2 [A] **M**

Symphony No. 11 in G min. (The Year 1905), Op. 103 Moscow
PO, Kondrashin
Melodiya/BMG 74321 19843-2 [A] **M**

*Symphonies: No. 12 in D min. (The Year 1917), Op. 112; No. 1 in
F min., Op. 10* Moscow PO, Kondrashin
Melodiya/BMG 74321 19848-2 [A] **M**

Symphony No. 13 in B♭ min. (Babi Yar), Op. 113 Rintzler (bs),
Concertgebouw O & Ch., Haitink
Decca 425 073-2 (US: London 425 073-2) [D] **M**

Symphonies: No. 14, Op. 135 ; No. 2 in B (To October), Op. 14
Tselovalnik (sop), Nesterenko (bs), Moscow PO, Kondrashin
Melodiya/BMG 74321 19844-2 [A] **M**

C *Cello Sonata in D min., Op. 40; Moderato* Harrell (vcl),
Ashkenazy (pno)
(+ Prokofiev: *Cello Sonata*)
Decca 421 774-2 (US: London 421 774-2) [D] **F**

**Piano Quintet in G min., Op. 67; Piano Trio No. 2 in E min.,
Op. 67* Beaux Arts Trio, *Drucker (vln), *Dutton (vla)
Philips 432 079-2 [D] **F**

String Quartets Nos. 1–15
EDITORS' CHOICE: Shostakovich Quartet
Olympia OCD 5009, 5 CDs [A] **M**

*String Quartets Nos. 1–15; *Piano Quintet* *Richter (pno),
Borodin Quartet
EMI CMS5 65032-2 (US: CDMB 65032), 6 CDs [A] **M**

String Quartets: Nos. 1, 3 & 4; 2 Pieces, Op. 36 Shostakovich
Quartet
Olympia OCD 531 [A] **F**

String Quartets Nos. 2, 5 & 7 Shostakovich Quartet
Olympia OCD 532 [A] **F**

String Quartets Nos. 6, 8 & 9 Shostakovich Quartet
Olympia OCD 533 [A] **F**

String Quartets Nos. 10, 11 & 15 Shostakovich Quartet
Olympia OCD 534 [A] **F**

String Quartets Nos. 12–14 Shostakovich Quartet
Olympia OCD 535 [A] **F**

Viola Sonata Bashmet (vla), Muntian (pno)
(+ Glinka: *Viola Sonata;* Roslavets: *Viola Sonata No. 1*)
RCA 09026 61273-2 [D] **F**

S *24 Preludes and Fugues, Op. 87* Nikolayeva (pno)
Melodiya/BMG 74321 19849-2, 3 CDs [A] **M**

24 Preludes, Op. 34
Mustonen (pno)
(+ Alkan: *25 Preludes*)
Decca 433 055-2 (US: London 433 055-2) [D] **F**

V *From Jewish Poetry, Op. 79a; 2 Fables of Krylov, Op. 4;
3 Romances on Poems by Pushkin, Op. 46a; 6 Romances on Verses
by Raleigh, Burns & Shakespeare, Op. 62/140* Orgonasova (sop),
Dyadkova (mez), Stutzmann (cont), Langridge (ten),
Leiferkus (bs), Gothenburg SO, Järvi
DG 439 860-2 [D] **F**

*Suite on Verses of Michelangelo, Op. 145; 4 Verses of Captain
Lebyadkin, Op. 146* Fischer-Dieskau (bar), Berlin RSO,
Ashkenazy
Decca 433 319-2 (US: London 433 319-2) [D] **F**

SIBELIUS, Jean (1865–1957) FINLAND

O *Belshazzar's Feast* (incidental music), *Op. 51: Alla marcia;
The Dryad* (tone poem), *Op. 45/1; Pan and Echo* (dance
intermezzo), *Op. 53; Swanwhite* (incidental music), *Op. 54:
The Peacock* Gothenburg SO, Järvi
BIS BIS-CD 359 [D] **F**

*Violin Concerto in D min. (1903/4 version); Violin Concerto in D
min., Op. 47* Kovakos (vln), Lahti SO, Vanska
BIS BIS-CD 500 [D] **F**

Violin Concerto in D min., *Op. 47*
Heifetz (vln), CSO, Hendl
(+ Glazunov: *Violin Concerto;* Prokofiev: *Violin Concerto No. 2*)
RCA RD 87019 (US: RCDI 7019) [A] **F**
Lin (vln), Swedish RSO, Salonen
(+ Nielsen: *Violin Concerto*)
Sony CD44548 [D] **F**
Little (vln), RLPO, Handley
(+ Brahms: *Violin Concerto*)
EMI Eminence CD-EMX 2203 (US: Classics for Pleasure CDEMX
2203) [D] **M**

En Saga, *Op. 9; Scènes historiques: Suites Nos. 1, Op. 25, & 2,*
Op. 66 Gothenburg SO, Järvi
BIS BIS-CD 295 [D] **F**

Finlandia, *Op. 26; Legends, Op. 22: The Swan of Tuonela;*
Tapiola (tone poem), *Op. 112; Valse Triste, Op. 44/1* BPO,
Karajan
DG 413 755-2 [D] **F**

Kullervo, *Op. 7* Saarinen (mez), Hynninen (bar), Estonian
State Academic Male Ch., Helsinki University Male Ch.,
Helsinki PO, Berglund
EMI CDM5 65080-2 (US: CDM 65080) [D] **M**

4 Legends (Lemminkäinen Suite), Op. 22 Gothenburg SO, Järvi
BIS BIS-CD 294 [D] **F**

Pohjola's Daughter (symphonic fantasia), *Op. 49; Rakastava,*
Op. 14; Tapiola (tone poem), *Op. 112; Andante lirico*
Gothenburg SO, Järvi
BIS BIS-CD 312 [D] **F**

Scènes historiques: Suites Nos. 1, Op. 25, & 2, Op. 66 Gothenburg
SO, Järvi
BIS BIS-CD 295 [D] **F**

Symphonies Nos. 1–7 VPO, Maazel
Decca 430 778-2 (US: London 430 778-2), 3 CDs [A] **M**

Symphony No. 1 in E min., Op. 39; Finlandia, Op. 26; Karelia
Suite, Op. 11 Oslo PO, Jansons
EMI CDC7 54273-2 (US: Angel CDC 54273) [D] **F**

Symphony No. 2 in D, Op. 43; Finlandia, Op. 26; Karelia Suite,
Op. 11 Philharmonia O, Ashkenazy
Decca 430 737-2 (US: London 430 737-2) [D] **M**

Symphonies: No. 3 in C, Op. 52; No. 5 in E♭, Op. 82 LSO, C.
Davis
RCA 09026 61693-2 [D] **F**

Symphonies: No. 3 in C, Op. 52; No. 6 in D min., Op. 104
Philharmonia O, Ashkenazy
Decca 436 478-2 (US: London 436 478-2) [D] **M**

Symphonies: No. 4 in A min., Op. 63; No. 7 in C, Op. 105;
Valse triste, Op. 44 BPO, Karajan
DG 439 527-2 [A] **M**

Symphonies: No. 5 in E♭, Op. 82; No. 6 in D min., Op. 104;
The Swan of Tuonela BPO, Karajan
DG 439 982-2 [A] **M**

Symphony No. 7 in C, Op. 105; Oceanides (tone poem), *Op. 73;*
Pelléas et Mélisande (incidental music), *Op. 46; Tapiola* (tone

poem), *Op. 112* RPO, Beecham
EMI CDM7 63400-2 (US: Angel CDM 63400) [A] **M**

O *Tapiola* BPO, Karajan
(+ Nielsen: *Symphony No. 4*)
DG 445 518-2 [D] **M**

C *Piano Quintet in G min.; String Quartet in D min., Op. 56 (Voces
intimae)* Goldstone (pno), Gabrieli Quartet
Chandos CHAN 8742 [D] **F**

   2 Pieces, Op. 77; 4 Pieces, Op. 78; Malinconia, Op. 20 Mork (vcl)
   Thibaudet (pno)
   (+Grieg: *Cello Sonata in A min., Op. 36; Intermezzo)*
   Virgin VC5 45034-2 (US: 45034) [D] **F**

S *The Cavalier; 5 Esquisses, Op. 114; Morceau romantique; 8 Pieces,
Op. 99; 5 Pieces, Op. 101; 5 Pieces, Op. 103* Tawastsjerna (pno)
BIS BIS-CD 278 [D] **F**

   *6 Finnish Folksongs; 6 Impromptus, Op. 5; 4 Lyric Pieces, Op. 74;
   Piano Sonata in F, Op. 12* Tawastsjerna (pno)
   BIS BIS-CD 153 [D] **F**

   3 Lyric Pieces, Op. 41; Sonatines Nos. 1–3, Op. 67 Gould (pno)
   (+ Bizet: *Nocturne No. 1; Variations chromatiques, Op. 3;* Grieg:
   Piano Sonata)
   Sony CD 52654, 2 CDs [A] **M**

   *4 Lyric Pieces, Op. 74; Pieces, Op. 76; 2 Rondinos, Op. 68;
   3 Sonatinas, Op. 67* Tawastsjerna (pno)
   BIS BIS-CD 196 [D] **F**

   10 Pensées lyriques, Op. 40; 10 Pieces, Op. 58 Tawastsjerna (pno)
   BIS BIS-CD 195 [D] **F**

   10 Pieces, Op. 24; 10 Pieces, Op. 34 Tawastsjerna (pno)
   BIS BIS-CD 169 [D] **F**

V *Arioso, Op. 3; Narcissus; Pelléas et Mélisande* (incidental music),
*Op. 46: Three blind sisters; Row, row duck; 7 Songs, Op. 17; 6
Songs, Op. 36; 5 Songs, Op. 37; 6 Songs, Op. 88* von Otter (mez)
Forsberg (pno)
BIS BIS-CD 457 [D] **F**

   Luonnotar, Op. 70; 13 songs Hynninen (bar), Häggander (sop)
   Gothenburg SO, Panula
   BIS BIS-CD 270 [D] **F**

   24 Songs Krause (bar), Djupsjobacka (pno)
   Finlandia 4509 96871-2 [D] **F**

SIMPSON, Robert (born 1921) ENGLAND

O *Energy; The Four Temperaments; Introduction and Allegro on a
Bass by Max Reger; Volcano; Vortex* Desford Colliery Caterpillar
Band, Watson
Hyperion CDA 66449 [D] **F**

   Symphonies Nos. 2 & 4 Bournemouth SO, Handley
   Hyperion CDA 66505 [D] **F**

   Symphonies Nos. 3 & 5 RPO, Handley
   Hyperion CDA 66728 [D] **F**

   Symphony No. 6; Symphony No. 7 RLPO, Handley
   Hyperion CDA 66280 [D] **F**

O *Symphony No. 9* (including talk by the composer)
Bournemouth SO, Handley
Hyperion CDA 66299 [D] **F**

Symphony No. 10 RLPO, Handley
Hyperion CDA 66510 [D] **F**

C *String Quartet No. 1; String Quartet No. 4* Delmé Quartet
Hyperion 66419 [D] **F**

String Quartet No. 2; String Quartet No. 5 Delmé Quartet
Hyperion 66386 [D] **F**

String Quartet No. 3; String Quartet No. 6; String Trio (Prelude, Adagio and Fugue) Delmé Quartet
Hyperion 66376 [D] **F**

String Quartet No. 7; String Quartet No. 8 Delmé Quartet
Hyperion 66117 [D] **F**

String Quartet No. 9 (32 Variations and a Fugue on a Theme of Haydn) Delmé Quartet
Hyperion 66127 [D] **F**

String Quartet No. 10; String Quartet No. 11 Coull Quartet
Hyperion CDA 66225 [D] **F**

String Quartet No. 12; String Quintet Coull Quartet, Bigley (vla)
Hyperion CDA 66503 [D] **F**

String Quartets Nos. 14 & 15; 2-Clarinet Quintet Vanburgh
Quartet, Farral (cl), Cross (bs cl)
Hyperion CDA 66626 [D] **F**

SMETANA, Bedřich (1824–1884) BOHEMIA

O *Hakon Jarl, Op. 16; Prague Carnival; Richard III, Op. 11; Wallenstein's Camp, Op. 14* Bavarian RSO, Kubelik
(+ Janáček: *Sinfonietta*)
DG 437 254-2 [A] **M**

Má Vlast (complete) Czech PO, Kubelik
Supraphon 11 1208-2 [D] **F**

Vltava Boston SO, Kubelik
(+Dvorak: *Symphonies Nos. 7–9*, etc.)
DG 439 663-2, 2 CDs [A] **B**

C *Piano Trio in G min. B104* Fontenay Trio
(+ Chopin: *Piano Trio*)
Teldec 2292 43715-2 [D] **F**

String Quartets: No. 1 in E min. (From my Life); No. 2 in D min.
Lindsay Quartet
(+ Dvořák: *Romance; Waltzes*)
ASV CDDCA 777 [D] **F**

S *Macbeth and the Witches; Dreams; 3 Salon Polkas; 3 Poetic Polkas; Memories of Bohemia in the Form of Polkas, Opp. 12 & 13* Kvapil
(pno)
Unicorn-Kanchana DKPCD 9152 [D] **F**

SMYTH, Ethel (1858–1944) ENGLAND

O *The Wreckers* (opera): *Overture* SNO, Gibson
(+ German: *Welsh Rhapsody*; Harty: *With the Wild Geese*;
MacCunn: *Land of Mountain and Flood*)
Classics for Pleasure CD CFP 4635 [A] **B**

V *Mass in D; The Boatswain's Mate* (opera): *Mrs Water's Aria;*
March of the Women Harrhy (sop), Hardy (mez), Dressen (ten),
Bohn (bar), Plymouth Music Series O & Ch, Brunelle
Virgin VC7 59022-2 (US: CDC 59022) [D] **F**

SORABJI, Kaikhosru (1892–1988) ENGLAND

S *Opus clavicembalisticum* Ogdon (pno)
Altarus AIR-CD-9075, 4 CDs [D] **F**

Piano Sonata No. 1 Hamelin (pno)
Altarus AIR-CD-9050 [D] **F**

Organ Symphony No. 1 Bowyer (org)
Continuum CCD 1001/2, 2 CDs [D] **F**

SOUSA, John Philip (1854–1932) USA

O *Famous Marches* Eastman Wind Ensemble, Fennell
Philips Mercury 434 300-2 [A] **M**

SOWERBY, Leo (1895–1968) USA

C *Trio* (1953); *Trio in C♯ min.* Musica Gioiosa Trio
New World NW 365-2 [D] **F**

S *Fantasy for Flute Stops; Requiescat in pace; Symphony in G*
Crozier (org)
Delos DE 3075 [D] **F**

Passacaglia; Piano Sonata; Suite for Piano Quillman (pno)
New World NW 376-2 [D] **F**

SPOHR, Louis (1784–1859) GERMANY

O *Clarinet Concerto No.1 in C min., Op.26* Ottensamer (cl), VPO,
Colin Davis
(+ Mozart: *Clarinet Concerto*; Weber: *Clarinet Concerto No. 2*)
Philips 438 868-2 [D] **F**

Symphonies: No. 6 in G (Historical), Op. 116; No. 9 in B min.
(Seasons), Op. 143 Bavarian RSO, Rickenbacher
Orfeo CO94841A [D] **F**

C *Double Quartets: No. 1 in D min., Op. 65; No. 2 in E♭, Op. 77*
ASMF Chamber Ensemble
Hyperion CDA66141 [D] **F**

Double Quartets: No. 3 in E min., Op. 87; No. 4 in G min., Op. 136
ASMF Chamber Ensemble
Hyperion CDA 66142 [D] **F**

Octet in E♭, Op. 32; Nonet in F, Op. 31 Gaudier Ensemble
Hyperion CDA 66699 [D] **F**

Piano and Wind Quintet in C min., Op. 52; Septet in A min.,
Op. 147 Brown (pno), Nash Ensemble
CRD 3399 [A] **F**

String Quartet in A, Op. 93; String Quartet in B min., Op. 84/3
New Budapest Quartet
Marco Polo 8.223252 [D] **F**

String Quartets: in D min., Op. 11; in G min., Op. 27; in E♭,
Op. 15/2 New Budapest Quartet
Marco Polo 8.223254 [D] **F**

2 String Quartets, Op. 4; String Quartet in D, Op. 15/4 New
Budapest Quartet
Marco Polo 8.223253 [D] **F**

C *String Quartets, Op. 29 Nos. 1 & 2* New Budapest Quartet
Marco Polo 8.223255 [D] **F**

String Quartets, Op. 84 Nos. 1 & 2 New Budapest Quartet
Marco Polo 8.223251 [D] **F**

V *German Songs, Op. 25 Nos. 2 & 5: Schottisches Lied; Zigeunerlied; 6 German Songs, Op. 37 No. 5: Lied beim Rudetanz; 6 German Songs, Op. 41 Nos. 3 & 6: An Mignon & Vanitas!; 6 German Songs, Op. 72 No. 6: Schlaflied; 6 German Songs, Op. 103; 6 Songs, Op. 154* Fischer-Dieskau (bar), Varady (sop), Sitkovetsky (vln), Schoneberger (cl), Höll (pno)
Orfeo C103841A [D] **F**

STAINER, John (1840–1901) ENGLAND

V *The Crucifixion* (oratorio) Davies (ten), Wilson-Johnson (bar), St. Paul's Cathedral Ch, Scott (org), Lucas
Conifer CDCF 193 [D] **F**

STANFORD, Charles Villiers (1852–1924) IRELAND/ENGLAND

O *Piano Concerto No. 2 in C min., Op. 126; Concert Variations on 'Down around the Dead Men', Op. 71* Fingerhut (pno), Ulster O, Handley
Chandos CHAN 8736 [D] **F**

*Piano Concerto No. 2; Irish Rhapsody No. 4; Becket: Funeral March *Binns (pno), *LSO, *Braithwaite; LPO, Boult
Lyrita SRCD219 [A] **F**

Irish Rhapsodies Nos. 1–6; *Concert Piece, Op. 181; Oedipus tyrannus: Prelude; **Clarinet Concerto *Weir (org), **Hilton (cl), Wallfisch (vcl), Mordkovitch (vln), Ulster O, Handley
Chandos CHAN 9264/5, 2 CDs [D] **M**

Symphonies Nos. 1–7 Ulster O, Handley
Chandos CHAN 9279-82, 4 CDs [D] **F**

Symphony No. 1 in B♭; Irish Rhapsody No. 2 Ulster O, Handley
Chandos CHAN 9049 [D] **F**

Symphony No. 2 in D min. (Elegiac); *Clarinet Concerto in A min., Op. 80 *Hilton (cl), Ulster O, Handley
Chandos CHAN 8991 [D] **F**

Symphony No. 3 in F min. (Irish), Op. 28; Irish Rhapsody No. 5 in G min., Op. 147 Ulster O, Handley
Chandos CHAN 8545 [D] **F**

Symphony No. 4 in F, Op. 31; *Irish Rhapsody No. 6; Oedipus Tyrannus (incidental music), *Op. 29: Prelude* *Mordkovitch (vln), Ulster O, Handley
Chandos CHAN 8884 [D] **F**

Symphony No. 5 in D (L'Allegro ed il penseroso), Op. 56; Irish Rhapsody No. 4 in F, Op. 31 Ulster O, Handley
Chandos CHAN 8581 [D] **F**

Symphony No. 6 in E♭ (In memoriam G.F. Watts), Op. 94; Irish Rhapsody No. 1 in D min., Op. 78 Ulster O, Handley
Chandos CHAN 8627 [D] **F**

Symphony No. 7 in D min., Op. 124; *Concert Piece, Op. 181; **Irish Rhapsody No. 3, Op. 137 *Weir (org), **R. Wallfisch (vcl), Ulster O, Handley
Chandos CHAN 8861 [D] **F**

C   *Serenade (nonet) in F* Capricorn
(+ Parry: *Nonet in Bb*)
Hyperion CDA 66291 [D] **F**

Cello Sonata No. 2 Lloyd Webber (vcl), McCabe (pno)
(+ Bridge: *Elegy; Scherzetto;* Ireland: *Cello Sonata*)
ASV CDDCA 807 [D] **F**

Clarinet Sonata, Op. 129 King (cl), Benson (pno)
(+ Ferguson: *4 Short Pieces, Op. 6;* Finzi: *5 Bagatelles;*
Hurlstone: *4 Characteristic Pieces*)
Hyperion CDA 66014 [D] **F**

V   *Evening Service in A (Magnificat and Nunc dimittis), Op. 12; For
Io, I rise up; The Lord is My Shepherd; 3 Latin Motets, Op. 38; 3
Motets, Op. 135 Nos. 1 & 3: Ye Holy Angels; Powerful God; O living
Will; Ye Choirs of Jerusalem* Worcester Cathedral Ch, Hunt
Hyperion CDA 66030 [D] **F**

STANLEY, John (1712–1786) ENGLAND

O   *6 Organ Concerti, Op. 10* Gifford (org/dir), Northern Sinfonia
CRD 3365 [A] **F**

6 String Concerti, Op. 2 Parley of Instruments, Goodman
Hyperion CDA 66338 [D] **F**

STENHAMMER, Wilhelm (1871–1927) SWEDEN

O   *Piano Concerto No. 1 in Bb min., Op. 1; Symphony No. 3: fragment*
Widlund (pno), Stockholm PO, Rozhdestvensky
Chandos CHAN 9074 [D] **F**

*Piano Concerto No. 2 in D min., Op. 23; *Serenade in F, Op. 31;
**Florez och Blanzeflor, Op. 3* Solyom (pno), Munich PO,
Westerberg; **Wixell (bar), *Swedish RSO, Westerberg
EMI CDM5 65081-2 (US: CDM 65081) [A] **M**

*Excelsior! (symphonic overture), Op. 13; Symphony No. 2 in G
min., Op. 34* Gothenburg SO, Järvi
BIS BIS-CD 251 [D] **F**

Symphony No. 1 in F Gothenburg SO, Järvi
BIS BIS-CD 219 [D] **F**

C   *String Quartet No. 1 in C, Op. 2; *String Quartet No. 2 in C min.,
Op. 14* Fresk Quartet; *Copenhagen Quartet
Caprice CAP 21337 [A] **F**

*String Quartet No. 3 in F, Op. 18; String Quartet No. 4 in A min.,
Op. 25* Gotland Quartet
Caprice CAP 21338 [A] **F**

*String Quartet No. 5 in C (Serenade), Op. 29; *String Quartet No. 6
in D min., Op. 35* Gotland Quartet; *Copenhagen Quartet
Caprice CAP 21339 [A] **F**

V   *30 Songs* von Otter (mez), Hagegård (bar), Forsberg (pno),
Schuback (pno)
Musica Sveciae MSCD 623 [A] **F**

STERNDALE BENNETT, William (1816–1875) ENGLAND

O   *Piano Concertos: No. 1 in D min., Op. 1; No. 3 in C min., Op. 9;
Caprice in E, Op. 22* Binns (pno), LPO, Braithwaite
Lyrita SRCD 204 [D] **F**

*Piano Concertos: No. 2 in Eb, Op. 4; No. 5 in F min.; Adagio for
Piano and Orchestra* Binns (pno), LPO, Braithwaite
Lyrita SRCD 205 [D] **F**

O *Piano Concerto No. 4 in F min.; Symphony in G min.; Fantasia in A, Op. 16* Binns (pno), Milton Keynes CO, Wetton
Unicorn-Kanchana UKCD 2032 [D] **M**

STEVENS, Bernard (1916–1983) ENGLAND

O *Cello Concerto, Op. 18; A Symphony of Liberation* Baillie (vcl), BBC PO, Downes
Meridian CDE 84124 [D] **F**

*Violin Concerto, Op. 4; Symphony No. 2, Op. 35 *Kovacic (vln), BBC PO, Downes
Meridian CDE 84174 [D] **F**

C *Lyric Suite, Op. 30; String Quartet No. 2, Op. 34; Theme and Variations, Op. 11* Delmé Quartet
Unicorn-Kanchana DKPCD 9097 [D] **F**

V *Mass for Double Choir* Finzi Singers, Spicer
(+ Howells: *Mass in the Dorian Mode*, etc.)
Chandos CHAN 9021 [D] **F**

STEVENSON, Ronald (born 1928) ENGLAND/SCOTLAND

O *Piano Concertos Nos. 1 & 2* McLachlan (pno), Chethams SO, Clayton
Olympia OCD 429 [D] **F**

S *Beltane Bonfire; Scottish Ballads Nos. 2 & 3* McLachlan (pno)
(+ piano works by Center, Scott)
Olympia OCD 264 [D] **F**

Passacaglia on DSCH; Recitative and Air; Prelude and Fugue on Themes from Busoni's 'Doktor Faust' Stevenson (pno)
Altarus AIR-CD-9091 [D] **F**

STILL, William Grant (1895–1978) USA

O *Symphony No. 1 ('Afro-American')* Detroit SO, Järvi
(+ Ellington: *The River: Suite*)
Chandos CHAN 9154 [D] **F**

Symphony No. 2 (Song of a New Race) Detroit SO, Järvi
(+ Dawson: *Negro Folk Symphony;* Ellington: *Harlem*)
Chandos CHAN 9226 [D] **F**

C *Summerland; Quit Dat Fool'nish; Pastorela; Folk Suite No1 for String Quartet, Flute & Piano; Suite (excpts); Prelude for Flute, String Quintet & Piano; Here's One; If You Should Go; Song for the Lonely; Bayou Home* A Still (fl), Smith (pno), New Zealand Quartet
Koch 3-7192-2 [D] **F**

STOCKHAUSEN, Karlheinz (born 1928) GERMANY

S *Klavierstücke XII–XIV* Wambach (pno)
Koch Schwann 3-1001-5 [D] **F**

9 Klavierstücke: I–IV, IX & X Wambach (pno)
Koch Schwann 3-1001-6 [D] **F**

V *Stimmung* Songcircle, Rose
Hyperion CDA 66115 [D] **F**

STRAUSS FAMILY

O *Viennese New Year's Day Concerts*
1987: Battle (sop), VPO, Karajan
DG 419 616-2 [D] **F**
1988: VPO, Abbado

DG 423 662-2 [D] **F**
1989: VPO, C. Kleiber
Sony CD 45938 [D] **F**
1990: VPO, Mehta
Sony CD 45808 [D] **F**
1991: VPO, Abbado
DG 431 628-2 [D] **F**
1992: VPO, C. Kleiber
Sony CD 48376 [D] **F**
1993: VPO, Muti
1995: VPO, Mehta
Sony CD 66860 [D] **F**

STRAUSS, Eduard (1835–1916) AUSTRIA

O *Bahn frei* VPO, Boskovsky
(+ orchestral works by Johann Strauss I, Johann Strauss II &
Josef Strauss)
Decca 425 426-2 (US: London 425 426-2) [A] **M**

Fesche Geister VPO, Boskovsky
(+ orchestral works by Johann Strauss I, Johann Strauss II &
Josef Strauss)
Decca 425 425-2 (US: London 425 425-2) [A] **M**

Mit Extrapost VPO, Boskovsky
(+ orchestral works by Johann Strauss I, Johann Strauss II &
Josef Strauss)
Decca 425 429-2 (US: London 425 429-2) [A] **M**

STRAUSS, Johann I (1804–1849) AUSTRIA

O *Beliebte Speri-Polka* VPO, Boskovsky
(+ orchestral works by Johann Strauss II & Josef
Strauss)
Decca 425 427-2 (US: London 425 427-2) [A] **M**

Loreley-Rhein-Klänge VPO, Boskovsky
(+ orchestral works by Eduard Strauss, Johann Strauss II &
Josef Strauss)
Decca 425 429-2 (US: London 425 429-2) [A] **M**

Piefke und Pufke; Radetzky March VPO, Boskovsky
(+ orchestral works by Eduard Strauss, Johann Strauss II &
Josef Strauss)
Decca 425 426-2 (US: London 425 426-2) [A] **M**

Wettrennen VPO, Boskovsky
(+ orchestral works by Eduard Strauss, Johann Strauss II &
Josef Strauss)
Decca 425 425-2 (US: London 425 425-2) [A] **M**

STRAUSS, Johann II (1825–1899) AUSTRIA

O *Accelerationen; Bitte schön!; Kaiser (Emperor) Waltz; Leichtes
Blut; Persischer Marsch; Rosen aus dem Süden; 's gibt nur a
Kaiserstadt; Schneeglöckchen; Tik-Tak; Vergnügungszug* VPO,
Boskovsky
(+ orchestral works by Eduard Strauss, Johann Strauss I &
Josef Strauss)
Decca 425 429-2 (US: London 425 429-2) [A] **M**

*Annen Polka; Auf der Jagd; An der schönen, blauen Donau
(Blue Danube); Carnevals-Botschafter; Ägyptischer Marsch;
Pizzicato Polka; Tritsch-Tratsch; Frühlingsstimmen* VPO,
Boskovsky
(+ orchestral works by Eduard Strauss, Johann Strauss I &

Josef Strauss)
Decca 425 425-2 (US: London 425 425-2) [A] **M**

O *Cinderella* (ballet); *Ritter Pasman; Le Beau Danube* (ballet)
National PO, Bonynge
Decca 430 852-2 (US: London 430 852-2), 2 CDs [D/A] **M**

Künstlerleben; Banditen-Galop; Champagne; Eljen a Magyar!; Jubel Marsch; Liebeslieder; Morgenblätter; Neue Pizzicato; Russischer Marsch; Unter Donner und Blitz; Wiener Blut; Wiener Bonbons VPO, Boskovsky
(+ Josef Strauss: *Auf Ferienreisen; Dorfschwalben aus Österreich*)
Decca 425 428-2 (US: London 425 428-2) [A] **M**

Demolirer; Du und Du; Freuet euch des Lebens; Lagunen Walzer; Perpetuum Mobile; Spanischer March; Stürmisch in Lieb' und Tanz; Geschichten aus dem Wienerwald VPO, Boskovsky
(+ orchestral works by Eduard Strauss, Johann Strauss I & Josef Strauss)
Decca 425 426-2 (US: London 425 426-2) [A] **M**

Explosionen; Im Krapfenwald'; Lob der Frauen; Napoleon Marsch; Seid umschlungen Millionen; So ängstlich sind wir nicht; 1001 Nacht; Wein, Weib und Gesang; Wo die Zitronen blüh'n VPO, Boskovsky
(+ Johann Strauss I: *Beliebte Speri-Polka*; Josef Strauss: *Heiterer Muth; Libelle; Moulinet; Transaktionen*)
Decca 425 427-2 (US: London 425 427-2) [A] **M**

STRAUSS, Josef (1827–1870) AUSTRIA

O *Aquarellen; Brennende Liebe; Eingesendet; Frauenherz* VPO, Boskovsky
(+ orchestral works by Eduard Strauss, Johann Strauss I & Johann Strauss II)
Decca 425 426-2 (US: London 425 426-2) [A] **M**

Auf Ferienreisen; Dorfschwalben aus Österreich VPO, Boskovsky
(+ Johann Strauss II: *Orchestral works*)
Decca 425 428-2 (US: London 425 428-2) [A] **M**

Delirien; Die Emanzipierte VPO, Boskovsky
(+ orchestral works by Eduard Strauss, Johann Strauss I & Johann Strauss II)
Decca 425 429-2 (US: London 425 429-2) [A] **M**

Dynamiden; Feuerfest!; Jockey; Schwätzerin; Sphärenklänge VPO, Boskovsky
(+ orchestral works by Eduard Strauss, Johann Strauss I & Johann Strauss II)
Decca 425 425-2 (US: London 425 425-2) [A] **M**

Heiterer Muth; Libelle; Moulinet; Transaktionen VPO, Boskovsky
(+ orchestral works by Johann Strauss I & Johann Strauss II)
Decca 425 427-2 (US: London 425 427-2) [A] **M**

STRAUSS, Richard (1864–1949) GERMANY

○ *Eine Alpensinfonie, Op. 64; Aus Italien, Op. 16; Divertimento; *Don Quixote, Op. 35; Macbeth, Op. 23; Metamorphosen* *P. Tortelier (vcl), *Rostal (vla), Dresden Staatskapelle, Kempe
EMI CMS7 64350-2 (US: CDZC 64350), 3 CDs [A] **M**

An Alpine Symphony; Die Frau ohne Schatten: Symphonic Fantasy CSO, Barenboim
Erato 2292 45997-2 [D] **F**

O *Also sprach Zarathustra, Op. 30; Ein Heldenleben, Op. 40* CSO, Reiner
RCA 09026 61494-2 [A] **M**

*Also sprach Zarathustra, Op. 30; Der Burger als Edelmann: Suite; *Violin Concerto in D min., Op. 8; Josephslegende (ballet), Op. 63: Symphonic Fragment; Der Rosenkavalier (opera): Waltzes; Salome (opera): Dance of the 7 Veils; Schlagobers (ballet): Waltz; Sinfonia Domestica, Op. 53; Tod und Verklärung, Op. 24* *Hoelscher (vln), Dresden Staatskapelle, Kempe
EMI CMS7 64346-2 (US: CDZC 64346), 3 CDs [A] **M**

Also sprach Zarathustra, Op. 30; Till Eulenspiegels lustige Streiche, Op. 28; Salome (opera): Dance of the 7 Veils BPO, Karajan
DG 415 853-2 [A] **M**

Le bourgeois gentilhomme: Suite, Op. 60; Divertimento, Op. 86 Orpheus CO
DG 435 871-2 [D] **F**

*Burleske in D min.; Horn Concertos: No. 1 in E♭, Op. 11; No. 2 in E♭; Oboe Concerto; Don Juan, Op. 20; **Duet-Concertino; Ein Heldenleben, Op. 40; Panathenaenzug; ***Parergon, Op. 73; Till Eulenspiegels lustige Streiche, Op. 28 *Frager (pno), Damm (hn), Clement (ob), **Weise (cl), **Liebscher (bsn), ***Rosl (pno), Dresden Staatskapelle, Kempe
EMI CMS7 64342-2 (US: CDZC 64342), 3 CDs [A] **M**

Horn Concertos Nos. 1 & 2 Baumann (hn), LGO, Masur
(+ Weber: *Horn Concertino*)
Philips 412 237-2 [D] **F**

Oboe Concerto de Lancie (ob), LSO, Previn
(+ Ibert: *Symphonie Concertante*; Françaix: *L'horloge de flore*; Satie: *Gymnopédies Nos. 1 & 3*)
RCA GD 87989 (US: 7989-2) [A] **M**

Violin Concerto in D min., Op. 8 Wei (vln), LPO, Glover
(+ Headington: *Violin Concerto*)
ASV CDDCA 780 [D] **F**

Don Juan, Op. 20; Ein Heldenleben, Op. 40 BPO, Karajan
DG 429 717-2 [A] **M**

*Don Quixote, Op. 35; Tod und Verklärung, Op. 24 *Fournier (vcl), *Cappone (vla), BPO, Karajan
DG 429 184-2 [A] **M**

Metamorphosen; *Four Last Songs; **Oboe Concerto *Janowitz (sop), **Koch (ob), BPO, Karajan
DG 423 888-2 [A] **M**

Metamorphosen; Tod und Verklärung, Op. 24 BPO, Karajan
DG 410 892-2 [D] **F**

Symphonia Domestica, Op. 53; Tod und Verklärung, Op. 24 CSO, Reiner
RCA GD 60388 (US: 60388-2) [A] **M**

Symphony in F min., Op. 12; *Romance in F, AV75 *Fujiwara (vcl), Tokyo Metropolitan SO, Wakasugi
Denon CO-75860 [D] **F**

C *Complete Music for Wind Ensemble* London Winds
Hyperion CDA 66731/2, 2 CDs [D] **F**

Cello Sonata in F, Op. 16 Rolland (vcl), Hamelin (pno)
(+Thuille: Cello Sonata)
ASV CDDCA 913 [D] **F**

String Quartet in A, Op. 2 Delmé Quartet
(+ Verdi: *String Quartet in E min.*)
Hyperion CDA 66317 [D] **F**

Violin Sonata in Eb, Op. 18 Chung (vln), Zimerman (pno)
(+ Respighi: *Violin Sonata in B min.*)
DG 427 617-2 [D] **F**

*Piano Sonata, Op. 5; 5 Piano Pieces, Op. 3; *Ophelia Lieder,
Op. 67; **Enoch Arden, Op. 38* *Schwarzkopf (sop), **Rains
(narr), Gould (pno)
Sony CD 52657, 2 CDs [A] **M**

23 Lieder Popp (sop), Sawallisch (pno)
EMI CDC7 49318-2 (US: Angel CDC 49318) [D] **F**

140 Lieder Fischer-Dieskau (bar), Moore (pno)
EMI CMS7 63995-2 (US: Angel CDMF 63995), 6 CDs [A] **M**

*Der Abend, Op. 34/1; An den Baum Daphne; Deutsche Motette,
Op. 62; Die Göttin im Putzzimmer; Hymne, Op. 34/2* Soloists,
Copenhagen Boys' Ch, Danish National Ch & Chamber Ch,
Parkman
Chandos CHAN 9223 [D] **F**

*Four Last Songs; Das Bächlein; Freundliche Vision; Die heiligen drei
Könige; Meinem Kinde; Morgen; Muttertändelei; Das Rosenband;
Ruhe, meine Seele; Waldseligkeit; Wiegenlied; Winterweihe;
Zueignung* Schwarzkopf (sop), Berlin RSO, LSO, Szell
EMI CDC7 47276-2 (US: Angel CDC 47276) [A] **F**

Four Last Songs Studer (sop), Dresden State O, Sinopoli
(+Wagner: *Wesendonck Lieder; Tristan und Isolde: Prelude &
Liebestod*)
DG 439 865-2 [D] **F**

TRAVINSKY, Igor (1882–1971) RUSSIA/FRANCE/USA

The Stravinsky Edition (near-complete works under the
composer's direction or supervision) Various artists and
orchestras, Stravinsky, Craft
Sony CD 46290, 22 CDs [A] **M**

Ballets: Agon; Apollo; Le Baiser de la fée; Bluebird pas-de-deux
(arr.); *Jeu de cartes; Orpheus; Pulcinella; Scènes de ballet* LA
Festival SO, Columbia SO, Cleveland O, Chicago SO, CBC
SO, Stravinsky
Sony CD 46292, 3 CDs [A] **M**

*Circus Polka; Concerto for Chamber Orchestra; Concerto in D for
String Orchestra; 4 Études; Greeting Prelude; 8 Instrumental
Miniatures; 4 Norwegian Moods; Suites Nos. 1 & 2 for Small
Orchestra* CBC SO, Stravinsky
Sony CD 46296 [A] **F**

Violin Concerto in D Mutter (vln), BBC SO, Lutoslawski
(+ Lutoslawski: *Chain II; Partita*)
DG 423 696-2 [D] **F**
Lin (vln), LAPO, Salonen
(+Prokofiev: *Violin Concertos Nos. 1 & 2*)
Sony CD 53969 [D] **F**

O *Divertimento from 'Le Baiser de la fée'* (symphonic suite); *Octet;
2 Suites for small orchestra; L'Histoire du soldat: Concert Suite*
London Sinfonietta, Chailly
Decca 433 079-2 (US: London 433 079-2) [D] **F**

Ebony Concerto Stolzman (cl), Woody Herman's Thundering
Herd
(+ Bernstein: *Prelude, Fugue & Riffs;* Copland: *Clarinet Concerto;*
Corigliano: *Clarinet Concerto*)
RCA 09026 61360-2 [D] **F**

The Firebird (ballet); *Fireworks* (fantasy), *Op. 4; L'Histoire du
soldat: Concert Suite; Les Noces (4 choreographic scenes); Petrushka*
(ballet); *Renard* (burlesque); *The Rite of Spring* (ballet); *Scherzo
à la Russe; *Scherzo fantastique, Op. 3* Various artists, *CBC SO,
Columbia SO, Stravinsky
Sony CD 46291, 3 CDs [A] **M**

*Firebird; Petrushka; Rite of Spring; *Apollon musagète* LPO,
Haitink; *LSO, Markevitch
Philips 438 350-2, 2 CDs [A] **M**

The Firebird (ballet); *Chant du rossignol; Fireworks; Scherzo à la
Russe; Tango* LSO, Dorati
Philips Mercury 432 012-2 [A] **M**

Ballets: *Orpheus; Jeu de cartes* Royal Concertgebouw O, Järvi
Chandos CHAN 9014 [D] **F**

Ballets: *Petrushka; *Le Sacre du printemps* Cleveland O,
*NYPO, Boulez
Sony CD 64109 [A] **M**

Ballets: *Pulcinella; Jeu de cartes* *Berganza (mez), *Davies
(ten), *Shirley-Quirk (bar), LSO, Abbado
DG 423 889-2 [A] **M**

Pulcinella (ballet): *Suite* ASMF, Marriner
(Bizet: *Symphony in C;* Prokofiev: *Symphony No. 1*)
Decca 417 734-2 (US: London 417 734-2) [A] **M**

The Rite of Spring (ballet); *Persephone* *Rolfe Johnson (ten),
*Fournet (narr), *Tiffin Boys' Ch, LPO & *Ch, Nagano
Virgin VCK7 59077-2 (US: 59077), 2 CDs [D] **M**

*The Rite of Spring; *Pulcinella* *Berganza (mez), Davies (ten),
Shirley-Quirk (bar), LSO, Abbado
DG 439 433-2 [A] **B**

*Symphony in C; Symphony in Eb, Op. 1; Symphony in Three
Movements; *Symphony of Psalms* *CBC SO, Columbia SO,
Stravinsky
(+ rehearsal sequences)
Sony CD 46294, 2 CDs [A] **M**

C *Ballad; Berceuse; Chanson russe; Duo concertant; L'Histoire du
soldat: Suite; Pastorale; Prélude et Ronde des princesses; Scherzo*
American Chamber Players
Koch 3-7078-2 [D] **F**

*Concerto for 2 Pianos; Sonata for 2 Pianos; Scherzo à la Russe;
Le Sacre du printemps* Ashkenazy (pno), Gavrilov (pno)
Decca 433 829-2 (US: London 433 829-2) [D] **F**

S *3 Movements from Petrushka* Pollini (pno)
(+ Boulez: *Piano Sonata No. 2;* Prokofiev: *Piano Sonata No. 7;*
Webern: *Variations*)
DG 447 431-2 [A] **M**

Anthem ('The Dove Descending Breaks the Air'); Ave Maria; Babel; Cantata; Canticum Sacrum; Chorale-Variations on 'Von Himmel Hoch'; Credo; Introitus 'T.S. Eliot in memoriam'; Mass; Pater Noster; A Sermon, a Narrative and a Prayer; Threni Various artists, Stravinsky
Sony CD 46301, 2 CDs [A] **M**

Mass; Les Noces (4 choreographic scenes) Various artists, English Bach Festival O & Ch, Bernstein
DG 423 251-2 [A] **M**

Mass; Symphony of Psalms; Ave Maria; *Canticum sacrum ad honorem Sancti Marci nominus; Credo; Pater Noster *Ainsley (ten), *Roberts (bar), Westminster Cathedral Ch, O'Donnell
Hyperion CDA 66437 [D] **F**

SUK, Josef (1874–1935) BOHEMIA

Asrael (symphony), *Op. 27* RLPO, Pešek
Virgin VC7 59638-2 (US: 59638) [D] **F**

Ripening (symphonic poem), *Op. 34; Praga* (symphonic poem), *Op. 26* RLPO, Pešek
Virgin VC7 59318-2 (US: 59318) [D] **F**

Piano Quartet in A min., Op. 1 Domus
(+ Dvořák: *Bagatelles;* Martinů: *Piano Quartet*)
Virgin VC7 59245-2 (US: CDC 59245) [D] **F**

String Quartets: No. 1 in Bb, Op. 11; No. 2, Op. 31; Meditation on an Old Czech Hymn (St Wenceslas), Op. 35a; Ballade in D min., Op. 3/1; Balada in D min. Suk Quartet
CRD 3472 [D] **F**

Piano Pieces, Op. 7; About Mother, Op. 28; Lullabies, Op. 33; Spring, Op. 22a; Summer, Op. 22b; Things lived and dreamt, Op. 30 Fingerhut (pno)
Chandos CHAN 9026/7, 2 CDs [D] **F**

SULLIVAN, Sir Arthur (1842–1900) ENGLAND

Cello Concerto in D; *Symphony in E (Irish); *Overture di ballo Lloyd Webber (vcl), LSO, Mackerras; *RLPO, Groves
EMI CDM7 64726-2 (US: Angel CDM 64726) [A] **M**

Overtures: *Di Ballo; The Gondoliers; HMS Pinafore; Iolanthe; Patience; The Pirates of Penzance; Princess Ida; Ruddigore; The Sorcerer; The Yeoman of the Guard* Scottish CO, Faris
Nimbus NI 5066 [D] **F**

SUPPÉ, Franz von (1819–1895) AUSTRIA

Overtures: *The Beautiful Galatea; Boccaccio; Light Cavalry; Morning, Noon and Night in Vienna; Pique Dame; Poet and Peasant* Detroit SO, Paray
(+ Auber: *Overtures: The Bronze Horse; Fra Diavolo; La Muette de Portici*)
Philips Mercury 434 309-2 [A] **M**

SVENDSEN, Johan (1840–1911) NORWAY

Symphonies: No. 1 in D, Op. 4; No. 2 in Bb, Op. 15; Swedish Folk Tunes Gothenburg SO, Järvi
BIS BIS-CD 347 [D] **F**

SZYMANOWSKI, Karol (1882–1937) POLAND

Symphonies: No. 2 in Bb, Op. 19; *No. 3 (Song of the Night), Op. 27; Concert Overture in E, Op. 12 Polish National RSO,

Kasprzyk, *Semkow
EMI CDM5 65082-2 (US: CDM 65082) [A] **M**

O *Symphony No. 3, Op. 27 (Song of the Night); **Stabat Mater,
Op. 53; ***Litania do Marii Panny, Op. 59 *Garrison (ten),
/*Szmytka (sop), **Quivar (mez), **Connell (bs), CBSO
& Ch., Rattle
EMI CDC5 55121-2 (US: CDC 55121) [D] **F**

C *String Quartets: No. 1 in C, Op. 37; No. 2, Op. 56*
Varsovia Quartet
(+ Lutoslawski: *String Quartet;* Penderecki: *String Quartet No. 2*)
Olympia OCD 328 [A] **F**
Carmina Quartet
(+ Webern: *Langsamer Satz*)
Denon CO-79462 [D] **F**

S *Études, Op. 4; Fantasy, Op. 14; Masques, Op. 34; Métopes, Op. 29*
Lee (pno)
Hyperion CDA 66409 [D] **F**

*9 Preludes, Op. 1; Variations in Bb min., Op. 3; 4 Studies, Op. 4;
Piano Sonata No.1 in C min., Op. 8; Variations on a Polish Folk-
Theme, Op. 10; Fantasia in C, Op. 14; Prelude and Fugue in C#
min. (1909); Piano Sonata No. 2 in A, Op. 21* Jones (pno)
Nimbus NI 5405/6, 2 CDs [D] **F**

TAKEMITSU, Toru (born 1930) JAPAN

O *Fantasma/Cantos; Water-Ways; Waves; Quatrain II* Various
artists
RCA 09026 62537-2 [D] **F**

*A Flock Descends into the Pentagonal Garden; Quatrain; Ring;
Sacrifice; Stanza I; Valeria* Various artists, Boston SO, Ozawa
DG 423 253-2 [A] **M**

Rain Coming; Rain Spell; Riverrun; Tree Line London
Sinfonietta, Knussen
Virgin VC7 59020-2 (US: 59020) [D] **F**

V *12 Songs for Mixed Chorus* Shin-Yu Kai Ch., Sekiya
Philips 438 135-2 [D] **F**

TALLIS, Thomas (c.1505–1585) ENGLAND

V Responds: *Audivi vocem; Candidi facti; Dum transisset; Hodie
nobis; Homo quidam; Honor, virtus; In pace; Loquebantur; Spem in
alium; Videte miraculum* Taverner Ch & Consort, Parrott
EMI CDC7 49555-2 (US: Angel CDC 49555) [D] **F**

*Gaude gloriosa; In jejunio; Lamentations of Jeremiah I & II;
Miserere nostri; O nata lux; O sacrum convivium; Salvatore mundi,
salva nos I & II; Suscipe quaeso Dominus; Te lucis I* Taverner
Ch & Consort, Parrott
EMI CDC7 49563-2 (US: Angel CDC 49563) [D] **F**

*Gaude gloriosa; Loquebantur variis linguis; Miserere nostri;
Salvator mundi, salve nos I & II; Sancte Deus; Spem in alium*
Tallis Scholars, Phillips
Gimell CDGIM 006 [D] **F**

*Spem in alium; Ecce tempus idoneum; Gaude gloriosa; Loquebantur
variis linguis; O nata lux de lumine* Clerkes of Oxenford,
Wulstan
(+ Sheppard: *Gaude Maria*, etc.)
Classics for Pleasure CD-CFP 4638 [A] **B**

TANEYEV, Sergey (1856–1915) RUSSIA

O   *Symphony No. 4; The Oresteia (opera): Overture* Philharmonia O, Järvi
Chandos CHAN 8953 [D] **F**

C   *Piano Quintet in G min., Op. 30* Lowenthal (pno), Rosenthal (vln), Kamei (vln), Thompson (vla), Kates (vcl)
Arabesque Z6539 [D] **F**

     Piano Trio in D, Op. 22 Borodin Trio
Chandos CHAN 8592 [D] **F**

TARTINI, Giuseppe (1692–1770) ITALY

O   *Violin Concerto E min., D56; Violin Concerto in A, D96; Violin Concerto in A min., D113* Ughi (vln), Solisti Veneti, Scimone
Erato 4509 92188-2 [A] **M**

C   *Violin Sonata in G min. (Devil's Trill); 12 Violin Sonatas and Pastorale, Op. 1 Nos. 2, 8, 10, 12 & 13* Locatelli Trio
♦ Hyperion CDA 66430 [D] **F**

     Violin Sonatas: in A, BA4; in B♭, BB5 (Op. 5/6); in B♭, BD1; in D, BD19 E. Wallfisch (vln), Locatelli Trio
♦ Hyperion CDA 66485 [D] **F**

TAUSKY, Vilem (born 1910) CZECHOSLOVAKIA/ENGLAND

O   *Concertino* Reilly (harmonica), ASMF, Marriner
(+Jacob: *5 Pieces;* Moody: *Little Suite;* Vaughan Williams: *Romance*)
Chandos CHAN 8617 [D] **F**

TAVENER, John (born 1944) ENGLAND

O   *Eternal Memory* Isserlis (vcl), Moscow Virtuosi, Spivakov
(+Bloch: *From Jewish Life*)
RCA 09026 61966-2 [D] **F**

     The Protecting Veil; Thrinos (solo cello) Isserlis (vcl), LSO, Rozhdestvensky
(+Britten: *Cello Suite No. 3*)
Virgin VC7 59052-2 (US: 59052) [D] **F**

     The Repentant Thief A. Marriner (cl), LSO, Tilson Thomas
Collins 20052 [D] **M**

C   **The Last Sleep of the Virgin; The Hidden Treasure* *Simrock (handbells), Chilingirian Quartet
(Pärt: *Fratres; Summa*)
Virgin VC5 45023-2 (US: 45023) [D] **F**

     Funeral Ikos; *Ikon of Light; Little Lamb, who made thee? Tallis Scholars, *Chilingirian Quartet, Phillips
Gimell CDGIM 005 [D] **F**

     Eonia; God is with us; Hymn for the Dormition; Hymn to the mother of God; Little Lamb; Love bade me welcome; Magnificat; Nunc Dimittis; Ode of St. Andrew; The Tiger; Today the Virgin; The Uncreated Eros St. George's Chapel Ch, Robinson
Hyperion CDA 66464 [D] **F**

     *Ikon of Light; 2 Hymns to the Mother of God; The Lamb; The Tiger *Duke Quartet members, The Sixteen, Christophers
Collins 14052 [D] **F**

     Thunder entered her Dunnett (org), Winchester Cath. Ch., Hill
Virgin VC5 45035-2 (US: 45035) [D] **F**

V *We Shall See Him As He Is* Various artists, BBC Welsh SO, Hickox
Chandos CHAN 9128 [D] **F**

TAVERNER, John (c.1490–1545) ENGLAND

V *Audivi vocem; Missa Gloria tibi Trinatis* The Sixteen, Christophers
Hyperion CDA 66134 [D] **F**

Dum transisset Sabbatum; Ex eius tumba; Missa Sancti Wilhelmi; O Wilhelme The Sixteen, Christophers
Hyperion CDA 66427 [D] **F**

Gaude plurimum; In pace in idipsum; Missa Corona Spinia The Sixteen, Christophers
Hyperion CDA 66360 [D] **F**

Kyrie; Missa O Michael The Sixteen, Christophers
Hyperion CDA 66325 [D] **F**

Mater Christi; Missa Mater Christi; O Wilhelme Christ Church Cathedral Ch, Darlington
Nimbus NI 5218 [D] **F**

Mass 'The Western Wynde'; Alleluia, veni electa mea; O splendor gloriae; Te deum The Sixteen, Christophers
Hyperion CDA 66507 [D] **F**

TAYLOR, Deems (1885–1966) USA

O *Through the Looking Glass (suite)* Seattle SO, Schwarz
(+Griffes: *Pleasure-Dome of Kubla Khan*, etc.)
Delos DE 3099 [D] **F**

TCHAIKOVSKY, Pyotr (1840–1893) RUSSIA

O *Piano Concerto No. 1 in B♭ min., Op. 23; Theme and Variations, Op. 19/6* Gavrilov (pno), Philharmonia O, Muti
(+ Balakirev: *Islamey;* Prokoviev: *Piano Concerto No. 1,* etc.)
EMI CDM7 64329-2 (US: CDM 64329) [A] **M**

*Piano Concerto No. 1 in B♭ min., Op. 23; *Violin Concerto in D, Op. 35* Argerich (pno), RPO, Dutoit; *Milstein (vln), VPO, Abbado
DG 439 420-2 [A] **B**

Piano Concerto No. 1 in B♭ min., Op. 23 Wild (pno), RPO, Fistoulari
(+ Dohnányi: *Variations on a Nursery Tune, Op. 25,* etc.)
Chesky CD 13 [A] **F**

Piano Concertos: No. 2 in G, Op. 44; No. 3 in E♭, Op. 73 Donohoe (pno), Bournemouth SO, Barshai
EMI CDC7 49940-2 (US: Angel CDC 49940) [D] **F**

1812 Overture, Op. 49; Francesca da Rimini (symphonic fantasia), *Op. 32; Marche Slave, Op. 31; Romeo and Juliet* (fantasy overture) RLPO, Edwards
EMI Eminence CD-EMX 2152 (US: Classics for Pleasure CDEMX 2152) [D] **M**

*Festival Overture on the Danish National Hymn in D, Op. 15; *Hamlet: Incidental Music, Op. 67a; Mazeppa* (opera): *Battle of Poltava, Cossack Dance; Romeo and Juliet* (fantasy overture – 1869 version); *Serenade for Nikolas Rubinstein's Name Day* *Kelly (sop), *Hammond-Stroud (bar), LSO, Simon
Chandos CHAN 8310/1, 2 CDs [D] **F**

Francesca da Rimini (symphonic fantasia), *Op. 32; Hamlet* (fantasy overture), *Op. 67* New York Stadium SO, Stokowski
Dell'Arte CDDA9006 [A] M

Manfred Symphony, Op. 58; The Tempest, Op. 18 Russian National O, Pletnev
DG 439 891-2 [D] F

The Nutcracker (ballet), *Op. 71* LSO, Previn
Classics for Pleasure CFPD 4706, 2 CDs [A] B

The Nutcracker (ballet), *Op. 71; *The Sleeping Beauty* (highlights), *Op. 66* Concertgebouw, Dorati; *LSO, Fistoulari
Philips 442 562-2, 2 CDs [A] B

Suites from: *The Nutcracker; Sleeping Beauty; Swan Lake* BPO, Rostropovich
DG 429 097-2 [A] M

Serenade for Strings in C, Op. 48
BPO, Karajan
(+ Dvořák: *Serenade for Strings*)
DG 400 038-2 [D] F
Moscow Soloists, Bashmet
(+ Grieg: *Holberg Suite, Op. 40; 2 Norwegian Melodies, Op. 63*)
RCA RD 60368 (US: 60368-2) [D] F

Sleeping Beauty (ballet), *Op. 66* National PO, Bonynge
(+ Meyerbeer: *Les Patineurs*)
Decca 425 468-2 (US: London 425 468-2), 3 CDs [A] M

The Snow Maiden, Op. 12 (complete incidental music)
Mishura-Lekhtman (mez), Grishko (ten), University Society Choral Union, Detrot SO, Järvi
Chandos CHAN 9324 [D] F

Swan Lake (ballet), *Op. 20* National PO, Bonynge
(+ Massenet: *Le Cigale*)
Decca 425 413-2 (US: London 425 413-2), 3 CDs [A] M

Symphonies Nos. 1–6; Francesca da Rimini, Op. 32; Serenade for Strings in C, Op. 48; Romeo and Juliet (fantasy overture); Fate, Op. 77; Capriccio italien, Op. 45; The Tempest, Op. 18; Voyevoda, Op. 78; Andante cantabile, Op. 1 USSR SO, Svetlanov
RCA 74321 17101-2, 6 CDs [A/D] M

Symphonies Nos. 1–6 BPO, Karajan
DG 429 675-2, 4 CDs [A] M

Symphony No. 2 in C min., Op. 17 (Little Russian) (original version)*; Serenade for Nikolas Rubinstein's Name Day; Mazeppa* (opera): *Battle of Poltara & Cossack Dance; Festival Overture on the Danish National Anthem in D, Op. 15* LSO, Simon
Chandos CHAN 9190 [D] F

Symphony No. 3 in D (Polish), Op. 29; Capriccio italien, Op. 45 BPO, Karajan
DG 419 178-2 [A] F

Symphonies Nos. 4–6 Leningrad PO, Mravinsky
DG 419 745-2, 2 CDs [A] F

Symphony No. 4 in F min., Op. 36; Capriccio italien, Op. 45 BPO, Karajan
DG 419 872-2 [A] M

O *Symphony No. 5 in E min., Op. 64; *Marche Slave, Op. 31;
Eugene Onegin (opera): Polonaise & Waltz LSO, *Minneapolis
SO, Dorati
Philips Mercury 434 305-2 [A] **M**

Symphony No. 5 in E min., Op. 64; *Nutcracker Suite, Op. 71a
Leningrad PO, Mravinsky; *BPO, Karajan
DG 439 434-2 [A] **B**

Symphony No. 6 in B min. (Pathétique), Op. 74 BPO, Karajan
DG 419 486-2 [A] **M**

Symphony No. 6; *Swan Lake: Suite Leningrad PO, Mravinsky;
*BPO, Karajan
DG 439 456-2 [A] **B**

Variations on a Rococo Theme, Op. 33 Rostropovich (vcl), BPO,
Karajan
(+ Dvořák: *Cello Concerto*)
DG 447 413-2 [A] **M**

Variations on a Rococo Theme (original version); *Andante
Cantabile, Op. 11; Nocturne, Op. 19/4; Pezzo Capriccioso, Op. 62*
Isserlis (vcl), COE, Gardiner
Virgin CUV5 61225-2 (US: 61225) [D] **M** (see collection –
Music for Cello and Orchestra)

C *String Quartets Nos. 1–3; String Quartet in B♭; *Souvenir de
Florence, Op. 70* Borodin Quartet, *Yurov (vla), *Milman (vcl)
Teldec 4509 90422-2, 2 CDs [D] **F**

String Quartets: No. 1 in D, Op. 11; No. 2 in F, Op. 22 Keller
Quartet
Erato 2292 45965-2 [D] **F**

String Quartet No. 3 in E♭, Op. 30; Adagio Molto in B♭
Shostakovich Quartet
(+ Grechaninov: *String Quartet No. 1*)
Olympia OCD 522 [A] **F**

String Quartet No. 3 in E♭, Op. 30; *Souvenir de Florence, Op. 70
Keller Quartet; *Kashkashian (vla), Perenyi (vcl)
Erato 4509 94819-2 [D] **F**

Souvenir de Florence, Op. 70 Raphael Ensemble
(+ Arensky: *Quartet in A min.*)
Hyperion CDA 66648 [D] **F**

S *Complete Piano Works* Postnikova (pno)
Erato 2292 45969-2, 7 CDs [D] **F**

Album for the Young, Op. 39; *Album for the Young, Op. 39 (arr.
Dubinsky) Edlina (pno), *Dubinsky (vln), Zweig (vln),
Horner (vla), Turovsky (vcl)
Chandos CHAN 8365 [D] **F**

The Seasons, Op. 37b Edlina (pno)
(+Borodin: *Petite Suite*)
Chandos CHAN 9309 [D] **F**

The Seasons, Op. 37b; 6 Piano Pieces, Op. 21 Pletnev (pno)
Virgin VC5 45042-2 (US: 45042) [D] **F**

Piano Sonata in G, Op. 37; The Seasons, Op. 37b Katin (pno)
Olympia OCD 192 [D] **F**

Sleeping Beauty: Suite (arr. Pletnev) Pletnev (pno)
(+ Mussorgsky: *Pictures at an Exhibition*)
Virgin VC7 59611-2 (US: 59611) [D] **F**

Piano Recital Richter (pno)
Olympia OCD 334 [D] F

22 Songs Rodgers (sop), Vignoles (pno
Hyperion CDA 66617 [D] F

28 Songs Söderström (sop), Ashkenazy (pno)
Decca 436 204-2 (US: London 436 204-2) [A/D] M

Songs: *Op. 6/4 & 6; Op. 25/1; Op. 28/6; Op. 38/1; Op. 60/4 & 11; Op. 632; Op. 73/6* Hvorostovsky (bar), Boshniakovich (pno)
(+ Rachmaninov: *Songs*)
Philips 432 119-2 [D] F

EDITORS' CHOICE: *19 Songs* Borodina (mez), Gergieva (pno)
Philips 442 013-2 [D] F

TCHEREPNIN, Alexander (1899–1977) RUSSIA

Piano Concertos Nos. 2, 3 & 5 McLachlan (pno), Chethams SO, Clayton
Olympia OCD 439 [D] F

TELEMANN, Georg Philipp (1681–1767) GERMANY

Chandos Telemann Edition Various artists, Collegium Musicum 90, Standage (vln/dir)
Volume 1: La Changeante
✧ **CHAN 0519 [D] F**
Volume 2: Ouverture burlesque
✧ **CHAN 0512 [D] F**
Volume 3: Domestic Music
✧ **CHAN 0525 [D] F**
Volume 4: Orchestral Music
✧ **CHAN 0547 [D] F**
Volume 5: Sonates Corellisantes, etc.
✧ **CHAN 0549 [D] F**

Flute Concerto No. 4 in D; Recorder and Flute Concerto in E min.; Trumpet Concerto in D; Violin, Cello and Trumpet Concerto in D; Concerto No. 1 in D min. for 2 Chalumeaux; Concerto for 3 Oboes and 3 Violins in Bb Soloists, Cologne Musica Antiqua, Goebel
✧ **DG Archiv 419 633-2 [D] F**

Flute, Oboe d'amore and Viola d'amore Concerto in E; Recorder and Flute Concerto in E min.; Concerto for Strings in G (Polonais); Concerto No. 1 in D for 3 Trumpets; Quartet in Bb Soloists, AAM, Hogwood
✧ **L'Oiseau-Lyre 411 949-2 [D] F**

Horn Concerto in D; Concerto for 2 Horns in Eb; Concerto No. 1 for 2 Horns and 2 Oboes in D; Concerto for 3 Horns and Violin in D; Overture-suite in F for 2 Horns Baumann (hn), T. Brown (hn), Hill (hn), ASMF, I. Brown
Philips 412 226-2 [D] F

Oboe Concertos: No. 2 in C min.; No. 3 in D; No. 4 in D min.; No. 6 in E min.; No. 8 in F min. Holliger (ob), ASMF, Brown
Philips 412 879-2 [D] F

Recorder and Bassoon Concerto in F; Recorder and Flute Concerto in E min.; Overture-suite in A min. Petri (rec), Bennett (fl), Thunemann (bsn), ASMF, Brown
Philips 410 041-2 [D] F

Violin Concertos: No. 2 in D; No. 3 in E; No. 9 in G; No. 10 in G min.; No. 14 in Bb Brown (vln/dir), ASMF
Philips 411 125-2 [D] F

O *2 Oboe and Trumpet Concerto No. 1* Wilbraham (tpt), ASMF,
Marriner
(+ Albinoni: *Trumpet Concerto in C*; Haydn: *Trumpet Concerto in
Eb*; Hummel: *Trumpet Concerto in Eb*; L. Mozart: *Trumpet
Concerto in D*)
Decca 417 761-2 (US: London 417 761-2) [A] **M**

Darmstadt Overtures; Tafelmusik (excerpts) Concerto
Amsterdam, Brüggen; VCM, Harnoncourt
◇ Teldec 2292 42723-2, 3 CDs [A] **M**

Tafelmusik (Produktions Nos. 1–3) VCM, Harnoncourt
◇ Teldec 2292 44568-2, 4 CDs [D] **F**

Tafelmusik: Overtures Concerto Amsterdam, Brüggen
◇ Teldec 2292 43546-2 [A] **M**

C *Concerto da camera in A min.; Quartet in F; Quartet in G min.;
Trio sonatas in D min.; in F; in G min.* Chandos Baroque
Players
◇ Hyperion CDA 66195 [D] **F**

*6 Paris Quartets Nos. 1 & 3; 6 'Nouveaux' Paris Quartets
Nos. 2 & 6* Hazelzet (fl), Trio Sonnerie
◇ Virgin VC7 59049-2 (US: 59049) [D] **F**

*6 'Nouveaux' Paris Quartets Nos. 3 & 4; Quadri: Concerto secondo
& Première Suite* Hazelzet (fl), Trio Sonnerie
◇ Virgin VC5 45020-2 (US: 45020) [D] **F**

*Recorder Sonatas in A; in C; in C; in D min.; in F; in F min.; in F
min.* Schneider (rec), Zipperling (gmba), Hoeran (hpd)
◇ DHM GD 77153 (US: Editio Classica 77153-2) [A] **M**

12 Sonate Melodische (nos. 3–7 & 10) Brüggen (rec), de Vries
(ob), Bylsma (vcl), Moller (vcl), Leonhardt (hpd), van Asperen
(hpd), Boston Museum Trio
◇ RCA GD 71957 (US: Editio Classica 71957-2) [A] **M**

6 Sonates sans basses for 2 recorders Petri (rec), Selin (rec)
RCA RD 87903 (US: 7903-2) [D] **F**

Trio Sonatas in A min.; in C min.; in C min.; in E min.; in F; in F
Cologne Camerata
◇ DHM GD 77017 (US: Editio Classica 77017-2) [A] **M**

V *Die Donner Ode* (cantata); *Deus judicum tuum* (motet) Kwella
(sop), Denley (alt), Tucker (ten), Roberts (bs), George (bs),
Collegium Musicum 90, Hickox
◇ Chandos CHAN 0548 [D] **F**

Die Tageszeiten (cantata) Bach (sop), Georg (mez), Blochwitz
(ten), Mannov (bs), Freiburg Collegium Musicum,
Hengelbrock
◇ DHM RD 77092 (US: 7092-2) [D] **F**

THOMSON, Virgil (1896–1989) USA

O *Film Music: Louisiana Story (Suite); The Plow that Broke the
Plains (Suite); Power Among Men (Fugues & Cantilenas)* New
London O, Corp
Hyperion CDA 66576 [D] **F**

THUILLE, Ludwig (1861–1907) GERMANY

C *Cello Sonata,Op. 22* Rolland (vcl), Hamelin (pno)
(+R. Strauss: *Cello Sonata*)
ASV CDDCA 913 [D] **F**

TICHELI, Frank (born 1958) USA

O   *Radiant Voices; Postcard* Pacific SO, St. Clair
(+ Corigliano: *Piano Concerto*)
Koch 3-7250-2 [D] **F**

TIPPETT, Michael (born 1905) ENGLAND

O   **Piano Concerto; Triple Concerto* *Tirimo (pno), Kovacic (vln),
Caussé (vla), Baillie (vcl), BBC PO, Tippett
Nimbus NI 5301 [D] **F**

Symphony No. 1; *Piano Concerto *Shelley (pno), Bournemouth
SO, Hickox
Chandos CHAN 9333 [D] **F**

Symphony No. 2; Suite from New Year Bournemouth SO,
Hickox
Chandos CHAN 9299 [D] **F**

Symphony No. 3; Praeludium Robinson (sop), Bournemouth
SO, Hickox
Chandos CHAN 9276 [D] **F**

*Symphony No. 4; *Fantasia on a Theme of Handel; Fantasia
Concertante on a Theme of Corelli* *Shelley (pno), Bournemouth
SO, Hickox
Chandos CHAN 9233 [D] **F**

C   *String Quartets Nos. 1–4* Britten Quartet
Collins 70062, 2 CDs [D] **F**

String Quartet No. 4 Lindsay Quartet
(+ Britten: *String Quartet No. 3*)
ASV CDDCA 608 [D] **F**

String Quartet No. 5 Lindsay Quartet
(+ Wood: *String Quartet in A min.*, etc.)
ASV CDDCA 879 [D] **F**

S   *Piano Sonatas Nos. 1–4* Crossley (pno)
CRD 3430/1, 2 CDs [D] **F**

V   *Bonny at Morn; Crown of the Year; Dance, Clarion Air; Music;
5 Negro Spirituals from 'A Child of our Time'; The Weeping Babe*
Christ Church Cathedral Ch, Darlington
Nimbus NI 5266 [D] **F**

*Boyhood's End; The Heart's Assurance; Music; Songs for Achilles;
Songs for Ariel; 5 arrangements of songs by Purcell* Hill (ten), Ball
(pno), Ogden (pno)
Hyperion CDA 66749 [D] **F**

A Child of our Time (oratorio) Robinson (sop), Walker (mez),
Garrison (ten), Cheek (bs), CBSO & Ch, Tippett
Collins 13392 [D] **F**

Choral Works Finzi Singers, Spicer
Chandos CHAN 9265 [D] **F**

A Mask of Time Robinson (sop), Walker (mez), Tear (ten),
Cheek (bs), BBC Singers, BBC SO, A. Davis
EMI CMS7 64711-2 (US: CDMB 64711), 2 CDs [D] **F**

TOMKINS, Thomas (1572–1656) WALES

V   *Above the Stars; Almighty God; Behold, the hour cometh; Glory be to
God; My beloved spake; My Shepherd is the living Lord; O God, the
proud; O sing unto the Lord; Sing unto God; Then David mourned;
Third Service; When David heard* St. George's Chapel Ch,

Robinson
Hyperion CDA 66345 [D] **F**

TORELLI, Giuseppe (1658–1709) ITALY

O *Concerti grossi, Op. 8: Nos. 2, 3, 6, 8, 9 & 12* I Musici
Philips 432 118-2 [D] **F**

TORKE, Michael (born 1961) USA

O *Adjustable Wrench; *Rust; Slate; Vanada; *The Yellow Pages*
Torke (pno), London Sinfonietta, Nagano, *Miller
Argo 430 209-2 [D] **F**

Ash; Bright Blue Music; Ecstatic Orange; Green; Purple Baltimore
SO, Zinman
Argo 433 071-2 [D] **F**

*Music on the Floor; *Four Proverbs; Monday; Tuesday* London
Sinfonietta, Zagrosek; *Bott (sop), Argo Band, Torke
Argo 443 528-2 [D] **F**

TUBIN, Eduard (1905–1982) ESTONIA

O *Ballade for Violin and Orchestra; Double-bass Concerto; Violin
Concerto No. 2; Estonian Dance Suite; Valse triste* Garcia (vln),
Ehren (db), Gothenburg SO, Järvi
BIS BIS-CD 337 [D] **F**

Balalaika Concerto; Music for Strings; Symphony No. 1
Sheynkman (balalaika), Gothenburg SO, Järvi
BIS BIS-CD 351 [D] **F**

*Piano Concerto; Sinfonietta on Estonian Motifs; Symphony No. 7
*Pöntinen (pno), Gothenburg SO, Järvi
BIS BIS-CD 401 [D] **F**

*Violin Concerto No. 1; Prélude solennel; Suite on Estonian Dances
*Lubotsky (vln), Gothenburg SO, Järvi
BIS BIS-CD 286 [D] **F**

Symphonies Nos. 2 & 6 Swedish RSO, Järvi
BIS BIS-CD 304 [D] **F**

Symphonies Nos. 3 & 8 Swedish RSO, Järvi
BIS BIS-CD 342 [D] **F**

*Symphonies Nos. *4 & 9; Toccata* *Bergen SO, Gothenberg SO,
Järvi
BIS BIS-CD 227 [D] **F**

Symphony No. 5; Kratt Bamberg SNO, Järvi
BIS BIS-CD 306 [D] **F**

*Symphony No. 10; Requiem for Fallen Soldiers *Gothenberg
SO, Lundin (cont), Rydell (bar), Hardenberger (tpt), Lund
Choral Society, Järvi
BIS BIS-CD 297 [D] **F**

TURINA, Joaquín (1882–1949) SPAIN

O *Danzas fantásticas, Op. 22; La Procesión del Rocío, Op. 9; Ritmos
(fantasía coreográfica), Op. 43; Sinfonía Sevillana, Op. 23*
Bamberg SO, Almeida
RCA RD 60895 (US: 60895-2) [D] **F**

C *Piano Trio No. 1, Op. 35* Borodin Trio
(+ Debussy: *Piano Trio;* Martin: *Piano Trio*)
Chandos CHAN 9016 [D] **F**

TURNAGE, Mark Anthony (born 1960) ENGLAND

O *Drowned Out; *Kai; Three Screaming Popes; Momentum* *Heinen (vcl), CBSO, Birmingham Contemporary Music Group, Rattle
EMI CDC5 55091-2 (US: CDC 55091) [D] **F**

TYE, Christopher (c.1505–c.1572) ENGLAND

V *Christ rising again; Deliver us; From the depth; Give alms; Gloria laus; I lift my heart; In pace; Kyrie; Mass Euge Bone; Nunc dimittis; Omnes gentes; Quaesumus; To Father* Cambridge University Chamber Ch, Brown
Gamut GAMCD 519 [D] **F**

Mass: Western Wynde; Christ rising again; My trust, O Lord; Omnes gentes, plaudite; Peccavimus cum patribus New College Ch, Higginbottom
CRD 3405 [A] **F**

VAINBERG, Moysey (born 1919) POLAND

O *Golden Key: Ballet Suites* Bolshoi Theatre O, Ermler
Olympia OCD 473 [D] **F**

*Symphonies Nos. 6 & *10* Moscow PO, Kondrashin; *Moscow CO, Barshai
Olympia OCD 471 [A] **F**

*Symphonies Nos. 7 & *12* Moscow CO, Barshai; *USSR TV & Radio O, M. Shostakovich
Olympia OCD 472 [A] **F**

C *Piano Quintet; String Quartet No. 12* *Vainberg (pno), Borodin Quartet
Olympia OCD 473 [D] **F**

VARÈSE, Edgar (1883–1965) FRANCE/USA

O *Ameriques; Arcana; Ionisation; Intégrales; *Density 21.5; Offrandes* Yakar (sop), NYPO, Ensemble InterContemporain, Boulez; *Beauregard (fl)
Sony CD45844 [A/D] **M**

VAUGHAN WILLIAMS, Ralph (1872–1958) ENGLAND

O *Oboe Concerto; Fantasia on a Theme by Thomas Tallis; Fantasia on Greensleeves; The Lark Ascending; 5 Variants of Dives and Lazarus; The Wasps: Overture* Maurice Bourgue (ob), English String O, Boughton
Nimbus NI 7013 [D] **F**

Piano Concerto in C Shelley (pno), RPO, Handley
(+ Foulds: *Dynamic Triptych*)
Lyrita SRCD 211 [A] **F**

Double Piano Concerto; Symphony No. 5 in D *Markham (pno), *Broadway (pno), RPO, Menuhin
Virgin VJ5 61105-2 (US: 61105) [D] **M**

English Folksong Suite; Fantasia on Greensleeves; In the Fen Country; The Lark Ascending; Norfolk Rhapsody No. 1; Serenade to Music NPO, LPO, LSO, Boult
EMI CDM7 64022-2 (US: Angel CDM 64022) [A] **M**

Fantasia on a Theme by Thomas Tallis; Fantasia on Greensleeves *Allegri Quartet, Sinfonia of London, Barbirolli
(+ Elgar: *Introduction and Allegro; Serenade in E min.*)
EMI CDC7 47537-2 (US: Angel CDC 47537) [A] **F**

○ *Fantasia on a Theme by Thomas Tallis; Fantasia on Greensleeves;*
Norfolk Rhapsody No.1; *The Lark Ascending; 5 Variants of 'Dives
and Lazarus'; In the Fen Country *H. Shaham (vln), New
Queen's Hall O, Wordsworth
◇ Argo 440 116-2 [D] **F**

Job (a masque for dancing) Nolan (vln), LPO, Handley
Classics for Pleasure CD-CFP 4603 [D] **B**

*The Lark Ascending; 5 Variants on 'Dives and Lazarus'; The
Wasps (Aristophanic Suite) *Nolan (vln), LPO, Handley
EMI Eminence CD-EMX 9508 (US: Classics for Pleasure CDEMX
9508) [D] **M**

Romance in D♭ Reilly (harmonica), ASMF, Marriner
(+ Jacob: *5 pieces;* Moody: *Little Suite;* Tausky: *Concertino*)
Chandos CHAN 8617 [D] **F**

Symphonies Nos. 1–9; Flos campi; Serenade to Music
EDITORS' CHOICE: Various soloists, RLPO, Handley
EMI Eminence CD-BOX VW1 (US: Classics for Pleasure CDBOX
VW1), 6 CDs [D] **M**

Symphony No. 1 (A Sea Symphony) Harper (sop), Shirley-Quirk
(bar), LSO & Chorus, Previn
RCA GD 90500 (US: 60580-2) [A] **M**

Symphony No. 2 (A London Symphony); *Concerto accademico in D
min.; The Wasps (Aristophanic Suite): Overture *Buswell (vln),
LSO, Previn
RCA GD 90501 (US: 60581-2) [A] **M**

Symphonies: No. 2 (A London Symphony); No. 8 in G min. Hallé
O, Barbirolli
EMI CDM7 64197-2 (US: Angel CDM 64197) [A] **M**

Symphonies: No. 3 (A Pastoral Symphony); No. 4 in F min. LSO,
Previn
RCA GD 90503 (US: 60583-2) [A] **M**

Symphonies: No. 4 in F min.; No. 5 in D BBC PO, A. Davis
Teldec 4509 90844-2 [D] **F**

Symphony No. 5 in D; Elizabeth of England (film music): *Suite*
LSO, Previn
RCA GD 90506 (US: 60586-2) [A] **M**

Symphonies: No. 5 in D; No. 6 in E min. Philharmonia O,
Slatkin
RCA RD 60556 (US: 09026 60556-2) [D] **F**

Symphony No. 6 in E min.; Fantasia on a Theme by Thomas Tallis;
*The Lark Ascending *Little (vln), BBC SO, A. Davis
Teldec 9031 73127-2 [D] **F**

Symphonies: No. 6 in E min.; No. 9 in E min. LSO, Previn
RCA GD 90508 (US: 60588-2) [A] **M**

Symphony No. 7 (Sinfonia Antarctica) Armstrong (sop), LPO &
Ch, Haitink
EMI CDC7 47516-2 (US: Angel CDC 47516) [D] **F**

Symphonies: No. 7 (Sinfonia Antarctica); No. 8 in D min.
Richardson (narr), Harper (sop), LSO & Ch, Previn
RCA GD 90510 (US: 60590-2) [A] **M**

Symphonies: No. 8 in D min.; No. 9 in E min. LPO, Boult
EMI CDM7 64021-2 (US: Angel CDM 64021) [A] **M**

○ *The Wasps (Aristophanic Suite): Overture* LSO, Previn
(+ Walton: *Symphony No. 1*)
RCA GD 87830 (US: 7830-2) [A] **M**

C **Phantasy Quintet; String Quartets Nos. 1 & 2* *Blume (vla),
English Quartet
Unicorn-Kanchana DKPCD 9076 [D] **F**

String Quartet No. 1; *On Wenlock Edge *Langridge (ten),
*Shelley (pno), Britten Quartet
(+ Ravel: *String Quartet*)
EMI CDC7 54346-2 (US: Angel CDC 54346) [D] **F**

6 Studies in English Folksong Hilton (cl), Swallow (pno)
(+ Bax: *Clarinet Sonata*; Bliss: *Clarinet Quintet*)
Chandos CHAN 8683 [D] **F**

V **10 Blake Songs; **Songs of Travel; Songs: Linden Lea; Orpheus
with his Lute; Silent Noon; The Water Mill* Tear (ten), *Black
(ob), **Ledger (pno)
(+ Butterworth: *A Shropshire Lad*)
Decca 430 368-2 (US: London 430 368-2) [A] **M**

*3 Choral Hymns; The Hundredth Psalm; Magnificat; The
Shepherds of the Delectable Mountains; A Song of Thanksgiving*
Gielgud (spkr), Dawson (sop), Wyn-Rogers (cont), Bowen
(ten),
J. Best (bs), Corydon Singers, City of London Sinfonia, Best
Hyperion CDA 66569 [D] **F**

*Dona nobis pacem; 4 Hymns; O Clap your Hands; Lord, Thou hast
been our refuge; Toward the Unknown Region* Howarth (sop),
Ainsley (ten), Allen (bar), Corydon Singers & O, Best
Hyperion CDA 66655 [D] **F**

Dona nobis pacem; Sancta civitas Kenny (sop), Langridge (ten),
Terfel (bs-bar), LSO & Ch., Hickox
EMI CDC7 54788-2 (US: CDC 54788) [D] **F**

Hodie (A Christmas Cantata); Fantasia on Christmas Carols Gale
(sop), Tear (ten), Roberts (bs), LSO & Ch, Hickox
EMI CDC7 54128-2 (US: Angel CDC 54128) [D] **F**

*Lord, Thou hast been our refuge; Prayer to the Father of Heaven;
A Vision of Aeroplanes* Finzi Singers, Spicer
(+ Howells: *Requiem*, etc.)
Chandos CHAN 9019 [D] **F**

Mass in G min.; Te Deum in G Corydon Singers, Best
(+ Howells: *Requiem*)
Hyperion CDA 66076 [A] **F**

On Wenlock Edge Thompson (ten), Delmé Quartet, Burnside
(pno)
(+ Gurney: *Ludlow and Teme; Western Playland*)
Hyperion CDA 66385 [D] **F**

*Serenade to Music; *Flos campi; Fantasia on Christmas Carols;
5 Mystical Songs* *Imai (vla), Allen (bar), Corydon Singers,
Soloists, ECO, Best
Hyperion CDA 66420 [D] **F**

*5 Tudor Portraits; *Benedicite; **5 Variants of 'Dives and
Lazarus'* Bainbridge (sop), Carol Case (bar), *Harper (sop),
Bach Ch, NPO, *LSO, Willcocks; **Jacques O, Willcocks
EMI CDM7 64722-2 (US: CDM 64722) [A] **M**

VERDI, Giuseppe (1813–1901) ITALY

O   Opera Overtures and Preludes: *Un ballo in maschera; La Battaglia di Legnano; Il Corsaro; Ernani; La forza del destino; Luisa Miller; Macbeth; I Masnadieri; Nabucco; Rigoletto; La Traviata; I Vespri Siciliani* BPO, Karajan
DG 419 622-2 [A] **F**

C   *String Quartet in E min.* Delmé Quartet
(+ R. Strauss: *String Quartet in A*)
Hyperion CDA 66317 [D] **F**

V   **Messa da Requiem; **4 Sacred Pieces* *Orgonasova (sop), *von Otter (mez), *Canonici (ten), *Miles (bs), **Brown (sop), Monteverdi Ch., Orchestre Révolutionnaire et Romantique, Gardiner
Philips 442 142-2, 2 CDs [D] **F**

VICTORIA, Tomás Luis de (1548–1611) SPAIN

V   *Ascendens Christus; Missa Ascendens Christus; Missa O magnum mysterium; O magnum mysterium* (motet) Westminster Cathedral Ch, Hill
Hyperion CDA 66190 [D] **F**

Ave Maria; Ave maris stella; Missa Vidi speciosam; Ne timeas; Sancta Maria; Vidi speciosam Westminster Cathedral Ch, Hill
Hyperion CDA 66129 [D] **F**

Missa Ave maris stella; Missa O Quam gloriosum; O Quam gloriosum (motet) Westminster Cathedral Ch, Hill
Hyperion CDA 66114 [D] **F**

Nigra sum Tallis Scholars, Phillips
(+ De Silva: *Nigra sum;* Lhéritier: *Nigra sum;* Palestrina: *Missa Nigra sum*)
Gimell CDGIM 003 [D] **F**

Officium defunctorum Westminster Cathedral Ch, Hill
Hyperion CDA 66250 [D] **F**

Officium Hebdomadae Sanctae (Tenebrae responses)
Tallis Scholars, Philips
Gimell CDGIM 022 [D] **F**
Westminster Cathedral Ch, Hill
Hyperion CDA 66304 [D] **F**

VIERNE, Louis (1870–1937) FRANCE

C   *Piano Quintet in C min., Op. 42; Violin Sonata, Op. 23* Charlier (vln), Hubeau (pno), Viotti Quartet
Erato 2292 45524-2 [D] **F**

S   *Organ Symphonies: No. 1 in D min., Op. 14; No. 2 in E min., Op. 20* Sanger (org)
Meridian CDE 84192 [A] **F**

Organ Symphonies: No. 3 in F♯ min., Op. 28; No. 4 in G min., Op. 32 Sanger (org)
Meridian CDE 84176 [A] **F**

Organ Symphonies: No. 5 in A min., Op. 47; No. 6 in B min., Op. 59 Sanger (org)
Meridian CDE 84171 [A] **F**

VIEUXTEMPS, Henry (1820–1881) BELGIUM

⊃ *Cello Concertos: No. 1 in A min., Op. 46; No. 2 in B min., Op. 50*
Schiff (vcl), Stuttgart RSO, Marriner
EMI CDC7 47761-2 (US: Angel CDC 47761) [D] **F**

Violin Concerto No. 5 in A min. (Grétry), Op. 37 Lin (vln),
Minnesota O, Marriner
(+Bruch: *Violin Concerto No.1; Mendelssohn: Violin Concerto in E min.*)
Sony CD 64250 [D] **M**

Fantasia appassionata, Op. 35 Kremer (vln), LSO, Chailly
(+ Chausson: *Poème;* Milhaud: *Le Boeuf sur le toit: Le printemps;*
Satie: *Choses vues à droite et à gauche*)
Philips 432 513-2 [A] **F**

VILLA-LOBOS, Heitor (1887–1959) BRAZIL

⊃ **Guitar Concerto; 12 Études; 5 Preludes* Bream (gtr), LSO,
Previn
RCA 09026 61604-2 [A] **M**

Piano Concertos Nos. 1–5 Ortiz (pno), RPO, Gómez-
Martínez
Decca 430 628-2 (US: London 430 628-2), 2 CDs [D] **F**

: *Assobio a jato; Bachianas Brasileiras No. 6; Canção do amor;
Chôros No. 2; Distribuição de flores; Modinha; Wind Quintet; Wind
Trio* Bennett (fl), Tunnell (vcl), O'Neill (bsn), Wynberg (gtr),
King (cl), Black (ob), Knight (cor ang)
Hyperion CDA 66295 [D] **F**

*Bachianas Brasileiras Nos. 1 & *5; Preludes and Fugues from
Bach's 48; Suite for Voice and Violin* *Gomez (sop), Manning
(vln), Pleeth Cello Octet
Hyperion CDA 66257 [D] **F**

**Violin Sonatas Nos. 1–3; Danças características africanas; Suite
floral* *Yao (vln), Heller (pno)
Etcetera KTC 1101 [D] **F**

String Quartets Nos. 1–3 Bessler-Reis Quartet
Chant du Monde LDC 278 1052 [D] **F**

String Quartets Nos. 4–6 Bessler-Reis Quartet
Chant du Monde LDC 278 901 [D] **F**

String Quartets Nos. 15–17 Bessler-Reis Quartet
Chant du Monde LDC 278 948 [D] **F**

*Bachianas Brasileiras No. 4; Chôros No. 5; Cicio brasileiro; Valsa
da dor* Petchersky (pno)
ASV CDDCA 607 [D] **F**

*Caixinha de musica quebrada; Prole do bebe: Book I; Cirandinhas;
Carnaval das crianças* Bratke (pno)
Olympia OCD 455 [D] **F**

*Alleluia; Ave Maria; Bendita sabedoria; Cor dulce, cor amabile;
Magnificat; Missa São Sebastião; Panis angelicus; Pater noster;
Praesepe; Sub tuum* Corydon Singers, Best
Hyperion CDA 66638 [D] **F**

VIVALDI, Antonio (1678–1741) ITALY

The Vivaldi Edition (Opp. 1–12) Various artists
Philips 426 925-2, 19 CDs [A] **M**

○ *12 Concerti, Op. 3 (L'Estro armonico)*
English Concert, Pinnock
◇ DG Archiv 423 094-2, 2 CDs [D] **F**

12 Concerti, Op. 3 (L'Estro armonico); 4 Wind Concerti ASMF,
Marriner
Decca 443 476-2 (US: London 443 476-2), 2 CDs [A] **B**

12 Concerti, Op. 4 (La Stravaganza)
ASMF, Marriner
Decca 430 566-2 (US: London 430 566-2), 2 CDs [A] **M**
◇ AAM, Hogwood
◇ L'Oiseau-Lyre 417 502-2, 2 CDs [D] **F**

6 Violin Concerti, Op. 6 Carmirelli (vln), I Musici
Philips 426 939-2 [A] **M**

12 Concerti, Op. 8 Accardo (vln), Holliger (ob), I Musici
Philips 426 940-2, 2 CDs [A] **M**

4 Concerti, Op. 8 Nos. 1–4 (Four Seasons) Loveday (vln),
ASMF, Marriner
Decca 414 486-2 (US: London 414 486-2) [A] **F**

12 Concerti, Op. 9 (La Cetra) Standage (vln), AAM, Hogwood
◇ L'Oiseau-Lyre 421 366-2, 2 CDs [D] **F**

6 Flute Concerti, Op. 10 Beznosiuk (fl), English Concert,
Pinnock
◇ DG Archiv 423 702-2 [D] **F**

6 Concerti, Op. 11 Ritchie (vln), de Bruine (ob), AAM,
Hogwood
◇ L'Oiseau-Lyre 436 172-2 [D] **F**

6 Violin Concerti, Op. 12 Accardo (vln), I Musici
Philips 426 951-2 [A] **M**

Complete Bassoon Concerti, RV466–504 Smith (bsn), ECO,
Ledger; Zagreb Soloists, Ninic
ASV CDDCX 615, 6 CDs [D] **M**

*Cello Concerti: in C, RV399; in C min., RV401; in D min., RV405;
in B♭, RV423; in F, RV538: Largo; *Concerto for Cello and
Bassoon in E min., RV409* Harnoy (vcl), *McKay (bsn),
Toronto CO, Robinson
RCA RD 87774 (US: 7774-2) [D] **F**

*Cello Concerti: in C min., RV402; in D, RV403; in D min., RV406;
in F, RV412; in G, RV414; in A min., RV422; in B min., RV424*
Harnoy (vcl), Toronto CO, Robinson
RCA RD 60155 (US: 60155-2) [D] **F**

*Cello Concerti: in C min., RV401; in F, RV412; in G, RV413; in C
min., RV416; in A min., RV418; in B min., RV424* Coin (vcl),
AAM, Hogwood
◇ L'Oiseau-Lyre 421 732-2 [D] **F**

*Flute Concerti: in D, RV427; in D, RV429; in E min., RV431; in
E min., RV432; in G, RV436; in G, RV438a; in G, RV438; in A
min., RV440; in C min., RV441* Rampal (fl), I Solisti Veneti,
Scimone
Sony/CBS CD 45623, 2 CDs [D] **M**

*Mandolin Concerto in C, RV425; Double Mandolin Concerto in G,
RV532; Viola d'amore and Lute Concerto in D min., RV540;
Chamber Concertos in D, RV93; Trio Sonatas in C, RV82; in G
min., RV85* Jeffrey (mandolin), O'Dette (mandolin), Parley of

Instruments, Goodman, Holman
◇ Hyperion CDA 66160 [D] **F**

*Oboe Concerti: in C, RV446; in C, RV447; in C, RV452; in A min.,
RV461* Holliger (ob), I Musici
Philips 411 480-2 [D] **F**

*Recorder Concerti: in C min., RV441; in F, RV442; in C, RV443;
in C, RV444; in A min., RV445; Chamber Concerto, RV108*
Holstag (rec), Parley of Instruments, Holman
◇ Hyperion CDA 66328 [D] **F**

String Concerti: RV117, 134, 143, 159, 413, 418, 547, 549 & 575
Tafelmusik, Lamon
◇ Sony CD 48044 [D] **F**

*Viola d'amore Concerti: in D, RV392; in D min., RV393; in D min.,
RV394; in D min., RV395; in A, RV396; in A min., RV397* Paris
(gmba), I Musici
Philips 422 051-2 [D] **F**

*Violin Concerti: in C min. (Il sospetto), RV199; in D
(L'inquietudine), RV234; in E (Il riposo), RV270; in E
(L'amoroso), RV271; in E min. (Il favorito), RV277* Vicari (vln),
Gallozi (vln), Cotogni (vln), Ayo (vln), Michelucci (vln),
I Musici
Philips 422 493-2 [A] **M**

*Double Concerti for: 2 Violins, RV505; 2 Oboes, RV535; 2 Violins,
RV511; 2 Cellos, RV531; 2 Violins, RV523; Oboe & 2 Violins,
RV554* Comberti (vln), Coe (vcl), Watkin (vcl), Robson (ob),
Lartham (ob), Collegium Musicum 90, Standage (vln/dir)
◇ Chandos CHAN 0528 [D] **F**

*Lute and Viola d'amore Concerto in D min., RV540; Chamber
Concerto for Lute and 2 Violins, RV93; Trio Sonata for Violin, Lute
and Continuo, RV82* Fernández (gtr), ECO, Malcolm
(+ Giuliani: *Guitar Concerto in A*)
Decca 417 617-2 (US: London 417 617-2) [D] **F**

*Chamber Concerti: in C, RV88; in D, RV90 (Il Gardellino); in D,
RV94; in F, RV99; in G min., RV106; in G min., RV107* London
Harpsichord Ensemble, Francis
Unicorn-Kanchana DKPCD 9071 [D] **F**

*Cello Sonatas: in A min., RV43; A min., RV44; in Bb, RV46; in Bb,
RV47; in E min., RV40; in F, RV41* Coin (vcl), Hogwood
◇ L'Oiseau-Lyre 421 060-2 [D] **F**

*Cello Sonatas: in Bb, RV45; in Eb, RV39; in G min., RV42; *Cello
Concertos: in G min., RV402; in D min., RV406; in G, RV414*
Coin (vcl), Ferre (baroque gtr), Hogwood (hpd); *Coin (vcl),
AAM, Hogwood
◇ L'Oiseau-Lyre 433 052-2 [D] **F**

Cello Sonatas Nos. 1–6, RV 40–41, 43 & 45–47 Harnoy (vcl),
Tilney (hpd), Tetel (vcl cont)
RCA 09026 60430-2 [D] **F**

12 Trio Sonatas, Op. 1 Accardo (vln), Gulli (vln), Canino (hpd),
de Saram (vcl)
Philips 426 926-2 [A] **M**

*12 Trio Sonatas, Op. 1 Nos. 8 in D min., 9 in Ab & 11 in B min.;
Trio Sonatas: in F, RV68; in Bb, RV77; Violin Sonatas: in C, RV2;
in C min., RV6* Purcell Quartet
◇ Chandos CHAN 0511 [D] **F**

C   *Trio Sonatas: in Eb, RV65; in F, RV70; in G, RV71; in G min., RV72; in Bb, RV76; in Bb, RV78; Violin Sonata in A, RV29* Purcell Quartet
◇ Chandos CHAN 0502 [D] **F**

12 Violin Sonatas, Op. 2 Accardo (vln), Canino (hpd), de Saram (vcl)
Philips 426 929-2 [A] **M**

6 Violin Sonatas, Op. 5 Accardo (vln), Gazeau (vla), Canino (hpd), de Saram (vcl)
Philips 426 938-2 [A] **M**

12 'Manchester' Violin Sonatas Manze (vln), Toll (hpd), North (lte)
◇ HM HMU90 7089/90, 2 CDs [D] **F**

V   *Beatus vir, RV597; Credo, RV592; Magnificat, RV610* Soloists, John Alldis Ch, ECO, Negri
Philips 420 651-2 [A] **M**

Beatus Vir, RV598; Dixit Dominus, RV594; Introduzione al Dixit: Canta in prato in G, RV636; Magnificat in G min. (ed. Negri) Soloists, John Alldis Choir, ECO, Negri
Philips 420 649-2 [A] **M**

Crediti propter quod, RV105; Credo, RV591; Introduction to Gloria, RV639; Gloria, RV588; Kyrie, RV587; Laetatus sum, RV607 Soloists, John Alldis Ch, ECO, Negri
Philips 420 650-2 [A] **M**

Gloria in D, RV642; Introduction to Gloria, RV642; Lauda Jerusalem, RV609; Laudate Dominum in D min., RV606; Laudate pueri Dominum in A, RV602 Soloists, John Alldis Ch, ECO, Negri
Philips 420 648-2 [A] **M**

Gloria in D, RV589 Argenta (sop), Attrot (sop), Denley (mez), English Concert O & Ch, Pinnock
(+ A. Scarlatti: *Dixit Dominus*)
◇ DG Archiv 423 386-2 [D] **F**

*Gloria in D, RV589; Magnificat in G min., RV611 *Vaughan (sop), *Baker (mez), King's College Ch, ASMF, *Willcocks, Ledger
(+ Pergolesi: *Magnificat*)
Decca 425 724-2 (US: London 425 724-2) [A] **M**

Gloria in D, RV589; Ostro picta, RV642 Kirkby (sop), Bonner (sop), Chance (alt), Collegium Musicum '90 O & Ch, Hickox
(+ J.S. Bach: *Magnificat*)
◇ Chandos CHAN 0518 [D] **F**

Juditha Triumphans (oratorio) Finnilä (mez), Springer (mez), Hamari (cont), Ameling (sop), Berlin CO, Negri
Philips 426 955-2, 2 CDs [A] **M**

VOLANS, Kevin (born 1949) SOUTH AFRICA

C   *String Quartets Nos. 2 & 3* Balanescu Quartet
Argo 440 687-2 [D] **F**

VOŘÍŠEK, Jan Vaclav (1791–1825)

S   *Piano Sonata in Bb min., Op. 20; Fantasia, Op. 12; 6 Impromptus, Op. 7; Variations in Bb, Op. 20* Kvapil (pno)
Unicorn-Kanchana DKPCD 9145 [D] **F**

WAGNER, Richard (1813–1883) GERMANY

◯ Opera excerpts: *Rienzi; Der fliegende Holländer; Lohengrin; Tannhäuser; Tristan und Isolde* Philharmonia O, Klemperer
CDM7 63617-2 (US: Angel CDM 63617) [A] **M**

Opera excerpts: *Götterdämmerung; Die Meistersinger; Parsifal; Das Rheingold; Siegfried; Die Walküre* Philharmonia O, Klemperer
CDM7 63618-2 (US: Angel CDM 63618) [A] **M**

Opera excerpts: *Die Meistersinger; Tannhäuser; Tristan und Isolde* BPO, Karajan
DG 413 754-2 [D] **F**

✓ *Wesendonck Lieder; Tristan und Isolde: Prelude & Liebestod* Studer (sop), Dresden State O, Sinopoli
(+R. Strauss: *Four Last Songs*)
DG 439 865-2 [D] **F**

WALTON, William (1902–1983) ENGLAND

◯ *Capriccio burlesco; The First Shoot; Galop Final; Granada Prelude; Johannesburg Festival Overture; Music for Children; Portsmouth Point Overture; Prologo e fantasia; Scapino Overture* LPO, Thomson
Chandos CHAN 8968 [D] **F**

*Cello Concerto; Improvisations on an Impromptu of Benjamin Britten; Partita; *Passacaglia for Solo Cello *R. Wallfisch (vcl), LPO, Thomson
Chandos CHAN 8959 [D] **F**

Viola Concerto in A min.; Violin Concerto in B min. Kennedy (vla/vln), RPO, Previn
EMI CDC7 49628-2 (US: Angel CDC 49628) [D] **F**

Façade (An Entertainment) Scales, West (speakers) LMP, Glover
(+ Sitwell: *Poems*)
ASV CDDCA 679 [D] **F**

Façade (An Entertainment): Suites Nos. 1 & 2 English Northern PO, Lloyd-Jones
(+ Bliss: *Checkmate*; Lambert: *Horoscope*)
Hyperion CDA 66436 [D] **F**

Henry V (film score); *A Shakespeare Scenario* (arr. Palmer) Plummer (narr), Westminster Cathedral Ch, ASMF, Marriner
Chandos CHAN 8892 [D] **F**

Film score excerpts: *Macbeth; Major Barbara; Richard III (Shakespeare scenario)* Gielgud (narr), ASMF, Marriner
Chandos CHAN 8841 [D] **F**

The Quest (ballet); *The Wise Virgins* (ballet): *Suite* LPO, Thomson
Chandos CHAN 8871 [D] **F**

Sinfonia concertante Stott (pno), RPO, Handley
(+ Bridge: *Phantasm*; Ireland: *Piano Concerto*)
Conifer CDCF 175 [D] **F**

Symphonies: No. 1 in Bb minor; *No. 2 LPO; *LSO, Mackerras
EMI Eminence CD-EMX 2206 (US: Classics for Pleasure CDEMX 2206) [D] **M**

O   *Symphony No. 1 in Bb min.* LSO, Previn
(+ Vaughan Williams: *Wasps Overture*)
RCA GD 87830 (US: 7830-2) [A] **M**

Symphony No. 2; Partita; Variations on a Theme of Hindemith
Cleveland O, Szell
Sony/CBS CD46732 [A] **M**

C   *Piano Quartet; Violin Sonata* Sillito (vln), Smissen (vla), Otton
(vcl), Milne (pno)
Chandos CHAN 8999 [D] **F**

String Quartet (1919–22); String Quartet in A min. Gabrieli
Quartet
Chandos CHAN 8944 [D] **F**

S   *Passacaglia for Solo Cello* R. Wallfisch (vcl)
(+ Bax: *Rhapsodic Ballad;* Bridge: *Cello Sonata;* Delius: *Cello
Sonata*)
Chandos CHAN 8499 [D] **F**

V   *All this time; Cantico del Sole; Jubilate Deo; King Herod and the
Cock; A Litany; Magnificat and Nunc dimittis; Make we joy now in
this feast; Missa brevis; Set me as a seal* (antiphon); *The Twelve;
What cheer? Where does the uttered music go?* Trinity College Ch.
Marlow
Conifer CDCF 164 [D] **F**

*Anon in love; Christopher Columbus: Suite; Daphne; Long steel
grass; Old Sir Faulk; A song for the Lord Mayor's table; Through
gilded trellises; The Twelve* Finnie (mez), Davies (ten), Hill
(ten), Gomez (sop), Westminster Singers, City of London
Sinfonia, Hickox
Chandos CHAN 8824 [D] **F**

*Belshazzar's Feast (cantata); *Improvisations on an Impromptu o
Benjamin Britten; Portsmouth Point Overture; Scapino Overture*
*Shirley-Quirk (bar), LSO & Ch, Previn
EMI CDM7 64723-2 (US: CDM 64723) [A] **M**

Belshazzar's Feast (cantata); *In Honour of the City of London*
Wilson-Johnson (bar), LSO & Ch, Hickox
EMI Eminence CD-EMX 2225 (US: Classics for Pleasure CDEMX
2225) [D] **M**

*Gloria; Te Deum; Façade Suites Nos. 1 & 2; Crown Imperial; Orb
and Sceptre* CBSO & Ch, Frémaux
EMI CDM7 64201-2 (US: CDM 64201) [A] **M**

WARLOCK, Peter (1894–1930) ENGLAND

O   *Capriol Suite; Serenade for Frederick Delius's 60th Birthday*
Ulster O, Handley
(+ Moeran: *Serenade in G; Nocturne*)
Chandos CHAN 8808 [D] **F**

V   *34 Songs* Ainsley (ten), Vignoles (pno)
Hyperion CDA 66736 [D] **F**

WEBER, Carl Maria von (1786–1826) GERMANY

O   *Andante e Rondo ungarese in C min.; Bassoon Concerto in F*
Thunemann (bsn), ASMF, Marriner
(+ Hummel: *Bassoon Concerto*)
Philips 432 081-2 [D] **F**

*Clarinet Concertos: No. 1 in F min.; No. 2 in Eb; Clarinet
Concertino*

Pay (cl), Age of Enlightenment O
✧ Virgin VC7 59002-2 (US: 59002) [D] **F**
Neidich (cl), Orpheus CO
(+ Rossini: *Introduction, Theme and Variations*)
DG 435 875-2 [D] **F**

O *Clarinet Concerto No.2 in E♭* Ottensamer (cl), VPO, Colin
Davis
(+ Mozart: *Clarinet Concerto*; Spohr: *Clarinet Concerto No. 1*)
Philips 438 868-2 [D] **F**

Horn Concertino in E min. Baumann (hn), LGO, Masur
(+ R. Strauss: *Horn Concertos Nos. 1 & 2*)
Philips 412 237-2 [D] **F**

Invitation to the Dance (orch. Berlioz); Opera overtures: *Abu
Hassan; Euryanthe; Der Freischütz; Oberon; Peter Schmoll; Ruler of
the Spirits* BPO, Karajan
DG 419-070-2 [A] **M**

Overtures: *Abu Hassan; Euryanthe; Der Freischütz; Oberon; Peter
Schmoll; Ruler of the Spirits; Invitation to the Dance* (orch. Berlioz)
Hanover Band, Goodman
✧ Nimbus NI 5154 [D] **F**

Symphonies: No. 1 in C; No. 2 in C ASMF, Mariner
ASV CDDCA 515 [D] **F**

C *Clarinet Quintet in B♭; Flute Trio* Nash Ensemble
CRD 3398 [A] **F**

*Clarinet Quintet in B♭, Op. 34; Introduction, Theme and Variations,
Op. posth.; Grand duo concertant in B♭; Variations, Op.33*
Ensemble Walter Boeykens
Harmonia Mundi HMC90 1481 [D] **F**

S *Piano Sonatas: No. 1 in C; No. 2 in A♭; Rondo brillante in E♭ (La
gaieté); Invitation to the Dance* Milne (pno)
CRD 3485 [D] **F**

Piano Sonatas: No. 3 in D min.; No. 4 in E min.; Polacca brillante
Milne (pno)
(+ Liszt: *Polonaise brillante: Introduction*)
CRD 3486 [D] **F**

WEBERN, Anton (1883–1945) AUSTRIA

O *Passacaglia, Op. 1; 5 Pieces, Op. 5; 6 Pieces, Op. 6; 5 Pieces, Op. 10;
Symphony, Op. 21; Variations, Op. 40; 6 Bagatelles, Op. 9;
Concerto for 9 Instruments, Op. 24; 3 Little Pieces, Op. 11;
5 Movements, Op. 5; 4 Pieces, Op. 7; Quartet, Op. 22; String
Quartet, Op. 28; String Trio, Op. 20; Variations, Op. 27; Das
Augenlicht, Op. 26; 5 Canons, Op. 16; Cantatas Nos. 1 & 2;
Entflieht auf leichten Kähnen; 5 Sacred Songs; 5 Songs, Op. 4; 2
Songs, Op. 8; 4 Songs, Op. 12; 4 Songs, Op. 13; 6 Songs, Op. 14; 3
Songs, Op. 18; 2 Songs, Op. 19; 3 Songs, Op. 25; 5 Songs, Op. 3; 3
Songs from 'Viae inviae'; 3 Traditional Rhymes, Op. 17* Various
artists, Boulez
Sony CD 45845, 3 CDs [A] **M**

*5 Movements, Op. 5; Passacaglia, Op. 1; 6 Pieces, Op. 6; Symphony,
Op. 21* BPO, Karajan
(+ Berg: *Lyric Suite*, etc.; Schoenberg: *Pelleas und Melisande*, etc.)
DG 427 424-2, 3 CDs [A] **M**

5 Pieces, Op. 10 LSO, Dorati
(+ Berg: *3 Orchestral Pieces; Lulu: Symphonic Suite*; Schoenberg:

5 Orchestral Pieces)
Philips Mercury 432 006-2 [A] **M**

C *6 Bagatelles, Op. 9; 5 Movements, Op. 5; String Quartet (1905);
String Quartet, Op. 28* LaSalle Quartet
(+ Berg: *Lyric Suite; String Quartet, Op. 3;* Schoenberg: *String
Quartet in D; String Quartets Nos. 1–4*)
DG 419 994-2, 4 CDs [A] **M**

Langsamer Satz Carmina Quartet
(+ Szymanowski: *String Quartets Nos. 1 & 2*)
Denon CO-79462 [D] **F**

*Piano Quintet (1907); ***Entflieht auf leichten Kahnen, Op. 2;
Lieder; Opp. *8, *13, *14, **18 & ***19; 5 Pieces for Orchestra,
Op. 10; **5 Sacred Songs, Op. 15; **5 Canons, Op. 16; **3
Traditional Rhymes, Op. 17; Quartet, Op. 22; Concerto, Op. 24*
*Pollet (sop), **Oelze (sop), ***BBC Singers, Aimard (pno),
Ensemble InterContemporain, Boulez
DG 437 786-2 [D] **F**

*String Trio, Op. 20; Movement for String Trio; Piano Quintet
(1907); Rondo for String Quartet (1906)* Litwin (pno), LaSalle
Quartet
(+ Schoenberg: *Ode to Napoleon Bonaparte*)
DG 437 036-2 [A] **M**

S *Variations, Op. 27* Pollini (pno)
(+ Boulez: *Piano Sonata No. 2;* Prokofiev: *Piano Sonata No. 7;*
Stravinsky: *3 Movements from Petrushka*)
DG 447 431-2 [A] **M**

V *8 Lieder* Fischer-Dieskau (bar), Reimann (pno)
(+ Berg: *4 Lieder, Op. 2;* Schoenberg: *Gurrelieder, 8 Lieder*)
DG 431 744-2, 2 CDs [A] **M**

WEELKES, Thomas (1576–1623) ENGLAND

V *Alleluia; Evening Service a 5; Evening Service No. 9; Give ear; Give
the king; Gloria in excelsis; Hosanna; O Lord, arise; When David
heard* Christ Church Cathedral Ch, Darlington
Nimbus NI 5125 [D] **F**

WEILL, Kurt (1900–1950) GERMANY/USA

O **Violin Concerto; Kleine Dreigroschenmusik* *Lidell (vln),
London Sinfonietta, Atherton
DG 423 255-2 [A] **M**

Symphonies Nos. 1 & 2 Lisbon Gulbenkian O, Swierczewski
Nimbus NI 5283 [A] **F**

V *Songs* Lemper (sop), Berlin Radio Ensemble, Mauceri
Volume 1
Decca 425 204-2 (US: London 425 204-2) [D] **F**
Volume 2
Decca 436 417-2 (US: London 436 417-2) [D] **F**

*The Seven Deadly Sins; Songs from: Lady in the Dark; Happy End;
One Touch of Venus; 5 Lieder* von Otter (mezzo), Forsberg
(pno), NDR SO, Gardiner
DG 439 894-2 [D] **F**

WESLEY, Samuel (1766–1837) ENGLAND

O *Symphonies: in B♭; in D; in E♭; in A* Milton Keynes CO,
Wetton
Unicorn-Kanchana DKPCD 9098 [D] **F**

WESLEY, Samuel Sebastian (1810–1876) ENGLAND

✔ *Ascribe unto the Lord; Blessed be the God; Cast me not away; Let us Lift; Thou wilt keep him; The Wilderness* Worcester Cathedral Ch, Partington (org), Hunt
Hyperion CDA 66446 [D] **F**

The face of the Lord; Man that is born; O give thanks; O Lord, thou art my God; Praise the Lord; Wash me thoroughly Worcester Cathedral Ch, Partington (org), Hunt
Hyperion CDA 66469 [D] **F**

WESTLAKE, Nigel (born 1958) AUSTRALIA

❍ *Antarctica* (Suite for Guitar and Orchestra) Williams (gtr), LSO, Daniel
(+Sculthorpe: *Nourlangie*, etc.)
Sony CD 53361 [D] **F**

WIDOR, Charles-Marie (1844–1937) FRANCE

C *Piano Quintet No. 1 in D min., Op. 7; Piano Trio in B♭, Op. 19* Prunyi (pno), New Budapest Quartet
Marco Polo 8.223193 [D] **F**

S *Organ Sonatas Nos: 1–10* (complete) Kaunzinger (org)
Novalis 150 105-2, 5 CDs [D] **F**

Organ Symphonies: No. 1 in C min., Op. 13/1; No. 2, Op. 13/2 Kaunzinger (org)
Novalis 150 073-2 [D] **F**

Organ Symphonies: No. 5 in F min., Op. 42/1; No. 6 in C min., Op. 42/2; No. 8, Op. 42/4; No. 9 in C min. (Gothic), Op. 70; 3 Nouvelles pièces, Op. 87 Trotter (org)
Argo 433 152-2 [D] **F**

Organ Symphonies: No. 5 in F min., Op. 42/1; No. 6 in C min., Op. 42/2 Kaunzinger (org)
Novalis 150 015-2 [D] **F**

Organ Symphonies: No. 9 in C min. (Gothic), Op. 70; No. 10 (Roman), Op. 73 Kaunzinger (org)
Novalis 150 038-2 [D] **F**

WIENIAWSKI, Henryk (1835–1880) POLAND

❍ *Violin Concertos: No. 1 in F♯ min., Op. 14; No. 2 in D min., Op. 22; Légende, Op. 17* Shaham (vln), LSO, Foster
(+ Sarasate: *Zigeunerweisen*)
DG 431 815-2 [D] **F**

WILBRANDT, Thomas (born 1952) GERMANY

C *Mono Tones (12 Studies in Silence)* Wilbrandt (pno), Ernest (pno)
Argo 440 228-2 [D] **F**

WIRÉN, Dag (1905–1986) SWEDEN

❍ *Serenade for Strings, Op. 11* English String O, Boughton
Nimbus NI 5347 [D] **F** (see collections – *String Favourites*)

WOLF, Hugo (1860–1903) AUSTRIA

✔ *9 Lieder* von Otter (mez), Gothoni (pno)
(+ Mahler: *Lieder selection*)
DG 423 666-2 [D] **F**

27 Goethe & Morike Lieder Auger (sop), Gage (pno)
Hyperion CDA 66590 [D] **F**

V *Italienisches Liederbuch* Bonney (sop), Hagegard (bar), Parsons (pno)
Teldec 9031 72301-2 [D] **F**

Mörike Lieder (selection) Fassbaender (cont), Thibaudet (pno)
Decca 440 208-2 (US: London 440 208-2) [D] **F**

Spanisches Liederbuch Schwarzkopf (sop), Fischer-Dieskau (bar), Moore (pno)
DG 423 934-2, 2 CDs [A] **M**

WOLF-FERRARI, Ermanno (1876–1948) ITALY

O Overtures: *L'amore medico; La Dama Boba; Il Campiello; I Gioielli della Madonna; I quattro Rusteghi; Il Segreto di Susanna* ASMF, Marriner
EMI CDC7 54585-2 (US: Angel CDC 54585 [D] **F**

WOOD, Charles (1866–1926) ENGLAND

C *String Quartet in A min.* Lindsay Quartet
(+ Tippett: *String Quartet No. 5*, etc.)
ASV CDDCA 879 [D] **F**

V *St. Mark Passion* Kendall (ten), Harvey (bs), Gonville & Caiu College Ch, Webber
(+ Holloway: *Since I Believe*)
ASV CDDCA 854 [D] **F**

WOOD, Hugh (born 1932) ENGLAND

O *Cello Concerto, Op. 12; Violin Concerto, Op. 17* Welsh (vcl), Parikian (vln), RLPO, Atherton
Unicorn-Kanchana UKCD 2043 [A] **M**

String Quartets Nos. 1–4 Chilingirian Quartet
Conifer CDCF 239 [D] **F**

WORDSWORTH, William (1908–1988) ENGLAND

O *Symphonies: No. 2 in D, Op. 34; No. 3 in D, Op. 48* LPO, Braithwaite
Lyrita SRCD 207 [D] **F**

WRIGHT, Maurice (born 1949) USA

S *Piano Sonata* Hamelin (pno)
(+ Ives: *Piano Sonata No. 2 'Concord Mass'*)
New World NW378-2 [D] **F**

XENAKIS, Iannis (born 1922) ROMANIA/FRANCE

O *A l'île de Gorée; Komboï; Khoai; Naama* Chojnacka (hpd), Xenakis Ensemble, Kertens
Erato 2292 45030-2 [D] **F**

S *Palimpsest; Dikhthas; Epeï; Akanthos* Various artists
Wergo WER 6178-2 [D] **F**

YSAŸE, Eugène (1858–1931) BELGIUM

S *6 Sonatas for Solo Violin, Op. 27* Shumsky (vln)
Nimbus NI 5039 [D] **F**

ZELENKA, Jan (1679–1745) BOHEMIA

O *Capriccios Nos. 1–5; Concerto in G; Hipocondrie in A; Overture in F; Sinfonia No. 8 in A min.* Berne Camarata, Wijnkoop
DG Archiv 423 703-2, 3 CDs [A] **M**

C 6 Trio Sonatas Holliger (ob), Bourgue (ob), Thunemann (bsn), Gawriloff (vln), Buccarella (db), van der Meer (bs)
DG Archiv 423 937-2, 2 CDs [A] M

V The Lamentations of Jeremiah Chance (alt), Ainsley (ten), George (bs), Chandos Baroque Players
✧ **Hyperion CDA 66426 [D] F**

Litanae Lauretanae; Missa dei fili Argenta (sop), Chance (alt), Prégardien (ten), Jones (bs), Stuttgart Chamber Ch, Tafelmusik, Bernius
✧ **DHM RD 77922 (US: 7922-2) [D] F**

ZELINSKI, Wladyslaw (1837–1921) POLAND

C Piano quartet in C min., Op. 61 Polish Piano Quartet
(+ Noskowski: Piano Quartet)
Olympia OCD 381 [D] F

ZEMLINSKY, Alexander von (1871–1942) AUSTRIA

O Lyrische Symphonie, Op. 18; *Symphonische Gesänge, Op. 20 Marc (sop), Hagegard (bar), *White (bs-bar), Royal Concertgebouw O, Chailly
Decca 443 569-2 (US: London 443 569-2) [D] F

Symphony No. 2 in Bb; Psalm 23, Op. 14 Ernst-Senff Chamber Ch, Berlin RSO, Chailly
Decca 421 644-2 (US: London 421 644-2) [D] F

C Piano Trio in D min., Op. 3 Beaux Arts Trio
(+ Korngold: Piano Trio)
Philips 434 072-2 [D] F

String Quartets Nos. 1–4 LaSalle Quartet
(+ Apostel: String Quartet No. 1)
DG 427 421-2, 2 CDs [A] M

V Lieder: Gesänge, Op. 5 Books 1 & 2; 6 Gesänge, Op. 6; 5 Gesänge, Op. 7; 4 Gesänge, Op. 8; 6 Gesänge, Op. 10; 6 Gesänge, Op. 13; Lieder, Op. 2 Books 1 & 2; 6 Lieder, Op. 22; 12 Lieder, Op. 27; Schummerlied Blochwitz (ten), Bonney (sop), von Otter (mez), Schmidt (bar), Garben (pno)
DG 427 348-2, 2 CDs [D] F

Collections

○ *American Orchestral Music* Babbitt, Cage, Carter, etc.
Chicago SO, Levine
DG 431 698-2 [D] **F**

American Orchestral Music Barber, Piston, Griffes, etc.
Eastman-Rochester O, Hanson
Philips Mercury 434 307-2 [A] **M**

Ernest Ansermet Edition Various composers
OSR, Ansermet
Decca 433 803-2 (US: London 433 803-2), 12 CDs [A] **M**

The Art of Itzhak Perlman Brahms, Sibelius, Bach, etc.
Perlman (vln), Various artists
EMI CMS7 64617-2 (US: ZDMD 64617), 4 CDs [A/D] **F**

Baroque Recorder Concertos Telemann, Vivaldi, etc.
Petri (rec), ASMF, Sillito
Philips 412 630-2 [D] **F**

Brass music Britten, Carter, Tippett, etc.
Wallace Collection, Wallace
Collins 12292 [D] **F**

British Trombone Concertos Jacob, Howarth & Bourgeois
Lindberg (tbn), BBC Welsh National O, Llewellyn
BIS BIS-CD 658 [D] **F**

A Chance Operation . . . A John Cage Tribute
Various artists
Koch 3-7238-2, 2 CDs [D] **F**

Contemporary Orchestral Music Boulez, Ligeti, Nono, etc.
VPO, Abbado
DG 429 260-2 [D] **F**

Early Romantic Overtures Berlioz, Mendelssohn, etc.
LCP, Norrington
✧ EMI CDC7 49889-2 (US: Angel CDC 49889) [D] **F**

Estonian Music Eller, Lemba, Pärt, Tormis, etc.
SNO, Järvi
Chandos CHAN 8656 [D] **F**

L'Éventaille de Jeanne (ballet by 10 French composers);
Les Mariés de la Tour Eiffel (ballet by five of Les Six)
Philharmonia O, Simon
Chandos CHAN 8356 [D] **F**

Fête à la française Bizet, Chabrier, Dukas, etc.
Montreal SO, Dutoit
Decca 421 527-2 (US: London 421 527-2) [D] **F**

Flute Concerto Collection Honegger, Ibert, Mozart, etc.
Stinton (fl), Browne (hp), Brewer (pno), Scottish CO, ECO,
Philharmonia O, Bedford, Vásáry
Collins 70052, 2 CDs [D] **M**

The Four Seasons Milhaud, Rodrigo, Chaminade, Serebrier
Guttman (vln), RPO, Serebrier
ASV CDDCA 855 [D] **F**

French Orchestral Works Fauré, Bizet, Delibes, etc.
RPO, Beecham
EMI CDM7 63379-2 (US: CDM 63379) [A] **M**

○ *The Great Guitar Concertos* Giuliani, Rodrigo, etc.
Williams (gtr), ECO, Philharmonia O, LSO, Barenboim,
Previn, Frémaux
Sony/CBS CD 44791, 2 CDs [A/D] F

The Bernard Haitink Symphony Edition: Beethoven, Brahms,
Bruckner, Mahler, etc.
Royal Concertgebouw O, Haitink
Philips 442 355-2, 35 CDs [D/A] F

Harp Music Beethoven, Boieldieu, Handel, etc.
Robles (hp), ASMF, Marriner
Decca 425 723-2 (US: London 425 723-2) [A] M

The Jascha Heifetz Complete Edition
Heifetz (vln), Various Os, conductors & accompanists
RCA 09026 61778-2, 65 CDs [A] Mono/Stereo F

The Vladimir Horowitz Edition
Horowitz (pno), Various artists
RCA 09026 61655-2, 22 CDs [A] Mono/Stereo F

One Hundred Years of Dutch Orchestral Music
Het Residentie Orchestra, Various conductors
Volume 1: Schuyt, Sweelinck, Rosier, etc.
Olympia OCD 500 [A] F
Volume 2: Hellendaal, Lentz, Graaf, etc.
Olympia OCD 501 [A] F
Volume 3: Wilms, vam Bree, Verhulst
Olympia OCD 502 [A] F
Volume 4: Verhey, Zweers
Olympia OCD 503 [A] F
Volume 5: Wagenaar, Pijper, Andriessen, etc.
Olympia OCD 504 [A] F
Volume 6: Vermeulen, Ketting, De Leeuw, etc.
Olympia OCD 505 [A] F
Volume 7: Escher, Janssen, Laman, etc.
Olympia OCD 5006 [A] F
Volume 8: Diepenbrock, Badings, Andriessen, etc.
Olympia OCD 507 [D] F

Lollipops Berlioz, Chabrier, Debussy, Delius, etc.
RPO, Beecham
EMI CDM7 63412-2 (US: CDM 63412) [A] M

The Pierre Monteux Edition Beethoven, Debussy, etc.
SFSO, CSO, Boston SO, Monteux
RCA 09026 61893-2, 15 CDs [A] M

Music for Cello and Orchestra Cui, Glazunov, Tchaikovsky, etc.
Isserlis (vcl), COE, Gardiner
Virgin CUV5 61225-2 (US: 61225) [D] M

Music for String Orchestra Respighi, Wirén, Walton, etc.
English String O, Boughton
Nimbus NI 5347 [D] F

Música Mexicana: Volume 1 Chávez, Ponce, Revueltas
RPO, Bátiz
ASV CDDCA 738 [D] F

Música Mexicana: Volume 2 Chávez, *Ponce, Revueltas
*Szeryng (vln), Mexico PO, RPO, Bátiz
ASV CDDCA 866 [D] F

Música Mexicana: Volume 3 *Halffter, Moncayo, Ponce,
Revueltas

*Szeryng (vln), Mexico PO, Bátiz
ASV CDDCA 871 [D] **F**

○ *Música mexicana: Volume 4* López, Ruiz, Reves, etc.
Mexico City PO, Bátiz
ASV CDDCA 893 [D] **F**

Música Mexicana: Volume 5 Revueltas, Halffter, Ponce, etc.
Mexico City PO, Bátiz
ASV CDDCA 894 [D/A] **F**

The New York Album Albert, Bartok & Bloch
Ma (vcl), Baltimore SO, Zinman
Sony CD57961 [D] **F**

Overtures Berlioz, Mendelssohn, Rossini, Suppé, etc.
RPO, Beecham
EMI CDM7 63407-2 (US: CDM 63407) [A] **M**

Popular Baroque Albinoni, Bach, Corelli, Pachelbel, etc.
Orpheus CO
DG 429 390-2 [D] **F**

Popular Baroque Pachelbel, Handel, Vivaldi, etc.
AAM, Hogwood
✧ L'Oiseau-Lyre 410 553-2 [D] **F**

Prometheus – The Myth in Music Beethoven, Nono, Liszt &
Scriabin
BPO, Abbado
Sony CD 53978 [D] **F**

The Complete Recordings Michael Rabin
Rabin (vln), Various accompanists, Os & conductors
EMI CMS7 64123-2 (US: Angel CDMF 64123), 6 CDs [A]
Stereo/Mono **M**

Romantic Overtures Humperdinck, Schumann, Weber, etc.
NPO, Philharmonia O, Klemperer
EMI CDM7 63917-2 (US: Angel CDM 63917) [A] **M**

Scandinavian Suite Grieg, Nielsen, Wirén, etc.
Guildhall String Ensemble
RCA RD 60439 (US: 60439-2) [D] **F**

The Spirit of England Delius, Elgar, Holst, etc.
English String O, Boughton
Nimbus NI 5210/3, 4 CDs [D] **F**

The Stokowski Sound Bach, Debussy, Albéniz, etc.
Cincinnati Pops O, Kunzel
Telarc CD 80129 [D] **F**

String Favourites Arensky, Wirén, Respighi, Walton,
Ireland, etc.
English String O, Boughton
Nimbus NI 5347 [D] **F**

The Ultimate Guitar Collection The Julian Bream Edition
Bream (gtr), Various artists
RCA 09026 61583-2, 28 CDs [D/A] **M**

Victorian Concert Overtures Macfarren, Sullivan, etc.
English Northern Philharmonia, Lloyd-Jones
Hyperion CDA 66515 [D] **F**

Viola music Hindemith, Reger, Schnittke, etc.
Bashmet (vla/dir), Moscow Soloists
RCA RD 60464 (US: 60464-2) [D] **F**

O *Bruno Walter – The Edition: Volume. 1* Mahler, Beethoven,
Wagner & Mendelssohn
Various artists, NYPO, Columbia SO, Walter
Sony CD66246, 10 CDs [A] **M**

Works for Cello and Orchestra Fauré, Lalo, etc.
Rose (vcl), Philadelphia, Ormandy
Sony CD 48278 [A] **F**

Works for Flute and Orchestra Godard, Ibert, Saint-Saëns, etc.
Milan (fl), City of London Sinfonia, Hickox
Chandos CHAN 8840 [D] **F**

Works for Horn and Orchestra Dukas, Glière, etc.
Baumann (hn), LGO, Masur
Philips 416 380-2 [D] **F**

C *An American Recital* Barber, Copland, Hanson, etc.
Stinton (fl), Martineau (pno)
Collins 13852 [D] **F**

American Works for Piano Trio Rorem, Baker, Rochberg
Beaux Arts Trio
Philips 438 866-2 [D] **F**

Bream and Williams Live Albéniz, Granados, Sor, etc.
Bream (gtr), Williams (gtr)
RCA RD 89645 (US: 9645-2) (US: 9645-2) [A] **F**

British Cello Music Arnold, Britten, Ireland, etc.
Lloyd Webber (vcl), McCabe (pno)
CDDCA 592 [D] **F**

British Clarinet Music Vaughan Williams, Bax, Bliss, etc.
Johnson (cl), Martineau (pno), Howarth (sop)
ASV CDDCA 891 [D] **F**

British Works for Flute Arnold, Delius, Elgar, etc.
Smith (fl), Rhodes (pno)
Volume 1: Summer Music
ASV CDDCA 739 [D] **F**
Volume 2: Folk & Fantasy
ASV CDDCA 768 [D] **F**

La Clarinette française Poulenc, Ravel, etc.
Johnson (cl), Back (pno)
ASV CDDCA 621 [D] **F**

A Contemporary Flute Collection Alwyn, Demase, Jolivet, etc.
Stinton (fl), Brewer (pno)
Collins 12972 [D] **F**

Contemporary Irish String Quartets Beckett, Boydell,
Kinsella, etc.
Vanburgh Quartet
Chandos CHAN 9295 [D] **F**

Elizabethan and Jacobean Consort Music
Julian Bream Consort
RCA RD 87801 (US: 7801-2) [D] **F**

Encore Beethoven, Ravel, etc.
Midori (vln), McDonald (pno)
Sony CD 52568 [D] **F**

Encores Volume 2 Milhaud, Rameau, Babin, Templeton, etc.
Johnson (cl), Drake (pno)
ASV CDDCA 910 [D] **F**

C   *English Clarinet Music* Arnold, Finzi, Ireland, etc.
de Peyer (cl), Pryor (pno)
Chandos CHAN 8549 [D] **F**

English Music for Piano Duet Berners, Walton, Lambert, etc.
Lawson, MacLean (pno duet)
Albany TROY 142 [D] **F**

English Music for Viola Britten, Grainger, Bridge, etc.
Coletti (vla), Howard (pno)
Hyperion CDA 66687 [D] **F**

First and Foremost Nyman, Corea, Bedford, etc.
Apollo Saxophone Quartet
Argo 443 903-2 [D] **F**

Flute Fantasie Fauré, Gaubert, etc.
Milan (fl), Brown (pno)
Chandos CHAN 8609 [D] **F**

French Clarinet Music Debussy, Poulenc, Saint-Saëns, etc.
de Peyer (cl), Pryor (pno)
Chandos CHAN 8526 [D] **F**

French Violin Music Fauré, Poulenc, Ravel, etc.
Heifetz (vn), Smith (pno)
RCA GD 87707 (US: 7707-2) [A] **M**

Glyndebourne Wind Serenades Harvey, Osborne, Saxton, etc.
LPO members, Age of Enlightenment O members, Dove,
Pay, Parrott
EMI CDC7 54424-2 (US: CDC 54424) [D] **F**

Heart's Ease Viol Consort Music by Byrd, Gibbons, etc.
Fretwork
✧ Virgin VC7 59667-2 (US: 59667) [D] **F**

Italian Recorder Music Cima, Frescobaldi, Merula, etc.
Amsterdam Loeki Stardust Quartet (recs)
✧ L'Oiseau-Lyre 430 246-2 [D] **F**

Kiss on Wood MacMillan, Schnittke, Copland, etc.
Bachmann (vln), Klibonoff (pno)
RCA 09026 62668-2 [D] **F**

The Lindsays: 25 Years Barber, Wirén, Wood, etc.
Lindsay Quartet
ASV CDDCA 825 [A] **F**

Loopholes Barber, Harris, Wolfe, etc.
Piano Circus
Argo 443 527-2 [D] **F**

Midori Live at Carnegie Hall Beethoven, Ravel, etc.
Midori (vln), McDonald (pno)
Sony CD 46742 [D] **F**

Piano Circus Volans, Reich, etc.
Piano Circus
Argo 440 294-2 [D] **F**

Piano Music for Four Hands Dvořák, Rachmaninov, etc.
Duo Tal & Groethuysen
Sony CD 47199 [D] **F**

Russian Miniatures Borodin, Glazunov, Tchaikovsky, etc.
Borodin Quartet
Teldec 4509 94572-2 [D] **F**

Souvenir Bach, Telemann, Jacob, etc.
Petri (recs), Hannibal (lte/gtr)
RCA 09026 62530-2 [D] **F**

Terminal Velocity Bryars, Gordon, Lang, etc.
Icebreaker
Argo 443 214-2 [D] **F**

Three Parts Upon a Ground: Sonatas and other works for 3 violins
Hollaway, Ritcie, Manze (vlns), Toll (hpd), North (lte)
HM HMU90 7091 [D] **F**

Together Albéniz, Lawes, Sor, etc.
Bream (gtr), Williams (gtr)
RCA 09026 61450-2 [A] **M**

Together Again Albéniz, Carulli, Giuliani, etc.
Bream (gtr), Williams (gtr)
RCA 09026 61452-2 [A] **M**

Violin Recital Bartók, Brahms, Falla, etc.
Takezawa (vln), Moll (pno)
RCA 09026 60704-2 [D] **F**

The Virtuoso Violin Brahms, Ravel, Shostakovich, etc.
Little (vln), Lane (pno)
EMI Eminence CD-EMX 2196 (US: Classics for Pleasure CDEMX 2196) [D] **M**

The Winged Lion Castello, Vitali, Vivaldi, etc.
Palladian Ensemble
Linn CKD 015 [D] **F**

American Piano Classics Garner, Ives, Nancarrow, etc.
MacGregor (pno)
Collins 12992 [D] **F**

Baroque Guitar Bach, Scarlatti, Weiss, etc.
Bream (gtr)
RCA 09026 61592-2 [A] **M**

Jorge Bolet Live Liszt, Franck, etc.
Bolet (pno)
Decca 436 648-2 (US: London 436 648-2) [D] **F**

Carnegie Hall Debut Liszt, Schumann, etc.
Kissin (pno)
RCA 09026 61202-2 [D]**F**

Classic Guitar Diabelli, Giuliani, Sor, etc.
Bream (gtr)
RCA 09026 61593-2 [A] **M**

The Complete Masterworks Recordings (1962–73)
Horowitz (pno)
Sony CD 53456, 13 CDs [A] **M**

Echoes of a Waterfall Alvars, Glinka, Spohr, etc.
Drake (hp)
Hyperion CDA 66038 [D] **F**

The Essential Harpsichord Arne, Rameau, Scarlatti, etc.
Black (hpd)
Collins 50242 [D] **F**

Fandango Virtuoso Sonatas from 18th Century Spain
Puyana (hpd)
L'Oiseau-Lyre 417 341-2 [D] **F**

S   *Guitarra* Granados, Mudarra, Narváez, Sanz, Sor, etc.
Bream (gtr)
RCA 09026 61610-2 [D] **M**

The Harmonious Blacksmith Bach, Handel, Rameau, etc.
Pinnock (hpd)
DG Archiv 413 591-2 [D] **F**

Horowitz in Moscow Mozart, Rachmaninov, Scarlatti, etc.
Horowitz (pno)
DG 419 499-2 [D] **F**

Horowitz at the Met Chopin, Liszt, Rachmaninov, etc.
Horowitz (pno)
RCA 09026 61416-2 [D] **M**

Horowitz: The Private Collection Bach, Clementi, Mendelssohn
Chopin, etc.
Horowitz (pno)
RCA 09026 62643-2 [D] **F**

The Last Romantic Bach, Mozart, Schubert, Rachmaninov, etc.
Horowitz (pno)
DG 419 045-2 [D] **F**

Late Russian Romantics Rachmaninov, Scriabin, etc.
Horowitz (pno)
Sony CD 53472 [A] **F**

Live at the Wigmore Hall Haydn, Scarlatti, Berg, etc.
Demidenko (pno)
Hyperion CDA 66781/2, 2 CDs [D] **F**

Live at the Wigmore Hall Alkan, Medtenr, Godowsky, etc.
Hamelin (pno)
Hyperion CDA 66765 [D] **F**

Live in London Chopin, Schumann, Scriabin
Horowitz (pno)
RCA 09026 61414-2 [D] **M**

Netherlands Harpsichord Music Bustijn, Sweelinck, etc.
van Asperen (hpd)
Sony CD 46349 [D] **F**

The Nimbus Recordings Mussorgsky, Rachmaninov, etc.
Cherkassky (pno)
Nimbus NI 1793 [D] **F**

Organ Fireworks Herrick (org)
Volume 1
Hyperion CDA 66121 [D] **F**
Volume 2
Hyperion CDA 66258 [D] **F**
Volume 3
Hyperion CDA 66457 [D] **F**
Volume 4
Hyperion CDA 66605 [D] **F**
Volume 5
Hyperion CDA 66676 [D] **F**

Organ Spectacular Franck, Karg-Elert, Widor, etc.
Hurford (org)
Decca 430 710-2 (US: London 430 710-2) [D] **F**

A Paganini Ernst, Milstein, Rochberg, Schnittke
Kremer (vln)
DG 415 484-2 [D] **F**

S *The Piano Album 1* Godowsky, Paderewski, etc.
Hough (pno)
Virgin VC7 59509-2 (US: 59509) [D] **F**

The Piano Album 2 Tausig, Levitzki, etc.
Hough (pno)
Virgin VC7 59304-2 (US: 59304) [D] **F**

Popular French Romantics Franck, Gigout, Widor, etc.
Parker-Smith (org)
Volume 1
ASV CDDCA 539 [D] **F**
Volume 2
ASV CDDCA 610 [D] **F**

Rare Piano Encores Bizet, Gershwin, Rossini, etc.
Howard (pno)
Hyperion CDA 66090 [D] **F**

Rêverie Brahms, Debussy, Godowsky, etc.
Fergus-Thompson (pno)
ASV CDWHL 2066 [D] **M**

The Sviatoslav Richter Edition
Richter (pno)
Philips 442 464-2, 21CDs [A] **M**

Russian Piano Music Balakirev, Borodin, Mussorgsky, etc.
Fingerhut (pno)
Chandos CHAN 8439 [D] **F**

Spanish Guitar Music Albéniz, de Falla, Granados, etc.
Williams (gtr)
Sony CD 46347 [A] **B**

Spanish Piano Music Albéniz, de Falla, Granados, Halffter,
Mompou, Soler, Turina, etc.
de Larrocha (pno)
Volume 1
Decca 433 920-2 (US: London 433 920-2), 2 CDs [A/D] **M**
Volume 2
Decca 433 923-2 (US: London 433 923-2), 2 CDs [A/D] **M**
Volume 3
Decca 433 926-2 (US: London 433 926-2), 2 CDs [A] **M**
Volume 4
Decca 433 929-2 (US: London 433 929-2), 2 CDs [A/D] **M**

The Studio Recordings (1962–3) Chopin, Liszt, etc.
Horowitz (pno)
Sony CD 53457, 2 CDs [A] **F**

Tchaikovsky and his Friends Arensky, Lyadov, Glazunov, etc.
Fingerhut (pno)
Chandos CHAN 9218 [D] **F**

Theme & Variations 1 Brahms, Mendelssohn, Mozart, etc.
Brendel (pno)
Philips 426 272-2 [D] **F**

Virtuoso Guitar Transcriptions
Hall (gtr)
Decca 430 839-2 (US: London 430 839-2) [D] **F**

Virtuoso Piano Showpieces Godowsky, Moszkowski, etc.
Jones (pno)
Nimbus NI 5326 [D] **F**

S *Virtuoso Transcriptions* Tausig, Balakirev, etc.
Fowke (pno)
CRD 3396 [A] **F**

Virtuoso Victoriana
Schiller (pno)
ASV CDWHL 2051 [D] **M**

Wagneriana Transcriptions by Busoni, Raff, Wagner, etc.
Katsaris (pno)
Sony CD 58973 [D] **F**

Works for Solo Cello Britten, Crumb, Ligeti, Reger
Haimowitz (vcl)
DG 431 813-2 [D] **F**

V *Abelard: Hymns and Sequences for Héloïse*
Cambridge Schola Gregoriana, Winchester Cathedral
Choristers, Berry
Herald HAVPCD 168 [D] **F**

Airs de Cour French Court Music of the 17th Century
Vallin (sop), van Egmond (bar), Kirchof (lte)
◊ Sony CD 48250 [D] **F**

American Collection Barber, Fine, Reich, etc.
The Sixteen, Christophers
Collins 12872 [D] **F**

An Evening with Victoria de los Angeles
de los Angeles (sop), Parsons (pno)
Collins 12472 [D] **F**

Anthology of Gregorian Chant
Various choirs & directors
DG Archiv 435 032-2, 4 CDs [A] **M**

Avis Maris Stella: Life of the Virgin Mary in Plainsong
Niederaltaicher Scholaren, Ruhland
Sony CD 45861 [D] **F**

Awake, Sweet Love Campion, Dowland, Ford, etc.
Bowman (alt), Miller (lte), Kings Consort
Hyperion CDA 66447 [D] **F**

Cantus Selecti: Gregorian Chant
Choralschola of the Niederaltaicher Scholaren, Ruhland
Sony CD 53372 [D] **F**

Carmina Burana
Bott (sop), George (bs), New London Consort, Pickett
L'Oiseau-Lyre 442 143-2, 4 CDs [D] **M**

Carnaval Offenbach, Massenet, Hérold, Messager, etc.
Jo (sop), ECO, Bonynge
Decca 440 679-2 (US: London 440 679-2) [D] **F**

Codex Las Huelgas (Music from 13th Century Spain)
Huelgas Ensemble, Van Nevel
Sony CD 53341 [D] **F**

Christmas Music from Mediaeval and Renaissance Europe
The Sixteen, Christophers
Hyperion CDA 66263 [D] **F**

Collectio Argentea: An Anthology of Early Music
Various artists
DG 437 070-2, 20 CDs [A] **B**

V *Crown of Thorns* Browne, Davy, Sheryngham, etc.
The Sixteen, Christophers
Collins 13162 [D] F

The Dante Troubadours Daniel, Faidit, Vidal, etc.
Martin Best Medieval Ensemble
Nimbus NI 5002 [D] F

La Dissection d'un Homme armé Six Masses
Huelgas Ensemble, Van Nevel
Sony CD 45860 [D] F

Divas in Song Britten, Rachmaninov, Granados, Brahms, etc.
Horne (mez), Caballé (sop), Donath (sop), Fleming (sop),
Swenson (sop), von Stade (mez), Bjarnason (ten), Ramey (bs),
Levine (pno)
RCA 09026 62547-2 [D] F

Elizabethan Lute Songs Pears (ten), Bream (gtr)
RCA 09026 61602-2 [A] M

Elizabethan Songs 'The Lady Musick'
Kirkby (sop), Rooley (lte)
L'Oiseau-Lyre 425 892-2 [D] F

The English Anthem Volume 1 Gardiner, Stainer, Wood, etc.
St. Paul's Cathedral Ch, Lucas (org), Scott
Hyperion CDA 66374 [D] F

The English Anthem Volume 2 Bainton, Finzi, Stanford, etc.
St. Paul's Cathedral Ch, Scott
Hyperion CDA 66519 [D] F

España Antigua: Popular Spanish Music 1200–1700
Hesperion XX, Savall
Virgin VM5 61179-2 (US: 61179) [A] M

Febus Avant! (Music at the Court of Gaston Febus)
Huelgas Ensemble, Van Nevel
Sony CD 48195 [D] F

The Girl with the Orange Lips Falla, Ravel, etc.
Upshaw (sop)
Elektra-Nonesuch 7559 79262-2 (US: 79262-2) [D] F

Goethe Lieder Mozart, Schubert, Schumann & Wolf
Upshaw (sop), Goode (pno)
Elektra-Nonesuch 7559 79317-2 (US: 79317-2) [D] F

Thomas Hampson Live at the Usher Hall, Edinburgh Schumann,
Beethoven, Loewe, etc.
Hampson (bar), Parsons (pno)
EMI CDC5 55147-2 (US: CDC 55147) [D] F

Ikos Gorecki, Pärt & Tavener
King's College Ch., S. Cleobury
EMI CDC5 55096-2 (US: CDC 55096) [D] F

In Praise of Woman Lehmann, Smyth, Clarke, etc.
Rolfe Johnson (ten), Johnson (pno)
Hyperion CDA 66709 [D] F

In Morte di Modanna Laura Madrigal cycle on Petrarca
Huelgas Ensemble, Van Nevel
Sony CD 45942 [D] F

V *Italian Songs*
Bartoli (mez), Schiff (pno)
Decca 440 297-2 (US: London 440 297-2) [D] **F**

Lieder Recital Berg, Korngold, R. Strauss
Von Otter (mez), Forsberg (pno)
DG 437 515-2 [D] **F**

Madrigals and Wedding Songs for Diana Weelkes, etc.
Kirkby (sop), Thomas (bs), Consort of Musicke, Rooley
Hyperion CDA 66019 [D] **F**

The Medieval Romantics
Gothic Voices, Page
Hyperion CDA 66463 [D] **F**

Miserere Allegri, Parry, Schubert, etc.
Trinity College Ch, Marlow
Conifer CDCF 219 [D] **F**

Mozart Portraits
Bartoli (mezzo), VCO, Fischer
Decca 443 452-2 (US: London 443 452-2) [D] **F**

Music for the Lion-Hearted King
Gothic Voices, Page
Hyperion CDA 66336 [D] **F**

Music from Renaissance Portugal Lobo, Carreira, Fernandez, etc.
Cambridge Taverner Ch, Rees
Herald HAVPCD 155 [D] **F**

Music from the Court of King Janus at Nicosia (1374–1432)
Huelgas Ensemble, Van Nevel
Sony 53976 [D] **F**

Music from the Time of the Crusades
Early Music Consort, Munrow
Decca 430 264-2 (US: London 430 264-2) [A] **M**

Music of the Gothic Era
Early Music Consort, Munrow
DG Archiv 415 292-2 [A] **M**

Music of the Italian Renaissance Alberti, de Roré, etc.
Huelgas Ensemble, Van Nevel
Sony CD 48065 [D] **F**

Music of the Portuguese Renaissance Morago, Melgas
Pro Antiqua Musica, Brown
Hyperion CDA 66715 [D] **F**

My Restless Soul Tchaikovsky, Borodin, Rachmaninov, etc.
Hvorostovsky (bar), Arkadiev (pno)
Philips 442 536-2 [D] F

Nights Black Bird Consort Music by Byrd & Dowland
Fretwork, Wilson
Virgin VC7 59539-2 (US: 59539) [D] **F**

La Procession – 80 Years of French Song Chausson, etc.
Varcoe (bar), Johnson (pno)
Hyperion CDA 66248 [D] **F**

Amanda Roocroft Handel, Mozart, Dvořák, R. Strauss, etc.
Roocroft (sop), LPO, Welsor-Most
EMI CDC5 55090-2 (US: CDC 55090) [D] **F**

V *The Rose and the Ostrich Feather* Browne, Cornyshe, etc.
The Sixteen, Christophers
Collins 13142 [D] **F**

Russian Romances Tchaikovsky, Mussorgsky, Cui, Glinka, etc.
Ghiaurov (bs), Dokovska (pno)
RCA 09026 62501-2 [D] **F**

Russian Romances, Volume 2
Hvorstovsky (bar), Arkadiov (pno)
Philips 442 536-2 [D] **F**

The Sea Borodin, Debussy, Ireland, etc.
Walker (mez), Allen (bar), Vignoles (pno)
Hyperion CDA 66165 [D] **F**

Shakespeare's Kingdom Brahms, Schubert, Schumann, etc.
Walker (mez), Johnson (pno)
Hyperion CDA 66136 [D] **F**

Song Collection Borodin, Glinka, Mussorgsky, etc.
Vishnevskaya (sop), Rostropovich (pno)
Erato 2292 45643-2, 2 CDs [D] **F**

Songs and Dances of Death Rimsky-Korsakov, Mussorgsky,
Rubinstein, etc.
Hvorstovsky (bar), Kirov O, Gergiev
Philips 438 872-2 [D] **F**

Songs by Finzi and his Friends Finzi, Gill, Milford, etc.
Partridge (ten), Roberts (bar), Benson (pno)
Hyperion CDA 66015 [A] **F**

A Spanish Songbook Bizet, Delibes, Rodrigo, Obradors, etc.
Gomez (sop), Constable (pno)
Conifer CDCF 243 [D] **F**

The Spirits of England and France, Volume. 1: Pykini, Machaut,
Perotin, etc.
EDITORS' CHOICE: Gothic Voices, Page
Hyperion CDA 66739 [D] **F**

Sweet Power of Song Brahms, Chausson, Fauré, etc.
Lott (sop), Murray (mez), Johnson (pno)
EMI CDC7 49930-2 (US: Angel CDC 49930) [D] **F**

The Three Tenors in Concert, 1994
Carreras (ten), Domingo (ten), Pavarotti (ten), LA Music
Center Ch., LAPO, Mehta
Teldec 4509 96200-2 [D] **F**

War's Embers Butterworth, Finzi, Gurney, etc.
George (bs), Hill (ten), Varcoe (bar), Benson (pno)
Hyperion CDA 66261/2, 2 CDs [D] **F**

50 Historical Recordings

For the purposes of this Guide we have labelled any recording in monaural sound (in the great majority of cases pre-1956) as 'historical'. Although a certain degree of tolerance is often called for in terms of the recorded quality, and a number of CD transfers of this material have proved less than entirely successful in the past, the artistic endeavour enshrined therein is often of a uniquely compelling quality. Listed below is a selection of 50 recommended 'historical' CDs, chosen not so much for the actual repertoire but for the outstanding quality of musicianship displayed by the artists involved. This is not intended as a 'league' table, nor have we been able to include a number of distinguished artists whom we both greatly admire; however, we feel that it provides an excellent starting point for any collector, and hope that it will encourage further exploration of this musical treasure trove. Opera recordings and recitals will be found in our companion guide, *Opera Music on CD*.

BACH, Johann Sebastian (1685–1750) GERMANY

Goldberg Variations
Gould (pno)
Sony CD 52594 [A] M

The Well-Tempered Clavier (complete)
Fischer (pno)
EMI CHS7 63188-2 (US: CDHC 63188), 3 CDs [A] M

Landowska plays Bach
Landowska (hpd)
Pearl GEMMCD 9489 [A] M

BARTÓK, Bela (1881–1945) HUNGARY/USA

Bartók Performs Bartók – *Contrasts, Mikrokosmos
Bartók (pno), *Goodman (cl), *Szigeti (vln)
CBS/Sony CD 47676 [A] M

BAX, Arnold (1883–1953) ENGLAND

Symphony No. 3
Hallé O, Barbirolli
(+ Ireland: *These Things Shall Be; Forgotten Rite; April*)
EMI CDH7 63910-2 (US: CDH 63910) [A] M

BEETHOVEN, Ludwig van (1770–1827) GERMANY

Piano Concertos Nos. 1-5; Rondos, Op. 51
Kempff (pno), BPO, van Kempen
DG 435 744-2, 3 CDs [A] M

Symphony No. 3 in E♭ (Eroica), Op. 55
Concertgebouw O, E. Kleiber
Decca 433 406-2 (US: London 433 406-2) [A] M

Symphonies: No. 5 in C min., Op. 67; No. 7 in A, Op. 92
BPO, Furtwängler
DG 427 775-2 [A] M

String Quartets: No. 7 in F (Razumovsky), Op. 59/1; No. 13 in B♭, Op. 130
Busch Quartet
CBS/Sony CD 47687 [A] M

The Complete Piano Sonatas
Schnabel (pno)
EMI CHS7 63765-2 (US: CDHH 63765), 8 CDs [A] M

RAHMS, Johannes (1833–1897) GERMANY

Violin Concerto in D, Op. 77
Neveu (vln), Philharmonia O, Dobrowen
(+ Sibelius: *Violin Concerto*)
EMI CDH7 61011-2 (US: CDH 61011) **[A] M**

Wilhelm Backhaus Plays Brahms – Ballades, Rhapsodies, Scherzo, etc.
Backhaus (pno)
Pearl GEMMCD 9385 **[A] M**

CHOPIN, Frédéric (1810–1849) POLAND

Cortot plays Chopin
Cortot (pno)
Biddulph LHW 001 **[A] M**

Artur Rubinstein plays Chopin, Volume 2
Rubinstein (pno)
EMI CHS7 64697-2 (US: CDHB 64697), 2 CDs **[A] M**

DEBUSSY, Claude (1862–1918) FRANCE

Préludes (complete)
Gieseking (pno)
EMI CDH7 61004-2 (US: CDH 61004) **[A] M**

DELIUS, Frederick (1862–1934) ENGLAND

*Brigg Fair; In a Summer Garden; On Hearing the First Cuckoo in Spring; Summer Night on the River; *Sea Drift; Koanga: La Calinda*
*Brownlee (bar), RPO, Beecham
Sir Thomas Beecham Trust BEECHAM 3 **[A] M**

ELGAR, Edward (1857–1934) ENGLAND

*Violin Concerto in B min., Op. 61; *Cello Concerto in E min., Op. 85*
Menuhin (vln), LSO, Elgar; *Harrison (vcl), New SO, Elgar
EMI CDH7 69786-2 (US: CDH 69786) **[A] M**

Symphonies Nos. 1 & 2; Falstaff; Dream of Gerontius (excerpts); *Music Makers* (excerpts); *Civic Fanfare; National Anthem* (arr.)
LSO, Royal Albert Hall O, Elgar
CDS7 54560-2 (US: CDHC 54560), 3 CDs **[A] M**

IRELAND, John (1879–1962) ENGLAND

These Things Shall Be; Forgotten Rite; April
Jones (ten), Hallé Ch & O, Barbirolli
(+ Bax: *Symphony No. 3*)
EMI CDH7 63910-2 (US: CDH 63910) **[A] M**

KORNGOLD, Erich (1897–1957) AUSTRIA-HUNGARY/USA

Violin Concerto
Heifetz (vln), LAPO, Wallenstein
(+ Rozsa: *Violin Concerto;* Waxman: *Carmen Fantasy*)
RCA GD 87963 (US: 7963-2) **[A] M**

KREISLER, Fritz (1875–1962) AUSTRIA

Kreisler plays Kreisler
Kreisler (vln), Various accompaniments
EMI CDH7 64701-2 (US: CDH 64701) **[A] M**

MAHLER, Gustav (1860–1911) AUSTRIA

Das Lied von der Erde
Ferrier (cont), Patzak (ten), VPO, Walter
Decca 414 194-2 (US: London 414 194-2) [A] **F**

MOZART, Wolfgang Amadeus (1756–1791) AUSTRIA

Horn Concertos Nos. 1–4
Brain (hn), Philharmonia O, Karajan
EMI CDH7 61013-2 (US: CDH 61013) [A] **M**

MUSSORGSKY, Modest (1839–1881) RUSSIA

Complete Songs
Christoff (bs), Labinsky (pno), FRNO, Tzipine
EMI CHS7 63025-2 (US: CDHC 63025), 3 CDs [A] **M**

PAGANINI, Nicolò (1782–1840) ITALY

24 Caprices, Op. 1
Rabin (vln)
EMI CDM7 64560-2 (US: Angel CDM 64560) [A] **M**

RESPIGHI, Ottorino (1879–1936) ITALY

Fountains of Rome; Pines of Rome; Roman Festivals
NBC SO, Toscanini
RCA GD 60262 (US: 60262-2) [A] **M**

SCHUMANN, Robert (1810–1856) GERMANY

Dichterliebe, Op. 48; Frauenliebe und Leben, Op. 42
Lehmann (sop), Walter (pno)
CBS/Sony CD 44840 [A] **M**

SIBELIUS, Jean (1865–1957) FINLAND

Violin Concerto in D min., Op. 47
Neveu (vln), Philharmonia O, Susskind
(+ Brahms: *Violin Concerto*)
EMI CDH7 61011-2 (US: CDH 61011) [A] **M**

TCHAIKOVSKY, Pyotr (1843–1893) RUSSIA

Piano Concerto No. 1 in B♭ min., Op. 23
Horowitz (pno), NBC SO, Toscanini
(+ Beethoven: *Piano Concerto No. 5*)
RCA GD 87992 (US: 7992-2) [A] **M**

COLLECTIONS

The Young Claudio Arrau Liszt, Schumann, Debussy, Chopin
Arrau (pno)
Pearl GEMMCD 9928 [A] **M**

Simon Barere At Carnegie Hall, Volume 2 Balakirev, Bach,
Schumann, etc.
Barere (pno)
APR CDAPR 7008, 2 CDs [A] **M**

Caruso in Song Di Capua, Rossini, Pergolesi, etc.
Caruoso (ten), Various accompaniments
Nimbus NI 7809 [A] **M**

Cziffra – The Hungaraton Recordings 1954–56 Liszt, Schumann,
Grieg, etc.
Cziffra (pno), Various Os and conductors
APR CDAPR 7021, 2 CDs [A] **M**

Mischa Elman – Solo Recordings 1921–24 Brahms, Schubert, Lalo, etc.
Elman (vln), various accompaniments
Biddulph LAB 038 [A] **M**

Feuermann – The Columbia Recordings – Volume 1 Haydn, Chopin, Schubert, etc.
Feuermann (vcl), various accompaniments
Pearl GEMMCD 9442 [A] **M**

Godowsky – UK Columbia Recordings 1928–30 Beethoven, Schumann, Grieg, Chopin
Godowsky (pno)
APR CDAPR 7010, 2 CDs [A] **M**

Josef Hassid and Ginette Neveu – Selected Recordings Kreisler, Dvořák, Sarasate, etc.
Hassid (vln), Neveu (vln), various accompaniments
Testament SBT 1010 [A] **M**

Klemperer in Amsterdam Schoenberg, Mendelssohn, Mozart, etc.
Concertgebouw O, Klemperer
Memories HR 4248/9, 2 CDs [A] **M**

Dinu Lipatti – Piano Recital Bach, Scarlatti, Mozart, etc.
Lipatti (pno)
EMI CDH7 69800-2 (US: CDH 69800) [A] **M**

A. B. Michelangeli – Early Recordings Bach, Scarlatti, Grieg, etc.
Michelangeli (pno)
EMI CDH 64490-2 (US: CDH 64490) [A] **M**

Nathan Milstein – American Columbia Recordings Tchaikovsky, Beethoven, etc.
Milstein (vln), Chicago SO, Stock; Balsam (pno)
Biddulph LAB 063 [A] **M**

Benno Moiseiwitsch – Solo Piano Recordings 1938–50 Liszt, Mussorgsky, Debussy, etc.
Moiseiwitsch (pno)
APR CDAPR 7005, 2 CDs [A] **M**

The Art of Gregor Piatigorsky Brahms, Shostakovich, Weber, etc.
Piatigorsky (vcl), Stewart (pno), Newton (pno)
Music & Arts MACD-644 [A] **M**

Sergei Rachmaninov – The Complete RCA Recordings
Rachmaninov, Chopin, Mendelssohn, etc.
Rachmaninov (pno/cond), Kreisler (vln) Philadelphia O, Ormandy, Stokowski
RCA 09026 61265-2, 10 CDs [A] **M**

The Art of Segovia – The HMV Recordings 1927–1939 Bach, Albéniz, Ponce, etc.
Segovia (gtr)
EMI CHS7 61047-2 (US: CDHB 61047), 2 CDs [A] **M**

A Stokowski Fantasia Mussorgsky, Tchaikovsky, Dukas, etc.
Philadelphia O, Stokowski
Pearl GEMMCD 9488 [A] **M**

The Art of Joseph Szigeti, Volume I Bach, Paganini, Dvořák, etc.
Szigeti (vln), Ruhrseits (pno)
Biddulph LAB 005/6, 2 CDs [A] **M**

Index of Selected Works